MW01194591

SHIFTING IMAGES OF THE HASMONEANS

Shifting Images of the Hasmoneans

*Second Temple Legends and Their Reception in
Josephus and Rabbinic Literature*

VERED NOAM

Translated by
DENA ORDAN

OXFORD
UNIVERSITY PRESS

OXFORD
UNIVERSITY PRESS

Great Clarendon Street, Oxford, OX2 6DP,
United Kingdom

Oxford University Press is a department of the University of Oxford.
It furthers the University's objective of excellence in research, scholarship,
and education by publishing worldwide. Oxford is a registered trade mark of
Oxford University Press in the UK and in certain other countries

© Vered Noam, 2018

The moral rights of the author have been asserted

First Edition published in 2018

All rights reserved. No part of this publication may be reproduced, stored in
a retrieval system, or transmitted, in any form or by any means, without the
prior permission in writing of Oxford University Press, or as expressly permitted
by law, by licence or under terms agreed with the appropriate reprographics
rights organization. Enquiries concerning reproduction outside the scope of the
above should be sent to the Rights Department, Oxford University Press, at the
address above

You must not circulate this work in any other form
and you must impose this same condition on any acquirer

Published in the United States of America by Oxford University Press
198 Madison Avenue, New York, NY 10016, United States of America

British Library Cataloguing in Publication Data
Data available

Library of Congress Control Number: 2017939642

ISBN 978-0-19-881138-1

Links to third party websites are provided by Oxford in good faith and
for information only. Oxford disclaims any responsibility for the materials
contained in any third party website referenced in this work.

Preface

In recent years I have been engaged in a collaborative project with Tal Ilan, with the participation of Daphne Baratz, Meir Ben Shahar, and Yael Fisch, that seeks to closely examine the phenomenon of parallel traditions on Second Temple-period history found in the writings of Flavius Josephus and rabbinic literature. The fruits of this study produced a two-volume Hebrew work that scrutinizes some thirty-five parallels treating the Second Temple period in both corpora. The first volume studies events that took place during the four centuries from the Alexandrine conquest to the eve of the First Jewish Revolt. The second volume addresses the dramatic events of the four-year revolt, until the destruction of the temple.

On the completion of this project I realized that, from the traditions I analyzed in its context, it was possible to extract a defined group of stories that touch on the history of the Hasmonean dynasty. Examination of these stories has added value beyond the overall question of the relationship between the Josephan and the rabbinic corpora, and between them and their presumed sources. These stories provide a valuable key to, and a new perspective on, the reflection of the Hasmonean image in the eyes of their contemporaries and following generations, the manner in which the illustrious Second Temple-period historian judged the generations of the dynasty, and on the viewpoint of the creators of rabbinic literature vis-à-vis the last Jewish commonwealth that preceded their period. In that sense, this book belongs to the scholarly discipline of reception history.

This fresh look at Hasmonean traditions required revision of five chapters that appeared in the Hebrew book, the fleshing out of a chapter that discusses an additional tradition, and mainly the writing of Chapter 7, the concluding chapter. This final chapter unfolds my conclusions regarding the legends recounted of the Hasmoneans in Second Temple-period Jerusalem, the genres to which they belonged, and their political rationales and aims. Based on the attempt to reconstruct the original stories, this chapter redefines Josephus's attitude toward the Hasmonean rule in the past, and consequently, re-explores the question of his sectarian identity, which has long been a subject of scholarly debate. It also suggests a new resolution of the long-standing question of the rabbinic attitude toward the Hasmonean dynasty.

This initiative would not have come to fruition without the professional expertise, rich experience, devotion, and friendship of Dena Ordan, who translated the text from Hebrew into English, and whose good advice accompanied all stages of the creation and polishing of this book. Working with Dena was a distinct pleasure.

I would also like to thank the Oxford University Press for undertaking to publish this book. I have found its staff, Karen Raith in particular, to be unfailingly helpful. I must also express my appreciation to the anonymous readers for the press, whose comments helped make this a better book.

It is my pleasant task to thank the Israel Institute for Advanced Studies, where I spent the 2014–15 academic year, and its director, Michal Linial, for the supportive, congenial atmosphere that facilitated the writing of this book. Nor can I fail to thank my colleagues who advised me on many matters, including my partner to the Hebrew project, Tal Ilan. Daniel R. Schwartz assisted on historical matters; Yoel Elitzur, Elisha Qimron, and Noam Mizrahi provided advice on linguistic issues; Bezalel Bar-Cochva enlightened me on Hellenistic matters; and Daphna Baratz assisted me on issues pertaining to the Greek texts. I owe my ability to pursue my academic career over the years to Elhanan, who stands by my side in love and friendship, and to the large family that happily supports my efforts.

בריך רחמנא דסייען.

Jerusalem,
Adar 5777/March 2017

Contents

List of Abbreviations

AIU	Alliance Israélite Universelle
Ant.	Josephus, *Jewish Antiquities*
b., BT	Bavli; Babylonian Talmud
BL	British Library
CD	*Damascus Document*
DSS	Dead Sea Scrolls
m.	Mishnah
Macc	Maccabees
NT	New Testament
Scholion O	Oxford, Bodleian Library, Michael 388 (Neubauer 867)
Scholion P	Parma, Biblioteca Palatina 2298 (De Rossi 117)
SP	Samaritan Pentateuch
ṭ	Tosefta
War	Josephus, *The Jewish War*
y., YT	Yerushalmi; Jerusalem Talmud

Mishnah, Tosefta, Talmud

'Abod. Zar.	*'Abodah Zarah*
B. Bat.	*Baba Batra*
B. Qam.	*Baba Qamma*
Ber.	*Berakhot*
'Ed.	*'Eduyot*
Git.	*Gittin*
Ḥag.	*Ḥagigah*
Ḥal.	*Ḥallah*
Ḥul.	*Ḥullin*
Ker.	*Keritot*
Ketub.	*Ketubbot*
Ma'as. Sh.	*Ma'aser Sheni*
Meg.	*Megillah*
Menaḥ.	*Menaḥot*
Naz.	*Nazir*

Pesaḥ.	*Pesaḥim*
Qidd.	*Qiddushin*
Rosh Hash.	*Rosh Hashanah*
Sanh.	*Sanhedrin*
Shabb.	*Shabbat*
Sheqal.	*Sheqalim*
Taʿan.	*Taʿanit*
Ter.	*Terumot*
Yad.	*Yadayim*
Yeb.	*Yebamot*
Zebaḥ	*Zebaḥim*

Midrash and Other Works

'Abot R. Nat.	*'Abot de Rabbi Nathan*
ALD	*Aramaic Levi Document*
Cant. Rab.	*Canticles Rabbah*
Eccl. [Qoh.] Rab.	*Ecclesiastes[Qohelet] Rabbah*
Gen. Rab.	*Genesis Rabbah*
L.A.B.	*Liber antiquitatum biblicarum* (Pseudo Philo)
Lam. Rab.	*Lamentations Rabbah*
Lev. Rab.	*Leviticus Rabbah*
Meg. Taʿan.	*Megillat Taʿanit*
Num. Rab.	*Numbers Rabbah*
Pesiq. Rab.	*Pesiqta Rabbati*
Pesiq. Rab Kah.	*Pesiqta de Rab Kahana*
Sifre Deut.	*Sifre Deuteronomy*
Sifre Num.	*Sifre Numbers*
Tg. Onq.	*Targum Onqelos*
Tg. Ps.-J.	*Targum Pseudo-Jonathan*
T. Levi	*Testament of Levi*

Abbreviations of Journals and Series Names

AGJU	Arbeiten zur Geschichte des antiken Judentums und des Urchristentums

AJP	*American Journal of Philology*
ANRW	*Aufstieg und Niedergang der römischen Welt: Geschichte und Kultur Roms im Spiegel der neueren Forschung.* Part 2, *Principat.* Ed. Hildegard Temporini and Wolfgang Haase. Berlin: de Gruyter, 1972–
BJS	Brown Judaic Studies
CEJL	Commentaries on Early Jewish Literature
CRINT	Compendia Rerum Iudaicarum ad Novum Testamentum
DJD	Discoveries in the Judaean Desert
DSD	*Dead Sea Discoveries*
HDR	Harvard Dissertations in Religion
HSS	Harvard Semitic Studies
HTR	*Harvard Theological Review*
HUCA	*Hebrew Union College Annual*
IEJ	*Israel Exploration Journal*
JAJSup	Supplements to the *Journal of Ancient Judaism*
JBL	*Journal of Biblical Literature*
JJS	*Journal of Jewish Studies*
JQR	*Jewish Quarterly Review*
JSJ	*Journal for the Study of Judaism in the Persian, Hellenistic, and Roman Periods*
JSJSup	Supplements to the *Journal for the Study of Judaism*
JSNTSup	Journal for the Study of the New Testament Supplement Series
JSOTSup	Journal for the Study of the Old Testament Supplement Series
JSP	*Journal for the Study of the Pseudepigrapha*
JSPSup	Journal for the Study of Pseudepigrapha Supplement Series
JSQ	*Jewish Studies Quarterly*
JTS	*Journal of Theological Studies*
LCL	Loeb Classical Library
LSJ	Liddell, Henry George, Robert Scott, Henry Stuart Jones, *A Greek–English Lexicon.* 9th edn. with revised supplement. Oxford: Clarendon Press, 1996
PAAJR	*Proceedings of the American Academy of Jewish Research*
PVTG	Pseudepigrapha Veteris Testamenti Graece
RB	*Revue biblique*
RE	*Realencyklopädie für protestantische Theologie und Kirche*
REJ	*Revue des études juives*
RevQ	*Revue de Qumran*

SJ	Studia Judaica
SJLA	Studies in Judaism in Late Antiquity
STDJ	Studies on the Texts of the Desert of Judah
StPB	Studia Post-biblica
SubBi	Subsidia Biblica
SVTP	Studia in Veteris Testamenti Pseudepigraphica
TSAJ	Texte und Studien zum antiken Judentum
VTSup	Supplements to Vetus Testamentum
WUNT	Wissenschaftliche Untersuchungen zum Neuen Testament

Translator's Note

The translator of works in the field of Judaica faces many challenges. One relates to consistency in transliteration and spelling. In general, I have used the *SBL Handbook of Style* (2nd edn.) as a guide for transliteration and spelling; however, several changes have been introduced: thus, for example, *shin* is transliterated *sh* (not *š*) and no distinction is made between *tet* and *taf*; halakhah was preferred over halakah, and *Sifre* over *Sipre*. Abbreviations largely follow the *SBL Handbook*.

With respect to translations of the primary works cited throughout the book, the base text for Josephus in English has been the Loeb Classical Library edition. Where provided, the Greek text of Josephus has been cited from Niese's full critical edition. For rabbinic works, I relied on the existing translations as found in the bibliography. Divergences from the original translations, such as the spelling of names, or modernization or standardization of biblical quotes, have not been noted. With respect to personal names the more usual spellings of names were employed: thus Zakkai, not Zaqqai; Yitzhak, not Yiṣḥaq; Simeon ben Shataḥ, not Shimon. In citing rabbinic works, preference has been given to use of the Hebrew form of names; for example, Yehudah and not Judah.

Theirs was a splendid and renowned house
because of both their lineage and their priestly office,
as well as the things which its founders achieved
on behalf of the nation.
But they lost their royal power
through internal strife...

(*Antiquities* 14.490–1)

"Neither did I abhor them" [Lev 26:44]
—in the days of the Greeks,
when I raised up for them Simeon the Righteous
and Hasmonai and his sons, and Mattathias the High Priest...

(*b. Megillah* 11a)

Introduction

A. THE IMAGE OF THE HASMONEANS: A FRESH PERSPECTIVE FROM AN UNRECOGNIZED CORPUS

This book stands at the charged interface between literature and history; more precisely, between memory and historiography. It traces a series of discrete Jewish stories of varying lengths that describe cruxes in the history of the Hasmonean revolt and the Hasmonean kingdom. These are not sequential historical narratives, but rather distinct, "closed" literary units, whose creation was as much fueled by historical curiosity as by conceptual, esthetic, and literary considerations. Despite their fragmentary, at times fictional, nature these legends are embedded here and there in the rational-professional narrative of the historian of the age, Flavius Josephus. And they are, on the other hand, also scattered throughout the extensive halakhic-exegetical compositions known as rabbinic literature, redacted and compiled centuries later.

A compelling aspect of the much-studied history of the Maccabean revolt and the Hasmonean commonwealth has been the question of the image of the Hasmoneans in the eyes of their contemporaries and later generations, up to the present. Sharply debated from antiquity,[1] the discussion of this issue extends into modern scholarship, whose own attitude toward the Hasmoneans was no little influenced by changing trends and worldviews.[2]

Unlike recent significant contributions to the research of this period,[3] the present volume examines the Hasmoneans neither from a historical nor an

---

[1] On the attitude of ancient non-Jewish authors toward the Hasmoneans and Jews in the Hasmonean period, see Bar-Kochva, *Image of the Jews in Greek Literature*, 253–541. See also the brief survey in Shatzman, "The Hasmoneans in Greco-Roman Historiography," 8–11.

[2] See e.g. Efron, "Hasmonean Revolt," 1–32; and from the opposite perspective, D. R. Schwartz, "Pharisaic Opposition," 44–56.

[3] Recently, the scholarly literature on the Hasmoneans has been enriched by new studies that illumine the period from new perspectives. Eyal Regev ("Hasmoneans' Self Image," 5–30; idem, *Hasmoneans*, passim) studies the self-image and ideology of the Hasmoneans themselves: namely, how they styled themselves, formulated their goals, and sought to bequeath their history to coming generations. Uriel Rappaport (*House of the Hasmoneans*) has written an updated Hebrew monograph that summarizes the history of the dynasty. Chris Seeman (*Rome and*

internal Hasmonean perspective, but rather from the viewpoint of reception history.[4] It investigates their image as preserved in the collective Jewish consciousness. It asks how their Jewish contemporaries and the following generations apprehended the image of the Hasmonean dynasty and its history from its legendary founders, through its achievement of full sovereignty, to its eventual downfall.

The trajectory of this book differs from previous studies in three respects:

1. If past studies examined the overall attitude of entire corpora—such as the Dead Sea Scrolls (DSS),[5] Josephus,[6] or rabbinic literature[7]—to the Hasmoneans, the current study examines a series of Jewish folktales from the Second Temple period that treats figures and events from the Hasmonean era.

As demonstrated here, these stories, preserved in both the Josephan and rabbinic corpora, are remnants of a lost Jewish literature. Most likely transmitted orally, this literature handed down snippets of Second Temple period collective memory, but not in the form of a historical sequence grounded in documents and facts, such as the works of Nicolaus or Josephus. Rather, it was relayed by means of assorted minimalistic historical or legendary anecdotes that use brief comments or witticisms to characterize and judge the heroes of that age and enfold a historiosophical or theological view of events. As opposed to sequential historiography which reflects the worldview of the historian and his sources (Maccabees, Josephus), and redacted collective corpora that recruited and

---

Judea in Transition) studies Roman–Judean political relations during the Hasmonean reign. Sylvie Honigman (*Tales of High Priests and Taxes*) analyzes how the two books of Maccabees describe the Maccabean rebellion and argues that they present social and economic events and confrontation as having temple and religious features. Vasile Babota (*Hasmonean High Priesthood*) investigates the Hasmonean high priesthood in the context of the Jewish-traditional and the Hellenistic-Seleucid cultural spheres until 140 BCE. Kenneth Atkinson (*History of the Hasmonean State*) investigates the political history of the Hasmonean state and kingdom from 152 to 63 BCE, drawing on papyrological documentation, inscriptions, archeological evidence, numismatics, Dead Sea Scrolls, pseudepigrapha, and textual sources from the Hellenistic to the Byzantine periods (but not on Jewish legends embedded in Josephus's works and rabbinic literature).

[4] On the boom in reception studies at large and reception history in antiquity in particular, see Porter, "Reception Studies," and his observation: "It can be no accident that Greek and Roman studies have themselves been moving along a path that parallels reception studies. Only there the object has been something like the reception of antiquity within antiquity, without being so named. More and more scholars are turning to the ways in which antiquity conceived its own histories. And more and more it is becoming apparent that our sense of the past is shaped by its sense of its own past" (471). For general surveys of the history of reception theory since its inception in the so-called Konstanz School, see the bibliography cited in ibid. 474, 481.

[5] For compilation and analysis of all references to the Hasmonean commonwealth and contemporary events in Qumran literature, see H. Eshel, *Dead Sea Scrolls and the Hasmonean State*. For discussion of the attitude toward the Hasmoneans displayed by the DSS, see the literature cited in D. R. Schwartz, "Pharisaic Opposition," 45 n. 5.

[6] On Josephus's attitude toward the Hasmoneans, see e.g. Efron, "Simeon Ben Shataḥ and Jannaeus," 161–75; Cohen, *Josephus in Galilee and Rome*, 44–7; Gafni, "Josephus and I Maccabees," 116–31; Feldman, "Josephus' Portrayal of the Hasmoneans," 41–68; Fuks, "Josephus and the Hasmoneans," 166–76; Mason, *Josephus on the Pharisees*, 83–4, 213–30, 246–59; D. R. Schwartz, "Josephus on Hyrcanus II," 210–32; Regev, *Hasmoneans*, 28–31, 69–73; Tuval, *Jerusalem Priest to Roman Jew* (see n. 74 and text there).

[7] See later discussion.

reworked historical events for their own propaganda or didactic aims (DSS, rabbinic literature), these stories are set apart by chronological proximity to events and their vibrant, folk nature. Evidently recounted orally, they circulated in the streets of Jerusalem during the century-long leadership of the Hasmonean dynasty and for 130 years after its downfall, until the destruction of the Second Temple.

2. To date, the scholarship has examined Josephus's attitude toward the Hasmoneans based on his writings and his treatment of his historiographical sources: 1 Maccabees,[8] Nicolaus of Damascus,[9] and Strabo,[10] as well as from the perspective of his use of material from his previous book, *The Jewish War*, in composing *Jewish Antiquities*.[11] For its part, the rabbinic attitude toward the Hasmoneans is usually surveyed through compilation of halakhic and aggadic statements from tannaitic and amoraic sources that touch on the Hasmoneans.[12]

However, as shown throughout the current study, the Second Temple-period Jewish traditions concerning the Hasmoneans have yet to be decisively defined as an early, independent source that was secondarily introduced into both corpora. Thus the scholarship has been flawed on two accounts: first, by its failure to make chronological distinctions between texts; second, by its lack of recognition of the redactional role assumed by Josephus and rabbinic literature. Let me clarify my argument. With respect to chronology, the traditions cited were incorrectly perceived as representing the viewpoint of the corpus in which they were found. Thus, for example, the traditions of the pelting of Janneus with citrons, the questioning of his lineage, and his deathbed instructions to his wife (*Ant*. 13.372–3, 399–404) were perceived as Josephus's attempt to defend the Pharisees or alternatively Janneus.[13]

---

[8] See Cohen, *Josephus in Galilee and Rome*, 44–7 and the wide-ranging bibliographical references in the notes; Gafni, "Josephus and I Maccabees"; Feldman, "Josephus' Portrayal of the Hasmoneans"; Sievers, *Synopsis*; idem, "Josephus, First Maccabees, Sparta," 241–51.

[9] Starting with the groundbreaking work of Hölscher, *Quellen des Josephus*; idem, "Josephus," 1934–2000. For subsequent research, see Stern, "Nicolaus of Damascus," 445–64 and the bibliographical references in the notes. On Nicolaus, see Stern, *Greek and Latin Authors*, 1:227–60; Shatzman, "The Hasmoneans in Greco-Roman Historiography," 40–2. See also Cohen, *Josephus in Galilee and Rome*, 48–58; D. R. Schwartz, "Josephus and Nicolaus," 157–71; Ilan, *Integrating Women*, 85–125; idem, "David, Herod and Nicolaus," 195–240.

[10] See Shatzman, "The Hasmoneans in Greco-Roman Historiography," 34–40; Bar-Kochva, *Image of the Jews in Greek Literature*, 401–2. On the Josephan treatment of specific selections from Strabo, see e.g. ibid. 399–435. See also D. R. Schwartz's description of Karl Albert's isolation of passages from Strabo in Josephus's works as a means of understanding the latter's attitude toward Hyrcanus II ("Josephus on Hyrcanus II," 211–12).

[11] The first to undertake such a comprehensive comparison between *War* and *Antiquities* was Laqueur, *Jüdische Historiker Flavius Josephus*. On the mixed reception of Laqueur's conclusions in the scholarship, see D. R. Schwartz, "Josephus on Hyrcanus II," 213 n. 5. For a survey of the state of the comparative research of *War* and *Antiquities*, see Cohen, *Josephus in Galilee and Rome*, 48–66; Mason, *Josephus on the Pharisees*, 187–95. Regarding Josephus's relationship to the Hasmoneans based on a comparison of the two, see e.g. Fuks, "Josephus and the Hasmoneans"; D. R. Schwartz, "Josephus on Hyrcanus II."

[12] See e.g. Alon, "Did the Jewish People and Its Sages Cause the Hasmoneans to Be Forgotten?" 1–17; Efron, "Hasmonean Revolt," 29–32; Stemberger, "The Maccabees in Rabbinic Tradition," 193–203; Gafni, "Ha-ḥashmonaim be-sifrut ḥazal," 261–76, and see also further discussion in this Introduction.

[13] See Morton Smith, "Palestinian Judaism," esp. 75–6, for the first assumption; Fuks, "Josephus and the Hasmoneans," 169–71 for the second.

The story of Onias's refusal to support one of the parties in the internecine Hasmonean conflict was interpreted as the Josephan stance regarding the need for separation between political positions and the sacred values of good and evil.[14] On the other hand, the legend of the rupture with the Pharisees—in its talmudic version—was understood as a singular instance of the rabbis addressing history,[15] and the demand that the Hasmonean ruler relinquish the high priesthood as representing the rabbinic viewpoint.[16] To my mind, all of these stories preceded both Josephus and rabbinic literature and feature their own messages. Moreover, at times the corpus in which the tradition is cited imposes a contrary view on the story, either through its incorporation in a conflicting framework, or through interpolation of subversive statements into the original story.

I maintain that a fresh perspective on the shifting attitudes toward the Hasmoneans can be gained by correctly distinguishing between the ancient embedded stories and their purposeful redaction. Such an approach facilitates characterization of the attitude toward the Hasmoneans in temple times and the changes reflected in the Josephan reworking, on the one hand, and in the redaction and transmission of rabbinic literature, on the other. Comparison of the versions of the story found in the two corpora assists identification of these reworkings. The following example demonstrates the advantages of this strategy. Some scholars claim that the absence of Judas Maccabeus and his brothers from rabbinic literature does not evidence tendentiousness or deliberate censorship, because this literature was not intended to serve as a historical witness: "The Hasmoneans' impact on that tradition is not inferior, and their part is not reduced in comparison with the Pharisees of their time."[17] This argument is undoubtedly correct when we examine rabbinic literature as a whole. However, when we look at the corresponding versions of a specific ancient tradition that concerns Judas's bravery, which was embedded in the books of Maccabees, *Antiquities*, and several rabbinic sources, we discover the blatant omission of the hero's name only in the rabbinic versions. This supports a claim of deliberate censorship. This example will be treated in Chapter 1.

3. Another innovative feature of this study lies in its consideration of the "attitude toward the Hasmoneans" by generation, rather than collectively. Most studies take an overall view of their portrayal in rabbinic sources; here I try to divide them into periods, looking at each generation separately. Naturally, I differentiate between the military account of Judas's victory over Nicanor and the miracle-legend of

---

[14] D. R. Schwartz, "Josephus on Hyrcanus II," 225–6.

[15] Yerushalmi, *Zakhor*, 24–5.

[16] This is a widely made claim. See e.g. Tcherikover, *Hellenistic Civilization and the Jews*, 254–61; D. R. Schwartz, "Pharisaic Opposition," 48–9; Kalmin, *Jewish Babylonia*, 57. Alon ("Did the Jewish People and Its Sages Cause the Hasmoneans to Be Forgotten?" 7–8) used the more tempered description of Janneus in the ancient story in order to demonstrate the forgiving rabbinic attitude toward the Hasmoneans.

[17] Efron, "Hasmonean Revolt," 30. See also Herr, "Conception of History," 141–2; Gafni, "Ha-ḥashmonaim be-sifrut ḥazal," 265.

John Hyrcanus in the temple, and between the latter and the totally different genre that echoes the internal conflicts of Janneus and his sons.[18]

An additional objective of this book is to decipher the nature of the relationship between the parallel stories preserved in Josephus and in rabbinic literature: dependence, as some argue, or mutual reliance on traditions and memory available to both, which is the thesis proposed here. In other words, the existence of these similar stories facilitates examination of the relationship between these substantially different libraries and worlds, specifically from the perspective of where they touch, and of the disparities, different emphases, reworking, and unique orientations typical of each. On the other hand, this comparison can, at the same time, enable partial reconstruction of these corpora's shared cultural memory and backdrop.

B. THE CORPORA: A COMPARISON

Before proceeding to an examination of specific episodes that appear in Josephus and rabbinic literature, a closer consideration of the two corpora in which the stories of the Hasmoneans appear is warranted. Of the works by Flavius Josephus, two are regarded as the primary, most important, historical source for Second Temple-period Jewish history: his *Jewish War* (usually dated between 75 and 79 CE)[19] and *Jewish Antiquities* (c.94 CE). Composed in Rome by a Jerusalem priest who witnessed or participated in many of the events, they employ the Greek language and the historical format bequeathed by Hellenistic culture. Although his other two works, *The Life* and *Against Apion*, also provide much information on contemporary events, the autobiographical nature of the first and the polemical-apologetic nature of the second make them less relevant to the discussion here. *War* recounts the history of the First Jewish Revolt against the Romans, prefaced by a précis of previous events, starting with the Hasmonean revolt. Here Josephus aspired to commend "to posterity the history of one's own time," and to make "the framework of the history his own," "with all the detail and elaboration at my command" (*War* 1.15, 18). In *Jewish Antiquities* Josephus's declared intention was to "embrace our entire ancient history and political constitution," for it was the author's belief that "the whole Greek-speaking world will find it worthy of attention" (*Ant.* 1.5).

---

[18] Gafni followed this path (see his "Ha-ḥashmonaim be-sifrut ḥazal," 261–2 and the organization of the article as a whole), but did not distinguish clearly between the embedded Second Temple-period fragments and their rabbinic reworking.

[19] But may have undergone later revision. For a discussion and references, see D. R. Schwartz, "Josephus, Catullus," 331–52, esp. 331–4.

The impress of the Second Temple period is also fragmentarily scattered throughout rabbinic literature. As the most prominent, comprehensive, post-biblical Jewish oeuvre—preserved as the main asset of the Jewish people for future generations—rabbinic literature manifests religious law, lifestyles, beliefs, and opinions, and even traces of events experienced during that period and afterwards.[20] Considering the Second Temple period with hindsight, this literature depicts a religious world concerned mainly with observance of the commandments and Torah study, the temple rites, the transmission of the Oral Law, halakhah, and exegesis. In this world the rabbis are the heroes and leaders, and the stormy events outside its walls are conveyed non-sequentially, arbitrarily, and incidentally, cloaked in legend and filtered through a theological prism.[21]

The two corpora in question are fundamentally different. Josephus's writings plainly belong to the historiographical genre as practiced in Hellenistic-Roman culture; whereas, as many have noted, rabbinic literature is religious, didactic-exegetical, and ahistorical in nature. Notice of the lack of interest in history in general and Jewish history in particular in the "sea of the Talmud" was already taken in the nineteenth century, by Joseph Derenbourg.[22] Currently, we still find in the scholarship such observations as "the rabbis showed no interest in historiography ..."; "the talmudic story manifests a literary reality, and the fundamental inchoate historical material is not important to the author"; "among the rabbis... one should not search for a critical-historical approach aimed at

[20]   Naturally, historians of this period have at their disposal many additional sources, such as the Apocrypha, Qumran literature, the NT, and archeological and epigraphic findings.

[21]   Exceptions are three short works on the margins of rabbinic literature: (1) *Seder olam rabbah*, which calculates the years between biblical events, with the addition of a single short but obscure chapter that calculates the years between Nehemiah and Alexander the Great's conquest, and from Alexander to the Bar Kokhba revolt. Defined as chronography in the scholarship, it contains no post-bibilical historiography (see Milikowsky, *Seder Olam: Critical Edition, Commentary, and Introduction*; idem, "Seder 'Olam"); (2) *Megillat Ta'anit*, an Aramaic list from the late Second Temple period, which enumerates dates on which it is forbidden to fast or eulogize the dead because of propitious events that took place on that day. Its aim is halakhic and it is organized calendrically, not chronologically; the varied historical events are mentioned laconically, without explanation or dating. Here too we do not have historiography, but *Megillat Ta'anit* undoubtedly represents the deliberate preservation of collective memory through ritual (see the observations of Halbwachs, Yerushalmi, and Nora as surveyed in section G of this chapter). On the one hand, this work pre-dated the rabbinic world and does not represent its culture. On the other hand, its later adoption into rabbinic literature and halakhah somewhat tempers the determination that the rabbis lacked interest in postbiblical history; and (3) the Scholion, the late Hebrew commentary on *Megillat Ta'anit*, which has survived in several editions, one of which was already known to the redactors of the *sugyot* in the BT (on *Megillat Ta'anit* and the Scholion, see Noam, *Megillat Ta'anit*). This is an exegetical work and its materials came from pseudo-historical traditions on Second Temple-period times. Yet, the very creation of commentary on *Megillat Ta'anit*, and the collection and preservation of these traditions, indicates historical curiosity and accessibility to pools of Jewish memory on the part of this text's creators.

[22]   "Car, en faisant quelques excursions sur le terrain, ou, comme disent les docteurs, 'sur la mer du Thalmud'... on aperçoit de suite du peu de place qu'y occupe, nous ne disons pas l'histoire en général, mais l'histoire du peuple juif lui-même ..." (Derenbourg, *Essai*, 2).

preserving for coming generations information on 'what really happened.' "[23] Different explanations have been proposed for this lack: that, for the rabbis, the centrality of biblical exegesis and the creation of halakhah supplanted historical study; that they perceived the Bible as a sufficient pattern for all of history; that, for them, history lacked educational-religious value; that a theological viewpoint regarding the eternity of the Written and Oral Law overrode the relativity of the historical perspective; or that the lack of sovereignty pushed the Jews out of their place as active participants in history, among others.[24] Recently Inbar Raveh suggested that the absence of sequential historical narrative in rabbinic literature manifests "a fragmentary perception of the universe...a sort of poetic refusal to respond to the explanatory function of seeing events in sequence."[25] I am in agreement with, and my research supports, the already suggested need for a more nuanced reading of the rabbinic indifference to history;[26] nonetheless, it is the case that the genre of straightforward historiography is not found in rabbinic literature.

Indeed, Josephus and rabbinic literature present surprisingly different pictures of the world and of the stamp of events from the same period. In Josephus we find rich military and political descriptions and stormy political life; his protagonists are people of action: generals, rulers, Jewish and gentile high office-holders, rebels, and soldiers. In rabbinic literature we find halakhic, exegetical, and aggadic discourse against the backdrop of the temple and the study house: its protagonists are rabbis, priests, and religious leaders. It suffices to touch on some outstanding disparities between the two; for example, the various genres of rabbinic literature over the ages make no mention of the names or deeds of the Hasmonean brothers, including Judas Maccabeus himself,[27] whereas Josephus devotes nearly 400 sections to their bravery.[28] On the other hand, Josephus does not even allude to the important schools of Beit Hillel and Beit Shammai, which, according to the rabbis, flourished during the final century of the Second Temple period, whereas they receive over 250 mentions in the Mishnah alone. Nor is Josephus familiar with his contemporary, the religious leader Yoḥanan ben Zakkai, to whom rabbinic testimony attributes responsibility for revitalizing post-destruction Judaism. The reader may

---

[23] Cited respectively (in translation by the author) from Herr, "Conception of History," 142; Fraenkel, "Hermeneutic Problems," 145 (see also Fraenkel, *Darkhei ha-aggadah ve-ha-midrash*, 235–8); Gafni, "Research on the Second Temple," ix. See also Boyarin, "Ha-midrash ve-ha-ma'aseh," 105–17; Friedman, "La-aggadah ha-historit," 119–64, esp. 162; Cohen, "The Destruction," 18–19; Raveh, *Fragments of Being*, 12–14. See also the references in Yassif, *Hebrew Folktale*, 492 n. 66.

[24] For a survey of the state of the research and references, see Gafni, "Talmudic Historiography," 295–6 and more recently in great detail, Ben Shahar, "Biblical and Post-biblical History," 29–35.

[25] Raveh, *Fragments of Being*, 54.   [26] Gafni, "Research on the Second Temple."

[27] See Chap. 1, "Nicanor's Defeat."   [28] *Ant.* 12.265–13.229.

justifiably wonder how a single historical reality spawned such divergent portraits.

Another difference, apart from those grounded in the expected gap between historiographical and halakhic-conceptual-didactic literature, lies in the proximity of composition to the events in question. Josephus's works were composed not long after the end of this period, and he personally witnessed its concluding events. But the editing of what is broadly referred to as "rabbinic literature" spanned some 700 years, and the earliest composition—the Mishnah—was completed around 130 years after the destruction of the temple. Moreover, the work with the greatest number of parallels to Josephus—the Babylonian Talmud—was formulated not only at a temporal but also at a pronounced geographical, cultural, and political distance from events in the Second Temple-period land of Israel.

Still another dichotomy between the two lies in orientation: Josephus is outer-directed; rabbinic literature is inner-directed. As the French historian Pierre Nora has stated: "Memory wells up from groups that it welds together...By contrast, history belongs to everyone and to no one and therefore has a universal vocation."[29] Josephus, the historian, wrote in Greek, primarily for a non-Jewish audience, whereas the Hebrew-Aramaic rabbinic literature is a definitive example of the internal discourse of an enclave within an enclave: the circles of the rabbis and their disciples, who comprised but one stratum of Jewish society.[30] Its audience was a closed religious group with shared, self-evident values, beliefs, and cultural infrastructure.

Yet another decisive difference is the ability to identify the author. At the outset of *War*, Josephus designates himself as follows: "I—Josephus, son of Matthias, a Hebrew by race, a native of Jerusalem and a priest, who at the opening of the war myself fought against the Romans and in the sequel was perforce an onlooker" (1.3). Josephus's voice surfaces in each and every sentence in *War* and *Antiquities*, and his account interweaves personal and more general history. He again places himself in the forefront in the conclusion of *Antiquities*, his history of the Jewish people: "And now I take heart from the consummation of my proposed work to assert that no one else, either Jew or gentile, would have been equal to the task, however willing to undertake it, of issuing so accurate a treatise as this for the Greek world" (20.262). Typically, the book ends by marking both a conventional and a personal date: "which belongs to the thirteenth year of the reign of Domitian Caesar and to the fifty-sixth of my life" (20.267). It is therefore not surprising that Josephus regarded his autobiography, the *Life*,

---

[29] Nora, *Realms of Memory*, 3. See further discussion in this Introduction.

[30] For studies that downplay rabbinic influence on the surrounding Jewish society, see e.g. Levine, *Rabbinic Class*, 21–2, 117–33; Goodman, *State and Society*, 93–111; Cohen, "The Rabbi," 959–71; and the more extreme position taken by Seth Schwartz, *Imperialism and Jewish Society*. But see also the recent, more balanced, convincing reservations put forth by Schremer, "Religious Orientation of Non-Rabbis," 319–41.

as an appendix to, and continuation of, *Antiquities*, the biography of the entire Jewish people.[31] In contrast, rabbinic literature is collective and partially anonymous, spanning many generations and locales, and reflects numerous, mostly unnamed, voices, redactors, and transmitters.[32]

The history of their reception constitutes another substantive difference between the corpora, as Yosef Hayim Yerushalmi notes:

> Sometime between 75 and 79 C.E. Josephus published his account of the *Jewish War* against Rome and then went on to an elaborate summation of the history of his people in the *Jewish Antiquities*. The latter work was published in 93/94, that is, less than a decade before the rabbis held the council at Yabneh. By coincidence the two events were almost contemporaneous. Yet in retrospect we know that within Jewry the future belonged to the rabbis, not to Josephus.[33]

If rabbinic literature shaped the collective memory of the Jewish past by consigning the historian's works to oblivion—and to non-Jews[34]—the historical awareness that emerged in modernity, among Jews and non-Jews alike, granted Josephus unquestioned priority in the reconstruction of history over what were now seen as fragmentary legends embedded in a late, folk creation. Accordingly, we can state that the rabbis shaped Jewish collective memory over the generations, whereas Josephus shaped modern scholarly historical perceptions.

C. THE PARALLELS BETWEEN JOSEPHUS AND RABBINIC LITERATURE

Notwithstanding the significant differences outlined above, the two corpora nonetheless reflect a shared platform of historical events, *realia*, Jewish lifestyle, and also an early cultural heritage of halakhah, aggadah, and exegesis that left

---

[31] On *Life* as the continuation of *Antiquities*, see D. R. Schwartz, *Vita*, 3–4.

[32] On anonymity as a feature of rabbinic literature, see Sussmann, "Torah she-be-al peh," 350–1. See also Drory, *Jewish–Arabic Literary Contacts*. 72. Raveh (*Fragments of Being*, 73–5) correctly argues that the scholarship has neglected to investigate the underlying reasons for this phenomenon. In her view, it is grounded in a sense that God is hiding his face and that the era of revelation has ended: in other words, when the creator of the world no longer reveals himself, the creator of the text hides as well. Meir Ben Shahar (oral communication) describes an opposite development: rabbinic literature represents a transitional stage of gradual moving away from the anonymity characteristic of many Second Temple works: Qumran and most of the apocryphal literature (though there are exceptions, such as Ben Sira, 2 Maccabees, Philo, and Josephus himself, and the Hellenistic-Jewish literature cited by Eusebius). This literature concealed its protagonists, using cognomens such as the Teacher of Righteousness, or hid behind pseudepigraphy (Enoch, the Testaments of the Twelve Patriarchs, and the like), whereas rabbinic literature, which passed the scepter from those who received divine revelation and inspiration to the human sphere of the rabbis, partially revealed the names of its speakers, even if it chose to conceal the identity of its redactors.

[33] Yerushalmi, *Zakhor*, 16.

[34] With the exception of indirect familiarity through the mediation of *Josippon* in the Middle Ages.

its mark on both. More or less comprehensive attention has been devoted to the hermeneutic aspects shared by both corpora;[35] however, one type of parallel has yet to be considered from an overall perspective or collected in its entirety. I refer here to the striking storehouse of anecdotal traditions concerning post-biblical persons and events from the Second Temple period, from the conquest of Alexander the Great to the destruction of the temple. The historical and legendary figures who are the foci of the parallels include Alexander the Great, John Hyrcanus, Alexander Janneus, his wife Alexandra, Hyrcanus and Aristobulus, Herod and Mariamne, and the caesars Gaius Caligula, Vespasian, and Titus, among others. The anecdotes related both by Josephus and by the rabbis take place against the backdrop of Alexander's conquest; the Hasmonean revolt and the Hasmonean commonwealth—which is our topic here; the rule of Herod and the procurators; and the First Jewish Revolt against Rome. Although the majority have evoked scholarly interest from the days of the *Wissenschaft des Judentums* to the present, and the most prominent have been treated from a variety of perspectives, neither the phenomenon as a whole nor its attendant questions have been fully studied in light of the entire inventory.

The last attempt to extract rabbinic material on the Second Temple period and compare it to Josephus took place in the latter half of the nineteenth century. This was Joseph Derenbourg's *Essai sur l'histoire et la géographie de la Palestine d'après les Thalmuds et les autres sources rabbiniques* (1867), a naive attempt to reconstruct the history of that era from data contained in both corpora, within the confines of the then current knowledge. In recent decades, the sole over-arching survey of the subject was a groundbreaking, insightful eight-page article by Shaye D. Cohen,[36] intended as an introduction to a comprehensive study that was never carried out.

Although aware of the existence of parallels between Josephus and rabbinic literature, *wissenschaftliche* scholars and their followers did not devote much attention either to their comparison or to the question of their relationship. Often they took a harmonistic approach that grafted the two traditions to create a historical reconstruction.[37] This simplistic perspective ignored the dubious

---

[35] On biblical exegesis and aggadot treating biblical heroes and events, see S. Rappaport, *Agada und Exegese*, and especially Louis Feldman's monumental works: Feldman, *Josephus' Rewritten Bible*; idem, *Josephus's Interpretation of the Bible*; and Attridge, *Biblical History in the Antiquitates Judaicae*. On halakhah in Josephus's writings, see Goldenberg, "Halakha in Josephus"; and the comprehensive survey in Feldman, *Josephus and Modern Scholarship*, 492–527. See also Nakman, "Halakhah in the Writings of Josephus"; Noam, "Josephus and Early Halakhah," 133–46. On descriptions of the temple in the Mishnah and Josephus, see Kaufman, *Temple Mount*; Levine, "Josephus' Description of the Jerusalem Temple," 233–46, and the earlier literature cited by both.

[36] Cohen, "Parallel Historical Tradition," 7–14. For a compilation of parallel traditions concerning the destruction of the temple only, see Taran, "Flavius and the Destruction of the Second Temple," 141–57.

[37] Several of the stories studied in detail here have received such treatment. With regard to the stories of the feast and the rift between John Hyrcanus/Janneus and the Pharisees (*Ant.* 13.288–98; *b. Qidd.* 66a—see Chap. 3), and of the pelting of Janneus with citrons on the Sukkot festival as

historical validity of these aggadic traditions, their underlying political agendas, and possible corruptions that influenced the shaping of the tradition in Josephus or rabbinic literature. In many instances, scholarly literature ignored the doubtful nature of the very similitude of the stories.

Later, more sophisticated scholarly approaches turned from historical reconstruction to a consideration of the presumptive messages and aims of each tradition. In the spirit of the day, they exchanged the search for the history reflected *in* the text for the history *of* the text, raising in that context the question of the relationship between the parallel versions of the stories in Josephus and rabbinic literature.[38] Many disparate theories regarding the meaning of the parallels between Josephus and the rabbis, and their similarities and differences, are found in the scholarship and no consensus has been reached on this focal topic.

One nineteenth-century hypothesis attributed the rabbinic traditions to an early version of *War*, which Josephus attests that he originally composed in his "vernacular tongue" and sent to the "barbarians" in the East.[39] Although this theory was abandoned shortly thereafter, twentieth-century scholars also intuitively assumed that it was necessary to seek the "source" in the early, "historical" Josephan context and that rabbinic writings relied on some version of Josephus, viewing the rabbinic versions as later, and more biased. Because it lacked historical awareness, the aggadah as found in rabbinic sources was assumed to always be later and reworked.

In this spirit, Shaye J. D. Cohen declared "that in not a single case is the rabbinic version earlier than the Josephan," and that the Josephan traditions can provide a control for the parallel embedded in rabbinic literature, but never the opposite; namely, a rabbinic aggadah cannot teach us anything about the nature of Josephus's works.[40] He suggested that isolated stories in rabbinic literature

recounted in Josephus (*Ant.* 13.372–4)/ the episode of the priest who misperformed the water libation according to the rabbis (*m. Sukkah* 4:9, *t. Sukkah* 3:16; *b. Sukkah* 48b), scholars unified the Josephan and the rabbinic versions of each of these traditions into a single narrative (see Chap. 4). Lieberman (*Tosefta Ki-fshutah*, 4:881) also accepted the latter identification. Joseph Derenbourg attributed Janneus's hatred of the Pharisees to the colorful rabbinic aggadah regarding halakhic debates between him and Simeon ben Shataḥ (*Gen. Rab.* 91:4–5; *Eccl. Rab.* 7:11; *y. Naz.* 5:5, 54b; *b. Ber.* 48a), combining it with the description of the Pharisaic rebellion against Janneus as recounted by Josephus (*War* 1.88–98; *Ant.* 13.372–83). Similarly, he described the circumstances of Janneus's deathbed instructions conveyed to his wife in Transjordan in the wake of Josephus (*Ant.* 13.398–404), but copied its contents from a rabbinic tradition (*b. Sotah* 22b) (Derenbourg, *Essai*, 96–102). Graetz and Klausner also conflated the two stories; see Chap. 5. Others incorporated the testimony of the two parallels on the Hasmonean civil war into their historical reconstructions, weaving the talmudic episode of the pig (*b. Sotah* 49b; *b. B. Qam.* 82b; *b. Menaḥ.* 64b) into Josephus's description (*Ant.* 14.25–8; see Chap. 6).

[38] Shaye J. D. Cohen declared his questions more historiographical than historical in nature: namely, his concern is to establish which tradition is more original, the Josephan or the rabbinic one; how Josephus and the rabbis treat the traditions available to them; and whether the rabbis use Josephus or his sources ("Parallel Historical Tradition," 8).

[39] See *War* 1.3. Graetz (*Geschichte*, 3:688) suggests that the story of the rupture with the Pharisees derives from this source. See, however, Chap. 3, section D regarding the unlikely nature of this suggestion and the contrary one raised by Graetz himself in that context.

[40] Cohen, "Parallel Historical Tradition," 14.

were drawn directly from Josephus, whereas others came from *Ur-Jossipon*, a conjectural collection of stories that was available to the rabbis in writing, resembling the much later, well-known medieval collection *Jossipon*.[41] Cohen exemplifies his method in the proposed analysis of the story of the pelting of Janneus with citrons. Whereas Josephus attributes the turmoil in the temple to political protest against King Janneus, the rabbinic description is of an anonymous Boethusian or Sadducean priest who is pelted because he refused to perform the water libation. This is regarded by Cohen as the "rabbinization" of events: the erasure of the historical character of a secular political tradition, which originated in Josephus, and its endowment with halakhic content.[42]

Other scholars support the viewpoint that stories found in rabbinic literature have their source in Josephus. Joshua Efron, for example, assumed that the talmudic story of Janneus's instructions to his wife was simply a reworking of a Josephan parallel, which was in turn derived from Nicolaus of Damascus, rather than from a Jewish source.[43] He, among others, also posited that the story of the Hasmonean civil war in the Babylonian Talmud (BT) relied on some version of Josephus. Efron suggested that the accounts of Janneus's scheme to assassinate Jewish sages following his death (Scholion P, 2 Shevat),[44] and of the trial of Janneus (*b. Sanh.* 19a–b),[45] were drawn from Josephus's account of Herod (*War* 1.659–60, 666 and *Ant.* 17.173–81, 193; *War* 1.203–5, 208–11; *Ant.* 14.158–60, 163–84, respectively) and that, as in other instances, the rabbis deliberately displaced the Herodian context, substituting for it a Jannean one. He even went so far as to suggest that the BT's source for the negative description of Janneus, as opposed to the Palestinian aggadah, was Josephus.[46] Günter Stemberger, as well, noted: "we may conclude with some certainty that there was direct dependence by the rabbis upon Josephus."[47] Yitzhak Baer was convinced that the author of the talmudic legends of the fall of Jerusalem read Josephus in the Greek, and many shared this view.[48]

Recently, Richard Kalmin has suggested that Josephus's writings or related traditions were transmitted from Palestine or elsewhere in the Roman Empire to Babylonia around the fourth century CE, where they were favorably received

---

[41] Ibid. 13. Evidently, the uncertainty that characterizes the scholarship regarding this question left its mark on this article as well.

[42] Cohen, "Parallel Historical Tradition," 12. See also idem, "Significance of Yavneh," 37 n. 23. With reference to the same tradition, Jeffrey L. Rubenstein (*Sukkot*, 121 n. 67; "Water Libation," 417–44) argues that the motif of pelting with citrons, which has its source in the "political" story of Janneus in Josephus, was incorporated into an obscure tradition of a minor halakhic tradition, thereby endowing it, unjustifiably, with a charged, principled nature. See Chap. 4.

[43] Efron, "Simeon Ben Shataḥ and Jannaeus," 186–90.

[44] Efron (ibid. 210–11) proposes that the author of the Scholion, which he ascribes to the Middle Ages, knew Josephus's story through *Sefer Jossipon*. See also Luria, *Mi-yannai ad hordus*, 112–13.

[45] Efron, "Simeon Ben Shataḥ and Jannaeus," 195–6.

[46] Ibid. 161–2.   [47] Stemberger, *Jewish Contemporaries of Jesus*, 109.

[48] Baer, "Jerusalem," 173 and esp. 180. For a list of similar viewpoints, see Taran, "Flavius and the Destruction of the Second Temple," 141 n. 2. For the legends, see *b. Git.* 55b–58a and parallels.

by the Babylonian rabbis. Amram Tropper puts forth a similar view.[49] Kalmin proposes that "it is not out of the question that Josephus himself was the rabbis' source" for the story of the rupture with the Pharisees in the BT,[50] and that the significant differences between the Josephan and the talmudic versions were the result of the reworking of the talmudic *sugya*.[51] Nonetheless, he also admits that the source of certain parallels between Josephus and the BT are not Josephan, but rather traditions utilized independently by Josephus on the one hand, and the BT on the other.[52]

The prominent scholar of rabbinic literature Günter Stemberger has correctly observed: "A frequently stated desideratum is the collection and analysis of all parallel traditions in Josephus and rabbinic literature. But as far as I am aware, no serious investigation of this complex of traditions has ever been published."[53] Recently, Jonathan Price noted: "This difficult, complex task [of systematic comparison of Josephus and rabbinic sources] has yet to be completed. Such a study would be invaluable and would assist in responding to two questions: to what extent was Josephus expert in the traditions known to us from rabbinic literature, and is it possible that the rabbis knew the writings of Josephus, directly or indirectly."[54]

Recently, in collaboration with Tal Ilan and three additional researchers, I have completed a comprehensive study in Hebrew that examines all of the parallel traditions in Josephus and rabbinic literature and spans the entire Second Temple period. This two-volume work is a response to the challenge posed by the scholars mentioned above.[55] Although related to the larger collective Hebrew project, the current study is an independent book devoted only to the traditions regarding the Hasmoneans. These traditions form the basis of a fresh approach to the changing image of the Hasmoneans over the generations.

D. APPROACHES TO JOSEPHUS AND HIS SOURCES

Shifting attitudes toward textual study have a bearing on the issue of the legitimacy of the study of Josephus's sources. This topic has been at the forefront of scholarly debate for several years. At one end of the spectrum, influenced by

---

[49] Kalmin, *Jewish Babylonia*, 149–68; Tropper, *Simeon the Righteous*, 113–56.

[50] Kalmin, *Jewish Babylonia*, 56. See also p. 167.

[51] Ibid. 53–9, 163. For a similar, prevalent viewpoint in the scholarship, which ascribes dependence on Josephus to the rabbinic legend regarding Herod (*b. B. Bat.* 3b–4a), see Rubenstein, "Herod in Ardashir's Court," 249–74. Rubenstein himself presents an underlying Sasanian source for the story, but he too assumes that its kernel is Josephan.

[52] Kalmin, *Jewish Babylonia*, 150, 167–8. See also further discussion in this Introduction.

[53] Stemberger, "Narrative Baraitot," 65.   [54] Price, "Introduction," 69–70.

[55] Tal Ilan and Vered Noam, in collaboration with Meir Ben Shahar, Daphne Baratz, and Yael Fisch, *Josephus and the Rabbis* (Hebrew; Jerusalem: Yad Ben-Zvi, 2017).

trends that had their inception in the mid-twentieth-century "new-criticism," we find scholars harshly critiquing the use of textual criticism to explain difficult Josephan passages and contradictions.[56] This trend intensified in the latter half of the century by virtue of the post-modern approach that negates the existence of any "truth"—even textual truth—at the foundation of texts and which denies our ability to reconstruct any process of creation—even of a literary work—as it was. Instead of the quest for the history of the text, redaction criticism seeks to uncover the redacted text's ideology and rhetoric and to discover its conjectural discourse function with respect to its audience.[57] This approach has been termed as "a shift from composition as *genesis* to composition as *poesis*,"[58] namely, abandonment of the question of how the texts were formed for consideration of the literary complex as it stands.

In his survey of the source-critical approach to Josephus's work, its main opponent, Steve Mason, observed: "This kind of analysis [*Quellenkritik*] did not dwell on the question of Josephus's aims and tendencies as an author because his contribution seemed trivial."[59] For Mason, such an approach does the original, creative Josephus an injustice, portraying him as a careless plagiarist incapable of checking his text and noting the inconsistencies he himself created. Naturally, Mason does not ignore Josephus's use of sources, but rather downplays the importance of their consideration for an understanding of Josephus.[60]

---

[56] A groundbreaking article considered representative of this trend, which called for a close reading of the text itself and dismissal of external data, including the history of its formation, is that of Wimsatt and Beardsley. For details, see Sternberg, *Poetics of Biblical Narrative*, esp. 7–23, and his critique of the radicalization of this approach.

[57] In the sphere of biblical studies the literary approach is justifiably identified primarily with Meir Sternberg's pioneering study. But see his critique (*Poetics of Biblical Narrative*, chap. 1) of those who followed in his wake, who moved in more extreme directions and simplified his approach. According to Sternberg, even a holistic literary approach to the Bible cannot ignore the conventions adhered to in the historical context in which the text was composed, or significant examples in which philology, not literary analysis, provides the desired solution. In the study of rabbinics as well we are witness to a shift from higher criticism to a synchronistic literary approach that studies the conceptual principles that underlie the redaction of entire sections. In the 1980s Peter Schäfer ("Research into Rabbinic Literature," 139–52) questioned the very feasibility of investigating defined compositions in rabbinic literature, as opposed to the sources and traditions embedded in them and their differing and competing traditions of redaction. An opposite stance was taken by Chaim Milikowsky ("The 'Status Quaestionis,'" 201–11), who argued that these edited compositions are defined, stable entities deserving of literary analysis as a body. A definitively literary consideration of the redaction principles of these compositions was renewed a decade later. See e.g. the works of Walfish, "Poetics of Mishnah," 153–89; "Approaching the Text," 21–79; and Zohar, *Secrets of the Rabbinic Workshop*. For a survey of this development in the study of the Mishnah, see Furstenberg, *Purity and Community*, 2–14.

[58] See e.g. Sternberg, *Poetics of Biblical Narrative*, 68.

[59] Mason, "Introduction to *Antiquities*," xiv. See especially idem, "Contradiction or Counterpoint?" 145–88. For a critical survey of this trend, see D. R. Schwartz, "Composition and Sources in *Antiquities* 18," 125–6, 143. See also the adjectives "German" and even "Bismarck's Germany" appended to speculations using the documentary thesis (Cohen, *Josephus in Galilee and Rome*, 59 and 44 n. 77. References cited from D. R. Schwartz, "Composition and Sources in *Antiquities* 18").

[60] For earlier reservations regarding the German tendency to *Quellenkritik*, see already Thackeray, *Josephus: The Man and the Historian*; Bilde, *Flavius Josephus*; Mader, *Josephus and the Politics of Historiography*. I thank Daniel R. Schwartz for some of the references in the preceding footnotes.

At the other end of the scholarly spectrum, not only does Daniel R. Schwartz see no inherent contradiction between study of Josephus's sources and investigation of his aims, he further argues that the first may significantly contribute to the second. An accurate mapping of the materials received by Josephus from his predecessors, determination of their reworking and integration into his text, and identification of Josephus's own contributions within the sequential narrative, clearly point to his attitudes and worldview, both as a writer and editor.[61] Although Schwartz has been under attack for this ostensibly conservative approach,[62] at present we are witnessing a renewed trend in several scholarly fields that similarly suggests an integrated approach to the study of ancient texts, which seeks to reapply source criticism alongside, and in addition to, the literary perspective.[63] Uniquely, by its very nature, the present study requires consideration of the question of sources at the most fundamental level, for it focuses not on *Quellenkritik* as a tool for understanding Josephus, but just the opposite, on Josephus as a tool for reconstructing the ancient Jewish materials that he used.

Josephus employed many sources in his writings, from the Bible to contemporary historians.[64] The Hasmonean period is described briefly in *War* (1.36–158) and in *Antiquities* at length: from 12.265 (Mattathias and the beginning of the revolt) to 14.77 (a summation of the loss of Jewish hegemony caused by the internecine war between the Hasmonean brothers).[65] Below I survey the prevailing scholarly consensus regarding Josephus's sources in this section of his works.

According to the majority scholarly view,[66] the lost world history of Herod's court historian, Nicolaus of Damascus, served as Josephus's main, almost

---

[61] This approach is implemented across the board in his work. See e.g. his early article, D. R. Schwartz, "Josephus' Source on Agrippa II," 241–68. For a principled statement of his stance, see especially, his "Composition and Sources in *Antiquities* 18," and more recently, "Josephus on Albinus," 291–309; "Clash between Samaritans and Galileans," 125–46.

[62] See e.g. Mason's critique ("Contradiction or Counterpoint?" 150–6). See also Shaye J. D. Cohen's comment: "Schwartz practices source criticism with a fervor and a certainty seldom seen outside of German dissertations of the nineteenth century" ("Modern Study of Ancient Judaism," 70 n. 18). On the other hand, Cohen himself makes extensive use of source criticism. See Cohen, "Alexander the Great," 41–68.

[63] Sternberg (*Poetics of Biblical Narrative*, 13) wonders: "Why anyone should wish to deny himself a universal resource for explaining a text's incongruities, whether by appeal to its transmission or to any other framework, remains a mystery." He continues to note that the abuse of source criticism by biblical scholars over the past two centuries has made it distasteful to their followers and this too is unjust, for "the excesses and fruitlessness of traditional source criticism no more legitimate the waving aside of its available data than they illegitimate its goals." In the continuation he suggests the interweaving of the different approaches in the study of biblical narrative. For a recent, similar approach to the study of rabbinic literature, see Rosen-Zvi, *Mishnaic Sotah Ritual*, 11–14; Furstenberg, *Purity and Community*, 6–7.

[64] For a useful survey and bibliography, see Cohen, *Josephus in Galilee and Rome*, 24–66.

[65] Cf. the similar summary after the conquest of Jerusalem in Herod's day, *Ant.* 14.487–91.

[66] See Stern, "Nicolaus of Damascus," 445–6 and the bibliography there. See also Cohen, *Josephus in Galilee and Rome*, 48–58; D. R. Schwartz, "Josephus and Nicolaus"; Ilan, *Integrating Women*, 85–125; idem, "David, Herod and Nicolaus."

exclusive, source in *War*, book 1,[67] up to the account of the death of Herod. One distinguishing feature of this source was its admiration for Herod as opposed to its hostility toward the Hasmonean dynasty.[68] Regarding Josephus's description of the decrees and the Hasmonean revolt in *Antiquities* (12.240–13.214), the accepted view identifies this as a direct paraphrase of 1 Maccabees 1–13, evidently its Greek version,[69] without the mediation of an intermediate source and without reliance on 2 Maccabees. With respect to events not addressed in 1 Maccabees, the assumption is that Josephus followed, in a relatively organized fashion, the main source on which he relied for *War*, book 1—Nicolaus of Damascus. Opinion is divided as to whether Josephus generally reworked what he wrote in *War* with the addition of other sources, or whether he returned to Nicolaus and imposed the reworkings and additions on his original source.[70] In the context of this book this question remains implicit. My main interest lies in Jewish stories integrated into a given infrastructure in *Antiquities*, making the question of whether this infrastructure was borrowed directly from Nicolaus, or copied from Josephus's reworked use of Nicolaus in his earlier work, *War*, less relevant.

Books 12 to 14 of *Antiquities*, in which the episodes included in this book are recounted, are much broader in scope than their parallel in *War*, book 1. Josephus evidently made wide use of other sources in addition to Nicolaus; some, like the Greek geographer Strabo, receive explicit mention. In many instances, however, his new sources remain unnamed, and the stories treated here undoubtedly belong to this pool of sources, as detailed below. But dissimilar use of sources is not the sole difference between the two Josephan works. Many scholars, foremost among them Richard Laqueur, have noted that, as compared to *War*, *Antiquities* displays a definitively Jewish perspective.[71] Whereas in *War* Josephus denounces the fomenters of the Jewish revolt that led to the destruction and praises the Flavian dynasty, which in Josephus's eyes was forced to destroy the temple against its will, in *Antiquities* Josephus takes upon himself the role of an advocate for persecuted, maligned Judaism. Daniel R. Schwartz has pointed out fresh proofs of Josephus's growing attachment to Jewish tradition while

---

[67] According to Bar-Kochva (*Judas Maccabaeus*, 186–90), Josephus wrote the short survey of the revolt and the decrees, until Simeon's day, in the opening of *War* (1.31–49) from memory and was influenced by 1 Maccabees, Nicolaus, and Daniel. He thinks that Nicolaus himself relied here on a Seleucid source and also on 1 Maccabees for his description of Eleazar's bravery. For a comprehensive treatment of Nicolaus's use of 1 Maccabees at this juncture, see Ilan, "David, Herod and Nicolaus," 222–4.

[68] See e.g. Stern, "Nicolaus of Damascus," 459–63.

[69] See Cohen, *Josephus in Galilee and Rome*, 44 n. 77; Bar-Kochva, "On Josephus," 115–17; Feldman, "Josephus' Portrayal of the Hasmoneans," 41–2 n. 3.

[70] For a discussion and bibliography, see Cohen, *Josephus in Galilee and Rome*, 50–1 n. 90.

[71] Laqueur, *Jüdische Historiker Flavius Josephus*. For a survey of the acceptance of his viewpoint in the scholarship, see D. R. Schwartz, "Josephus on Hyrcanus II," 212–16. See also idem, "Josephus on the Pharisees as Diaspora Jews," 137–46; for additional bibliography, see idem, "Josephus on Albinus," and the bibliography there, 302–3 nn. 19–20; idem, "Clash between Samaritans and Galileans," 136 n. 26.

composing *Antiquities*,[72] suggesting that the shift was grounded in the typical insight of Diaspora Jews that the taken-for-granted aspects of territory, language, and the desire for sovereignty no longer defined their national identity.[73] Moreover, Josephus notes the existence of Greek-speaking assistants who helped him in the composition of *War* (*Against Apion* 1.50). Many scholars have commented that the inferior stylistic quality of the Greek in *Antiquities* indicates that they were not at his side when he wrote the latter work, and Schwartz suggests that this too contributed to the different character of *Antiquities* as compared to the earlier *War*. Recently Michael Tuval devoted a comprehensive study to this topic. He traces Josephus's transformation from a Jerusalem priest whose Jewish identity was grounded in the temple and its cult, reflected in *War*, to a Diaspora Jew whose identity derived from ancestral tradition, canonical texts, and study and observance of Jewish law, found in *Antiquities*.[74]

E. THE PARALLELS BETWEEN JOSEPHUS AND RABBINIC LITERATURE: A PROPOSED CHARACTERIZATION

As noted above, the phenomenon of parallels between Josephus and rabbinic literature has sparked scholarly debate. There are two possible explanations for the presence in rabbinic literature of stories, or their variants, which are also found in Josephus's works. One is that the rabbis were familiar with Josephus's writings, or some earlier or later version of them from which they drew these stories. The other is that the parallels derive from an ancient repository of traditions that served the historian and also reached the redactors of rabbinic literature centuries later.[75] The first approach identifies every difference between the versions as grounded in redaction or corruption by the rabbis or the transmitters of their literature; the second judges the nature of the change according to specific context and views the parallels considered here as an opportunity to uncover and delineate that conjectural "repository of traditions."[76]

---

[72] Josephus underscores his commitment to the principles of Judaism and to Scripture in his introduction to *Antiquities* (1.12–17). For impressive examples manifesting the use of Jewish expressions in Greek transcription by Josephus in *Antiquities* as compared to *War*, see D. R. Schwartz, "Clash between Samaritans and Galileans."

[73] See the preceding notes. This approach is consistent with a central theme of Schwartz's thought with respect to the difference between Jewish life in the land of Israel and the Diaspora. See D. R. Schwartz, "Maqqabim aleph u-maqqabim bet," 11–20; idem, "Josephus on the Pharisees as Diaspora Jews."

[74] Tuval, *Jerusalem Priest to Roman Jew*, esp. 129–259.

[75] On the existence of narrative traditions from the Second Temple period in rabbinic literature, see Yassif, *Hebrew Folktale*, 89–132.

[76] Cf. Taran, "Flavius and the Destruction of the Second Temple," 144. For different elaborations of this question, see e.g. Neusner, "Josephus' Pharisees," 285; Cohen, "Parallel Historical

The approach that posits rabbinic dependence on Josephus has far-reaching implications for resolving the conundrum of the rabbinic attitude toward Second Temple literature. Scholars are divided regarding the question of whether the rabbis deliberately ignored, or were not familiar with, the extensive, varied Jewish literature of the Second Temple period, for, with the exception of Ben Sira,[77] they neither quote nor show signs of familiarity with any of these works.[78] Another scholarly debate revolves around the extent to which the rabbis knew Greek and their acquaintance with Hellenistic and Roman culture.[79] Possible rabbinic use of Josephus has definitive ramifications for these two worthy questions.

On the other hand, if most of the parallel traditions treated here come from a lost Second Temple era repository, on which both Josephus and the rabbis drew, then this study points the way to the reconstruction and characterization of an entire complex of lost Jewish stories from Second Temple times, a complex of which only a fraction has survived in the works of Josephus on the one hand, and in rabbinic works on the other. The consideration of these stories in Josephus and rabbinic literature, especially their literary features, supports the second option, as outlined below.

The above-mentioned, collaborative Hebrew study of the entire corpus of parallel stories in Josephus and rabbinic literature repeatedly countered the assumption of rabbinic dependence on Josephus in any form: classic rabbinic literature never used Josephus's writings, neither in an earlier version nor a later reworking. Almost without exception,[80] both corpora depend on an earlier, external pool of Jewish traditions. The hypothesis regarding a shared pool of traditions has been raised several times in the scholarship, albeit hesitantly,

Tradition," 8; Kalmin, *Jewish Babylonia*, 167; and recently, Noam, "Lost Historical Traditions," 991–1017.

[77] See Kister, "Notes on Ben-Sira," 125 n. 2; Ilan, "Ben Sira's Attitude to Women," 103–11; Labendz, "Ben Sira in Rabbinic Literature," 347–92, and the bibliography cited there. It is possible to argue for the existence of an additional case, even though it does not belong to the accepted category of "apocryphal" Second Temple Jewish literature. *Megillat Ta'anit*—probably a Pharisaic halakhic document—was composed before the destruction and was cited in later rabbinic literature. See Noam, *Megillat Ta'anit*, esp. 333–63.

[78] For rabbinic reservations regarding Second Temple-period works, see Ginzberg, "Attitude of the Synagogue," 115–36; Herr, "History," 177–8; Yassif, *Hebrew Folktale*, 89–90; and the bibliographical references there, 483 n. 21.

[79] See e.g. Lieberman, *Greek in Jewish Palestine*; idem, *Hellenism in Jewish Palestine*; Alon, "Ha-yevanit," 248–77; Morton Smith, "Palestinian Judaism"; Hengel, *Judaism and Hellenism*; and more recently, Edrei and Mendels, "Split Jewish Diaspora," 91–137. For a useful survey of the state of the research, see Levine, *Judaism and Hellenism*, 6–15. Although Josephus attests to an early Aramaic or Hebrew version of *War* (see previous discussion), however, as seen below, the definitive parallels between the corpora appear in *Antiquities*, not *War*.

[80] With the exception of the unusual tradition regarding the prophecy to Vespasian regarding his future appointment as emperor, attributed to Josephus in *War* and to Yoḥanan ben Zakkai in rabbinic literature ('*Abot R. Nat.* A:4, B:6; *Lam. Rab.* 4:5; b. *Git.* 56a–b; cf. *War* 3.399–408). Evidently, in this instance rumors of Josephus's history (but not parts of his book) were reworked into a legend on a figure from the rabbinic world.

partially, or locally, with reference to a particular tradition.[81] The time is ripe to make this an overarching assertion. In the following discussion I enumerate the features that led to the conclusion that Josephus exercised neither direct nor indirect literary influence on rabbinic literature, and that rather we are dealing with the vestiges of a shared infrastructure.[82]

Identifying Incongruent Traditions in Josephus

A number of features disclose the secondary interpolation of a foreign source into the Josephan sequence. First, because the traditions with parallels in rabbinic literature appear only in *Antiquities*, not in *War*, this indicates that, in Josephus's later work, they were interpolated into an existing narrative. Generally "closed" units with a beginning and end, they stand out in the context of the sequential Josephan historical narrative, and their removal from *Antiquities* does not affect the narrative flow,[83] in many cases leaving a narrative sequence almost identical to that found in *War*.[84]

Furthermore, the stories in question generally stand out as independent anecdotal traditions that are incongruent in the narrative context. If the broader context treats political and military events, the traditions in question treat internal Jewish matters, often connected to the temple and the temple cult, or the Pharisees, their sages, and their struggles. Thus, both the story of the heavenly voice heard by John Hyrcanus in the temple (*Ant.* 13.282) and the story of the feast and the rupture with Pharisees are anomalous in the context of the historical narrative that treats Hyrcanus's political-military reign. The latter stories take place in a closed, personal environment (a feast, a priest alone in

---

[81] Early scholars of Josephus already noted "Jewish sources" as the source for this type of tradition. See e.g. Hölscher, *Quellen des Josephus*, 81–5; idem, "Josephus," 1973. He thought them orally transmitted Pharisaic traditions. See also the opinions of various scholars who tried to reconstruct the foundations of the talmudic story of the rupture between John Hyrcanus/Janneus and the Pharisees as "a torn leaf from a lost Hebrew book, such as the chronicles of John Hyrcanus or some other Hasmonean chronicle" (see Chap. 3, section D). See also Dinur, "Historiographical Fragments," 142–3; Neusner, *Rabbinic Traditions about the Pharisees*, 1:176 (cf. his deliberations elsewhere: idem, "Josephus' Pharisees," 285); Goodblatt, *Monarchic Principle*, 113; D. R. Schwartz, "Josephus' Source on Agrippa II"; Taran, "Flavius and the Destruction of the Second Temple," 141 n. 1; Fox, "Biography," esp. 135–41. Such viewpoints were also cited doubtfully, or with respect to limited cases, by Cohen ("Parallel Historical Tradition"); and Kalmin (*Jewish Babylonia*). They also raised opposing views; see the survey above and the preceding notes.

[82] For another version of the following discussion see Noam, "Lost Historical Traditions."

[83] On occasion, Josephus inserts a pair or a cluster of separate Jewish traditions in one interpolation, as exemplified by the stories of the citron-pelting and the accusation that Janneus was descended from captives (*Ant.* 13.372–4), or the murder of Onias followed by the episode of the violation of the agreement concerning the sacrificial animals during the internecine Hasmonean war (*Ant.* 14.22–8).

[84] See Chaps. 2, 3, 4, and 5.

the temple) and not in the broader political-military arena of the surrounding narrative. In *Antiquities* the story of the pelting of Janneus with citrons incorporates internal Jewish temple anecdotes—sacrifice in the temple, the pelting with citrons, questioning the priesthood, constructing a fence in the temple—in a military narrative that treats an uprising and the founding of a troop of mercenaries. Only the "military" units have parallels in the earlier *War.* Similarly, this king's deathbed instructions, which appear only in *Antiquities*, are inserted in the description of his final battle in Transjordan and his ensuing death in this campaign, which is also found in *War.* The internal Jewish stories of Onias and the breaking of the agreement regarding the sacrificial animals, which take place against the backdrop of the Temple Mount and the temple rites, were inserted into the general historical description of the war between Hyrcanus and Aristobulus, which appears independently in *War.* These episodes can be detached from the sequence without impairing the surrounding narrative and are also clearly marked by artificial connective sentences.

Finally, at times the interpolated unit creates tension with, or contradicts, the surrounding narrative and diverges from the usual features of the Josephan narrative. This tension can take the form of disrupted order, duplication, or repetition. Thus, the episode of Hyrcanus and the heavenly voice (*Ant.* 13.282) is misplaced chronologically, for the event foretold by the voice was recounted by Josephus several sections earlier (13.277). The rupture between Janneus and the Pharisees contains many contradictions with the preceding and succeeding contexts, and also casts the Hasmonean ruler and the Pharisees in a different light from their descriptions elsewhere in Josephus. Janneus's deathbed instructions to his wife are also out of sequence, coming after the mention of his death.

These interpolations also have external markers, and the literary features that mark the seams between Josephus's sources have been noted in the scholarship. Some appear in the parallels studied here.[85]

Unrealized cross-references. In the late nineteenth century Justus von Destinon, and Gustav Hölscher in his wake, noted the phenomenon of unrealized cross-references in Josephus's writings, namely, places where Josephus sends the reader to further discussion of a matter, which in the final analysis does not appear elsewhere.[86] Subsequent research bore out Destinon's initial observation that such cross-references are related to the interpolation of foreign sources into the narrative. These sentences often mark the end of an interpolation, the seam between where Josephus finishes using one source and moves to another.[87]

---

[85] I thank Tal Ilan, who compiled the data and bibliographical references in the following.

[86] Destinon, *Quellen*, 21–9; Hölscher, "Josephus," 1970–82. On this phenomenon and its significance, see also Drüner, "Untersuchung," 70–6 and the appendix, 82–94; Petersen, "Literary Projects of Josephus," 247–59.

[87] See D. R. Schwartz, "Josephus' Source on Agrippa II," 245–6. This is exemplified in one of the sources examined here: the rupture with the Pharisees (*Ant.* 13.297). Tal Ilan has also found that

Ancestral tradition. On occasion, Josephus explicitly attributes a story to oral transmission, using forms of the verb "to say." The first two examples, λέγεται, φασί, appear in an anecdote treated in this book: John Hyrcanus and a heavenly voice.[88] Elsewhere in Josephus, in the context of other Jewish traditions with parallels in rabbinic literature not treated in this volume devoted to stories of the Hasmoneans, we also find the use of expressions such as φασί ("they say"),[89] and παρειλήφαμεν ("we have received").[90] In one instance Josephus explicitly attributes the source of his account to an ancestral Jewish tradition: καὶ τοῦτον τὸν λόγον οἱ πατέρες ἡμῖν παρέδωκαν ("and this story... our fathers have handed down to us"; *Ant.* 15.425).[91]

Recurring patterns. Another strategy that assists identification of the Josephan interpolation of a new source has been proposed by Hugh Williamson. Williamson outlines the following structure for Josephus's secondary interpolations: a brief précis of the contents of the interpolation, followed by the phrase: διὰ τοιαύτην αἰτίαν ("the reason for this was") and similar formulas, and then the source itself. He delineates the full model of this recurring pattern as follows: (1) the passage opens with the results of the affair; followed by (2) "the reason for this was"; (3) a detailed description of the reason, namely, the event itself; and (4) a summary that links the event to its outcome as specified in the opening. Williamson has amassed an impressive, convincing list of the occurrences of this pattern in *Antiquities*.[92]

Repetitive resumption. Daphne Baratz has noted the existence in Josephus of a phenomenon that resembles the biblical repetitive resumption.[93] After interpolating the passage, he returns to the concluding sentence of the previous unit. An example is the story of the war between the Hasmonean brothers, where, after inserting the episode of Onias (see Chapter 6), Josephus repeats that

recognizable cross-references that are "realized" at times mark the conclusion of an interpolated source. She notes the following instances: (1) *Ant.* 13.62 and 12.387 (Onias's flight to Egypt); (2) *Ant.* 13.298, a reference to a discussion of different Jewish sects; (3) *Ant.* 14.176 and 14.4 (Samaias); (4) *Ant.* 11.305 (the affair of Alexander the Great and the high priest). One of the sources in a series of Jewish traditions on King Janneus, which will be treated later, his pelting with citrons (*Ant.* 13.372), concludes with the following statement: "these [the use of palm branches and citrons on the Sukkot festival] we have described elsewhere"—in *Ant.* 3.245.

[88] *Ant.* 13.282. For λέγεται see also 14.36; and 15.425, both insertions into Josephus's narrative which do not deal with the Hasmoneans and therefore are not included in this volume.

[89] *Ant.* 15.367: the story of Herod disguising himself and mingling with the people to hear what was being said about him. For a rabbinic parallel, see *b. B. Bat.* 4a.

[90] *Ant.* 14.491: the end of the Hasmonean dynasty.

[91] In the context of the miracle of the rainfall in Herod's day.

[92] See Williamson, "Historical Value," 51–5. Indeed, this pattern is beautifully exemplified in a Jewish story with a rabbinic parallel, which does not belong to the Hasmonean period which is my topic here (the story of the priest Joseph, son of Ellemus—*Ant.* 17.165–6; cf. *t. Yoma* [*Kippurim*] 1:4 and its parallels). A similar pattern appears in a story treated in Chap. 6 of this book: the story of the sacrificial animals during the fratricidal Hasmonean war (*Ant.* 14.25–8).

[93] See e.g. Gen. 39:1, which returns to 37:36.

the events took place on the Passover holiday (see *Ant.* 14.25, which repeats section 21).

"*About this time.*" In 1982 Daniel Schwartz noted another feature in Josephus that can signal transition to a new source: the opening formula κατὰ τοῦτον τὸν καιρόν ("about this time").[94] Indeed, this phrase appears in various places where Josephus interpolates sources, including Jewish sources.[95]

Given these data, we can only concur with Richard Kalmin's observation regarding the absurdity of the proposition that the rabbis perused Josephus's writings, deliberately choosing stories that were both missing from *War* and also contextually incongruent in *Antiquities*.[96] The findings surveyed above resoundingly show that we are not treating here a Josephan sequence from which the rabbis later "extracted" material which they then interpolated in their discourse, but rather a Jewish legend that is anomalous, secondary, and "marked" a priori within the historian's narrative. Its original form must then be sought not in one or the other but in an unknown pool of traditions that preceded Josephus just as it preceded rabbinic literature.

The Josephan traditions with rabbinic parallels sometimes contain details, data, and entire stories that shed light on the versions recounted in the Tosefta, the Midrash, and the Talmuds; round out the portrait of the protagonist in rabbinic literature; or reinforce a didactic rabbinic message. Nonetheless, these specific elements are missing from rabbinic literature. Again, this indicates that the rabbis were not familiar with the relevant passages in Josephus. Several examples are discussed in detail in the chapters: the story of John Hyrcanus and a heavenly voice (*Ant.* 13.282–3; *t. Sotah* 13:5 and parallels), in which we find striking topical and linguistic affinities to Josephus's version in the rabbinic sources, but no knowledge of the historical circumstances, which the rabbis could have drawn from Josephus had they known his works; the story of Onias (*Ant.* 14.22–8; *b. Sotah* 49b; *b. B. Qam.* 82b; *b. Menaḥ.* 64b; cf. *y. Ber.* 4:1, 7b = *y. Ta'an.* 4:8, 68c), in which the rabbinic sources parallel only the following anecdote found in Josephus, whereas the story of Onias's martyrdom has no traces there.[97] Also, consideration of the pelting of Janneus with citrons as recounted by Josephus (*Ant.* 13.372–4) showed this to be an etiological tale whose purpose

---

[94] See D. R. Schwartz, "Josephus' Source on Agrippa II."

[95] *Ant.* 20.17; 20.34, with respect to the conversion of the royal house of Adiabene, which is also related in rabbinic literature (*Gen. Rab.* 46:10); and *Ant.* 20.179, the tradition regarding the corrupt acts of the high priests in Agrippa II's day, which also has rabbinic parallels. See D. R. Schwartz, "Josephus' Source on Agrippa II." An indirect use of this expression is found in the story of the high priest and Alexander the Great, where it denotes the interpolation of a general historical source in a Jewish legend that serves as its background (*Ant.* 11.304). This element appears in the story treated in Chap. 2 (*Ant.* 13.284), but there the interpolation is not the legend concerning John Hyrcanus in which we are interested, but rather information that has its source in Strabo (*Ant.* 13.284–7).

[96] Kalmin, *Jewish Babylonia*, 167–8. Nonetheless, Kalmin does not refrain from suggesting that some version of Josephus reached fourth-century Babylonia. See previous discussion.

[97] See Chap. 6.

was to describe the circumstances leading to that king's construction of a wooden barrier in the temple. No such story exists in rabbinic literature. Given the rabbinic interest in the temple, its contents, and the dramas that unfolded there, it is difficult to imagine that they would have deleted this significant detail if their version of the story (*m. Sukkah* 4:9; *t. Sukkah* 3:16; *b. Sukkah* 48b) came from *Antiquities*, as Cohen and Rubenstein suggest.

The fact that not all the traditions from the pool of early Jewish traditions available to Josephus were equally available to the rabbis impacts Josephan research. Although the existence of a rabbinic parallel confirms the identification of a particular unit in Josephus as an early Jewish folk tradition, this is not a necessary condition for such identification. Namely, the traces of the lost pool of Jewish traditions in Josephus are not limited to instances for which we find a rabbinic parallel. Josephus's writings must be mined according to the above-mentioned criteria for additional instances in which he relies on lost Second Temple-period Jewish sources beyond the ones appearing in rabbinic literature.[98]

Early Features in Rabbinic Literature

The traditions cited in rabbinic literature often retain authentic early motifs that are both anomalous in rabbinic literature itself and are also missing from the Josephan version of the story, either because his reworking, or the fact that he wrote in Greek, uprooted basic features of the original Hebrew tradition. Because the transmitters and late redactors of rabbinic works could neither have drawn these linguistic or topical characteristics from Josephus nor arrived at them independently, we must assume that they had before them an early Hebrew or Aramaic source, and that this or some similar source, which rabbinic literature preserved in a form closer to the original, also served Josephus.

A definitive example of such a scenario is the story of Nicanor's defeat (*Ant.* 12.402–12). In this case, Josephus's report is a reworking of the account of this event found in 1 Maccabees—in its Greek version. However, for apologetic reasons, Josephus erased the abuse of Nicanor's corpse and the many biblical allusions that are still discernible in the Greek translation of 1 Maccabees. In contrast, the Hebrew tradition of Nicanor's defeat as found in rabbinic literature preserves the abuse of Nicanor's corpse; also, some of the sources contain

---

[98] Indeed, among the Jewish traditions in *Antiquities*, Hölscher ("Josephus," 1973–4) also noted stories without parallels in rabbinic literature, such as the description of the sects (*Ant.* 13.171–3); the release of Aristobulus I's brothers from imprisonment by his widow Alexandra/Salina/Salome (*Ant.* 13.320; for the variants of her name and her identity, see Marcus, *Jewish Antiquities* [LCL], ad loc., note *a*); John Hyrcanus's prophetic dream that his son Alexander (Janneus) was destined to be his successor (*Ant.* 13.321–2); the traditions regarding Samias and Pollion (*Ant.* 15.3, 370); the predictions of the Essene Manaēmus (Menahem) regarding Herod's future kingship (*Ant.* 15.373–9); Herod's plundering of David's Tomb (*Ant.* 16.179–82).

phrases and language close to that of 1 Maccabees, making rabbinic tradition closer to the original form of the story than to the Josephan reworking in *Antiquities*. Namely, it is closer to the source employed by Josephus than to Josephus himself. Another example treated in the chapters—of an Aramaic source—is the story of John Hyrcanus and a heavenly voice in the temple (*Ant.* 13.282–3; *t. Sotah* 13:5 and parallels). Here too it is obvious that the rabbinic version does not depend on Josephus, for direct borrowing from *Antiquities* would not have created the linguistic stratification found in the Tosefta between the ancient Aramaic kernel and the Hebrew legend into which it was incorporated.

In other instances we witness stylistic singularities which, although anomalous in rabbinic literature, cannot be attributed to the Josephan version because it was written in Greek. Thus, the story of the rupture between Pharisees and the Hasmonean rulers (*b. Qidd.* 66a) manifests a mixed style, an artificial mosaic of the biblical lexicon and syntax which was interwoven into a later linguistic stratum typical of Second Temple Jewish literature. The story's lexicon also draws on the late Second Temple-period sectarian polemic discourse known from Qumran and the New Testament, and even a common strategy of this discourse—the projection of biblical pericopes on current political events. If this story was drawn directly from Josephus, whose version lacks these characteristics, from whence did its tannaitic or amoraic transmitters derive this style and these expressions? (See Chapter 3.) This polemical background is also reflected in the story of Janneus's deathbed instructions (see Chapter 5), in the pointed epigram voiced by Janneus to his wife in the talmudic aggadah (*b. Sotah* 22b), which reveals familiarity with Second Temple-period discourse and does not appear in the Josephan parallel (*Ant.* 13.398–404). Nor does the biblical allusion, which projects a biblical context on a current political situation, appear in Josephus. It is difficult to imagine that some Babylonian raconteur could have invented such a version based on the Josephan one.

The BT's version (*b. Sotah* 49b; *b. B. Qam.* 82b; *b. Menaḥ.* 64b) of the story of the breaking of the agreement between the warring camps during the Hasmonean fratricidal conflict (*Ant.* 14.22–8) preserved the deeper axiom of the story: the importance of Jewish unity and the dangers of foreign language and culture (see Chapter 6). In the Josephan version this was deliberately obscured and replaced by a simplistic universal message.

Various forms of rich biblical allusions are another fundamental building-block of the shared traditions preserved only in rabbinic literature and eradicated by Josephus. These include: (1) hidden allusions by means of use of biblical language; and (2) explicit comparisons to biblical situations. Whereas explicit scriptural exegesis, which opens with a citation and continues with overt exegesis, characterizes rabbinic literature at its peak, the two phenomena just mentioned, infrequent in classic rabbinic literature, preserve Second Temple means of expression as found in the Pseudepigrapha and the Dead Sea

Scrolls.[99] We can therefore surmise that the linguistic allusions and explicit comparisons between the Bible and the current situation belong to the infrastructure of the original story, and that they are rare remnants of early exegetical strategies known from Qumran and apocryphal literature. The story of Nicanor's defeat belongs to the first type. To the second type belongs the story of Janneus's instructions to his wife, which explicitly mentions Zimri and Phinehas.[100] The Josephan parallels of these stories contain no homily. From this perspective the rabbinic version has here preserved a significant aspect of the original source.

Another consideration that assists the determination that we are dealing with shared traditions and not rabbinic dependence on Josephus are the significant differences between the parallels. Sometimes the identity of the protagonists differs.[101] Thus, in the story of Nicanor's defeat, Judas Maccabeus is not mentioned by name. Regarding the rupture with the Pharisees, we find different protagonists, and a reversal of the roles of Eleazar and Yonathan the Sadducee. In the story of the pelting of a priest with citrons in the temple, Josephus tells this tale of Janneus and rabbinic sources of an anonymous priest. With respect to the account of the internecine Hasmonean conflict, both Josephus and the BT refer to the same historical heroes, but in the Jerusalem Talmud (YT) the protagonists are the Maccabees, or the zealots from the First Jewish Revolt. Even if in some cases it could be argued that this is a deliberate reworking that moves the spotlight from Herod to Janneus, or from John Hyrcanus to Janneus, in other instances, when secondary, unknown heroes are involved, such as Yonathan the Sadducee or Yehudah ben

---

[99] See e.g. Kister, "Biblical Phrases," 27–39; Fraade, "Legal Midrash at Qumran," 169–92.

[100] For similar examples outside the context of this volume, see e.g. the story of the choosing of Phanni of Aphthia as high priest by lot (*War* 4.152–7). The rabbinic version of this episode (*t. Yoma* [*Kippurim*] 1:6 and parallels) compares his surprising appointment to this high office to the appointment of the prophet Elisha (1 Kgs 19). The piyyut that criticizes the corrupt priests of the Second Temple period (*b. Pesaḥ*. 57a; cf. *Ant.* 20.179–81, 205–7, 213–21; see also D.R. Schwartz, "Josephus' Source on Agrippa II") compares them to the biblical figures of the sons of Eli, whose sinfulness caused the destruction of the tabernacle at Shiloh (1 Sam 2).

[101] A similar phenomenon is evident in other Jewish traditions found in Josephus's works. In the story of the high priest and Alexander the Great, the priest is named Jaddūs in Josephus's account, and Simeon the Righteous in the rabbinic account (*Ant.* 11.302–47; Scholia O and P on *Meg. Ta'an.*, 21 Kislev and parallels); the story of Herod's trial before the Sanhedrin and the strong stand taken by the elder Samaias (*Ant.* 14.169–77) is related in the Talmud of King Janneus and Simeon ben Shataḥ (*b. Sanh.* 19a–b). Josephus's account of Herod's pre-death plot and how it was averted by his sister Salome (*War* 1.659–60, 666; *Ant.* 17.173–81, 193) is in the Scholion related of Janneus and his wife Shelamzion (Scholion P, 2 Shevat). Regarding the story of the conversion of the house of Adiabene, in Josephus the queen is Helena (*Ant.* 20.53–4); in rabbinic sources she is anonymous: even the name of the son/sons is different and the father of the family is associated in rabbinic midrash with King Ptolemy (*Gen. Rab.* 46:10). Regarding the woman who consumed her child during the siege of Jerusalem, she is named Miriam, daughter of Eleazar, by Josephus (*War* 6.199–218), and is anonymous in rabbinic sources, identified as the widow of Doeg ben Yosef (*Sifra: Beḥuqotai* 6:3 and parallels). In the testimony regarding the census under Cestius/Agrippa (*War* 6.423; *t. Pesaḥ*. 4:15 and parallels), the sources are divided as to who initiated the census.

Gedidya/Gudgeda in the story of the rupture with the Pharisees (Chapter 3), it is difficult to attribute the difference to reworking. Rather, it is more likely that these are essentially different versions of the tradition. In other instances the order of events differs,[102] or the stories differ to such an extent that the very existence of a parallel is doubtful.[103]

F. AN EARLY POOL OF TRADITIONS

In light of the above considerations, this book's thesis is that the parallels treated here were drawn from a shared pool of traditions rather than that they were the result of tannaitic or amoraic familiarity with some version of Josephus's writings. This fundamentally overturns the sweeping assumption that awards Josephus preference over the reworked rabbinic version. Rather, rabbinic literature is dependent on a collection of Jewish traditions that were also known centuries earlier to Josephus, in some version or other. Sometimes, notwithstanding its late date and ahistorical nature, it is the rabbinic version that preserves authentic, unique features that were lost or obscured in the Josephan reworking.[104] Accordingly, the rabbinic version may occasionally serve as a control for the Josephan one, revealing the nature of his reworking and his bias, and not just vice versa.

Awareness that a shared infrastructure underlies the parallels in Josephus and rabbinic literature has significant ramifications for both corpora. On the one hand, this indicates that Josephus drew on a pool of Jewish traditions and opens discussion of when and how he chose to use these traditions, how they are incorporated and treated in his narrative. On the other hand, by this means we also draw near a hidden treasure trove of pre-rabbinic materials that were available to the anonymous redactors of tannaitic and amoraic works. This raises the surprising possibility that late works, far removed in

---

[102] For example, the different order in *Antiquities* and the Talmud regarding the defamation of the king and the accusation of the Pharisees in the story of the rupture with the Pharisees (Chap. 3).

[103] In Josephus the story of "Alexander Janneus/The Priest Who Was Pelted with Citrons" is a tale of a political confrontation; in rabbinic literature it treats a halakhic dispute. Josephus recounts Janneus's instructions to his wife as a deathbed scene, whereas the talmudic text simply reports a conversation between them. The latter consists of a pithy aphorism, which has no parallel in Josephus. The story of the murder of Onias is missing from rabbinic literature; and finally, the matter of the sacrifices in the internecine Hasmonean conflict is recounted in several versions, some very different from that of Josephus and even placed in different historical settings. Similar phenomena are also attested in parallel traditions not treated in this volume; see Noam, "Lost Historical Traditions," 1014–15 nn. 76–8.

[104] Cf. Menahem Kister's observation: "It can also be the case that a more authentic version of a tradition was preserved in rabbinic sources, which are later [than the Second Temple literature parallel—VN]" (Kister, "Aḥor va-qedem," 231).

time and place, such as the Babylonian Talmud, preserved ancient materials, as Menahem Kister proposes:

> The significant similarity between the two libraries...teaches us that the founda-
> tions of talmudic literature are embedded in Second Temple Judaism, sometimes
> centuries before the redaction or transmission of the texts in rabbinic literature,
> and that many of the traditions and homiletic methods known to us from rabbinic
> literature were in wide use during temple days and even crossed the boundaries of
> the ideologies and sects that characterized this historical period.[105]

In general, the traditions examined here can serve as signposts and criteria for recognition of anomalous sources in both corpora. In Josephus, they stand out because of their distinctly Jewish nature; in rabbinic literature, because they are pre- and even extra-rabbinic.

More importantly, the compilation and characterization of these sources which were preserved by means of two such different conduits of transmission brings us closer to reconstruction of a lost literary continent, a hidden Jewish "Atlantis" whose existence is as yet unrecognized in the scholarship. For years scholars have been investigating the written library of the Second Temple period, searching for the fragments of early halakhah and pre-rabbinic exegesis embedded in this literature. An explicit statement regarding the existence of a wide pool of lost, probably oral, historical and pseudo-historical traditions dating to this period has yet to be made; nor has any attempt been undertaken to characterize the nature and conjectured origins of this collection.[106] Recently John Collins voiced the possibility that lost historical traditions, either oral or written, underlie the pesharim and other Qumran texts that allude to various unspecified historical events.[107] He suggests that these sources resembled the three very fragmentary calendrical texts, 4Q331–4Q333, which mention the names of the priestly courses and historical events. Some view them as lists of dates that must be observed yearly, similar to *Megillat Ta'anit*; others as a list of events with no halakhic purpose.[108] Collins proposes that, between the Hasmonean revolt and Josephus's day, these traditions were current among different Jewish circles, including the Qumran sectarians, proving that the sectarians were not entirely indifferent to historical memory.[109] Although this book posits a broader

---

[105] Ibid.

[106] For a very preliminary hypothesis regarding the existence of written traditions, different in nature and more extensive than what is described in this volume, see Dinur, "Historiographical Fragments." Günter Stemberger rejects the conjecture that oral traditions underlie rabbinic references to the Hasmoneans and suggests instead that this material was acquired from Christian communities in fourth-century Palestine and, with regard to the BT, from Arabs and Christians in Babylonia in the late Sasanian and early Islamic periods ("The Maccabees in Rabbinic Tradition," 202–3).

[107] For a comprehensive discussion of the historical allusions in the Dead Sea Scrolls, see H. Eshel, *Dead Sea Scrolls and the Hasmonean State*.

[108] On the contents of these calendrical texts and a detailed treatment of the scholarly hypotheses, see ibid. 124–31.

[109] Collins, "Historiography," 159–76.

scope of these lost "historical" sources, it is allied with Collins's scholarly intuition in seeking this literature, whose existence is gradually being affirmed from different directions.

G. MEMORY AND HISTORIOGRAPHY

The test case examined in this book constitutes an unusual, intriguing variation of the tension between traditional memory and critical historiography. The twentieth century saw a growing, sharp differentiation between these two poles by various sociologists and historians, among them the French sociologist Maurice Halbwachs. Halbwachs distinguishes between collective memory—which reflects a sense of a living, committed past that is the organic by-product of the present and of the needs of the living community that persistently nurtures this memory—and historical research—the frozen reconstruction of a dead past, to which the rememberer no longer bears an organic, experiential relationship. Implemented through commemorative ceremonies and holidays, collective memory represents a subjective reality that is destined to vanish. In contrast, history remains permanently fixed. The historian's efforts to achieve proof-based objectivity and to know the past-as-it-was sever him from the present and from the group to which he belongs, pushing him away from tribal consensus to the universal. In other words, history begins where tradition ends.[110]

Application of Halbwachs's insights to the specific case of Jewish historiography came in the 1980s, with the publication of the American-Jewish historian Yosef Hayim Yerushalmi's influential book *Zakhor*. A major assertion put forth in *Zakhor* was that Jewish historiographical creativity ceased with Josephus and was fully renewed only in modernity, with the beginnings of the *Wissenschaft des Judentums*.[111]

Shortly after the publication of *Zakhor*, Pierre Nora's seminal collection *Les Lieux de la mémoire* began to appear, in which Nora sought to reconstruct the lost French national memory from material and ceremonial "memory places" that preserved its last traces. In the introduction to this collection Nora laments: "What was left of experience, still lived in the warmth of tradition...has been

---

[110] Halbwachs, *Collective Memory*. In his wake Assman and Czaplicka ("Collective Memory and Cultural Identity," 125–33) introduced the notion of "cultural memory" (see their proposed new distinction between it and "communicative" memory), whose reconstruction of the past is incessantly changing. This type of memory, defined by its relationship to the group that shapes it, is molded and crystallized in the form of sacred texts and ceremonies and characterized by transcendentalism, which distinguishes it from the mundane. For a comprehensive survey of studies of collective memory from different perspectives, see Olick and Robbins, "Social Memory Studies," 105–40. I thank Meir Ben Shahar for bringing some of the studies mentioned here to my attention.

[111] Yerushalmi, *Zakhor*, 5–6.

swept away by a surge of deeply historical sensibility." Halbwachs's dichotomic description of memory vs. history receives poetic expression at Nora's hands:

> Memory is life, always embodied in living societies…Memory, being a phenomenon of emotion and magic, accommodates only those facts that suit it. It thrives on vague, telescoping reminiscences, on hazy general impressions of symbolic details…History, being an intellectual, nonreligious activity, calls for analysis and critical discourse. Memory situates remembrance in a sacred context. History ferrets it out; it turns whatever it touches into prose. Memory wells up from groups that it welds together…By contrast, history belongs to everyone and to no one and therefore has a universal vocation.

In Nora's view, the historical perspective destroys collective memory: "historiography sows doubt; it runs the blade of a knife between the heartwood of memory and the bark of history."[112]

The Hasmonean history fragmentarily preserved in the form of brief, colorful tales in Jewish recollection is an exceptional illustration of "the heartwood of memory." Whereas the writers cited above portray living memory as the product of pre-modern periods and historiography as definitively modern, here the representative of historiography is an ancient author, and the collective memory was preserved in works compiled centuries later. Moreover, if Halbwachs, Yerushalmi, and Nora describe historiography as murdering and inheriting living memory, in this instance the historian adopted and embedded vestiges of folk legend in his historiography. In the case of rabbinic literature, it was not history that ousted memory, but just the opposite: memory replaced historical sense.

In the scholarship penned after *Zakhor*, the dichotomic distinction between personal-collective memory and historiography was somewhat attenuated.[113] One kind of oblique critique emerged from post-modern skepticism, with its assessment of "the historical text as literary artifact," which blurred the distinction between allegedly objective historical writing and folktale.[114] The current

---

[112] Nora, *Realms of Memory*, 1:1–4. Intriguingly, Nora, who was evidently unfamiliar with Yerushalmi's monograph, made an observation surprisingly similar to its main theme: "Think of the Jews faithfully observing their traditional ritual: as the 'people of memory', history was of no concern of theirs until exposure to the modern world obliged them to discover a need for historians" (2).

[113] Funkenstein (*Perceptions of Jewish History*, 3–21) argues for a continuum between memory and historiography, since collective memory is not devoid of historical intuition, as manifested in creative thinking about the past and present and awareness of the relativity of time and place. Another critique of Halbwachs and Nora argues that folk memory, in spite of its characteristic hyperbolic creativity, still functions within the limitations of historical facticity (B. Schwartz, "Collective Memory and History," 469–96). For references to the response to Yerushalmi's thesis, see Ben-Shalom, *Facing Christian Culture*, 6 n. 10. For a survey of the scholarship on history and memory since the publication of *Zakhor*, see Miron, "Three Decades Since Zakhor," 107–21.

[114] White, "Historical Text as Literary Artifact," 81–100; idem, *Tropics of Discourse*. Other prominent thinkers also questioned the very feasibility of describing historical events, terming historical research an act of forming but not discovering the past. See L. Goldstein, *Historical Knowing*; de Certeau, *Writing of History*; Berkhofer, "Challenge of Poetics," 435–52; Ankersmit,

study also sheds new light on one of the main arguments typical of this approach, namely that historians impose the prevailing literary-cultural genres on the material at their disposal. "The historical narrative thus mediates between the events reported in it on the one side and pregeneric plot structures conventionally used in our culture to endow unfamiliar events and situations with meanings, on the other."[115] Familiarity with Jewish traditions scattered independently throughout rabbinic literature, and also embedded in a historical narrative, facilitates entry into the workshop in which anecdotal folk stories were transformed into a link in a historical narrative.

H. CONTENTS, AIMS, AND METHODOLOGY

This book singles out six stories relating to the Hasmoneans that appear both in Josephus and rabbinic literature. In most instances these are "literary parallels," namely, a parallel grounded in a formulated—but not necessarily written—source, rather than a shared memory of the same historical events. These traditions are closed, anecdotal episodes,[116] which take place on the margins of major events and clearly reflect "stories" absorbed by both libraries. Thus, for example, the biography of John Hyrcanus is part of the historical narrative of the Hasmonean period, but the anecdote regarding the heavenly voice he heard in the temple is a "story." This is also the case for the feast held by John Hyrcanus (or his son Janneus) with the Pharisees and the ensuing political rift. The figure of Janneus, his wars and conquests, have a central role in the history of the Hasmonean state, but his instructions to his wife regarding the Pharisees or his being pelted by citrons at the altar are "stories" that do not impact the events themselves. The Hasmonean civil war is a significant historical affair, but the murder of Onias/Ḥoni, the breaking of the agreement regarding sacrifices, the drought, and the legend of the pig are all miniatures appended to the main occurrence.

As treated here, the six anecdotes concerning the Hasmoneans are: Nicanor's defeat; John Hyrcanus and the heavenly voice in the temple; the rupture between John Hyrcanus/Janneus and the Pharisees; the pelting of Janneus/an

Narrative Logic. For a comprehensive survey of the impact of post-modern thought on the nuances of historical research, see Windschuttle, *Killing of History*, introduction, and p. 317 (I thank Isaiah Gafni for the last reference).

[115] White, "Historical Text as Literary Artifact," 88. For the struggle against this approach, see e.g. G. Himmelfarb, "Telling It As You Like It," 158–74; Windschuttle, *Killing of History*; Evans, *In Defence of History*.

[116] See D. R. Schwartz ("From Alexandria to Rabbinic Literature," 42) for an intriguing distinction between historiography, which documents sequential change, and a "story," which ends with the resolution of a crisis and restoration of a peaceful reality that has been disrupted. On the closed nature of aggadic stories, see Fraenkel, "Hermeneutic Problems."

anonymous priest with citrons in the temple; Janneus's instructions to his wife concerning the Pharisees; and the fratricidal war between Hyrcanus II and Aristobulus II that brought the downfall of the Hasmonean commonwealth.

For each set of parallels, I attempted to ascertain the underlying motivation for the creation of the story in question and its original message regarding the Hasmonean dynasty. From the literary perspective I assigned each story to a genre: a national myth of war and victory; a theodicean treatment of a national loss; an etiological story; a priestly legend set in the temple and its rites; a midrash grounded in a biblical pericope which is drafted to current needs; a polemical-political argument in literary garb; and the like. Each story's message, and also its idiosyncratic language, is considered against the backdrop of historical circumstances, literary topoi, and the world of images and expressions used in the extant Second Temple and rabbinic literature. The characterization of these early, pre-rabbinic and pre-Josephan traditions is part of the quest for the lost Second Temple oral Jewish literature, as described above.

This analysis is followed by exploration of the nature of the relationship between the Josephan and the rabbinic versions, in an attempt to reconstruct how the putative original traditions were adapted within the two corpora. These adaptations reflect the reception history of the pristine tales and thus disclose the shifting images of the Hasmoneans in later generations and within distinct contexts. Because the original tales were recounted in Hebrew and in Aramaic, rabbinic literature has preserved them in a form closer to the original—linguistically at least—than Josephus's Greek writings. I have therefore chosen to cite the Hebrew rabbinic sources in full, providing Greek words and phrases from Josephus only when pertinent to the discussion. The traditions are arranged chronologically, which is also how they appear in *Antiquities*.[117]

In order to assist the reader, appended to each story is a brief description of its historical background. It is *not* my intent, however, to reconstruct Hasmonean history based on these stories, but rather, as stated above, to trace the image of the Hasmonean dynasty in the collective memory of their contemporaries and the following generations, as this emerges from the Josephan and the rabbinic points of view. The general picture of this repository that emerges from analysis of the individual stories, its attitude toward the different generations of the Hasmoneans, and the deliberate changes detected within the two later corpora, will be discussed in the concluding chapter of this book.[118]

---

[117] In one instance, the traditions are divided, with different protagonists: John Hyrcanus in Josephus; Janneus in rabbinic literature (see Chap. 3). The chronological order is, however, according to Josephus.

[118] Some of the discussion has previously appeared in Vered Noam, "Lost Historical Traditions: Between Josephus and the Rabbis," in *Sibyls, Scriptures, and Scrolls: John Collins at Seventy*, ed. Joel Baden, Hindy Najman, and Eibert Tigchelaar, JSJSup 175 (Leiden: Brill, 2017), 2:991–1017.

1

Nicanor's Defeat

The initial episode analyzed here—the story of an outstanding Hasmonean victory over the Seleucid general Nicanor, which was subsequently marked by a holiday—is exceptional in the context of this book. As opposed to the other episodes treated here, for which the sole witnesses are the Josephan and rabbinic corpora, the existence of an additional source—1 Maccabees 7:26–50[1]—makes it possible to determine with certainty, in this instance at least, that the similarity between the Josephan and the rabbinic accounts does not testify to direct affinity between the two but rather lies in the use of sources or traditions pre-dating both corpora. Although the different renderings of this story within rabbinic literature are recounted in Hebrew, some of them also bear surprising similarity to the second-century BCE Greek version of 1 Maccabees. This substantiates the conjecture that rabbinic authors or redactors had access either to the Hebrew original of 1 Maccabees, or to some early historical Hebrew traditions that circulated in Judea even prior to the composition of this work. Moreover, based on the extant sources, it is possible to reconstruct the features of these lost Hebrew traditions, especially their flowery language and masterfully interpolated biblical associations and allusions. Although missing from the Josephan version, these attributes can still be discerned in the Greek text of 1 Maccabees, even if modified by translation, and in rabbinic literature, even if modified by redaction and transmission. The unique opportunity provided by this specific tradition to compare both the Josephan and the rabbinic narratives to a second-century BCE Jewish source (though veiled by a Greek translation) allows us to trace, with a large degree of certainty, the means by which these ancient traditions were integrated and adapted in Josephan works on the one hand, and in rabbinic sources on the other. One conclusion that emerges from this comparison was that rabbinic sources may have better preserved certain aspects of the ancient traditions than Josephus, both because he wrote in Greek and because of the aims that

---

[1] The parallel in 2 Macc 14:12–36, 15:1–36 did not influence the Josephan and rabbinic versions.

governed his reworking of the materials. The most significant conclusion for our purposes—the deliberate omission of Judas Maccabeus's name from the story in the rabbinic versions—may contribute to the long-debated question of the rabbinic attitude toward the Hasmoneans, and more generally to the inquiry at the heart of this book: the image of the Hasmoneans in various Jewish circles and generations in antiquity.

A. THE SOURCES

Antiquities 12.402-12; *Megillat Ta'anit*, 13 Adar; Scholia O and P, 13 Adar; *y. Ta'anit* 2:13, 66a; *y. Megillah* 1:6, 70c; *b. Ta'anit* 18b; [1 Maccabees 7:26–50; 2 Maccabees 14:12–36, 15:1–36]

Josephus, *Antiquities* 12.402–12

(402) Thereupon Demetrius, beginning to believe that it would be hazardous to his own interests also to do nothing about Judas' growing strength, sent out Nicanor, the most devoted and faithful of his Friends—for it was he who had escaped with him from the city of Rome—and giving him as large a force as he thought would be sufficient for him to use against Judas, ordered him to deal unsparingly with the nation. (403) But when Nicanor came to Jerusalem, he decided not to fight Judas immediately, but chose to get him into his power by deceit, and so he sent him offers of peace, saying that there was no necessity for their making war and facing danger, but he would give Judas his oath that he should suffer no harm; for he said, he had come with some friends to make clear to them what the intentions of King Demetrius were, and how he felt toward their race. (404) This offer, which was made by the envoys of Nicanor, was believed by Judas and his brothers, and not suspecting any treachery, they gave pledges to him, and received Nicanor with his force. But he, after greeting Judas, and while conversing with him, gave his men a certain signal by which they were to seize Judas. (405) He, however, saw through the plot, and dashing out, escaped to his own men. Accordingly, since his purpose and the trap had become known, Nicanor decided to make war on Judas; but the other, having organized his men and prepared for battle, engaged him at a certain village called Kapharsalama, and defeated him and forced him to flee to the Akra in Jerusalem.

(406) And again, as Nicanor was coming down from the Akra to the temple, he was met by some of the priests and elders, who greeted him and showed him the sacrifices which they said they were offering to God on behalf of the king. Thereupon he fell to cursing them (ὁ δὲ βλασφημήσας αὐτοὺς), and threatened that, if the people did not give Judas up to him, he would pull down the temple

when he returned. (407) After making these threats, he left Jerusalem, while the priests burst into tears in their distress over his words, and supplicated God to deliver them from their enemies. (408) Now after Nicanor had left Jerusalem, he came to a certain village called Bethoron, and there encamped, being joined by another force from Syria. And Judas encamped at Adasa,[2] another village thirty stades distant from Bethoron, with two thousand men[3] in all.[4] (409) These he exhorted not to be overawed by the numbers of their adversaries nor to reflect how many they were about to contend against, but to bear in mind who they were and for what prize they were facing danger, and bravely encounter the enemy; and then he led them out to battle. And engaging Nicanor, he defeated his adversaries after a severe fight, and killed many of them; finally Nicanor himself fell, fighting gloriously. (410) When he fell, his army did not stay, but having lost their commander, threw away all their armour, and turned to flight. But Judas pursued and slew them, and caused the trumpets to signal to the surrounding villages that he was defeating the enemy. (411) When their inhabitants heard this, they leaped to arms, and heading off the fugitives, met them face to face, and killed them, so that from this battle not a single man escaped out of the nine thousand who were in it. (412) Now the victory took place on the thirteenth of the month which is called Adar by the Jews, and Dystros by the Macedonians. And the Jews celebrate their victory every year in this month, and observe this day as a festival. But though the Jewish nation for a little while after that date had respite from war and enjoyed peace, thereafter it was again to undergo a period of struggle and danger.

Rabbinic Sources

Megillat Ta'anit, 13 Adar

[בתלת עשר ביה ניקנור[5]]

On the thirteenth thereof—Nicanor

Scholion P

‹אמרו› ניקנור פולמורדוס של מלכי יון היה והיה מניף ידו כנגד ירוש' וכנגד בית המקדש ומחרף
ומגדף מתי תפול בידי ואהרסנה. וכשתקפה יד בית חשמונאי ירדו לתוך חילותיו וחתכו את ראשו וקצצו
את איבריו ותלאום כנגד בית המקדש אמרו פה שדבר בגאיות ויד שהניפה כנגד בית המקדש נקמות
יעשה בהן יום שעשו כן עשאוהו יום טוב

---

[2] For proposals regarding the identification of Adasa, see Marcus, *Jewish Antiquities* (LCL), 7:212–13, note *c*. See also Bar-Kochva, *Judas Maccabaeus*, 363.

[3] Some manuscripts read "one thousand." In 1 Macc 7:40: "three thousand."

[4] The words "in all" are missing in several witnesses.

[5] See Noam, *Megillat Ta'anit*, 47 (and textual variants there).

[It was said[6] that] Nicanor was the (*polmordos*) [*polemarchos*][7] of the kings of Greece and he would raise his hand against Jerusalem and against the temple and blaspheme and curse: When will it fall into my hand so that I may destroy it? And when the Hasmonean dynasty prevailed they descended among his troops, severed his head, and cut off his limbs, and hanged them facing (*keneged*) the temple. They said: "The mouth that spoke arrogantly, the hand that was raised against the temple, vengeance shall be exacted on them." The day that they did so they declared a festival.

Scholion O

ומלכותא דיונאי. שהן מניפין ידיהן על ירושלם והר ציון וקבע אחד מבית חשמונאי ופסק ראשו ותלאום בשער ירושלם ואמר פה שדבר בגאיה תעשה בו נקמה וידים המניפות על ירושלם תקצצנה

And the kingdom of the Greeks. Who would raise their hands against Jerusalem and Mount Zion. And one [member] of the Hasmonean dynasty penetrated, severed his head and hanged them from the gate of Jerusalem. He said: "The mouth that spoke arrogantly, vengeance shall be exacted on it, and the hands that were raised against Jerusalem shall be cut off."

Y. Ta'anit 2:13, 66a [=Y. Meg. 1:6, 70c]

שלטון משלמלכות יוון עובר לאלכסנדרייאה וראה את ירושלם וחירף וגידף וניאץ ואמר בשובי בשלום אתוץ את המגדל הזה ויצא אליו אחד משלבית חשמונייי והיה הורג בחיילותיו עד שהגיע לקרוכין שלו וכיון שהגיע לקרוכין שלו קטע את ידו וחתך את ראשו ותחבן בעץ וכתב מלמטן הפה שדיבר באשמה והיד שפשטה בגאוה ותליין בקונטס נגד ירושלם[8]

A ruler of the kingdom of Greece [was] en route to Alexandria. And he saw Jerusalem and blasphemed and cursed and taunted, and said: "When I come back whole, I shall break down that tower." One [of the members] of the Hasmonean dynasty went forth toward him and killed members of his troops until he reached his chariot, and when he reached his chariot, he cut off his hand and severed his head, and stuck them on a pole, and wrote underneath

---

[6] It was said] In the Parma MS: אמר על, "He said of," probably a corruption. I corrected it according to the hybrid version: אמרו, literally: "they said."

[7] This appears to be a corruption of a term known from various biblical translations: pole-march, *polemarchos* (πολέμαρχος), which is the Greek for commander, the person who opens or leads a war (*LSJ*, http://stephanus.tlg.uci.edu/lsj/#eid=86949&context=lsj&action=from-search 1432), and warrior in rabbinic literature. See Sokoloff, *Jewish Palestinian Aramaic*, s.v. פולימרך (426). In Bar-Kochva's opinion (oral communication) the Scholion was more conversant with Greek than its parallels and, in seeking to aggrandize Nicanor's position in order to heighten his downfall, assigned him high military rank—*polemarchos*—which one copyist corrupted to *polmordos*.

[8] There are slight differences in the *y. Meg.* version.

them: "[Here is] the mouth that spoke wrongfully and the hand that stretched out arrogantly." These he set up on a pike facing Jerusalem.

B. *Ta'anit* 18b

ניקנור אחד מהפרכי⁹ יונים היה בכל יום ויום היה מניף ידו על יהודה וירושלם ואומר אימתי

יפלו בידי ואהרגם וכשגברו מלכי בית חשמנאי ונצחום נכנסו לחילות שלו וקיצצו בהונות ידיו

ורגליו ותלאום בשערי ירושלם אמרו פה שהיה מדבר בגאוה וידים שהיו מניפות על יהודה

וירושלם תיעשה בהן נקמה זאת¹⁰

Nicanor was one of the Greek generals. Every day he would raise his hand against Judah and Jerusalem and say, "When shall they[11] fall into my hands that I[12] may kill them?" But when the Hasmonean kings[13] proved victorious and triumphed over them,[14] they entered among his troops. They cut off his thumbs and his great toes and hanged them from the gates of Jerusalem. They said: "The mouth that spoke arrogantly and the hands that were raised against Judah and Jerusalem,[15] may this vengeance be exacted on them!"

B. HISTORICAL BACKGROUND

The frame of reference for Nicanor's defeat at the hands of Judas Maccabeus is the Judean power struggle against the Seleucid Empire.[16] Internal struggles within the realm between Antiochus V Eupator under the regency of Lysias (1 Macc 6:17; see also 1 Macc 3:32–3, 2 Macc 10:10–11, 11:1, 13:1–2) and another claimant to the throne, Demetrius, led to the former's execution. Having attained the throne in 162 BCE (1 Macc 7:1–4; 2 Macc 14:1–2),[17] Demetrius

---

[9] איפרכוס, איפרך, in rabbinic literature sometimes mistakenly spelled with *heh*. הפרכא is the Greek ἔπαρχος, or ruler of an eparchy, a Seleucid administrative unit that paralleled the Persian satrapy. This title continues to appear in Palestinian midrashim and in the BT with respect to the Roman period. See Sokoloff, *Jewish Palestinian Aramaic*, 53; idem, *Jewish Babylonian Aramaic*, 389. Bar-Kochva maintains that this title neither fits the Judean situation of the day nor Nicanor's status, who was a meridarch and not an eparch. Rather, in seeking to aggrandize his status, the sources portray him as possessing high military rank. See Avi-Yonah, *Historical Geography*, 45–8; Bar-Kochva, *Judas Maccabaeus*, 352–3.

[10] According to Jerusalem, MS Yad Harav Herzog 1.

[11] They] In several versions: יפול, תפול in the singular: masculine or feminine.

[12] I] in one version: ונהרגם meaning we, in the plural. In one manuscript: ואעשה בה מה שלבי חפץ, "and I shall do to her [probably meaning Jerusalem] whatever I wish." In most of the manuscripts: וארמסנה "and I shall trample her [Jerusalem]."

[13] The mention of "kings" is of course incongruent with the historical setting. Several versions have the equally incongruent reading מלכות "kingdom."

[14] Two manuscripts read ונצחוהו, "triumphed over him."

[15] Against Judah and Jerusalem] In the printed editions: "against Jerusalem."

[16] See Goldstein, "Hasmonean Revolt," 292–309.

[17] For a description of this event, see Polybius, *The Histories*, 31.11–12; Rappaport, *First Book of Maccabees*; D. R. Schwartz, *2 Maccabees*.

sought to promote the loyal high priest Alcimus,[18] and to eradicate Hasmonean superiority in Judea, to this end dispatching a large military force under Bacchides, who, according to 1 Maccabees 7:8, was in charge of the western sector of the Seleucid Empire and the king's confidant.

As recounted in the sources, neither these circumstances nor the campaign receive identical treatment. According to 1 Maccabees, at first certain Jewish circles were willing to recognize Alcimus as high priest. However, in the wake of renewed conflict precipitated by the cruelty of Bacchides and Alcimus (1 Macc 7:10–23), a senior Seleucid officer named Nicanor was dispatched to the region (1 Macc 7:26; 2 Macc 14:12). His precise identity, however, remains a disputed matter. Described as the former "commander of the elephant corps" (2 Macc 14:12), some scholars identify him as Nicanor, son of Patroclus (2 Macc 8:9), who is mentioned in the context of the battle at Emmaus;[19] however, the prevailing consensus is that this identification is incorrect. Many scholars follow Josephus (*Ant.* 12.402) and identify "our" Nicanor with the close friend of Demetrius I, who, according to Polybius, accompanied him from Rome.[20]

Bacchides's campaign is absent from the account in 2 Maccabees; there Nicanor's campaign occupies center stage from the start. In Daniel R. Schwartz's view this reflects a general thrust on the part of the author of 2 Maccabees: to highlight Nicanor's role.[21] He attributes both the emphasis on Nicanor's campaigns against the Jews, and the book's conclusion with the decree mandating the observance of Nicanor's day, to the author's desire to establish the holiday founded in commemoration of Nicanor's defeat.[22] 2 Maccabees places the initial clash between Nicanor and the Judeans near "the village of Dessau" (evidently Adasa, the final, decisive battlefield according to 1 Macc 7:40), recounting that Judas's brother Simeon suffered a "slight setback" in his encounter with Nicanor (2 Macc 14:12–17). According to this version, at this stage, deterred by the rebels' bravery, Nicanor reached an agreement with, and befriended, Judas.

---

[18] It is unclear from the sources whether Alcimus was appointed to the high priesthood in Lysias's day, or only after Demetrius came to power. See Goldstein, *II Maccabees*, 481.

[19] On the author or abridger's use of linguistic-structural means to create identity between the two Nicanors, see D. R. Schwartz, *2 Maccabees*, 7–10, 473 n. 12.

[20] For a survey of the opinions and the scholarship, see Bar-Kochva, *Judas Maccabaeus*, 352–3 (he disagrees with this identification); Goldstein, *II Maccabees*, 486–7; Rappaport, *First Book of Maccabees*, 214; D. R. Schwartz, *2 Maccabees*, 473–6.

[21] D. R. Schwartz, *2 Maccabees*, 473–6.

[22] Ibid. 3–10. Schwartz maintains that the letters at the beginning of the book, which call for the celebration of Hanukkah, and the description in 10:1–8 of the institution of Hanukkah after the purification of the temple, belong to a secondary reworking. Schwartz distinguishes between the Jerusalem-centric emphasis of the Diaspora author, who preferred Nicanor's Day, and the temple-centric emphasis of the Palestinian redactor, who preferred Hanukkah. However, below I will try to demonstrate that the Nicanor story is also grounded in a "temple" theme. Bar-Kochva (*Judas Maccabaeus*, 361) takes a more moderate stand. He views 2 Maccabees's detailed description of the battle at Adasa as an attempt to justify the declaration of Nicanor's Day, but does not see this as the underlying motivation for the composition of the book.

However, Alcimus's denunciation of Nicanor to Demetrius sparked renewed conflict (2 Macc 14:18–29).

This turn of events is not recounted in 1 Maccabees. There the circumstances differ: with his arrival in Judea, Nicanor sought to trick Judas Maccabeus by offering peace negotiations while actually plotting Judas's capture. Judas managed to escape, and two battles then ensued between Judas and his supporters and Nicanor and his forces. In the first, minor skirmish near Chaphar-salama, not far from Jerusalem,[23] Nicanor's forces suffered defeat and fled to the City of David, apparently, the Seleucid Akra.[24] At this stage, 1 Maccabees relates that, on seeking to appease Nicanor, the priests and elders received the following mocking reply: "Presumptuously he spoke, angrily swearing that 'Unless Judas and his army are delivered over into my hands immediately, upon my victorious return I shall burn this temple.' Then he went out, in a hot rage" (1 Macc 7:34–5). A decisive engagement then took place between the opposing forces at Adasa, near Beth Horon, in the hilly region north-west of Jerusalem. Judas enjoyed a great victory: Nicanor was killed in battle and Jerusalem was reconquered.

2 Maccabees does not recount the first clash at Chaphar-salama, only the decisive battle at which Nicanor met his death. It notes that, having reached an agreement with Judas, Nicanor was forced into a new conflict, making a treacherous attempt to capture Judas at Demetrius's behest. When Judas slipped away, Nicanor asked the temple priests to turn him over. On their declaring ignorance of Judas's whereabouts, he "stretched forth his right hand against the temple and swore, 'If you do not hand Judas over to me, I shall raze to the ground this shrine of your God, and tear down the altar, and I shall build in its place a fine temple to Dionysus!'" (2 Macc 14:33). 2 Maccabees 15 provides an expanded description of the battle of Adasa, without noting its location. Both books of Maccabees relate how parts of Nicanor's corpse were amputated and displayed in Jerusalem,[25] and how that date, the thirteenth of Adar, became

---

[23] Various proposals have been put forth for identifying this location with places whose Arabic names bear similarity to the name in the sources. See Bar-Kochva, *Judas Maccabaeus*, 356–8; Goldstein, *I Maccabees*, 339–40. However, 1 Maccabees does not indicate its location. Because the refugees fled to the City of David, it appears likely that it was not far from Jerusalem. Some scholars identify it as the Kefar Shalem mentioned in rabbinic literature. See Reeg, *Ortsnamen Israels*, 373.

[24] According to Josephus, *Ant.* 12.405, Nicanor defeated Judas, and Judas fled to the Akra. Because of the inconsistency with the testimony of 1 Maccabees, and because only Nicanor, not Judas, could have fled to the Seleucid stronghold, Dindorf emended the text. See Marcus, *Jewish Antiquities* (LCL), 7:210–11 and note *d*; Bar-Kochva, *Judas Maccabaeus*, 358.

[25] For parallels regarding post-mortem punishment in the ancient world, see Hallewy, *Ha-aggadah*, 47–9; Bar-Kochva, *Judas Maccabaeus*, 368–9, where he argues that decapitation and amputation was originally a Persian punishment. The books of Maccabees, and rabbinic sources, however, portray it as a "measure for measure" punishment for Nicanor's deeds, for having sinned with his hand and his mouth.

an annual holiday (1 Macc 7:47–9, 2 Macc 15:30–6).[26] Although this victory restored Hasmonean control of Judea, another twenty years would pass before full political independence was achieved.

C. THE ACCOUNTS OF NICANOR'S DEFEAT

Josephus and His Sources

The scholarly consensus assigns the opening of *War* (1.31–49), which summarizes the period of the Antiochian edicts and the revolt until Simeon's day, mainly to a Hellenistic source, most likely Nicolaus of Damascus,[27] whereas the description of the Antiochian persecution and the Maccabean revolt in *Antiquities* (12.240–13.214) is seen as a direct paraphrase of the Greek version of 1 Maccabees 1–13.[28] (It appears that Josephus made no use of 2 Maccabees.) Taking note of the many differences between 1 Maccabees and *Antiquities*, scholars attribute them to the Josephan reworking of his sources, noting a number of characteristic features: stylistic changes and simplification; omission of poetry; the use of indirect rather than direct speech to convey the contents of orations and creation of fictional speeches; the censoring of sections that might offend non-Jewish readers or detract from the image of the Hasmoneans; and the addition of geographical references based on personal knowledge. However, *Antiquities* also contains facts and figures not present in 1 Maccabees. Some view this as evidence of minor use of additional sources; others suggest that they were invented by Josephus.[29]

Isaiah Gafni notes another feature of the Josephan reworking of his sources: his goal of making them conform to the message he wished to convey to his

---

[26] Among the many differences between 1 and 2 Maccabees I note the significant additions in 2 Maccabees: the suicide of Razis (2 Macc 14:37–46); the debate regarding the conduct of war on the Sabbath between Nicanor and the Jews forced to accompany him (2 Macc 15:1–5); and Judas's dream of Onias, the late high priest (2 Macc 15:11–16). For further comparisons, see Goldstein, *I Maccabees*, 338–43; idem, *II Maccabees*, 486–93. Because these differences did not influence the Josephan version, and certainly not the rabbinic one, they have little bearing on the discussion here.

[27] According to Bar-Kochva (*Judas Maccabaeus*, 186–90), Josephus wrote his short survey of the revolt and the decrees from memory, influenced by 1 Maccabees, Nicolaus, and Daniel. With respect to the battle at Beth Zacharia (41–6), however, Bar-Kochva claims that Josephus used a written version of Nicolaus's book. Nicolaus himself relied on a Seleucid source and also on 1 Maccabees for his description of Eleazar's courageous act. For a comprehensive consideration of Nicolaus's use of 1 Maccabees for this point, see Ilan, "David, Herod and Nicolaus," 222–4.

[28] See Cohen, *Josephus in Galilee and Rome*, 44 n. 77; Bar-Kochva, "On Josephus," 115–17; Feldman, "Josephus' Portrayal of the Hasmoneans," 41–2 n. 3 and the bibliographical survey there.

[29] For topical and bibliographical surveys, see Gafni, "Josephus and I Maccabees," 116–31; Bar-Kochva, *Judas Maccabaeus*, 186–93; Feldman, "Josephus' Portrayal of the Hasmoneans"; Sievers, *Synopsis*; idem, "Josephus, First Maccabees, Sparta," esp. 246; Rappaport, *First Book of Maccabees*, 10–12, 69–70.

readers. These Josephan alterations include: the deletion of statements regarding the cessation of prophecy, because he believed that it still existed in his day;[30] the toning down of 1 Maccabees's dynastic emphasis; a shift from the theocentric worldview of his source to an anthropocentric one that places human ability at its center; and the highlighting of Jewish tenacity and willingness to die for ancestral law. Furthermore, Josephus underscores the notion that receiving divine assistance is contingent on the righteousness of those who yearn for deliverance, evidently in order to distinguish between the worthy, successful Hasmonean revolt and the misguided one of the zealots in his day.[31] In his study, Louis Feldman focuses on the similarities between the Josephan treatment of 1 Maccabees and the biblical text. For both, Josephus tends to reduce the divine role and empower the human protagonists, based on the belief, following Thucydides, that history is in essence the biography of great men and that strong leadership underlies the success of the state. In his 1 Maccabees-based account, Josephus censors statements praising zealotry, stresses Hasmonean hegemony and Hasmonean loyalty to their Syrian allies, while reducing manifestations of enmity toward non-Jews.[32] Many of these adaptations are evident in the case under discussion here, as elaborated later in the chapter.

Josephus and 1 Maccabees

In its brief account *War* 1 makes no reference to Nicanor. In contrast, notwithstanding the topical and stylistic differences detailed below, the version found in *Antiquities* evinces strong resemblance to the account in 1 Maccabees. Table 1.1 compares the accounts of Nicanor's defeat in *Antiquities* and 1 Maccabees (in English translation).[33]

As noted above, some of the features of the Josephan reworking of his sources appear in his reworking of 1 Maccabees. Of these varied features, only the erasure of biblical allusions, which has not been fully explored in the scholarship, will be treated here at length.

Anthropocentric rather than theocentric emphasis. In Maccabees, Judas turns to God for aid, making reference to divine deliverance from the Assyrians in the past (1 Macc 7:41–2, see below). In *Antiquities* Josephus mentions neither divine deliverance nor the historical precedent. Josephus replaces the appeal to God with Judas's appeal to the soldiers, grounding the future deliverance in

---

[30] See Chap. 2.

[31] Gafni, "Josephus and I Maccabees."

[32] Feldman, "Josephus' Portrayal of the Hasmoneans." Some of Feldman's observations—such as Josephus's emphasis on the human factor and Jewish willingness to die for ancestral laws—overlap Gafni's.

[33] For a comparative table of the accounts in the Greek original, see Sievers, *Synopsis*, 130–42.

Table 1.1. Comparison of *Antiquities* and 1 Maccabees

	1 Macc 7		*Ant.* 12
33	Some time thereafter, Nicanor *went up* to *Mount Zion* Some priests came out of the sanctuary along with some elders of the people to greet him peacefully and show him the burnt offering which was being sacrificed on behalf of the king.	406	And again, as Nicanor was *coming down* from the *Akra* to the temple he was met by some of the priests and elders, who greeted him and showed him the sacrifices which they said they were offering to God on behalf of the king.
34	*He, however, mocked them, laughing in their faces and rendering them unclean. Presumptuously he spoke*		Thereupon he fell to *cursing them,*
35	*angrily* swearing that "Unless Judas and his army are delivered over into my hands immediately, upon my victorious return I shall *burn* this temple." Then he went out, *in a hot rage.*		and threatened that, if the people did not give Judas up to him, *he would pull* down the temple when he returned.
		407	After making these threats, he left Jerusalem,
36	Thereupon, the priests went in *and stood before the altar and the nave.* Weeping they said,		while the priests burst into tears in their distress over his words,
37	*"You have chosen this house to bear Your name, to be a house of prayer and entreaty for Your people.*		and supplicated God to deliver them from their enemies.
38	*Take vengeance upon this man and upon his army, and make them fall by the sword. Remember their blasphemies, and let none of them survive."*		
39	Nicanor marched out from Jerusalem and encamped at Beth-Horon, where he was joined by a force from Syria.	408	Now after Nicanor had left Jerusalem, he came to a certain village called Bethoron, and there encamped, being joined by another force from Syria,
40	Judas encamped at Adasa with *three* thousand men. There Judas prayed,		
41–2	*"Long ago when a king's emissaries blasphemed, Your angel went forth and slew one hundred eighty-five thousand of the king's men. In the same manner crush this army before us today. Let all other men know that Nicanor has blasphemed against Your sanctuary. Pass judgment on him in accordance with his wickedness."*		
43	The armies joined battle *on the thirteenth of the month Adar,* and the army of Nicanor was defeated, he himself being the first to fall in battle.	409	…and then he led them out to battle. And engaging Nicanor, *he* defeated his adversaries after a severe fight, and killed many of them; *finally* Nicanor himself fell, fighting gloriously.

(Continued)

Table 1.1. (Continued)

	1 Macc 7		Ant. 12
44	When Nicanor's army saw that he had fallen, they threw away their arms and fled.	410	When he fell, his army did not stay, but having lost their commander, threw away all their armour, and turned to flight.
45	Judas and his men pursued them as far as the approaches of Gazera, one day's journey from Adasa, and sounded the signal trumpets in the enemy's rear.		But Judas pursued and slew them, and caused the trumpets *to signal to the surrounding villages that he was defeating the enemy.*
46	In response to the signal, men came out of all the neighboring villages of Judaea and struck all along the flanks of the enemy and then wheeled about to meet Judas and his men, so that the enemy all fell by the sword; not even one of them was left.	411	When their inhabitants heard this, they leaped to arms, and heading off the fugitives, met them face to face, and killed them, so that from this battle not a single man escaped out of the *nine thousand who were in it.*
47	*Taking the spoils and the booty, the victors cut off the head of Nicanor and his right hand, which he had so presumptuously raised in oath, and brought and raised them where they could be viewed from Jerusalem.*		
48–9	The people were overjoyed, and observed the day as a day of great rejoicing. They decreed that the day, the thirteenth of Adar, should be observed annually.	412	Now the victory took place on the thirteenth of the month which is called Adar by the Jews, and Dystros by the Macedonians. And the Jews celebrate their victory every year in this month, and observe this day as a festival.
50	There followed a brief period of peace for the land of Judah.		But though the Jewish nation for a little while after that date had respite from war and enjoyed peace, thereafter it was again to undergo a period of struggle and danger.

human righteousness and intent: "to bear in mind who they were and for what prize they were facing danger…" (*Ant.* 12.408–9).[34]

Aggrandization of Judas Maccabeus. On several occasions, Josephus shifts the spotlight from Judas and his camp as found in Maccabees and focuses on Judas alone. Thus, for example, as Feldman notes, whereas in 1 Maccabees (7:26) Demetrius dispatches Nicanor to "exterminate our people," in *Antiquities* (12.402) he sends him "against Judas" because of Judas's "growing strength." If in Maccabees (1 Macc 7:27–8), Nicanor's plot is directed at Judas and his brothers, in *Antiquities* (12.403) Judas alone is mentioned. Similarly, if in Maccabees

---

[34] Gafni, "Josephus and I Maccabees," 121–2. See also Feldman, "Josephus' Portrayal of the Hasmoneans," 64–5.

(1 Macc 7:35) Nicanor demands the surrender of Judas and his camp, in *Antiquities* (12.406) he asks only for Judas. 1 Maccabees 7:43 notes that the armies joined battle and Nicanor's army was defeated; Josephus stresses that Judas "led them into battle." Similarly, it was Judas "who defeated his adversaries...and killed many of them." Josephus heightens this victory, calling the battle in which Nicanor fell "a severe fight" (*Ant.* 12.409); this adjective is missing from 1 Maccabees. In 1 Maccabees, it is Judas's forces that pursue Nicanor (7:45), whereas in *Antiquities* Judas himself is the pursuer (12.410).[35]

Apologetic thrust. An outstanding difference between Josephus and his source is Josephus's omission of the taking of booty and the abusive treatment of Nicanor's corpse (1 Macc 7:47). "As usual, Josephus omitted details that were liable to hurt the feelings of the Greco-Roman reader or might depict the Jews in too unfavourable a light."[36]

Omission of prayers. It is noteworthy that the Josephan account omits both the prayer of the priests and Judas's pre-battle prayer (1 Macc 37–8, 41–2, respectively).

Additional details. Josephus provides geographical data for Adasa's location (section 408),[37] which is missing in 1 Maccabees. Moreover, he knows that Nicanor's forces numbered 9,000 men (section 411), a detail whose source is unknown.[38]

Other differences. There are further differences between Josephus and Maccabees that are not simply attributable to a free Josephan paraphrase of his source.[39] These include the strength of Judas's forces (Josephus: 2,000 or 1,000 according to one variant (section 408), instead of 1 Maccabee's 3,000 (7:40),[40] and Nicanor's threat to "pull down" the temple (section 406), instead of burning it (1 Macc 7:35). Josephus's description of the battle also differs. Whereas in Maccabees Nicanor is the first casualty (7:34), in Josephus he is the last (section 409).[41]

Deliberate omission of biblical allusions. I now devote closer attention to an additional, significant feature of the Josephan account: his omission of

---

[35] Feldman, "Josephus' Portrayal of the Hasmoneans," 53–4.

[36] Bar-Kochva, *Judas Maccabaeus*, 192 and n. 131. See also Feldman, "Josephus' Portrayal of the Hasmoneans," 66. Wilk ("Abuse of Nicanor's Corpse," 53 n. 3) notes additional instances where Josephus obscured or deleted biblical descriptions of abuse.

[37] For the proposed identifications of Adasa see this chapter, n. 2. Goldstein (*I Maccabees*, 341) thinks that Josephus was mistaken regarding this detail.

[38] See the suggestion by Bar-Kochva (*Judas Maccabaeus*, 192) that Josephus is relying here on external sources that he used in the past when writing *War*, perhaps Nicolaus of Damascus. Goldstein (*I Maccabees*, 341) suggests that perhaps this number appeared in the version of Maccabees consulted by Josephus.

[39] A difference that is simply stylistic is Josephus's terminology: he changed 1 Maccabees's verb "went up" (v. 33), which is ideological, biblical in nature, to "coming down" (section 406), which apparently reflects the actual topography (at least according to Josephus's consistent description of the Akra towering over the Temple Mount and the temple). On the problematic nature of this description, see Bar-Kochva, *Judas Maccabaeus*, 445–65. See Goldstein, *I Maccabees*, 340.

[40] Goldstein (*I Maccabees*, 341) suggests that this was a scribal error.

[41] For possible reasons for this change, see Tepper and Shahar, "He'arot," 6–23, esp. 9; Bar-Kochva, *Judas Maccabaeus*, 367; Goldstein, *I Maccabees*, 342.

biblical allusions. Only partly explored in the scholarship, this phenomenon
has ramifications for the other traditions treated in this book. That the Hebrew
source of 1 Maccabees was peppered with biblical phrases and allusions is still
discernible even in its Greek translation. With respect to the story of Nicanor
specifically, not all of these allusions have been noted. Although it is readily
apparent that Josephus strips his source of its biblical garb,[42] we could perhaps
argue that this is because Josephus uses the Greek translation of 1 Maccabees,
in which biblical resonance is reduced, and because he himself is writing in
Greek. I suggest, however, that this is a far more pervasive feature. Even where
the biblical context is explicit in the Greek version, Josephus chooses to erase it.
I begin by surveying the rich biblical allusions in 1 Maccabees 7.

a. *Hezekiah's rescue from the Assyrian forces* (2 Kgs 18–19; Isa 36–7). The
most pronounced biblical reference in 1 Maccabees 7—the reference to the
miraculous rescue of Jerusalem from the Assyrian forces under Rabshakeh—
appears explicitly in Judas's prayer: "Long ago when a king's emissaries blasphemed, Your angel went forth and slew one hundred eighty-five thousand of
the king's men. In the same manner crush this army before us today…" (vv. 41–2).
Nicanor and his army are compared here to the Assyrian forces under Sennacherib's emissary Rabshakeh, who was sent to Jerusalem "with a large force"
and was miraculously defeated by "an angel of the Lord." Given their shared
features, this association is not surprising: they include a threat to Jerusalem
from a strong kingdom to the north-east, the dispatch of a top military figure
to Jerusalem at royal command, the enemy's numerical superiority, and the
emissary's mocking, threatening stance. Moreover, "this is the sole instance in
the Bible in which God saves his city, temple, and people from a ruling power."[43]
The application of the biblical name "Assyria" to Syria and the Seleucid kingdom
during the Second Temple period further strengthens this link.[44] In the accounts
of the campaign against Nicanor (2 Macc 15:22),[45] and of the pre-battle situation

---

[42] Feldman ("Josephus' Portrayal of the Hasmoneans," 58 and n. 18) notes Josephus's deliberate
omission of references to King David, which he ascribes to political reasons. In my opinion, this
is a much broader phenomenon and does not just relate to biblical stories of David but to biblical
narrative in general.

[43] Kister, "Legends of the Destruction," 513.

[44] Flusser, "Apocalyptic Elements," 154; H. Eshel, *Dead Sea Scrolls and the Hasmonean State*, 171
and the bibliography cited in n. 27 there; Teeter, "Isaiah and the King of As/Syria," 169–99, esp.
187–9. See below on the use of this epithet in the *War Scroll*, which has אשור כתיי (*War* 1:2; Yadin,
War, 257), whom David Flusser and others in his wake identified with the Syrian Seleucids. For a
discussion of the identity of the Kittim in the DSS, see e.g. H. Eshel, *Dead Sea Scrolls and the
Hasmonean State*, 163–79; Lim, "Kittim," 469–71. For a different opinion, see Brooke, "Kittim,"
135–59; Sharon, "The Kittim and the Roman Conquest," 357–88.

[45] According to Kister ("Legends of the Destruction," 520), also embedded in 2 Maccabees is a
rejection of any possible parallel between the battle with Nicanor and the Babylonian siege of
Jerusalem which concluded in defeat and destruction; in Judas's dream it was therefore Jeremiah,
the prophet of destruction, who extended him the sword with which he would overcome his
enemies.

at Emmaus (8:19) in 2 Maccabees, Judas's prayers also recollect the defeat of Assyria in Hezekiah's day. This biblical pericope resonates in additional contexts in Second Temple literature.[46]

b. *Hezekiah's deliverance from the Assyrian forces* (Isa 10). Another biblical pericope understood as alluding to the Assyrian siege in ancient Jewish literature is Isaiah 10. One example is Ben Sira's (48:18) description of the events in Hezekiah's day, which combines phrases from Isaiah 10:32 with the language of 2 Kings 18–19, as Menahem Kister has shown.[47] In addition, *Pesher Isaiah* and other Qumran works applied verses from Isaiah 10 to the kingdom which they designated Kittim.[48] Thus, in antiquity, Isaiah 10 was understood as addressing both the biblical fall of Assyria and contemporary kingdoms.[49] Indeed, as we shall see below, this prophecy, alongside 2 Kings 18–19, resonates in almost all of the extant sources, including the rabbinic ones. The following phrases in 1 Maccabees 7 clearly echo Isaiah 10: the raising of the hand, blaspheming, and Mount Zion. 1 Maccabees 7:47 describes the severing of Nicanor's "right hand, which he had so presumptuously raised" (καὶ τὴν δεξιὰν αὐτοῦ, ἣν ἐξέτεινεν ὑπερηφάνως.). Nicanor's raising of his hand, which also figures dominantly in the rabbinic sources (ידיים המניפות, יד שהניפה), is no doubt an allusion to the above-mentioned Isaian prophecy: "at Nob he shall stand and wave his hand" (ינופף ידו, v. 32).

Another feature in 1 Maccabees with a biblical parallel is the blasphemous nature of Nicanor's remarks. In Maccabees, emphasis is placed on Nicanor's mocking, arrogant words through the use of four verbs in rhythmic sequence: "mocked them," "laughing in their faces," "rendering them unclean,"[50] "presumptuously he spoke" (καὶ ἐμυκτήρισεν αὐτοὺς καὶ κατεγέλασεν αὐτῶν καὶ ἐμίανεν αὐτοὺς καὶ ἐλάλησεν ὑπερηφάνως, v. 34). This type of disparaging remark, and the biblical parallel from the Assyrian period, is twice denoted

---

[46] See 3 Macc 6:5; Bar-Kochva, *Judas Maccabaeus*, 365; Teeter, "Isaiah and the King of As/Syria," 176–8, 198 n. 78; and recently Noam, "'Will this one never be brought down?'" According to Goldstein (*I Maccabees*, 261, 264), the difficult verse in 1 Macc 3:48 (and also 4:11) relies on the biblical narrative of Hezekiah and Sennacherib.

[47] Kister, "Aḥor va-qedem," 235. Other current scholarship also tends to a similar explication of this prophecy. See H. Eshel, *Dead Sea Scrolls and the Hasmonean State*, 97 n. 11.

[48] See H. Eshel, *Dead Sea Scrolls and the Hasmonean State*, 100, 172–3; Kister, "Legends of the Destruction," 514; Sharon, "The Kittim and the Roman Conquest"; Noam, "'Will this one never be brought down?'"

[49] For identification with the Seleucids and/or Romans, see this chapter, n. 44. Kister ("Legends of the Destruction," 512–17) argues that this prophecy later also served the messianic expectations of the Jerusalemites during the First Jewish Revolt.

[50] The nature of this impurity is not specified. According to the description in Josippon (24:27, Flusser ed., 1:104) of spitting opposite the temple, scholars postulate that Nicanor defiled the priests with his spit (see e.g. Goldstein, *I Maccabees*, 340, who relies on the fact that all the other actions described are performed with the mouth; Rappaport, *First Book of Maccabees*, 216); cf. *t. Yoma* [*Kippurim*] 3:20 and parallels. However, according to Wilk ("Abuse of Nicanor's Corpse," 55 n. 12), this verb is to be understood metaphorically and it was Nicanor's words that "defiled" the sacred precinct.

in 1 Maccabees 7:38, 41 using the same Greek root: δυσφημιῶν ("blasphemies") and ἐδυσφήμησαν ("blasphemed").[51] In both instances, the reconstruction of the Hebrew roots נא"ץ, גד"ף, חר"פ is supported by the rabbinic parallels (Scholion P, YT : מחרף ומגדף; וחרף וגידף; in YT also ניאץ) and by the biblical association. These Hebrew verbs, which appear in the account of the Assyrian siege of Jerusalem during Hezekiah's reign (2 Kgs 19:4, 6, 16, 22, 23; cf. Isa 37:4, 17, 23, 24), are occasionally translated by the LXX using the verb βλασφημέω (2 Kgs 19:4, 6, 22). Josephus, on the other hand, makes a single matter-of-fact use of a related verb: ὁ δὲ βλασφημήσας αὐτοὺς ("He fell to cursing them," 406).

The poetic-biblical designation for the Temple Mount—Mount Zion (καὶ μετὰ τοὺς λόγους τούτους ἀνέβη Νικάνωρ εἰς ὄρος Σιων: "Some time thereafter, Nicanor went up to Mount Zion," v. 33)—appears frequently in 1 Maccabees and probably reflects the Hebrew original.[52] However, because the allusion to Mount Zion was also preserved in the rabbinic tradition on Nicanor in Scholion O, "who raised their hands against Jerusalem and Mount Zion," it appears likely that the underlying biblical context is Isaiah 10:32: "This same day at Nob he shall stand and wave his hand. O mount of Fair Zion [בת ציון]! O hill of Jerusalem!" (see also Isa 10:12; 2 Kgs 19:31). Josephus simply substitutes "temple" for the biblical "Mount Zion,"[53] just as he substituted Akra for the biblical "City of David" (1 Macc 7:32; *Ant.* 12:405–6: see Table 1.1).[54]

Within this framework, the sole source lacking any implicit or explicit references to the Assyrian defeat is the Josephan reworking. Not only is Judas's prayer missing, but the motif of the "raising" of the hand, and additional allusions to both 2 Kings 18–19 (= Isa 36–7) and Isaiah 10 have disappeared entirely.[55]

c. *David's victory over Goliath* (1 Samuel 17). There is an associative link between this biblical story and Judas's victory over Nicanor: in both, the enemy is a single individual who threatens and intimidates the Israelites. In both, he is

---

[51] μνήσθητι τῶν δυσφημιῶν αὐτῶν; οἱ παρὰ τοῦ βασιλέως ὅτε ἐδυσφήμησαν, "remember their blasphemies" with respect to Nicanor and his camp (v. 38); "when a king's emissaries blasphemed" in referring to Sennacherib's messengers in the biblical story (v. 41).

[52] Goodblatt (*Ancient Jewish Nationalism*, 175–6) surveys the occurrences of this expression in 1 Maccabees, debating whether its concrete use to designate the locus of the temple represents an archaizing tendency or widespread use of this term in daily life. See also Bar-Kochva, *Judas Maccabaeus*, 461.

[53] Goodblatt (*Ancient Jewish Nationalism*, 187–9) suggests that the Josephan avoidance of the term "Zion" in his writings perhaps stemmed from its possible ideological significance for the rebels.

[54] On the identification of the Hellenistic Akra with the City of David in 1 Maccabees, see Bar-Kochva, *Judas Maccabaeus*, 445. This identification also emerges from Scholion O on *Meg. Ta'an.*, 23 Iyyar (see Noam, *Megillat Ta'anit*, 187–90).

[55] We find instead general words of encouragement by Judas to his men (*Ant.* 12:409). Daphne Baratz noted (oral communication) that the motif of the prize for which it is worth taking a risk (ἔπαθλον) is typical of Josephan reports of Judas's speeches. See also Judas's inspirational message in *Ant.* 12.304.

beaten by a weaker party,[56] the enemy is beheaded and brought to Jerusalem,[57] and the victor assumes the reins of leadership and founds a dynasty. In fact, we find explicit mention of the battle between David and Goliath elsewhere in 1 Maccabees, in Judas's prayer at Beth-Zur (1 Macc 4:30), alongside additional comparative allusions between Judas Maccabeus and King David.[58] In our narrative, the allusion to the biblical victory of David over Goliath is apparent in the description of the flight of the enemy forces and their pursuit: "When Nicanor's army saw that he had fallen, they threw away their arms and fled. Judas and his men pursued them as far as the approaches of Gazera…and sounded the signal trumpets…taking the spoils and the booty" (44–5, 47; cf. 1 Sam 17:51–3: "so David ran up and stood over the Philistine, grasped his sword and pulled it from its sheath; and with it he dispatched him and cut off his head. When the Philistines saw that their warrior was dead, they ran. The men of Israel and Judah rose up with a war cry and they pursued the Philistines all the way to Gai and up to the gates of Ekron; the Philistines fell mortally wounded along the road to Shaarim up to Gath and Ekron. Then the Israelites returned from chasing the Philistines and looted their camp."[59]

In fact, the two biblical sources of inspiration mentioned above, the story of David and Goliath and the Rabshakeh scene, are interrelated within the Bible itself. The phrase "to blaspheme the living God" (לחרף אלהים חי) used in the story of the Assyrian siege (2 Kgs 19:4, 16; Isa 37:4, 17) is an inner-biblical echo of David's clash with Goliath, where it is twice stated that Goliath "dares to defy the ranks of the living God" (חרף מערכות אלוהים חיים—1 Sam 17:26, 36). Moreover, the root חר"פ serves as a key word in that story, occurring no less than six times, five times in verbal, and once in nominal, form (1 Sam 17: 10, 25, 26 [see also the noun חרפה there], 36, 45). Hence, the repeated use of the verb חר"פ in the Hebrew original of 1 Maccabees (as reconstructed above), probably alludes not only to the story of the rescue of Jerusalem from the Assyrian forces under Rabshakeh, but also to the story of David and Goliath.

d. *Gideon's victory over the Midianites* (Judges 8). According to 1 Maccabees, Nicanor declares: "Upon my victorious return I shall burn this temple": καὶ ἔσται ἐὰν ἐπιστρέψω ἐν εἰρήνῃ, ἐμπυριῶ τὸν οἶκον τοῦτον (1 Macc 7:35). In the YT we find very similar wording: בשובי בשלום אתוץ את המגדל הזה ("when I come

---

[56] Tal Ilan commented (oral communication) that the motif of the strong falling before the weak, the many in the hands of few, is shared by 1 Maccabees (3:16–19, 39; 4:8, 28–9; 5:38; 6:29–30; 7:27, 40; 9:5–6, 9; see Rappaport, *First Book of Maccabees*, 32–33); Josephus (*Ant.* 12.290–1, 300, 307, 314, 409, 422–4); the rabbis (*Gen. Rab.* 99 [100 in MS Vatican 30]:2 [Theodor-Albeck ed., p. 1274]); and the *Al ha-Nissim* prayer. The image of David and Goliath fits this theme.

[57] On this detail, see also Abel, *Maccabées*, 143.

[58] Feldman, "Josephus' Portrayal of the Hasmoneans," 58.

[59] Goldstein (*I Maccabees*, 342) cites a different biblical context (1 Sam 14:21–2 and Judg 7:21–4).

back safe, I'll tear down this tower!" line 6), which has its source in Gideon's declaration to the people of Penuel (Judg 8:9).[60] Kister views this biblical citation in the YT as a secondary slip of the pen.[61] But the strong affinity of the YT to the language of 1 Maccabees indicates that the allusion to Judges 8 was not born in the YT, but was already embedded in the Hebrew original of the book of Maccabees.[62] Nor is the link to Gideon's campaign in Judges fortuitous. Here too the biblical story has to do with an unexpected victory of a young peasant leading a small unit of people over the large forces of a harsh enemy, due to the commander's bravery, initiative, and boldness, and of course to divine salvation. Note too that the prophecy in Isaiah 10, which served as the basis for different versions of the Nicanor story in the books of Maccabees and rabbinic sources, contains an inner-biblical allusion to Gideon's campaign against Midian: "The Lord of Hosts will brandish a scourge over him as when He beat Midian at the rock of Oreb" (Isa 10:26). It is almost superfluous to note that in this instance as well Josephus erases the key word εἰρήνη ("safely"), which provides the link to the biblical sources.

e. *Antiochus's defeat* (Daniel 11). A direct quotation found in 1 Maccabees 7 of an expression in Daniel (11:44–5) has not been noted in the scholarship: "Then he went out in a hot rage" (καὶ ἐξῆλθεν μετὰ θυμοῦ μεγάλου, v. 35). This is a clear allusion to the verse: "But reports from east and north will alarm him, and he will march forth in a great fury (וְיָצָא בְּחֵמָא גְדֹלָה) to destroy and annihilate many. He will pitch his royal pavilion between the sea and the beautiful holy mountain, and he will meet his doom with no one to help him" (Dan 11:44–5). In the LXX the translation of ויצא בחמא גדולה is almost identical to 1 Maccabees: καὶ ἐξελεύσεται ἐν θυμῷ ἰσχυρῷ. In antiquity, Jewish and non-Jewish sources applied these and the surrounding verses from Daniel to Antiochus Epiphanes.[63] But Scholion O on *Megillat Ta'anit* applies the same verses to an explanation of the 28th of Shevat, on which "Antiochus left Jerusalem,"[64] an event most scholars identify as the lifting of the siege of Jerusalem in Lysias and Antiochus V's day, just two years before Nicanor's attack. The use of this verse by the author of 1 Maccabees in the Nicanor pericope shows that it was understood as referring to different episodes from the Hasmonean period.[65] Indeed, Nicanor's threat

---

[60] The use of the word 'tower' in the biblical narrative evidently influenced the YT's (and earlier sources') use of 'tower' to refer to the temple. This makes it unnecessary to search for a Hasmonean tower in Jerusalem to which these remarks purportedly refer (see e.g. Hezser, "[In]significance of Jerusalem," 15).

[61] Kister, "Aḥor va-qedem," 236.   [62] See Goldstein, *I Maccabees*, 340 (note on v. 35).

[63] Flusser, "Apocalyptic Elements," 143–6. The entire article is devoted to the *War Scroll's* use of these verses from Daniel.

[64] See Noam, *Megillat Ta'anit*, 291.

[65] In the past, in line with the prevailing exegesis of the verse as applying to Antiochus Epiphanes, I surmised that Scholion O identified this date with the fall of this king, as opposed to those who argue that it marked the lifting of the siege by his son. However, as seen here, it appears that the verse in Daniel could be applied to different historical contexts in the Hasmonean period and it is possible that Scholion O was referring to Antiochus V Eupator.

against Jerusalem and his crushing defeat can certainly be applied to the verses from Daniel: "the beautiful holy mountain" and "will meet his doom with no one to help him." In the Qumran *War Scroll* the verses from Daniel fuel the description of a future apocalyptic war.[66] Nonetheless, note that there too the verses in Daniel are linked to "Assyria,"[67] just as the biblical association with Assyria appears in the above-mentioned sources on Nicanor. Intriguingly, 1 Maccabees, the Qumran *War Scroll*, and *War Rule* (4Q285) share some focal biblical contexts: the above-noted verses in Daniel 11 (*War Scroll* 1:1–12), the battle between David and Goliath (*War Scroll* 11:1–3), and Isaiah's oracle (Isa 10—*War Rule* 7:1–3).[68] As for the previous examples, here too the flowery phrase used in 1 Maccabees—even in its Greek version—is entirely missing from the Josephan paraphrase.

f. *The priests' prayer* (Joel 2). 1 Maccabees relates that: "Thereupon, the priests went in and stood before the altar and the nave. Weeping, they said…" (καὶ εἰσῆλθον οἱ ἱερεῖς καὶ ἔστησαν κατὰ πρόσωπον τοῦ θυσιαστηρίου καὶ τοῦ ναοῦ καὶ ἔκλαυσαν καὶ εἶπον, v. 36). Others have noted the close link to Joel 2:17: "Between the portico and the altar, Let the priests, the Lord's ministers, weep and say."[69] Josephus (407) not only omits the precise location of the priests while praying—near the altar and the nave—but also replaces the prayer itself with his own paraphrase, thereby erasing the allusion to the verse.

g. *The Solomonic prayer at the dedication of the temple* (1 Kgs 8). As Abel and Goldstein note, the priests' prayer in 1 Maccabees closely resembles the Solomonic prayer at the dedication of the temple. The priests open their plea with the statement: "You have chosen this house to bear Your name, to be a house of prayer and entreaty for Your people" (σὺ ἐξελέξω τὸν οἶκον τοῦτον ἐπικληθῆναι τὸ ὄνομά σου ἐπ᾽ αὐτοῦ εἶναι οἶκον προσευχῆς καὶ δεήσεως τῷ λαῷ σου, v. 37). King Solomon implores God: "May Your eyes be open day and night toward this House, toward the place of which You have said, 'My name shall abide there'; may You heed the prayers which Your servant will offer toward this place. And when You hear the supplications which Your servant and Your people Israel offer toward this place, give heed in Your heavenly abode" (1 Kgs 8:29–30).[70] In this instance as well, Josephus entirely omits the language of the prayer, providing a brief, dry paraphrase: "and supplicated God to deliver them from their enemies" (section 407).

---

[66] On the *War Scroll*'s use of verses from Daniel, see Yadin, *War*, 256–9; Flusser, "Apocalyptic Elements." For additional bibliography, see H. Eshel, *Dead Sea Scrolls and the Hasmonean State*, 168 nn. 20–1.

[67] H. Eshel, *Dead Sea Scrolls and the Hasmonean State*, 168–9.

[68] On this work, see Alexander and Vermes, "285. 4QSefer ha-Milḥamah," 228–48; H. Eshel, *Dead Sea Scrolls and the Hasmonean State*, 171–2 and n. 29.

[69] See Rappaport, *First Book of Maccabees*, 217 n. 6.

[70] See Abel, *Maccabées*, 141; Goldstein, *I Maccabees*, 340 on v. 37 (he also refers to 1 Kgs 8:43, 9:3).

h. *A period of peace following victory in the era of the Judges* (Judges 3, 5, 8). The concluding verse of the account in 1 Maccabees 7: "There followed a brief period of peace for the land of Judah" (καὶ ἡσύχασεν ἡ γῆ Ιουδα ἡμέρας ὀλίγας, v. 50), with its placement at the end of the episode, after the deliverance and joy, alludes, as Bar-Kochva notes, to the concluding formula found in the book of Judges—"and the land had peace for forty years"—in the pericopes of Othniel the Kenizzite (Judg 3:11), Deborah and Barak (5:31), and Gideon (8:28).[71] I have already noted an allusion to the Gideon cycle in our story.

The episode of Nicanor's defeat sheds light not only on the nature of Second Temple-period Jewish traditions but also on one of Josephus's main approaches to reworking his Jewish sources. Above I have noted the rich allusive biblical backdrop in this brief narrative in 1 Maccabees: Judges (twice), 1 Samuel, 2 Kings (twice), Isaiah, Joel, and Daniel. It is axiomatic that the Hebrew original of 1 Maccabees was pseudo-biblical in nature, poetic and flowery. Evidently, its account masterfully integrated a surprising number of biblical allusions in an early piyyut-like composition, perhaps preserving a specimen of a Jewish genre of that day whose other exemplars have not survived.

The intensive use of allusions to biblical stories of victory and divine salvation in 1 Maccabees places the Maccabean wars on the same footing as miraculous biblical events, and frames Judas Maccabeus as an heir to biblical heroes. Gideon and David serve as models of youthful enthusiasm, as individuals whose initiative, bravery, and devotion lead to the victory of the few over the many, but primarily as enjoying divine assistance which enables a small, enslaved people to escape conflict with more powerful enemies. If the contexts of the Assyrian siege in 2 Kings and Isaiah, and of the defeat of Antiochus alluded to in Daniel, underscore the defeat of a threatening northern empire, the allusions to Solomon's prayer in 1 Kings and to the priests' prayer in Joel shift the focus to the temple.

In essence, the story of Nicanor's defeat is our first encounter with a genre of early legends that centers on the temple and the priesthood.[72] One of its prominent motifs is an external threat to the temple and an admired high priest who stands in the breach at a moment of national distress, which is ultimately followed by salvation through divine instrumentality. There is a confrontation between two arenas in these stories: between an external military-political arena that poses a threat to Jewish lives, and the internal, also metaphysical,

---

[71] Bar-Kochva (*Judas Maccabaeus*, 374–5) views this as an antithetical allusion. Whereas the saviors in Judges granted the people years of peace, under Judas the land did not enjoy a lengthy period of tranquility. On the attempt by 2 Maccabees in particular to place the events of the revolt in a Judges-like framework, see ibid. 199.

[72] On priestly traditions that circulated during the Second Temple period and served Josephus as well, see Williamson, "Historical Value," 56 and n. 1, where he discusses similar scholarly assumptions. See also S. Schwartz, *Josephus and Judaean Politics*, 96.

arena of the divine–Israelite relationship. Symbolizing this latter arena, and the locus of its events, is the temple. As for the figure of the high priest, he combines the two arenas: he not only mediates the divine–Israelite relationship in the temple sphere but is also involved, directly or indirectly, in the political or military events. The temple as well connects the two spaces, for it is, on the one hand, the focus of the external threat and, on the other, it is also the stage for the divine–Israelite drama.

These stories' focal message is that history is determined not by world rulers and their emissaries, but by the God of Israel who resides in his temple. Accordingly, the real drama in these stories takes place not on the battlefield but in the temple, and their protagonist is not the great conqueror, the emperor, or his servant but rather the servant of God and the representative of the chosen people, namely, the high priest. In essence, this message is a direct continuation of the biblical viewpoint that portrays history from the perspective of dual causality, that is, a sequence of human events driven by a hidden divine hand, grounded in the relationship between God and Israel.[73]

The legend of the encounter between the high priest and Alexander the Great (*Ant.* 11.302–47; Scholia O and P, 21 Kislev [= *b. Yoma* 69a], among others) is a definitive example of this genre.[74] Interwoven with Alexander's conquests is a severe Samaritan threat to the temple. The legendary high priest, Simeon the Righteous according to the rabbinic version, or Jaddus in Josephus, comes to greet Alexander in priestly garb, and the great conqueror bows to him, for he has seen his image in a vision of his victory. According to Josephus, Alexander visits the temple and offers sacrifices there. The narrator of this legend wishes to highlight that the military successes of the great conqueror are in actuality dependent on the will of the God of Israel who resides in the Jerusalem temple. The dual role of the high priest as a religious-political ruler is striking. The episode treated in the next chapter ("John Hyrcanus and a Heavenly Voice"), which concerns a high priest who heard a message in the temple regarding a military victory, is another example of a temple legend.

In all its versions, the story of Nicanor's defeat also underscores the acute threat to the temple. Nicanor "raise[s] his hand against Jerusalem and against the temple" and threatens to destroy the temple on his return. With the exception of the censored Josephan version, all the versions of this story note the "measure for measure" punishment of the enemy. His hand, raised against the

---

[73] On the shaping and transmission of this concept, see the survey and new approach of Amit, "Dual Causality," 105–21. On the continuity of the biblical concept of divine providence into postbiblical literature, see Daube, "Typology in Josephus," 22–3. On a comparable religious viewpoint in Josephus, see D. R. Schwartz, "Josephus on Albinus." According to Schwartz, in *Antiquities* the Romans are an external force in the drama taking place between God and his sinful nation, which is punished.

[74] Much has been written on the various versions of this legend. For a survey of the scholarship and a reconsideration, see Tropper, *Simeon the Righteous*, 113–54; Ben Shahar, "The High Priest and Alexander the Great," 91–144.

temple/Jerusalem, and his head, with its mouth that had blasphemed the Judeans, were hung opposite the temple/in the gates of Jerusalem. Although no heroic priest figures prominently in the rabbinic version of this story (see below), the version found in 1 Maccabees, however, and Josephus in its wake, describes the bravery of Judas Maccabeus alongside the prayer of the priests in the temple and their attempt to conciliate Nicanor. In other words, the duality of the priestly role as representing the people before God in the temple and before the foreign military commander appears in this story as well. In this tradition, the victory is natural, not miraculous; nevertheless, its implicit message is that divine providence controls events. The prominent allusions to the biblical account of the miraculous fall of the Assyrian king Sennacherib on Hezekiah's day in 1 Maccabees, and the prayers of the priests and of Judas, certainly allude to this viewpoint.

For his part, Josephus flattens and waters down the text, removing its biblical ornamentation, arriving at a dry, matter-of-fact account. Although we might perhaps have anticipated that Josephus would here not alter his source, which preserved many stylistic features of the Hebrew original, this turns out not to be the case: Josephus consistently erases the biblical associations and the traces of Hebrew style from the Greek translation of Maccabees.

To what can we attribute these alterations? Certainly, Josephus had no objections to biblical stories; on the contrary, he recounted them at length in the first books of *Antiquities*. Evidently, he wished to make a sharp distinction between his paraphrases of biblical tales and his accounts of post-biblical historical events, which he sought to present factually, as a historian. Moreover, he was aware that his non-Jewish readers would in any event not recognize the biblical allusions embedded in his Jewish sources. To this we must add Kister's proposal that, because the story of the Assyrian siege of Jerusalem and the oracle in Isaiah 10 encouraged the Jerusalemites during the First Jewish Revolt against the Romans, Josephus opposed these biblical associations, presenting less optimistic alternatives.[75] If this is correct, it is then not surprising that Josephus erased from his account similar reliance on these biblical pericopes in the past.

As we shall see elsewhere, this is not the sole instance in which rabbinic literature has preserved some of the features of biblical language and usage that characterized ancient Jewish sources, whereas Josephus eliminates them totally.[76] This also forms an element of my argument for the possible superiority of certain rabbinic parallels over their Josephan counterparts for the reconstruction of Second Temple-period Jewish traditions, notwithstanding their inferiority in terms of date and genre.

---

[75] Kister, "Legends of the Destruction," 512–17.   [76] See Chaps. 3 and 5.

1 Maccabees and Rabbinic Sources

The shared foundation of all the variants of the rabbinic tradition and 1 Maccabees—as opposed to the Josephan version—is readily apparent. Like Maccabees, rabbinic tradition underscores the abuse of Nicanor's corpse. Also, if Nicanor's raising of his hand against the temple justifies its amputation and public display in Maccabees, this is similarly the case in the Scholia and the Talmuds (Scholia O and P, 13 Adar; *y. Ta'an.* 2:13, 66a; *y. Meg.* 1:6, 70c, *b. Ta'an.* 18b; cf. 1 Macc 7:47). Finally, the rabbinic traditions and the underlying Hebrew version reflected in the extant Greek of the book of Maccabees certainly shared several Hebrew expressions. These include הר ציון ("Mount Zion"—Scholion O, 13 Adar; cf. 1 Macc 7:33); וחרף / מחרף ("mocked"—Scholion P, 13 Adar; *y. Ta'an.* 2:13, 66a; cf. 1 Macc 7:38, 41); בשובי בשלום אתרץ את המגדל הזה ("When I come back whole, I shall break down that tower"—*y. Ta'an.* 2:13, 66a; cf. 1 Macc 7:35); וידבר בגאווה ("spoke arrogantly"—Scholion P, 13 Adar; *b. Ta'an.* 18b; *y. Ta'an.* 2:13, 66a; cf. 1 Macc 7:34, 47). The latter phrase is especially instructive. It does not derive from the biblical infrastructure of the fall of Assyria in 2 Kings and Isaiah, where the terms גאון or גאוה do not appear, but rather depends on an early extra-biblical tradition that attributed prideful speech to Rabshakeh, as seen from Ben Sira (48:18): ויט ידו על ציון ויגדף אל בגאונו ("he shook his fist at Zion and blasphemed God arrogantly").[77] Because none of these expressions survived in the Josephan account in their Greek forms, this rules out the existence of a direct parallel between Josephus and the rabbinic sources for the story of Nicanor's defeat. As they display greater affinity to Maccabees than to *Antiquities*, the variations of the tradition reflected in the rabbinic sources cannot be dependent on the Josephan account.

Of the different variants of the story in rabbinic sources, it is the version in the YT, with its exclusive features, that displays the greatest affinity to 1 Maccabees. These features include: the expression: בשובי בשלום אתרץ את המגדל הזה, which almost completely parallels what we find in 1 Maccabees, and the dual amputation of Nicanor's head and hand. Regarding the latter, Scholion O mentions only his head; Scholion P, his head and limbs; and the BT, whose reworking is based on a biblical association,[78] fingers and toes. Another phrase unique to the YT is היד שפשטה בגאוה ("and the hand that stretched out arrogantly"), which is the closest to 1 Macc 7:47: τὴν δεξιὰν αὐτοῦ, ἣν ἐξέτεινεν ὑπερηφάνως ("his right hand, which he had so presumptuously raised").[79] The other rabbinic versions have variations on the motif of "the raising of a hand." In the YT, Nicanor's head and hand are displayed "facing Jerusalem" (נגד ירושלים), similar to the version

---

[77] Kister, "Aḥor va-qedem," 235.

[78] Judg 1:6–7. See Noam, *Megillat Ta'anit*, 300; Kister, "Aḥor va-qedem," 236.

[79] On the Greek verb ἐκτείνω, which means 'spread out', see Bar-Kochva, *Judas Maccabaeus*, 370.

found in 1 Maccabees 7 (παρὰ τῇ Ιερουσαλημ [from Jerusalem], v. 47);[80] the other rabbinic sources place them at the gates of Jerusalem or opposite the temple.[81]

This similarity notwithstanding, a strange phrase in the YT still requires explanation: שלטון משלמלכות יון עובר לאלכסנדריה ("a ruler of the kingdom of Greece [was] en route to Alexandria"). The reference to Alexandria is unclear: some scholars suggest emendations; others maintain that it was introduced from a different historical context.[82] In Bar-Kochva's opinion, this phrase relies on the narrator's general knowledge of the wars between the Seleucids and the Ptolemies, in the course of which Seleucid rulers passed through Palestine en route to Egypt. The description of a Seleucid ruler passing through Palestine and promising future vengeance on his subjects on his return from his Egyptian military campaign is, according to Bar-Kochva, the outcome of a folk attempt to aggrandize Nicanor's importance.[83] According to Joshua Schwartz, a motif from the late anecdote concerning a different Nicanor—an Alexandrian Jew who donated doors to the Temple (*m. Yoma* 3:10; *m. Mid.* 2:3; *t. Yoma* [*Kippurim*] 2:4, and parallels)—at some point penetrated the early story on Seleucid Nicanor, and comprised the first stage of the amalgamation of these two traditions. In any event, this difficult phrase is found only in the YT.[84]

The above-mentioned affinities between the YT and 1 Maccabees prompted Bar-Kochva and Kister to suggest literary dependence between the YT and the Hebrew original of 1 Maccabees.[85] Scholars have assumed on this basis that the YT contains the most authentic version, whereas the Scholia and the BT are more distant reworkings.[86] However, the tradition in the BT and in the Scholia of *Megillat Ta'anit* is based on an early parent tradition, as Kister has shown. He grounds his argument in the phrase היה מניף ידו על ירושלים ("raised his hand

---

[80] Hezser ("[In]significance of Jerusalem," 14–15) surprisingly suggests that the story of Nicanor in the YT is a fabrication with no historical basis and with no link to the account in Maccabees.

[81] Bar-Kochva assesses these versions as less accurate (*Judas Maccabaeus*, 370). Kister ("Aḥor va-qedem," 236 n. 22), on the other hand, notes the parallel in 2 Macc 15:33, according to which the arm was hung opposite the sanctuary. J. Schwartz ("Nicanor Gate," 245–83) views this version as containing more viable historical testimony.

[82] For a survey of the different opinions, see Noam, *Megillat Ta'anit*, 299.

[83] Oral communication.

[84] J. Schwartz, "Nicanor Gate." Based on the evidence from Jossipon, Schwartz suggests that the Nicanor Gate in the temple was actually named for the Hasmonean victory over Nicanor, and not, as witnessed in the Mishnah and the Tosefta, for the door-donating philanthropist mentioned in a Greek inscription on an ossuary found on Mt Scopus. He also relies on the version found in Scholion P, and the testimony of 2 Macc 15:33, that Nicanor's limbs were hung opposite the temple. He therefore argues that the gate opposite the place where Nicanor's limbs were displayed was named for this event, per the tradition in Jossipon. This matter is beyond the scope of the discussion here.

[85] Bar-Kochva, *Judas Maccabaeus*, 370; Kister, "Aḥor va-qedem," 235. See also Noam, *Megillat Ta'anit*, 299.

[86] Bar-Kochva, *Judas Maccabaeus*, 369–70; Wilk, "Abuse of Nicanor's Corpse," 55–7; Noam, *Megillat Ta'anit*, 299.

against Jerusalem"—Scholion P; *b. Ta'an.* 18b), which he identifies as an allusion to Isaiah 10:32: ינפף ידו בת הר ציון גבעת ירושלים ("he shall stand and wave his hand. O mount of Fair Zion! O hill of Jerusalem!"), part of the Isaian prophecy which, as we have seen, forms the backdrop to all our sources.[87] In other words, two early branches of the Nicanor tradition are discernible in the extant sources. One is represented by the Hebrew original of 1 Maccabees, which evidently read ימינו אשר פשט בגאוה (τὴν δεξιὰν αὐτοῦ, ἣν ἐξέτεινεν ὑπερηφάνως, v. 47), and also by the similar tradition in the YT. The other tradition, which shares the biblical root נו"ף/נפ"ף, which is not documented in the first branch, is found in the BT and Scholion P. It then follows that the rabbinic traditions that use this root (BT and the Scholia) have preserved an ancient tradition *that is not dependent on 1 Maccabees*. Namely, this indicates that the Scholia and the BT had access to an authentic Hebrew version of the story that was not identical to the one found in 1 Maccabees.[88]

As attested in Scholion O, the corruption of the original text of the tradition is clearly recognizable. The Aramaic opening of the Hebrew commentary of the Scholion: ומלכותא דיונאי ("and the kingdom of the Greeks") is garbled: generally, narratives do not begin with conjunctive *waw*; it is also unusual to find a Hebrew passage with an Aramaic opening. Evidently, the original version was something like בימי מלכות יון, a frequent expression in Scholion O.[89] I concur with Menahem Kister's suggestion that an anonymous redactor, wishing to incorporate these words into the Aramaic *lemma* defining the date [בתליסר ביה נקנור—"On the thirteenth thereof Nicanor"], changed them into Aramaic: ניקנור ומלכותא דיונאי.[90] This reworking misled him or a later scribe into thinking that the subject of the passage was not Nicanor alone but rather Nicanor and "the Greek kingdom," leading to the incongruent use of the plural (שהן מניפין ידיהן על ירושלם—"who would raise their hands against Jerusalem and Mount Zion"), even though the continuation refers to an individual.[91]

Scholion P and the BT reflect corruptions due to transmission. As scholars have already noted,[92] the gradual empowerment of the Hasmonean dynasty

---

[87] Kister, "Aḥor va-qedem," 235–6 (quote, 236); see n. 22 there. Nonetheless, he also enumerates various corruptions and later reworkings in the versions in the BT and the Scholia. See ibid.

[88] Daphne Baratz has noted (oral communication) an additional difference between the rabbinic traditions and the books of Maccabees. The rabbinic traditions provide explanations for the revenge exercised against the head and the hand, whereas the books of Maccabees only mention the crime committed with the hand.

[89] See Scholion O, 27 Iyyar (Noam, *Megillat Ta'anit*, 67); 24 Av (ibid. 86); 17 Elul (ibid. 90); 3 Tishri (ibid. 94); 3 Kislev (ibid. 98); 28 Adar (ibid. 128). See also Scholion P, 25 Kislev (ibid. 105):...בימי יון נכנסו בני חשמונאי להר הבית; Scholia O and P, 13 Adar: מלכי יון/ומלכותא דיונאי. See Kister, "Scholia on Megillat Ta'anit," 461; Rosenthal, "Newly Discovered Leaf," 370 n. 55, 375, 382 n. 132. See also Chap. 6.

[90] Kister, "Aḥor va-qedem," 234 n. 11.

[91] For additional examples of content transferred between the Scroll and the Scholia, see Rosenthal, "Newly Discovered Leaf," 390–1.

[92] Wilk, "Abuse of Nicanor's Corpse," 57.

("and when the Hasmonean dynasty prevailed") does not match Judas Maccabeus's day; the phrase כשתקפה יד ("prevailed") is typical of Scholion P.[93] Accordingly, Kister suggests that these phrases "are not original, and attest to the corruption of the original text of the Scholion on this holiday and its replacement with the usual phrasing found in the Scholia of *Megillat Ta'anit*."[94]

The Erasure of Judas Maccabeus

As for the YT's version, if we assume that it is dependent on the Hebrew original of 1 Maccabees or a similar tradition, a striking phenomenon that contradicts that version requires explanation. Nicanor was pursued, according to both the YT and Scholion O, by "one of the [members of the] Hasmonean dynasty." This unique phrase is intriguing because it appears in no other rabbinic source. "Hasmonean dynasty," or "Hasmonean kingdom," are familiar terms, but not "one" of them. Who was this individual?

As it stands, the text conveys the impression that there has been a deliberate omission here, probably a censored name. Given the centrality of Judas Maccabeus in the parallel accounts of 1 Maccabees and Josephus, it is self-evident that the source underlying this tradition named Judas Maccabeus, assigning to him the responsibility for killing Nicanor. It follows that some rabbinic redactor wished to avoid specific mention of Judas, just as rabbinic literature in general avoids mention of this figure and his contemporaries. The absence of Judas Maccabeus from the celebration of victory on Nicanor Day in the Talmud was already noted by Joseph Klausner: "to our shame, the Talmud and the Midrash and the Hanukkah prayers mention Mattathias, John Hyrcanus, Alexander Janneus, but not Judas Maccabeus."[95] Tal Ilan has also indicated that the talmudic sources do not speak of the first Hasmonean generation. This is especially striking against her determination of the widespread currency of the names of the Hasmonean brothers among the Jewish population in the days of the Second Temple.[96]

If my suggested reconstruction is correct, this has far-reaching implications for a longstanding question touching on the topic of this volume: "Did the Jewish

[93] See Rosenthal, "Newly Discovered Leaf," 370 and n. 55. See the references to Kister in the following note.

[94] Kister, "Scholia on Megillat Ta'anit," 463; idem, "Aḥor va-qedem," 236 n. 23. On the unusual similarity between the BT and Scholion O regarding this point, see Kister, "Scholia on Megillat Ta'anit," 464 and n. 60. In the wake of the discovery of a new leaf of Scholion O, it became clear that the BT version resembles the Aa branch. See Rosenthal, "Newly Discovered Leaf," 370.

[95] Klausner, *Historiyah*, 3:47. See also Wilk, "Abuse of Nicanor's Corpse," 56.

[96] Ilan, "Names of the Hasmoneans," 240; see also 241 n. 27.

people and its sages cause the Hasmoneans to be forgotten?"[97] Simply raised here, this weighty question will be discussed in the concluding chapter.[98]

D. CONCLUSION

Fairly soon after the victory over Nicanor, and evidently even before the composition of 1 Maccabees, several Hebrew variants of the story of Nicanor's defeat were already current. Even though they differed in language and some details, all shared the presence of biblical allusions in general, to the Assyrian siege of Jerusalem in particular. One tradition was embedded in 1 Maccabees; others made their way to rabbinic sources, even if corrupted by editing and transmission.

1 Maccabees, in its turn, served as Josephus's source for his account of Nicanor's defeat. There is therefore no evidence for a direct parallel between the accounts in Josephus and in the rabbinic corpora, but rather attestation to use of 1 Maccabees by Josephus, on the one hand, and affinities between the rabbinic versions and 1 Maccabees, on the other. In other words, here the similarities between the rabbinic and Josephan versions do not stem from a direct link but are rather grounded in dependence on an earlier source.

Moreover, as many have noted, and as demonstrated above, the possibility of comparing Josephus to an existing source—a definitively Jewish source in this instance—discloses aspects of Josephus's treatment of no-longer-extant sources,[99] including all the Jewish traditions whose traces we seek. By the same token, the ability to compare rabbinic traditions to a second-century BCE text (even if in its Greek version and not the original Hebrew) facilitates the tracing of the preservation and reworking of ancient traditions in rabbinic literature. Marked features of the Josephan account are apologetic omissions and the obscuring of biblical allusions, whereas in two of the rabbinic sources it appears that we can restore the deliberate erasure of Judas Maccabeus's name.

---

[97] Alon, "Did the Jewish People and Its Sages Cause the Hasmoneans to Be Forgotten?" 1–17; Efron, "Hasmonean Revolt"; Noam, "Cruse of Oil," 191–226.

[98] The YT version differs from that of 1 Maccabees in other details as well. It describes "one of the members of the Hasmonean dynasty" as deliberately pursuing Nicanor. According to this predicated tradition, Nicanor met his death after his troops had suffered heavy casualties and was killed in his chariot by the Hasmonean hero. Finally, his limbs were impaled on a stake, and an inscription placed below his impaled limbs. None of these details comes from 1 Maccabees. We cannot yet determine if their source lies in a later reworking, the same reworking that erased the protagonist, Judas Maccabeus, from the story and inserted a Roman chariot in it, or whether what we have here is fundamentally a sister tradition to the one embedded in 1 Maccabees, which, although sharing close affinities, differed in some of its details.

[99] See e.g. Feldman, "Josephus' Portrayal of the Hasmoneans," 41–3.

Over time, the nuclear messages of the Nicanor traditions became the features of an entire topos of ancient stories. All share the themes of an external threat to the temple and fears for its future, priestly bravery and leadership, belief in divine providence as the moving force behind events, and miraculous heavenly deliverance. They appear in other stories treated in this book, such as John Hyrcanus and a heavenly voice,[100] and the fratricidal Hasmonean conflict and the murder of Onias.[101] Perhaps our account is an early prototype of this genre of "temple legends," which is also represented in the following chapter: a priestly temple legend centered on a Hasmonean victory. As opposed to the story of Nicanor's defeat, this legend has only been preserved in Josephus and a rabbinic parallel. However, the surprisingly close topical-linguistic affinity between them enables us to reconstruct with near certainty the source on which both were based.

---

[100] See Chap. 2. This story does not contain a direct threat to the temple, but does prominently feature an external threat to the land of Israel, priestly leadership by a person who is also a semi-prophet, and the centrality of the temple.

[101] See Chap. 6. Although this story contains an external threat to the temple, its thrust is mainly internal-Jewish. The priestly leaders from the Hasmonean house in this story are not heroes but the guilty party, and the righteous hero Ḥoni/Onias is a pietist, not a priest.

2

John Hyrcanus and a Heavenly Voice

Of the traditions in this book, the legend examined in this chapter is unique. The intriguing features preserved in its two versions provide a glimpse of a lost genre of Aramaic chronicles relating events in the Hasmonean era—a genre also attested in the Dead Sea Scrolls—which preceded the creation of the Jewish traditions on which Josephus relies. This Aramaic vestige was subsequently incorporated into a Hebrew, temple-centered story of a miraculous event involving John Hyrcanus, the Hasmonean high priest and ruler who reigned from 134 to 104 BCE, and belongs to the topos of temple legends described in the previous chapter. As we shall see, because it displays features of interpolation in both the Josephan and the rabbinic contexts, this again suggests that this story belonged to an earlier pool of traditions on which both corpora drew. In this case we have the good fortune to encounter yet another, later, layer of adaptation, namely the deliberate rabbinic reworking of the priestly temple legends into a rabbinic framework.

A. THE SOURCES

Antiquities 13.282–3; *t. Sotah* 13:5 (= *y. Sotah* 9:13, 24b; *b. Sotah* 33a; *Canticles Rabbah*, parashah 5)

Josephus, *Antiquities* 13.282–3

(282) Now about the high priest Hyrcanus an extraordinary story (παράδοξον) is told (λέγεται) how the Deity communicated with him, for they say (φασὶ γάρ) that on the very day (κατ᾽ ἐκείνην τὴν ἡμέραν) on which his sons fought with Cyzicenus, Hyrcanus, who was alone in the temple, burning incense as a high priest, heard a voice saying that his sons had just defeated Antiochus (οἱ παῖδες αὐτοῦ νενικήκασιν ἀρτίως τὸν Ἀντίοχον). (283) And on coming out of the

temple he revealed this to the entire multitude, and so it actually happened. This, then, was how the affairs of Hyrcanus were going.

Rabbinic Sources

T. Sotah 13:5

יוחנן כהן גדול שמע דבר[1] מבית קדש הקדשים, 1

נצחון (מרא)[2] טליא דאזלון לאגחא קרבא באנטכיא, 2

וכתבו אותה שעה ואותו היום, וכיונו ואותה שעה היתה שנצחו[3] 3

Yoḥanan the high priest heard a word from the house of the holy of holies: "The young men who went to wage war against Antioch have been victorious," and they wrote down the time and the day. And they checked, and the victory was at that very hour.

B. HISTORICAL BACKGROUND

John Hyrcanus I, the protagonist of this story, was the son of Simeon the Hasmonean and the grandson of Mattathias the priest. Hyrcanus began to rule and acceded to the high priesthood following Simeon's murder by the latter's son-in-law, Ptolemy son of Abubos, in 134 BCE. In both *War* and *Antiquities* Josephus recounts that Ptolemy held John's mother and two of his brothers hostage at the fortress of Dagon (Dok)[4] near Jericho. When Hyrcanus lifted his lengthy siege of the fortress because of the sabbatical year, Ptolemy seized the opportunity to escape to Philadelphia (Rabbat Ammon) in Transjordan, but not before he murdered his hostages (*War* 1.54–60; *Ant.* 13.228–35).

Shortly thereafter Antiochus VII Sidetes initiated a campaign against Judea and laid siege to Jerusalem, withdrawing however in 132 BCE in exchange for a pledge of loyalty and payment of tribute. Antiochus VII's death in battle against the Parthians in 129 BCE (*War* 1.61–2; *Ant.* 13.236–53) precipitated a long period of political instability in the Seleucid kingdom, which John Hyrcanus turned to his advantage, strengthening and expanding the boundaries of the Hasmonean state of Judea. He annexed Idumea, which lies south of Judea, converting

---

[1] דבר] missing in MS Erfurt, Evangelisches Ministerium, Or. 2° 1220.

[2] (מרא)]missing in MS Erfurt. Probably an error.

[3] שנצחו...וכתבו] MS Erfurt: וכיונו את אותה השעה וכיונו שנצחו אותה שעה.

[4] See Marcus, *Jewish Antiquities* (LCL), 7:343, note *g*.

its residents to Judaism; conquered Medaba in Transjordan; and subjugated the Samaritan region and its center at Shechem, also destroying the Samaritan temple on Mount Gerizim. The final years of his reign saw the conquest of the large Hellenistic cities of Samaria and Scythopolis (Beth-Shean) and the extension of his kingdom to the Jezreel Valley (*War* 1.62–6; *Ant.* 13.254–8, 275–81). As a means of further buttressing his status, John Hyrcanus also made overtures to the Roman Republic and Ptolemaic Egypt (*Ant.* 13.259–66; see also 284–7). The first ruler to mint coins for the independent state of Judea, they were stamped with the following legends: *yhwḥnn hkhn hgdwl wḥbr hyhwdym* ("Yehoḥanan the high priest and the *ḥbr* [council] of the Jews") or *yhḥnn hkhn hgdl rsh ḥbr hyhdym* ("Yehoḥanan the high priest and head of the council of the Jews").[5]

As reflected in various sources, these achievements made John a much-admired figure in his day. Josephus paints a portrait of an ideal ruler, one who combines civil and religious authority and marks the "apogee of Hasmonean glory."[6] Moreover, Josephus attributes prophetic powers to John Hyrcanus (treated at greater length below).

Josephus is not the sole source that portrays John as representing the coalescence of administrative and priestly authority. Another example comes from an ancient Aramaic midrash embedded in *Targum Pseudo-Jonathan*. Its exposition of Moses's blessing to the tribe of Levi—"Smite the loins of his foes; Let his enemies rise no more" (Deut 33:11)—was understood as referring to John as a victorious ruler and scion of the tribe of Levi. It is also feasible, as outlined below, that the apocryphal work *Testament of Levi* alludes to John's figure and his prophetic powers and that a Qumran document seeks to overturn this image.

Further indication of the importance of John's achievements in his contemporaries' eyes, and even in subsequent generations, comes from *Megillat Ta'anit*. Listed among its festive events are the exile of "the people of Beth-Shean and the Valley,"[7] the capture of the city of Samaria,[8] and "the day of Mount Gerizim."[9] Evidently all three refer to John's victories: the conquest of the Jezreel Valley and Beth-Shean and the exiling of their Syro-Hellenistic population, the conquest of Samaria, and the destruction of the Samaritan temple on Mount Gerizim, respectively. The espousal of the prohibition against fasting on these days for many generations attests to the lasting nature of John's favorable image, as

---

[5] Meshorer, *Jewish Coins*, 57–8, 63–8.
[6] See Mason, *Josephus on the Pharisees*, 225; Gray, *Prophetic Figures*, 16–23. See also Chap. 3 in the present volume.
[7] Noam, *Megillat Ta'anit*, 44, 196; idem, "Scroll of Fasting," 343.
[8] Noam, *Megillat Ta'anit*, 45, 243–9; idem, "Scroll of Fasting," 343.
[9] Noam, *Megillat Ta'anit*, 46, 262–5; idem, "Scroll of Fasting," 343.

Megillat Ta'anit underwent its final redaction close to the destruction of the temple, almost two centuries after John's reign.[10]

Rabbinic literature designates John Hyrcanus "Yoḥanan the high priest," and he receives respectful treatment in the majority of the sources. One mishnah portrays John as an exemplary figure (*Yad.* 4:6);[11] another attributes to him the issuing of temple regulations (*Ma'as. Sh.* 5:15 = *Sotah* 9:10);[12] a third enumerates him among the seven privileged individuals who prepared the purifying ash of the red heifer (*Parah* 3:5). A tradition embedded in the Scholion on *Megillat Ta'anit* and in the BT mentions the use of a date formula referencing the year of his reign on official documents: "In the year...of Yoḥanan, High Priest to the Most High God."[13] Also, the rabbinic tradition treated in this chapter attributes semi-prophetic powers to John Hyrcanus at a time when, according to the rabbis, prophecy had officially ceased among the Jews.

On the other hand, later rabbinic sources voice reservations regarding this figure and his actions. The YT casts some of his actions in a pejorative light,[14] and a baraita in the BT states: "Yoḥanan the high priest officiated as high priest for eighty years and in the end he became a Sadducee."[15] Note that Josephus describes a harsh rift between John Hyrcanus and the Pharisees, which led to the abrogation of Pharisaic law (*Ant.* 13.288–98). The parallel source in the Talmud, however, ascribes this event not to Hyrcanus but to his son Janneus. (This tradition is treated in detail in the next chapter.)

C. THE TRADITION

Thematic Features: Temple, Priest, and Prophetic Powers

The direct historical backdrop to this tradition touches on John Hyrcanus's conquest of the city of Samaria in 107 BCE following a lengthy siege, prolonged because both Antiochus IX Cyzicenus and Ptolemy IX Lathyrus, son of Egpyt's Cleopatra III, came to the city's aid. As noted above, this victory is probably also recorded in *Megillat Ta'anit* as the date on which Samaria and its wall were captured.[16] The tradition itself relates that, while in the temple, John Hyrcanus

---

[10] Noam, *Megillat Ta'anit*, 19–22, 28–33.   [11] Alon, "Attitude of the Pharisees," 26 n. 22.
[12] See also *t. Sotah* 13:10.
[13] Scholion P on *Meg. Ta'an.*, 3 Tishri (see Noam, *Megillat Ta'anit*, 94, 235–8); *b. Rosh Hash.* 18b.
[14] *Y. Ma'as. Sh.* 5:8, 56d; *y. Sotah* 9:11, 24a.
[15] *B. Ber.* 29a. According to Alon ("Attitude of the Pharisees," 26 n. 22) this is a late post-tannaitic baraita. Regarding the identification of Janneus and Yoḥanan in this talmudic passage, see Chap. 3.
[16] See n. 8.

heard a heavenly voice proclaim that his sons had achieved victory in battle. It subsequently turned out that his sons had indeed been victorious on that very day, at precisely that hour. From the Josephan context it is clear that the sons in question were John's sons Antigonus and Aristobulus, who engaged Antiochus Cyzicenus at Samaria (*Ant.* 13.277–9, 282).[17]

Based on the testimony that the voice emerged from the holy of holies, Rashi notes in his commentary on the parallel passage in the BT that John heard the voice "while performing the Day of Atonement ritual."[18] Ralph Marcus supports this conjecture, as Josephus reports that this event took place when Hyrcanus "was alone in the temple, burning incense as a high priest" (*Ant.* 13.282), which is consistent with the Day of Atonement ritual, and Lieberman also concurs with this conclusion.[19] On the other hand, there is a discrepancy between this testimony and *Megillat Ta'anit*, which assigns the conquest of Samaria to 25 Marheshvan.[20] Nonetheless, this is not necessarily a contradiction: the high priest could feasibly be alone in the temple other than on the Day of Atonement, and a voice could issue from the holy of holies without requiring the presence of the high priest there.

Like the story of Nicanor's defeat in the previous chapter, and the legend of the encounter between the high priest and Alexander the Great,[21] this story belongs to the priestly genre of temple legends.[22] Here too we encounter an esteemed high priest who stands in the breach at a time of national distress, and whose sons are responsible for victory in war. News of the victory, however, is relayed in the temple by the officiating priest and not by the warriors on the battlefield. Like the tale of Nicanor's defeat, this story also contains a confrontation between the external military-political arena and the internal temple one, which represents the metaphysical sphere of the divine–Israelite relationship. The two events conjoin in the figure of the priest: on the one hand, he mediates between God and his people through the symbolic incense offering;[23] on the other, he is involved in the events on the battlefield through his sons.[24] Clearly, the thrust of the legend is that the real drama occurs not on the battlefield but in the temple, and the true hero is not the Hasmonean military

---

[17] Even though in *War* 1.65 Josephus mistakenly refers to Antiochus VIII Aspendius.

[18] *B. Sotah* 33a, s.v. נ.יצחו...באנטוכיא. Rashi comments that the Hasmoneans went to war before the Day of Atonement.

[19] Lieberman, *Tosefta Ki-fshutah*, 8:739.

[20] Noam, *Megillat Ta'anit*, 45, 96, 243–9. See Marcus, *Jewish Antiquities* (LCL), 7:369, note *f*. Marcus, however, thinks that the rabbinic parallel does not allude to the date of the event.

[21] *Ant.* 11.302–47; Scholia O and P, 21 Kislev (= *b. Yoma* 69a, among others). See Chap. 1, text at n. 74.

[22] See Chap. 1, text at n. 72, and "Priestly Temple-Legends" in section A of Chap. 7.

[23] According to Josephus (section 282). See Exod 30:34–8; Lev 10:1–5, 16:12–13; Num 16:16–17, 38; 17:2–5, 11–13.

[24] See also Ben Sira 50:1–24.

commander but the servant of God and representative of the chosen people, that is, the high priest.

Alongside this particularistic Jewish approach, the Hyrcanus legend also represents a well-known universal topos in the contemporary literature. Similar stories were recounted by Roman historians regarding an individual who envisioned dramatic events at the very moment of their occurrence, such as the assassination of Domitian (96 CE).[25] The Romans also reported that a heavenly voice promised an individual that he would gain the consulship (Tacitus, *Annals* 11.21), that another mysterious voice proclaimed a Roman victory, and that oracles foretold the future appointment of Vespasian as emperor (69 CE).[26] In this context Lieberman mentions Josephus's story of his own prediction to Vespasian that he would become caesar and its rabbinic parallel that ascribes this prediction to Rabban Yoḥanan ben Zakkai.[27]

As the focus of our story is a prophetic message, I note that this is not the sole instance in which Josephus attributes the gift of prophecy to John Hyrcanus: it is prevalent elsewhere in his works and also appears in other Jewish sources. Josephus notes that Hyrcanus "was accounted by God worthy of three of the greatest privileges, the rule of the nation, the office of high-priest, and the gift of prophecy; for the Deity was with him and enabled him to foresee and foretell the future; so, for example, he foretold of his two elder sons that they would not remain masters of the state" (*Ant.* 13.299–300; cf. *War* 1.68).[28]

In arguing that Josephus drew a linguistic distinction between ancient biblical prophecy, for which he frequently used the root προφητεύω, and later manifestations of prophecy in the Second Temple period, to which he did not apply this root, Louis Feldman notes two exceptions: Cleodemus the prophet (*Ant.* 1.240) and John Hyrcanus, the protagonist of our story. Regarding Hyrcanus, Josephus notes that he was worthy of the gift of prophecy (προφητεία, *Ant.* 13.299). Feldman further maintains that Josephus used this term loosely and imprecisely and was perhaps influenced by an available Hasmonean source.[29] Indeed, this general statement regarding John Hyrcanus's gift of prophecy translates elsewhere in Josephus—in *Antiquities* rather than *War*—as several types of revelation, all inferior to classical biblical prophecy. One type is the heavenly voice that is at the heart of our story. Another is a revelatory dream:

[25] Lieberman, *Tosefta Ki-fshutah*, 8:739. Ibid. 980–90, Lieberman hints that the episode cited by Philostratus regarding the prediction of an attack on Domitian is "a late literary legend" that employed Josephus's testimony ad loc., changing the names of the people and places. I find this supposed dependence difficult to accept.

[26] Tacitus, *Histories* 5.13.2 (Stern, *Greek and Latin Authors*, 2:23, 31); Suetonius, *Lives of the Caesars* 8.4.5 (Stern, *Greek and Latin Authors*, 2:119–20).

[27] See Ben Shahar, "Prediction to Vespasian," 604–64.

[28] For a broader treatment of the "three greatest privileges" and their transformation by the rabbis into three "crowns," see Chap. 3.

[29] Feldman, "Prophets and Prophecy in Josephus." Cf. Marcus, *Jewish Antiquities* (LCL), 7:378 note *a*.

"and once when God appeared to him in his sleep, he asked Him which of his sons was destined to be his successor. And when God showed him the features of Alexander..." (*Ant.* 13.322). In this dream-oracle Hyrcanus poses a question and the divine answer is delivered in a vision.

A third type of oracular activity referred to by Josephus involves consultation of the Urim and Thummim. As Gedalyahu Alon has shown, Josephus evidently espoused the tradition that John Hyrcanus was the last high priest in whose day the stones of the breastplate announced divine intentions: this wonder ceased immediately after his tenure because of divine "displeasure at the transgression of the laws" (*Ant.* 3.218).[30] Rebecca Gray suggests that, given the much earlier dating of the cessation of predictions through the Urim and Thummim in rabbinic literature and in the *Lives of the Prophets*, this was an independent Josephan opinion motivated by his admiration for John Hyrcanus.[31] Intriguingly, the toseftan tradition on John Hyrcanus and the heavenly voice appears in the context of a discussion of the cessation of the Urim and Thummim (which had, according to this tradition, ceased centuries earlier—*t. Sotah* 13:2). There, the "word" heard by John Hyrcanus was one of several heavenly voices, perceived as the last vestiges of prophecy ("But even so, they made them hear [heavenly messages] through a *bat kol*," 13:3).

Apart from Josephus and the rabbinic sources, additional sources contain what can also be understood as references to John Hyrcanus and his prophetic powers. For example, that is how Charles interprets two statements from the *Testament of Levi*. One is a statement to the effect that a prophet to the Most High God will arise from the descendants of Levi.[32] The second is the announcement to Levi elsewhere in the *Testament* that in the future "the Lord will raise up a new priest, to whom all the words of the Lord will be revealed."[33] In the days of this priest the heavens will open: καὶ ἐκ τοῦ ναοῦ τῆς δόξης ἥξει ἐπ'

---

[30] The description of light shining from the stones on the high priest's shoulder (*Ant.* 3.214–17) is the Josephan version of the biblical Urim and Thummim. Josephus notes that the stones ceased to shine some two centuries before he wrote his work, namely, around the end of John Hyrcanus's reign. See Alon, "Attitude of the Pharisees," 26 n. 22. See also Gray (*Prophetic Figures*, 20) who views "two hundred years" as a round number and as indicating that the miracle reportedly ceased immediately after John Hyrcanus's death.

[31] Gray (*Prophetic Figures*, 17–19) argues that Josephus views consultation of the stones of the breastplate as a form of prophecy; accordingly, this explains his tendency to use the verb προφητεύω in its context.

[32] *T. Levi* 8:15. I thank Esther Eshel and Shlomi Efrati for their assistance with the *Testaments of the Twelve Patriarchs*. See de Jonge, *Testaments*, 34. For the Armenian version, see Stone, *Testament of Levi*, 87. According to a minority of manuscripts, the prophet is designated "high" and Hollander and de Jonge (*Testaments: Commentary*, 149, 150 n. 26) view this *lectio difficilior* as preferable. But based on the parallel between *T. Levi* 8:11 and *Aramaic Levi Document* 4:7—both of which treat the three offices granted to the descendants of Levi and mention priesthood and kingship (see Greenfield, Stone, and Eshel, *Aramaic Levi Document*, 37, 39, 66, 139)—it seems more likely that the phrase was "to the Most High God" (see Gen 14:18–20) as reconstructed in *Aramaic Levi* (4:7, 5:8, 8:6).

[33] *T. Levi* 18:2. See de Jonge, *Testaments*, 45; Stone, *Testament of Levi*, 123.

αὐτὸν ἁγίασμα μετὰ φωνῆς πατρικῆς ὡς ἀπὸ Ἀβραὰμ πατρὸς Ἰσαάκ ("from the temple of the glory there will come on him holiness by a voice of a father as from Abraham, Isaac's father").[34] Charles even links *T. Levi's* description of the voice heard by the priest from the temple with the story of the heavenly voice in Josephus and rabbinic sources.[35] Nonetheless, the scholarship after Charles expressed reservations regarding his tendency to identify multiple allusions to the Hasmoneans in the *Testaments*.[36] It is therefore possible that what we have here is simply a portrayal of an ideal priestly-prophetic figure. Still, we cannot ignore the key words ἐκ τοῦ ναοῦ ("from the temple") and μετὰ φωνῆς ("by a voice"), which at the very least indicate some literary link between this ancient image and the legend attributed at some point to the historical figure of John Hyrcanus. It is also possible that Christian motifs have secondarily penetrated this verse.[37]

An echo, albeit a negative one, of the tradition attributing prophetic powers to John Hyrcanus may have been preserved in a Qumran text. 4QTestimonia (4Q175) contains four biblical passages. The first passage, which comes from a harmonistic version of Exodus, interpolates the verses treating a false prophet in Deuteronomy 18:18–19. into Deuteronomy 5's or Exodus proto-SP 20's description of the giving of the Torah: "I will raise up for them a Prophet like you from among their brethren. I will put My words into his mouth and he shall tell them all that I command him" (4Q175 5–6).[38] The next passage, which treats a victorious future leader, comes from Balaam's prophecy (Num 24:15–17). The third passage, which addresses the superiority of the priesthood, contains Moses's blessing to Levi (Deut 33:8–11). The fourth is a pesher-like exposition of Joshua 6:26, which attributes Joshua's curse of the man who rebuilds Jericho to someone named by the author "a man of Belial," who would "again build [this city]" with his sons.[39]

Some scholars, Hanan Eshel among them, identify the "man of Belial," the builder of the city and his sons, as John Hyrcanus and his sons. Citing archeological evidence—a farm and a winter palace built by Hyrcanus at Jericho and fortified by his successors—Eshel proposes that John Hyrcanus's supporters interpreted the biblical descriptions of the exemplary figures found in the Qumran text—an ideal prophet, victorious leader, and righteous priest—as applying to John Hyrcanus. Antithetically, by juxtaposing to these pentateuchal

---

[34] De Jonge, *Testaments*, 49. According to Stone (*Testament of Levi*, 125): "From the Temple of his glory… as from Abraham to Isaac."

[35] See Charles, *Apocrypha and Pseudepigrapha*, 2:309, the commentary on vv. 14, 15; 314, commentary on v. 6; Urbach, "Matai paskah ha-nevu'ah," 11.

[36] See e.g. Segal, "Messianic King," 129–36.

[37] See Hollander and de Jonge, *Testaments: Commentary*, 179–80.

[38] Translation cited from H. Eshel, *Dead Sea Scrolls and the Hasmonean State*, 64.

[39] The reconstruction is also based on the parallel in 4Q379. For details, bibliography, and a comprehensive discussion, see H. Eshel, *Dead Sea Scrolls and the Hasmonean State*, 63–89. For a different opinion regarding the relationship between 4QTestimonia and 4Q Apocryphon of Joshua, see Berthelot, "4QTestimonia," 99–116; Dimant, *History*, 327–9. See also the discussion of this document in the context of the legend of Janneus and the Pharisees in Chap. 3.

pericopes a passage that, based on Joshua, cast the deeds of Hyrcanus and his sons in a negative light, the author of the Qumran pesher sought to reject these political midrashim.[40] If correct, this reconstruction evidences the familiarity of Hyrcanus's opponents within the Qumran *Yaḥad* with the prevailing notion that Hyrcanus merited the gift of prophecy. This political dispute between supporters and opponents of the dynasty accompanied the Hasmoneans throughout their entire reign, and its final metamorphosis will be explicated in the concluding chapter of this book.[41]

Linguistic Features

The Josephan and toseftan versions of this brief legend are nearly identical, as Shaye J. D. Cohen has noted.[42] Not just thematic, the similarities also extend to language. Even though composed and preserved in different languages, the two versions display discernible linguistic affinities. First, the two traditions share the exact message of the heavenly voice in its entirety:

נצחון טליא דאזלון לאגחא קרבא באנטכיא

οἱ παῖδες αὐτοῦ νενικήκασιν ἀρτίως τὸν Ἀντίοχον

Second, a striking linguistic affinity is the Aramaic word used by the heavenly voice in the tosefta: טליא "young men" or "children." This word was preserved by the rabbis even though they no longer understood its context, for rabbinic tradition no longer recollected that the message concerned John's two sons. Interestingly, traces of this word were preserved in the Josephan version of this story in *Antiquities*: παῖδες αὐτοῦ, "his children," rather than υἱοί, "sons."

Another similarity between Josephus and the tosefta is the title ἀρχιερεύς ("high priest") which Josephus attaches to Hyrcanus. In the Josephan narrative, this is exceptional: throughout his lengthy account of John Hyrcanus's life, Josephus *always* relates to him as Hyrcanus alone. *Only* within the current tradition does he also designate him "high priest," as in rabbinic literature, which always refers to him as Yoḥanan the high priest. This indicates the integration by Josephus of a Jewish, Hebrew source, a source that was also at the disposal of a later rabbinic editor.

Another linguistic parallel inheres in Josephus's use of the name Antiochus. Even though Josephus opens his narrative by noting that the event took place on the day that the sons faced Cyzicenus, in reporting the message of the heavenly

---

[40] H. Eshel, *Dead Sea Scrolls and the Hasmonean State*, 63–89.

[41] See Chap. 7, section C, "Reworking of the Hasmonean Stories: The Fourth Generation: Hyrcanus II and Aristobulus II."

[42] Cohen, "Parallel Historical Tradition," 9. Note the marginal notation in MS Vatican 133 of the YT near our story: "And this is found in Joseph ben Gurion's book."

voice heard by Hyrcanus he refers to Antiochus. This is also a vestige of the Hebrew/Aramaic Ur-text. Note that in the extant Hebrew sources the voice says באנטכיא/ באנטוכיא/ באנטוכיה[43]—the Seleucid city of Antioch in Syria (present-day southern Turkey). Their shared mention of Antioch is certainly an early corruption of the name Antiochus, as the Hasmoneans never fought at Antioch.[44] This corruption shows that, although the rabbis were not cognizant of the underlying historical or geographical circumstances, the rabbinic version has preserved a frozen echo of the ancient wording in this instance as well.

Note, however, the differences between the traditions. Josephus prefaces the story by recounting the historical circumstances, the clash with Cyzicenus (section 282), which is missing from the rabbinic versions. This was probably not part of the original tradition but rather an explanation added by Josephus to clarify the circumstances of the episode and its placement after the story of the Hasmonean brothers' battle against Antiochus Cyzicenus and the conquest of Samaria (sections 275–9). Another difference lies in the manner in which the tidings conveyed by the heavenly voice and, audible only to John, were disseminated: according to Josephus, he revealed the matter to the people upon leaving the temple; according to the tosefta, "they wrote down" the day and the time at which the voice was heard: namely, John revealed what he heard to some unidentified group of people, who then recorded it, even though this is not stated explicitly. In any event, both versions highlight the verification of the heavenly message: καὶ συνέβη οὕτως γενέσθαι ("and so it actually happened," *Ant.* 13.283); וכיונו ואותה שעה היתה שנצחו ("And they checked and the victory was at that very hour").[45]

D. THE PROVENANCE OF THE LEGEND

Contextual Considerations

It is readily apparent that the parallel traditions in Josephus and rabbinic literature were in this instance interpolated from an external source and did not originate in the works in which they are cited. In *Antiquities* the tradition follows a factual historical description of the conquest of Samaria, and is contextually incongruent in nature, date, and place. In nature, it is a "closed" legend on a miraculous event

---

[43] For the different versions, see Lieberman, *Tosefta: Nashim*, 231–2; and the various parallels in rabbinic sources: *y. Sotah* 9:13, 24b; *b. Sotah* 33a; *Cant. Rab.*, parashah 5.

[44] See Derenbourg, *Essai*, 74 n. 1. An indistinct recollection of the variant אנטיוכוס was preserved in MS Vatican 133, *y. Sotah* 9:13, 24b where it states in one place: באנדוכי(ס)[ה] (the *samekh* at the end of the word was at a second stage emended to *heh*).

[45] For exchanges in this sentence between the witnesses, see n. 3.

as opposed to a sequential, factual historical description;[46] in date, it returns to the moment of victory over Cyzicenus at a distance of several sections from its factual account (277) and after the mention of several intervening events (278–81); in place—the arena is the temple, not the battlefield. The story also stands out against the following section, another interpolation, evidently from Strabo, which surveys the condition of Egyptian Jews (284–7). This paragraph, which opens with a typical Josephan formula for such interpolations: κατὰ τοῦτον τὸν καιρόν ("at this time"), concludes with attribution of a quote to this historian (287).[47]

Comparison to *War* (see Table 2.1) shows that both these passages—the story of John Hyrcanus and the heavenly voice and the survey of Egyptian Jewry—were interpolated into an existing narrative in *Antiquities*. This is a further illustration of Josephus's addition of sources with parallels in rabbinic sources to his later work, as exemplified elsewhere in this book.

The expressions that frame its opening and closing also underscore the incongruity of the Hyrcanus story in this context. Josephus prefaces the story with an overall summary of its contents: "Now about the high priest Hyrcanus an extraordinary story is told how the deity communicated with him" (282).[48] Also, the use of λέγεται and the emphatic φασὶ γάρ ("for they say," section 282) indicate a folktale, as opposed to the preceding sequence.[49] Finally, Josephus closes the account of the tradition with the phrase καὶ συνέβη οὕτως γενέσθαι ("and so it actually happened") and then adds his own ending: καὶ τὰ μὲν περὶ Ὑρκανὸν ἐν τούτοις ἦν ("This, then, was how the affairs of Hyrcanus were going," section 283). This return to the interrupted sequence of his narrative typifies the Josephan interpolation of external sources.

But various features suggest that the tradition is anomalous not just in Josephus but also in the Tosefta. This is evidenced first and foremost by its

Table 2.1. Comparison of *Antiquities* and *War*

	Antiquities 13		*War* 1
275–81	Conquest of Samaria and Beth-Shean	64–6	Conquest of Samaria and Beth-Shean
282–3	John Hyrcanus and the heavenly voice		
284–7	Egyptian Jewry		
288	Hyrcanus's success and Jewish envy[a]	67	Hyrcanus's success and Jewish envy

Note: [a]This is followed in *Antiquities* by another interpolation. See Chap. 3.

[46] See Schürer, *History*, 1:51.
[47] See D. R. Schwartz, "Josephus' Source on Agrippa II," 249.
[48] Ibid. 246.   [49] See Gray, *Prophetic Figures*, 22.

inclusion of an Aramaic phrase, which is exceptional in this work. Infrequently cited in tannaitic literature, Aramaic expressions are typical of earlier strata, such as the ancient formulas of legal documents: the *ketubbah*, the *get*, and the like.

T. Sotah 13–15 contains lists of regulations that were cancelled or objects placed in storage in the wake of catastrophes such as the destruction of the temple and the death of the righteous.[50] They include, among others, the Davidic kingship, the Urim and Thummim, the Shamir-worm and the honey of *ṣufim*, industrious scholars, creators of parables, and men of deeds. In this context, *t. Sotah* 13:3 states: "When the latter prophets died, that is, Haggai, Zechariah, and Malachi, then the Holy Spirit came to an end in Israel." The tosefta continues: "But even so, they communicated with them by means of a *bat kol* (heavenly voice)." Four stories regarding messages from heavenly voices follow: sages gathered at Jericho during the time of Hillel the elder heard a heavenly voice declare, "There is a man among you who is worthy to receive the Holy Spirit" (13:3); at Jabneh a heavenly voice made a similar announcement, indicating Samuel the Small (13:4). The third tradition is the one concerning John Hyrcanus, our topic here (13:5). The fourth story concerns Simeon the Righteous[51] who heard a "word from the House of the holy of holies": שמעון הצדיק שמע דבר מבית קדש הקדשים: בטילת עבידתא די אמר סנאה לאיתאה להיכלא, ונהרג גסקלגס ובטלו גזרותיו ובלשון ארמי שמע ("'Annulled is the decree which the enemy planned to bring against the sanctuary, and Gasqelges [Caligula] has been killed and his decrees have been annulled.' And he heard [all this] in the Aramaic language"). This treats a different historical incident—the annulment of Caligula's decree mandating the bringing of an idol into the temple (13:6).[52]

---

[50] This is in the wake of a similar collection in *m. Sotah* 9, which opens with the abolishment of the rite of breaking the heifer's neck (mishnah 9), and continues with the ordeal of bitter water, the confession concerning the tithe, the singing at wedding feasts, the Urim and Thummim, and the good taste of produce, among others.

[51] This high priest, who allegedly lived in the days of Caligula, is evidently not to be identified either with "Simeon the Righteous" who is presented as the earliest sage in *m. 'Abot* 1:2–3 and mentioned elsewhere in tannaitic sources (*m. Parah* 3:5; *t. Naz.* 4:7; and in the current toseftan context, *t. Sotah* 13:7–8), or with the one who met with Alexander the Great, according to another legend (Scholia to *Meg. Ta'an.*, 21 Kislev; *b. Yoma* 69a, and elsewhere). This means that the toseftan chapter skips from one "Simeon the Righteous" (13:6) to another (13:7–8: "As long as Simeon the Righteous was alive…"), who had preceded him by several centuries (see Lieberman, *Tosefta Ki-fshutah*, 8:73). The Simeon of the Caligula story has been identified in scholarly literature with almost every figure named Simeon who lived in that period and was mentioned either in Second Temple-period Jewish literature, the New Testament, or rabbinic literature. Some scholars conjecture that the legend of Alexander and Simeon the Righteous caused the appellation "righteous" to be appended to the later Simeon in the Caligula story. Others surmise that the name "Simeon the Righteous" was a later insertion into the story that aimed to invoke the revered figure of a legendary high priest. For a review of the scholarship and references, see Tropper, *Simeon the Righteous*, 209–12.

[52] Philo, *Embassy* 186–348; Josephus, *Ant.* 18.257–309, *War* 2.184–203; Tacitus, *Histories* 5.9.15. For another mention of this event in rabbinic literature see *Meg. Ta'an.*, 22 Shevat (Noam, *Megillat Ta'anit*, 46, 112–14, 283–90).

For our purposes, we must note that these four stories are not cut from the same cloth. The first two, in line with the opening of the collection, use the term *bat kol*: "But even so, they communicated with them by means of a *bat kol* (heavenly voice)." These stories deal with the rabbis and are situated in the places where they gather. In them, the heavenly voice speaks Hebrew,[53] and the topic is a worthy attribute of an individual rabbi. In contrast, the term *bat kol* is missing from the latter two stories; what is heard is a *davar* ("word"), an ancient term that pre-dates *bat kol*.[54] Functionally closer to biblical prophecy, the *davar* in these stories treats dramatic national events—victory in war or annulment of a royal edict—not praise for a rabbi. Those who hear the "word" are high priests, not rabbis; it is delivered not where the rabbis gather but in the temple. Finally, the message of the "word" is delivered in identifiably Second Temple Middle Aramaic,[55] as an anonymous redactor notes at the conclusion of the story of Simeon the Righteous.

In conjunction, these features clearly indicate a different, earlier origin for these two stories as compared to the collection into which they were incorporated. Probably priestly traditions from the Second Temple period, they attribute the last vestiges of prophetic abilities to the priests. The inclusion in *Antiquities* of one of these two traditions is indeed clear evidence of its pre-rabbinic date. On the other hand, the first two stories concerning the *bat kol* at Jericho and Jabneh represent a secondary "rabbinic" stage of development in which such events were transferred to the rabbinic world. The heavenly voice received a fixed designation—*bat kol*—but it is a pale shadow of the original: it no longer proclaims dramatic national salvation but rather the spiritual attributes of a rabbi. Furthermore, the rabbis inverted the message of the *bat kol* stories—instead of heralding dramatic national salvation, as in the early *davar* traditions, the "rabbinic" heavenly voice proclaims the very cessation of prophecy.

---

[53] In these stories as well, the prophecy of Samuel the Small is conveyed in Aramaic: שמעון וישמעאל לקטלא ושאר חברוהי לחרבא... (halakhah 4; "Simeon and Ishmael are destined to be put to death, and the rest of the associates will die by the sword..."). It is possible that here too the words of the prophecy derive from an earlier, independent source. See the discussion below.

[54] Lieberman (*Tosefta Ki-fshutah*, 8:738) equates *davar* with *bat kol*. See his arguments there.

[55] The infinitive form לאגחא (a II-w verb in the causative stem) is typical of the Standard Literary Aramaic (SLA) of Hellenistic and Roman times. In later dialects, including Palestinian Jewish Aramaic, the infinitive of the derived stems is marked by an initial preformative /m-/. See Tal, "Infinitival Forms," 201–18, esp. 210–14. The perfect forms מצחו and אזלו, as correctly preserved in MS Erfurt and in the first printed edition of the Tosefta, align with the early stages of SLA, which continue Official Aramaic. In the Roman period, words with final long vowels were nasalized and the verbal paradigm acquired a paragogic *nun* in plural forms, especially in the perfect tense, as found in MS Vienna: (אזלון, נצחון), which tends to use Palestinian spellings, see Braverman, "Vienna and Erfurt Manuscripts," 153–70, esp. 161 and the literature cited there). See Tal, "Strata of Palestinian Jewish Aramaic," 165–84. I am indebted to Noam Mizrahi and Yoel Elitzur for their help on linguistic matters. See Lieberman's observation (*Tosefta Ki-fshutah*, 8:738) regarding the language of Samuel the Small's prophecy at the hour of his death, which is conveyed in Aramaic in *t. Sotah* 13:4: "It is in the ancient Aramaic of the Bible and legal documents (these documents themselves are also in ancient royal Aramaic, which was later used as flowery language)."

In other words, the purpose of this last vestige of prophecy, according to the rabbis, was in essence to indicate that the age of prophecy had ended. From now on, we are to infer, it is necessary to "bend your ear and listen to the words of the rabbis."[56]

The Components of the Tradition

Notwithstanding their status as autonomous literary units, the ancient stories regarding John and Simeon can be further broken down into layers. The language of the stories is Hebrew, but the "word" heard by the protagonists is in Aramaic. In the Tosefta the anonymous redactor of the story of Simeon attributes this phenomenon to the mysterious nature of the heavenly voice, which spoke Aramaic. The BT as well concludes that, as opposed to the angels, heavenly voices tended to speak Aramaic.[57] It is more likely, however, that the message was in Aramaic not because of its attribution to a heavenly voice but because it originated in a different, Aramaic-language, context. The ancient, "festive,"[58] Aramaic of these citations from this unknown source became a literary device for distinguishing the mysterious heavenly voice from the mundane voice of the narrator.

Support for this supposition comes from *Megillat Ta'anit*, in which each date is accompanied by a brief Aramaic explanation of the joyful event or victory that bars fasting on that day:[59] for example, איתוקם תמידא ("the daily sacrifice was settled"); נפקו בני חקרא מן ירושלם ("the men of the Akra [the fortress] left Jerusalem"); אחידת מגדל צר ("the Sher Tower was captured"); נטלו דימוסנאי מן ירוש' ("the 'Demosnaei' left Jerusalem"); עדא ספר גזרתא ("the book of decrees was removed"),[60] among others. The event for 22 Shevat is described as follows: בטילת עבידתא דאמיר סנאה לאיתאה להיכלא ("the [pagan] cult which the enemy ordered to bring into the temple was cancelled").[61] According to the scholarly consensus, this undoubtedly refers to the annulment of Caligula's decree, alluded to in our tosefta.[62]

---

[56] See *Seder Olam Rabbah* 30 (Milikowsky, *Seder Olam: Critical Edition, Commentary, and Introduction*, 1:322).

[57] *B. Sotah* 33a. Our baraita was interpolated into this sugya in order to question the proposition that the ministering angels do not understand Aramaic. The explanation tendered in the Talmud is that a *bat kol* differs from an angel, because its purpose is that it be understood by its addressees. The Talmud also proposes that it be identified as an angel that possesses expertise in many languages.

[58] Following Lieberman. See n. 55. [59] See Noam, *Megillat Ta'anit*, esp. 19–22.

[60] For the citations and variants, see ibid. 43–5. For the English translations here and below, see Noam, "Scroll of Fasting."

[61] Noam, *Megillat Ta'anit*, 46.

[62] Ibid. 283–90. See also Noam, "A Statue in the Temple," 454–86.

Note, however, that in *Megillat Ta'anit* this description stands independently, as a factual description of an event. It is neither placed in the mouth of a heavenly voice (or a "word"), nor interpolated into the story of Simeon in the temple.[63] Thus, it must have originally had an independent existence as a brief description of an event and was only secondarily placed in the mouth of a mysterious voice emanating from the holy of holies. Does this then mean that the author of the story of Simeon in the Tosefta took the language of the heavenly voice from *Megillat Ta'anit*? This appears unlikely as well, because the "word" heard by John Hyrcanus, so similar to that heard by Simeon, does not appear in *Megillat Ta'anit*. Thus, if the redactor of the story of John did not need *Megillat Ta'anit* as a source for words to place in the mouth of his heavenly voice, this makes it unlikely that he imported his Aramaic wording for the twin story of Simeon from this text.

Accordingly, I argue that the language used to define the holiday (22 Shevat) originated in an external context that pre-dated the redaction of *Megillat Ta'anit*. I have postulated elsewhere that this was characteristic of this work as a whole; namely, that the author of *Megillat Ta'anit* used existing, early linguistic phrases with which he was familiar and did not word the entire book *ex ante*. Indeed, this is exemplified in several instances.[64]

Comparison of the concise wording of the two "words" heard by the priests in the tosefta evidences impressive similarity between it and the language used to describe the events listed in *Megillat Ta'anit*. Note the following examples: נצחון טליא דאזלון לאגחא קרבא באנטוכיא (Tosefta: "the young men who went to wage war against Antioch have been victorious"); בטילת עבידתא די אמר סנאה לאיתאה להיכלא (Tosefta and *Meg. Ta'an.*: "the [pagan] cult which the enemy ordered to bring into the temple was cancelled"); and the following examples, all from *Megillat Ta'anit*: אתנטלת אדכרתא מן שטרא ("the mention was removed from the documents"); אחידת שומרון שורא ("Samaria was captured—the wall"); יתיבת כנשתא על דינא ("the 'Kenishta' took its seat for judgment"); נטל אנטיוכוס מן ירוש' ("Antiochus left Jerusalem").

These phrases bear the same stamp: all are in Middle Aramaic, open with a predicate followed by the subject, succinctly describe a historical event, and at times provide additional details, usually the place where the event occurred. In other words, they all appear to have emanated from an unknown Aramaic chronicle that listed victories and other happy events, which was probably begun during the Hasmonean period but was still dynamic and open to additions several decades before the destruction of the temple, as evidenced by

---

[63] Note that the story of Simeon the Righteous in the temple was incorporated into the Scholion, the commentary on *Megillat Ta'anit*, and that one of the editions of the Scholion, like the Tosefta, mentions the language of the heavenly voice. As noted, no mention of this appears in *Megillat Ta'anit* itself.

[64] The text citations are taken from Noam, *Megillat Ta'anit*, 284. For more on this matter, see ibid. 21, 338–9, 378.

its inclusion of the Caligula event from 41 CE. How many of the descriptions in *Megillat Ta'anit* were first worded by the author in a style already common before his day, and how many he derived from this Aramaic list of victories, is impossible to determine. With regard to the victory of John's sons at least, there is no doubt that it came from a separate source, for it is missing from *Megillat Ta'anit* altogether. This is also probably true of its "twin," the brief description of the annulment of Caligula's decree.

As noted in the Introduction, John Collins has recently suggested that lost historical traditions, either oral or written, underlie the pesharim and other Qumran texts that allude to unspecified historical events, and that these lost sources resembled the so-called annalistic texts: namely, 4Q331–4Q333. Some scholars view these fragments as lists of dates that must be observed annually, similar to *Megillat Ta'anit*; others as a list of events with no halakhic purpose.[65] Although the fragmentary annalistic texts from Qumran are not identical to the vestiges I have traced in the current chapter, they certainly provide further evidence of the existence of the genre Collins has described.

To sum up our findings: the story of John Hyrcanus took the phrasing of the "word" that announced the victory from an unknown source. This source probably also contained the "word" heard by Simeon. It appears likely that the redactor of *Megillat Ta'anit* also used that same source, at least for the wording of the entry for 22 Shevat, and almost certainly for other events.

E. CONCLUSION

Of the traditions shared by the Josephan and rabbinic corpora, the episode of John Hyrcanus and the "word" he heard in the temple exhibits the closest topical and linguistic affinities. Part of a wealth of allusions to prophetic powers ascribed to John Hyrcanus preserved in different Second Temple-period libraries and contexts, this tradition is anomalous in both Josephus and the Tosefta, and its origins in an earlier, probably oral, source are readily observed. Thus, as in the previous chapter, a comparison of the tradition as found in Josephus and in rabbinic sources demonstrates that there was no dependence between the two. Rather, both cited the same temple legend which incorporated Jewish motifs of temple, priesthood, and prophecy with the Hellenistic-Roman topos of heavenly signs that are harbingers of what will take place in the future or in distant places.

---

[65] On the contents of these calendrical texts and a detailed treatment of the scholarly hypotheses, see H. Eshel, *Dead Sea Scrolls and the Hasmonean State*, 136–44. See also the discussion and references in Collins, "Historiography," 171–6.

Through the language shift in the toseftan legend we can reconstruct the following three stages in the history of the tradition regarding John Hyrcanus and the heavenly voice. Its earliest stage is represented by the Aramaic message delivered by the heavenly voice. This laconic description of a Hasmonean military victory is in fact a rare vestige of a lost Aramaic document that enumerated a series of political events, of a type familiar to us from *Megillat Ta'anit* and from a similar story in the Tosefta. The Qumran library attests to the existence of other works of this genre. Incorporated into a priestly temple aggadah that was related in Hebrew in its second stage, the antiquity of this Aramaic sentence was used as a literary device to indicate the contents of the heavenly communication. This secondary story reached both Josephus and the rabbis, and was inserted into *Antiquities* in Greek translation, and later into the Tosefta in its original Hebrew and Aramaic. In spite of the language shift, the original form and wording of the Aramaic message that marks the climax of the story was astonishingly well preserved both within the Greek framework in *Antiquities* and within the Hebrew context of the Tosefta. Finally, the absorption of this Second Temple literary piece into the tannaitic context gave rise to a third stage of literary creativity. By composing emulative stories on heavenly voices whose arena was the study hall rather than the temple, and whose protagonists were rabbis rather than priests, the rabbis totally inverted the message of these legends. Instead of applying semi-prophetic powers to high priests, these later stories proclaimed the termination of the prophetic age and ordained the rabbis as the heirs of both the prophets and the priests. As demonstrated in the concluding chapter, this typifies the rabbinic treatment of John Hyrcanus's image as preserved in the Second Temple literary legacy.

"Yoḥanan the high priest," who received a divine message in the temple, was the last Hasmonean figure to enjoy the unstinting admiration of the Pharisaic circles who left their literary impress on the Josephan and rabbinic corpora. As we shall see in the following chapters, the Second Temple legends treating the next Hasmonean generations display ambivalence, conflict, and hostility.[66]

---

[66] For an abridged version of this chapter, see Vered Noam, "Why Did the Heavenly Voice Speak Aramaic? Ancient Layers in Rabbinic Literature," in *The Faces of Torah: Studies in the Texts and Contexts of Ancient Judaism in Honor of Steven Fraade*, ed. Michal Bar-Asher Siegal, Tzvi Novick, and Christine Hayes, JAJSup 22 (Göttingen: Vandenhoeck and Ruprecht, 2017), 157–68.

3

The Rupture with the Pharisees

The next episodes mark a departure from the positive attitude toward, and praise for, the Hasmonean dynasty that characterized the first two traditions examined here. In the rabbinic corpus, the episodes discussed in this and the following chapter relate to the figure of Janneus, the next generation of the Hasmonean dynasty, whereas in the Josephan version, the story treated in this chapter still concerns his father, John Hyrcanus.[1] In any case, this is a transitional story in both the Josephan and rabbinic versions: first, because it recounted either of the second generation of Hasmoneans and closed an era, or of a member of the third generation, and opened a new stage; second, because this story abruptly casts us from legends that reflect a Hasmonean "golden age" to legends in which the relations between the Hasmonean ruler and the people in general, and with the Pharisees in particular, move from misunderstandings and ambivalence to open hostility. Our episode pinpoints the opening of the rupture between the Pharisees and the Hasmonean dynasty.

Long a topic of scholarly discussion, this story appears only in *Antiquities* and in the BT. Apparently variants of a single tradition, the original form of these two parallel accounts can no longer be reconstructed in detail. What we do know is that this tradition is in fact an etiological tale whose purpose was to explain the evolution of certain historical circumstances, namely, the beginnings of the enmity between the Hasmonean dynasty and the Pharisees.[2] Typically for folktales seeking to explain historical processes, it ascribes the process to a one-time event in which personal intrigue and bad luck play a central role.[3] Significantly, the two versions of this story, and the one in the BT especially, reflect Second Temple sectarian debate in both content and language, so much so that I argue that it should be regarded as a lost fragment of an apologetic Pharisaic work.

---

[1] For historical background on John Hyrcanus, see Chap. 2; for background on Alexander Janneus, see Chap. 4.

[2] As opposed to Baumgarten ("Rabbinic Literature," 38–9), who suggests that the thrust of the story was to explain the need to reinforce the authority of Pharisaic halakhah after Janneus's death, I think that its purpose was to explain the development of the rupture between the Pharisees and the Hasmonean dynasty.

[3] See Neusner, *From Politics to Piety*, 59.

A. THE SOURCES

Josephus, *Antiquities* 13.288–98; *b. Qiddushin* 66a

Josephus, *Antiquities* 13.288–98

(288) As for Hyrcanus, the envy (φθόνος) of the Jews was aroused against him by his own successes (εὐπραγία) and those of his sons; particularly hostile to him were the Pharisees, who are one of the Jewish schools, as we have related above. And so great is their influence with the masses that even when they speak against a king or high priest, they immediately gain credence. (289) Hyrcanus too was a disciple of theirs, and was greatly loved by them. And once he invited them to a feast and entertained them hospitably, and when he saw that they were having a very good time, he began by saying that they knew he wished to be righteous and in everything he did tried to please God and them—for the Pharisees profess such beliefs; (290) at the same time he begged them, if they observed him doing anything wrong or straying from the right path, to lead him back to it and correct him. But they testified to his being altogether virtuous, and he was delighted with their praise. (291) However, one of the guests, named Eleazar, who had an evil nature and took pleasure in dissension (κακοήθης ὢν φύσει καὶ στάσει χαίρων), said, "Since you have asked to be told the truth, if you wish to be righteous, give up the high-priesthood and be content with governing the people" (τὴν ἀρχιερωσύνην ἀπόθου, καὶ μόνον ἀρκείτω σοι τὸ ἄρχειν τοῦ λαοῦ). (292) And when Hyrcanus asked him for what reason he should give up the high-priesthood, he replied, "Because we have heard from our elders that your mother was a captive in the reign of Antiochus Epiphanes." But the story was false, and Hyrcanus was furious with the man, while all the Pharisees were very indignant (καὶ πάντες δ᾽ οἱ Φαρισαῖοι σφοδρῶς ἠγανάκτησαν). (293) Then a certain Jonathan, one of Hyrcanus' close friends, belonging to the school of Sadducees, who hold opinions opposed to those of the Pharisees, said that it had been with the general approval of all the Pharisees that Eleazar had made his slanderous statement; and this, he added, would be clear to Hyrcanus if he inquired of them what punishment Eleazar deserved for what he had said. (294) And so Hyrcanus asked the Pharisees what penalty they thought he deserved—for, he said, he would be convinced that the slanderous statement had not been made with their approval if they fixed a penalty commensurate with the crime—, and they replied that Eleazar deserved stripes and chains; for they did not think it right to sentence a man to death for calumny, and anyway the Pharisees are naturally lenient in the matter of punishments. (295) At this Hyrcanus became very angry and began to believe that the fellow had slandered him with their approval. And Jonathan in particular inflamed his anger, and so worked upon him (296) that he brought him to join the Sadducaean party and desert the Pharisees, and to abrogate the regulations which they had established for the people, and punish those who

observed them. Out of this, of course, grew the hatred of the masses for him and his sons, (297) but of this we shall speak hereafter (περὶ μέντοι τούτων αὖθις ἐροῦμεν). For the present I wish merely to explain that the Pharisees had passed on to the people certain regulations handed down by former generations and not recorded in the Laws of Moses, for which reason they are rejected by the Sadducaean group, who hold that only those regulations should be considered valid which were written down (in Scripture), and that those which had been handed down by former generations (τὰ ἐκ παραδόσεως τῶν πατέρων) need not be observed. (298) And concerning these matters the parties came to have controversies and serious differences, the Sadducees having the confidence of the wealthy alone but no following among the populace, while the Pharisees have the support of the masses. But of these two schools and of the Essenes a detailed account has been given in the second book of my *Judaica*.

Rabbinic Sources

B. Qiddushin 66a[4]

דתניא:

1	מעשה בינאי המלך שהלך לכוחלית שבמדבר וכבש שם ששים כרכים
2	ובחזרתו היה שמח שמחה גדולה וקרא לכל חכמי ישר'<אל> ואמ' להם:
3	אבותינו היו אוכלים מלוחים בזמן שהיו עוסק<ים> בבניין בית המקדש
4	אף אנו נאכל מלוחי<ם> זכר לאבותינו
5	והעלו מלוחין על שולח<נות> של זה[ב] ואכלו
6	והיה שם אדם אחד לץ רע ובליעל ואלעזר בן פוערא שמו
7	ויאמר אלעזר בן פוער' לינאי המלך: ינאי המלך <לבם> של פרוש<ים> עליך
8	ומה אעשה? א'ל הקם להם בציץ שבין עיניך, הקים להם בציץ שבין עיניו
9	<היה שם זקן אחד ויהוד' בן גדירא שמו ויאמר יהוד' בן גדירא <לינאי המלך>:
10	<ינאי המלך> רב לך כתר מלכות הנח כתר כהונה לזרעו של אהרן
11	שהיו או': <אמו נשבית> במודעית
12	ויבקש הדבר ולא נמצא ויבדלו חכמי ישר<אל> בזעם
13	ויאמר אלע<זר> בן פועירא לינאי המלך:
14	ינאי המלך הדיוט שביש' כך הוא דינו ואתה מלך וכהן גדו' כך הוא דינך?
15	אמ' לו: ומה אעשה? אמ' לו: אם את שומ' לעצתי רומסם
16	אמ' לו: ותורה מה תהא עליה?
17	אמ' לו: והלא היא כרוכה ומונחת בקרן זוית וכל הרוצה ללמ<וד> יבא וילמד ⁵[...]
18	ותיו(ע)[צ]ץ הרעה על ידי אלעזר בן פוערא ועל ידי יהודה בן גדגדא
19	ויהרגו כל חכמי ישר' והיה <העולם משתומם>
20	עד שבא שמעון בן שטח והחזיר את התורה לישנה

⁴ The base text is according to MS Vatican, Biblioteca Apostolica, ebr. 111. In cases of abbreviation, deletion, or unique variants the text has been reconstructed based on other witnesses using angled brackets. For a fuller apparatus with textual variants, see Noam, "The Rift with the Pharisees," 255–85. Unusual words and expressions in the Hebrew have been incorporated into the English translation below in order to facilitate the discussion that follows.

⁵ Here a late amoraic conversation has been interpolated into the original tradition; see the discussion below.

…it was taught: It once happened that King Yannai [Janneus] went to Kohalith (כוחלית)[6] in the desert and conquered sixty towns there.[7] On his return he rejoiced exceedingly and invited all the sages of Israel. Said he to them, "Our forefathers ate mallows (מלוחים)[8] when they were engaged in the building of the [second] temple; let us too eat mallows in memory of our forefathers." So mallows were served on golden tables, and they ate.

Now, there was a man there, frivolous, evil,[9] and a scoundrel[10] (לץ רע ובליעל), named Eleazar ben Po'irah.[11] Said (ויאמר) Eleazar ben Po'irah to King Yannai. "O King Yannai, the hearts of the Pharisees are against thee (לבם של פרושים עליך)." "Then what shall I do?" He said to him: "Make them swear (הקם להם) by the plate (בציץ) between your eyes."[12] [So] he made them swear by the plate between his eyes.

---

[6] "Kohalith in the desert" is unknown and various suggestions have been made regarding its identification. Some find in it echoes of Janneus's campaign in Transjordan; others link it to [אזוב כן[ו]חלי]ת found in the Mishnah and halakhic midrashim as a type of hyssop plant, mentioned alongside "desert hyssop." Joshua Efron was of the opinion that this is not an authentic geographical location but rather an invention based on that halakhic phrase. For a survey of the various opinions see Efron, "Simeon Ben Shataḥ and Jannaeus," 178–9.

[7] Cf. Deut 3:4; see Efron, "Simeon Ben Shataḥ and Jannaeus," 178.

[8] Evidently a plant eaten by the poor in times of famine (cf. Job 30:4). Janneus seeks to under-score the gap between the poverty in the restoration era and the plenty in his own: "to be a remem-brance of the poverty of our forefathers and to give thanks to God who has granted us success and enriched us." (See Rashi on *b. Qidd.* 66a, s.v. בבנין עסוקים כשהיו. See also ibid., s.v. מלוחים; and Baumgarten, "Rabbinic Literature," 36–7 n. 84.) Perhaps the legend's author intended the ironic comparison of the golden tables and the symbolic asceticism Janneus wished to exemplify as a criticism of the latter.

[9] Usually translated "evil-hearted," according to the printed versions (both the Venice and Vilna editions read: לץ לב רע ובליעל), but in MSS Vatican 111; Oxford, Bodleian Library, Opp. 248 (Neubauer 367) (henceforth: Oxford 367); Munich, Bayerische Staatsbibliothek, Cod. hebr. 95 (henceforth: Munich 95) and the old, reliable Spanish printed edition (Guadalajara; c.1480) the word לב is missing. This word, as already suggested by Friedlaender ("Rupture," 446 n. 15), is a dittography from לץ.

[10] The *Hebrew–English Edition of the Babylonian Talmud* here translates Belial as "worthless," as do the English editions of the DSS on occasion (see e.g. Abegg et al., *Concordance*, 1:146; Steudel, "4QSapiential-Didactic Work B," 205). In my opinion, however, the renderings "wicked" or "a scoundrel," found in certain Bible translations, are better equivalents. For the biblical occur-rence of איש בליעל, see Prov 16:27.

[11] On the possible identification of this Eleazar with Eleazar ben Pachura, mentioned in the YT, see section G below, text near n. 151.

[12] On the expression הקם להם בציץ, see the discussion below. The description of the *ṣiṣ* as placed between the eyes is surprising, since it should be "on Aaron's forehead" (Exod 28:38). However, this expression appears elsewhere in rabbinic literature (*t. Ḥal.* 1:10; *Shir ha-Shirim Zuta* 4:3). For the ancient expression בין עיניים, "between the eyes," as a parallel to head in Ugaritic and in Jewish Aramaic, see Avishur, "Expressions," 15–19. I thank Noam Mizrahi for this reference. Yoel Elitzur referred me to *Tg. Onq.*, which translates the biblical words מצח אהרן, מצחו (Aaron's forehead, his forehead—Exod 28:38) as בית עינוהי. On the shift from בין to בית and vice versa in Rabbinic Hebrew, see Bar-Asher, "Ketav yad parma bet," 152–3; Breuer, *Pesaḥim*, 252–3, and the references cited in both.

Now, an elder, named Yehudah ben Gudgeda,[13] was present there. Said he (ויאמר) to King Yannai. "O King Yannai! let the royal crown suffice thee (רב לך כתר מלכות), and leave the crown of priesthood to the seed of Aaron." For it was rumored that his mother had been taken captive in Modi'im. [Accordingly,] the matter was investigated, but not sustained (ויבוקש הדבר ולא נמצא), and the Sages of Israel separated themselves in anger (ויבדלו חכמי ישראל בזעם).

Then said (ויאמר) Eleazar ben Po'irah to King Yannai: "O King Yannai! That is the law even for a commoner in Israel, and thou, a king and a high priest, shall that be thy law [too]?" "Then what shall I do?" He told him: "If thou wilt take my advice, trample them down (רומסם)." "But what shall happen with the Torah?" "Behold, it is bound up and lying in the corner (כרוכה ומונחת בקרן זוית), whoever wishes to study, let him come and study!" [...]

Straightway, the evil burst forth (ותוצץ הרעה)[14] through Eleazar ben Po'irah and through Yehudah ben Gudgeda.[15] All the Sages of Israel were massacred (ויהרגו כל חכמי ישראל), and the world was desolate until Simeon ben Shataḥ came and restored the Torah to its pristine [glory].

B. THE TRADITIONS: A COMPARISON

As they emerge from both variants, the basic elements of the tale are as follows: in the wake of a series of victories, the Hasmonean ruler invites the Pharisees (Josephus)/sages of Israel (Talmud) to a feast or a banquet. A crisis then ensues,

---

[13] In the printed versions: גדידיה, גדידיא. Baumgarten ("Rabbinic Literature," 45) suggests that the names are symbolic. The son of Po'ira opened a gap (פער) in Israel, whereas the son of Gedidiah caused the people to be divided into camps (see Deut 14:1, לא תתגדדו, according to the usual rabbinic interpretation: לא תעשו אגודות אגודות "do not divide yourselves into camps"). This interpretation, like Efron's above, is a homily. On the significance of the name Pachura, mentioned in the YT as a certain Eleazar's father (see below), see Lieberman, *Tosefta Ki-fshutah*, 8:748 n. 43, where he apparently considers פחורה in our text to be a variant of the same name. Efron ("Simeon Ben Shataḥ and Jannaeus," 179), prefers the MS Munich 95 version גריר' and interprets the name as denoting גרירה, being dragged, since Yehudah was influenced by Eleazar's advice. Both suppositions are far-fetched. Moreover, the MSS provide a variety of versions: גדירא (Vatican 111, twice); גזירא (Oxford 367, three times); גריר' (Munich 95 twice [the third time: גדיד']); גדריא (Guadalajara, twice). Genizah fragment Cambridge, CUL: T-S Misc. 28.265 begins with the second mention of the name, and has גודגדא twice. Vatican 111 also reads גודגדא in the third occurrence of the name. This version appears in Rashba too, as noted by Friedlaender, "Rupture," 447 n. 18; Efron, "Simeon Ben Shataḥ and Jannaeus," 180. I prefer this version since it is the reading in the Genizah fragment and is also attested in other versions. Moreover, the name Gudgeda is well known from the days of the Second Temple. On the early sage Yoḥanan ben Gudgeda, see *m. Ḥag.* 2:7; *m. 'Ed.* 7:9; *t. Ter.* 1:1; *t. Sheqal.* 2:14; *Sifre Num.* 116; *Sifre Zuta* 28:4, and elsewhere.

[14] Thus in Oxford 367 and in the printed editions. In the Genizah fragment ותיצץ, Munich 95 ותיעץ, Vatican 111 ותיון(ע)[צ]ץ, Spanish printed edition ותצץ. This verb is unique to this story. According to Elisha Qimron (oral communication), the vowel u in this verb does not indicate the passive, but rather an intransitive verb. Cf. Qimron, "עֲנוּת," 21–6.

[15] The words "and through Yehudah ben Gudgeda" are omitted in the printed editions (except for the old Spanish printed edition), but are extant in all the manuscripts. On the significance of this clause for the message of the story, see section E.

according to both versions, because of statements made by two of the guests: one enjoins the ruler to abandon the high priesthood and content himself with the government, for there is a rumor that his mother was a captive, making him ineligible for the priesthood. A woman married to a priest (such as the Hasmoneans) is forbidden to return to her husband if she has been held captive (cf. *m. Ketub.* 2:9; 4:8); if she does return, this renders any children born after her captivity unfit for the priesthood. According to Josephus this libel is false; according to the Talmud it was never proven, and it arouses the anger of the Pharisees/sages. Notwithstanding, another speaker states in the ruler's presence that the Pharisees oppose him,[16] and also opines that they believe the above-mentioned libel. In the wake of this accusation, a suggestion is made to test the Pharisees' true opinion. Finally, the ire of the ruler is aroused against the sages/Pharisees and he abolishes the statutes of the Pharisees (Josephus)/ murders all the sages of Israel (Talmud).

Apart from the fundamental similarity in the skeleton of the plot, the two versions also display surprisingly close affinities in its details. On occasion, notwithstanding their different languages—Greek and Hebrew—we can even discern linguistic-stylistic similarities between the versions.

One affinity is the name of the villain, Eleazar, which is identical in both versions; moreover, the narrative exposition applies a string of similar negative epithets to this figure. Note that this is unusual in talmudic literature: rabbinic aggadot generally do not explicitly characterize their protagonists in advance but rather portray them indirectly through their speech or actions.[17]

A second affinity is the similarity between the subversive statement by the opponent of the current ruler according to the baraita: רב לך כתר מלכות הנח כתר כהונה, which is nearly identical to the Greek version in *Antiquities*: τὴν ἀρχιερωσύνην ἀπόθου, καὶ μόνον ἀρκείτω σοι τὸ ἄρχειν τοῦ λαοῦ ("give up the high-priesthood and be content with governing the people," section 291).

Also, both versions classify the report that the ruler's mother was in captivity as a rumor ("we have heard from our elders" [292]/"it was rumoured"). This supposed captivity took place, according to both versions, during the Hasmonean

---

[16] לבם/לבן של פרושים עליך. Thus in MS Oxford 367, the Spanish printed edition, and later printed editions. Contextually, as Rashi notes ad loc., it means "they are your enemies." In this form, this expression is unknown elsewhere in rabbinic literature or any other Hebrew corpus. MSS Vatican 111 and Munich 95 read: בלבם, בלבן. This variant is similar to a phrase commonly found in the BT and late aggadic midrash (e.g. *b. Meg.* 16b; *Num. Rab.* 15:3):...אין בלב פלוני על /יש, which means that someone does/does not hate another. In tannaitic literature we find אין בלבנו מחלוקת על (*Sifre Deut.* 31), which is evidently the source of the later expression. Given the unusual linguistic features of the legend as a whole, it appears likely that the original phrase was לבם של פרושים עליך and בלבם was an emendation.

[17] "Not only are direct statements characterizing a figure few, but even the noting of factual details on prominent figures is extremely rare" (Meir, "Characters in the Stories of the Talmud," 330). On the economy of means employed by rabbinic legend in shaping its protagonists, see Raveh, *Fragments of Being*, 50–4.

revolt: the Josephan version notes the date—Antiochus Epiphanes's day; the baraita notes the place—Modiʿin/Modiʿit. We, who have been raised on what is recounted in the books of Maccabees, view the link between Modiʿin and the Hasmonean revolt as self-evident. Note, however, that nowhere in the vast canvas of rabbinic literature do we hear of Modiʿin as the birthplace of the Hasmonean dynasty or as the arena of the revolt; nor is this information found in any other context treating the Hasmoneans or the festival of Hanukkah, which suggests that the rabbis were not familiar with this detail.[18] In other words, here too we find a divergence from the usual practice in rabbinic literature.

Both accounts underscore that the libel regarding the ruler's patrimony was false and unsubstantiated ("but the story was false," section 292; "the matter was investigated, but not sustained"). Similarly, both stories highlight the anger of the Pharisees / the sages on hearing this libel (καὶ πάντες δ' οἱ Φαρισαῖοι σφοδρῶς ἠγανάκτησαν; ויבדלו חכמי ישראל בזעם). Here too the shared feature in the Josephan account and the baraita is anomalous in rabbinic literature, in which rabbinic anecdotes rarely describe the emotions accompanying events.

Moreover, even where the variants diverge it is possible to identify traces of the features of one in the other. The sentence: הדיוט שביש[ראל] כך הוא דינו ואתה מלך וכהן גדו[ל] כך הוא דינך ("That is the law even for a commoner in Israel, and thou, a king and a high priest, shall that be thy law [too]?") is difficult. No mention of the law of a commoner having been made earlier, the nature of Eleazar's comparison is unclear. As shown by Graetz, Derenbourg, and others,[19] there has been a deletion from the baraita. This deletion can be restored only in light of the parallel in *Antiquities*, where the Pharisees are tested by the need to devise a punishment for the libeler of John Hyrcanus. Hyrcanus, for his part, found their prescription of "stripes and chains" too lenient. This is the missing link in the baraita, for afterwards Eleazar's intention becomes plain: if the punishment for libeling an ordinary person is whipping and imprisonment, how much more severe should the punishment be for libeling a "king and high priest"?

Alongside these remarkable similarities, the two accounts exhibit many differences: according to the talmudic baraita, the king is Yannai (Janneus), whereas Josephus ascribes the event to Janneus's father, John Hyrcanus. Josephus speaks of Pharisees; whereas the baraita uses the typical designation of the Pharisees as "the sages of Israel," though the storyteller was evidently aware of the epithet "Pharisees" as well, since he clearly equates the two (for example, "the sages of Israel" are massacred as a result of Eleazar's instigation against "the

---

[18] I thank Tal Ilan for this significant observation. See also Ilan and Noam, "Pharisaic Apologetic Source," 122–3.

[19] Graetz, *Geschichte*, 3:688; Derenbourg, *Essai*, 80 n. 9; Neusner, *Rabbinic Traditions about the Pharisees*, 1:175, 3:250; Efron, "Simeon Ben Shataḥ and Jannaeus," 182–3; D. R. Schwartz, "Pharisaic Opposition," 48–9. For a different viewpoint, see Kalmin, *Jewish Babylonia*, 210 n. 101.

Pharisees").[20] Unique to the rabbinic version are the special symbolic nature of the menu (mallows) and the backdrop of the feast (golden tables), as well as the geographic setting of the leader's victory. On the other hand, some features appear only in the Josephan version. Josephus alone names the ruler a disciple of the Pharisees, and only there does the ruler ask the Pharisees to voice their opinion of him at the beginning of the feast, to which they respond with praise.

In both versions, the climax of the story involves two characters. One insults the Hasmonean ruler and demands that he abandon the high priesthood, while the other (a Sadducee, according to Josephus) informs the leader that the Pharisees oppose him and moreover endorse the slander regarding his mother's past captivity. However, the order in which these characters intervene is reversed and their names are partially inverted. The name Eleazar, including his description as a villain, is shared by both sources, but if in *Qiddushin* he is the inciter against the Pharisees, according to Josephus he is the slanderer of the ruler. The second character has a different name in each version, Jonathan/Yehudah ben Gudgeda, and is identified as a Sadducee in *Antiquities* alone.

In the rabbinic legend the defamation of the king, proclaimed following the incitement against the Pharisees, is understood as confirming the instigation. In the Josephan story, the accusation against the Pharisees is an outcome of the insult to the ruler. According to Josephus, this defamation is proven false; the talmudic source only states that it was never proven.

The two versions also propose different tests. According to Josephus, the test of the Pharisees is their proposed punishment for the person who insulted the ruler; according to *b. Qiddushin*, the test is: "'make them swear (הקם להם) by the plate (בציץ) between your eyes.' [So] he made them swear by the plate between his eyes." As already suggested by Abraham Krochmal,[21] and elaborated by Saul Lieberman,[22] the verb הקם in this context has nothing to do with standing, as

---

[20] As many have noted, tannaitic sources use the designation "Pharisees" only in disputational contexts, integrating this word into their opponents' arguments, whereas the storytellers always prefer the label "sages" (חכמים). See Rivkin, "Defining the Pharisees," 205–49 (esp. 213–17, 231–2, 247–8); Cohen, "Significance of Yavneh," 41 and n. 39; Flusser, "4QMMT," 97–103, esp. 99 (I am indebted to Yair Zoran for this reference). The exact connection between the post-70 rabbis and the pre-70 Pharisees is beyond the scope of the current discussion; see Cohen, "Significance of Yavneh," 36–42. In contrast to Cohen's conjecture (37, 39), I do not see any reason to ascribe the designation "sages of Israel" to later, Babylonian "rabbinization" processes. For Second Temple equivalents of this expression, see section H.

[21] See Krochmal, *Commentaries*, 218, who noted: "in my humble opinion, this does not concern either standing, or getting up, or sitting, or lying down…[but rather,] he should make them swear by the ṣiṣ that they accept his authority as a king and high priest." He was apparently preceded by Graetz (*Geschichte*, 3:687), who alluded to the fact that the verb הקם has a unique meaning here.

[22] Lieberman, *Tosefta Ki-fshutah*, 6–7: 397 n. 14.

ancients and moderns erroneously understood,[23] but rather means "to make someone swear," like the Aramaic root קו"ם. This verb appears, though rarely, in the meaning of "to swear" in Hebrew sources also, such as the DSS, the Mishnah,[24] and probably in the Hebrew original of several Jewish works from the Second Temple era, of which only the Greek translations have survived.[25] According to the story, Eleazar advised Janneus to make the Pharisees swear by the ṣiṣ, the golden plate that the high priest used to wear on his forehead, that they accepted his dual authority as king and high priest. Swearing by the temple worship, the high priest's clothes, and especially by the Tetragrammaton engraved on the ṣiṣ, was a common Jewish practice.[26] Because the ṣiṣ is the definitive symbol of the high priest, such an oath is especially appropriate in this context that calls the high priest's "crown of priesthood" into question.

Near the end of the story, only the baraita contains a conversation between Eleazar and Janneus regarding the fate of the Torah without the Pharisees. Eleazar alleviates the king's concerns regarding the trampling of the Pharisees by describing a tangible Torah scroll that is "bound up and lying in the corner," and accessible to study by all without the guidance of the Pharisees.[27] As the later talmudic sages

---

[23] See e.g. Rashi, s.v. הקם להם בציץ שבין עיניך: "Place the holy ṣiṣ on your forehead and they will stand because the Tetragrammaton is written on it and they will reveal their hearts." As Krochmal (*Commentaries*, 218) notes, understanding this verb as denoting taking an oath removes the doubts raised by Rashi ad loc., and by Tosafot, s.v. הקם, and other early authorities (see Efron, "Simeon Ben Shaṭaḥ and Janneus," 180–1) regarding the question of how Janneus allowed himself to wear the ṣiṣ during a secular feast. Taking an oath on the ṣiṣ does not require its presence, just as an oath by the temple service, the Torah, or Moses's name (Lieberman, *Tosefta Ki-fshutah*, 6–7: 397 n. 14) is an abstract oath that does not require the presence of a particular object.

[24] See Schiffman, *Sectarian Law*, 70–1 n. 80.

[25] See Alon, "Sefarim ḥiṣoniyyim," 189.

[26] See Lieberman, *Tosefta Ki-fshutah*, 6–7: 397 n. 14; Schiffman, *Sectarian Law*, 70–1 n. 80, as opposed to Efron, "Simeon Ben Shaṭaḥ and Janneus," 181–2.

[27] Based on an indirect witness, Urbach ("Ha-derashah," 65) proposed the reading כתובה ומונחת ("written and lying…") (but see Baumgarten, "Rabbinic Literature," 37 n. 87). This variant has no witnesses in the manuscripts and has been rejected by various scholars. In the wake of this proposed emendation, Menahem Kister ("Aggadic Traditions," 203 n. 65; idem, "Additions," 45) proposed that the original version was simply ומונחת <כתובה>. The marking of the place where it lay—זוית קרן—was added in the wake of the common expression מניח בקרן זוית, and the remark "whoever wishes to study, let him come and study" is a secondary addition by redactors from the rabbinic world. The reading כרוכה ומונחת is the one attested in the Genizah fragment (in opposition to the position taken by E. S. Rosenthal, "Ha-moreh," *8), in the manuscripts and printed editions (according to the Sol and Evelyn Henkind Talmud Text Databank of the Saul Lieberman Institute of Talmud Research of the Jewish Theological Seminary of America, the Spanish printed edition reads כתובה ומונחת; however, examination of the edition itself showed the correct reading to be כרוכה ומונחת). In my opinion, the preferred reading is כרוכה: a Torah scroll should be wrapped in a cloth; see *y. Ber.* 3:5, 6d: "A person should not have sexual intercourse when there is a Torah Scroll (ספר תורה) with him in the room […]. It is permitted if it is wrapped up in a cloth (כרוך במפה) or if it was placed in a window ten handbreadths high…" In our story, the metaphorical Torah is properly wrapped and lying in a corner.

already recognized,[28] Eleazar here stresses the existence of the Written Law and alludes to the lack of necessity for the Oral Law, which was the source of Pharisaic authority.[29] This polemical stance brings to mind the *Temple Scroll* (LVI:3–4), which replaces the word Torah in the verse עַל פִּי הַתּוֹרָה אֲשֶׁר יוֹרוּךָ (Deut 17:11) with the word pair ספר תורה, thereby stressing the exclusivity of the Written Law: וְעַל פִּי הדבר אשר יאמרו לכה מספר התורה ("and according what they say to you from the book of the law").[30] Although this conversation regarding the Written Law and the laws purveyed by the Pharisees is missing from the Josephan version, one can trace a surprising similarity. Immediately following our story Josephus reports:

> For the present I wish merely to explain that the Pharisees had passed on to the people certain regulations handed down by former generations and not recorded in the Laws of Moses, for which reason they are rejected by the Sadducaean group, who hold that only those regulations should be considered valid which were written down (in Scripture), and that those which had been handed down by former generations need not be observed. (297)[31]

This exemplifies an intriguing phenomenon: the surprising parallels between the later context in which the two versions appear, as if beyond the story itself both Josephus and rabbinic literature share a vague awareness of an underlying theoretical infrastructure.[32]

Besides the Josephan appendix, note also the insertion of various additions and "editorial notes" in both versions. In *Antiquities* these are short comments that clarify the background to the narrative: "for the Pharisees profess such beliefs" (13.289); "and anyway the Pharisees are naturally lenient in the matter of punishments" (13.294); and perhaps even the comment regarding the Sadducees: "who hold opinions opposed to those of the Pharisees" (13.293), which Josephus interpolated into the narrative. In the talmudic sugya a reaction by a fourth-generation amora was integrated into the story, in which Rav Naḥman bar Yitzḥak accuses King Janneus of heresy because of his failure to respond aptly to Eleazar.[33]

---

[28] See the amoraic conversation inserted in the baraita (according to the Genizah fragment): "for he should have replied. 'That is well for the Written Law; but what can be said of the Oral Law?'"

[29] I thank Steven Fraade for this observation.

[30] See Yadin's comment ad loc. (*Temple Scroll*, 2:251), and recently, for a different opinion see Fraade, "Between Constraining and Expanding," 416–18. See, however, Kister's reconstruction of a homiletic struggle from the *Temple Scroll*, LVI:3–4, and Scholion O on *Meg. Ta'anit*, 4/10 Tammuz (Noam, *Megillat Ta'anit*, 78–9, 206; also 209–10). Whereas the *Temple Scroll* places emphasis on the Written Law, the Scholion cites a homily that understands the words עַל פִּי as proving that study is oral. See Kister, "Marginalia Qumranica," 315.

[31] For a comprehensive discussion of this section and bibliographical references to prior research, see Mason, *Josephus on the Pharisees*, 230–45.

[32] See the introduction in Ilan and Noam, *Josephus and the Rabbis*, 12–13, where additional examples are noted that are not included in the present volume.

[33] Cf. the amoraic comment inserted into the story of the prediction to Vespasian (*b. Git.* 56b; see Ben Shahar, "The Prediction to Vespasian") which criticizes Rabban Yoḥanan ben Zakkai for not asking Vespasian for Jerusalem.

Finally, the conclusion of the story differs. According to the Josephan version the ruler abolishes the statutes of the Pharisees; in the rabbinic one, he murders their sages. Also missing from Josephus is the content of the baraita's concluding sentence regarding the rehabilitation of Torah study in Simeon ben Shatah's day, after the crisis described in the talmudic story.

C. THE STORY IN *ANTIQUITIES* AND *B. QIDDUSHIN*: A CONTEXTUAL CONSIDERATION

The "rupture" legend exhibits contextually incongruent features in both *Antiquities* and *Qiddushin*. Many scholars have noted the anomaly of the legend in the context of Josephus's running narrative in *Antiquities* and cite clear-cut signs of its artificial insertion from a different source.[34] I note first that the sequence of events in *Ant.* 13.288–300 is parallel to *War* 1.67–9. The opening is nearly identical in the two: "As for Hyrcanus, the envy of the Jews was aroused against him by his own successes" (*Ant.* 13.288); "the prosperous fortunes of John and his sons, however, provoked a sedition among his envious countrymen" (*War* 1.67), as are the key words success (εὐπραγία) and envy (φθόνος).[35] In *War* Josephus adds a sentence regarding the war started by John's opponents and their defeat, continuing with a description of John's successes, the length of his reign, the privileges he merited, his prophetic abilities, and the difference between his fate and that of his sons.

In *Antiquities*, however, the description of Jewish envy in the opening leads to the identification of John's opponents as the Pharisees: "particularly hostile to him were the Pharisees," and to the noting of their influence on the masses (288). This progresses to the story of the rupture with the Pharisees (289–96), followed by a brief appendix regarding the dispute between Pharisees and the Sadducees with respect to the unwritten laws handed down by former generations (298). After adding that John put an end to the sedition (Ὑρκανὸς δὲ παύσας τὴν στάσιν), Josephus returns to the narrative sequence known from *War*: John lived happily thereafter, ruled for thirty-one years, merited three privileges, and so on (299–300). Table 3.1 compares the parallel sections in *War* and *Antiquities*.

[34] See e.g. Levine, "Political Struggle," 70–2; Efron, "Simeon Ben Shatah and Jannaeus," 161–3; D. R. Schwartz, "Josephus' Source on Agrippa II," 244; Neusner, "Josephus' Pharisees," 286; Mason, *Josephus on the Pharisees*, 215–16, 218–22 (Table 3.1 is in the wake of Mason there, 215); Kalmin, *Jewish Babylonia*, 56, 167. For an opposing view see Rappaport, *House of the Hasmoneans*, 260, where he proposes that this internal Jewish story reached one of the Hellenistic authors, and from there via Nicolaus to Josephus.

[35] Scholars have noted Josephus's tendency to employ the conceptual triplet εὐπραγία, φθόνος, and εὐδαιμονία ("success," "envy," "fortune"). Honora Chapman ("Josephus and Greek Poetry," 133–7) proposed that this language embeds an allusion to the poet Pindar. For previous studies and her proposal, see ibid.

Table 3.1. Comparison of *War* and *Antiquities*

War 1.67–9	*Ant.* 13.288–300
The envy (φθόνος) aroused by the prosperous fortunes (εὐπραγίας) of John and his sons, however, provoked a sedition (στάσιν) among his countrymen, large numbers of whom held meetings to oppose them and continued to agitate, until the smouldering flames burst out into open war	As for Hyrcanus, the envy (φθόνον) of the Jews was aroused against him by his own successes (εὐπραγία) and those of his sons; particularly hostile to him were the Pharisees, who are one of the Jewish schools . . .
	289–98: Interpolation—Hyrcanus and the Pharisees
and the rebels were defeated. For the rest of his days John lived in prosperity (ἐν εὐδαιμονίᾳ), and, after excellently directing the government (τὰ κατὰ τὴν ἀρχὴν κάλλιστα διοικήσας) for thirty-one whole years, died leaving five sons; truly a blessed individual and one who left no ground for complaint against fortune as regards himself. He was the only man to unite in his person three of the highest privileges: the supreme command of the nation, the high priesthood, and the gift of prophecy (τήν τε ἀρχὴν τοῦ ἔθνους καὶ τὴν ἀρχιερωσύνην καὶ προφητείαν).	And so Hyrcanus quieted the sedition (τὴν στάσιν),[a] and lived happily (εὐδαιμόνως) thereafter; and when he died after administering the government excellently (τὴν ἀρχὴν διοικησάμενος τὸν ἄριστον τρόπον) for thirty-one years, he left five sons. Now he was accounted by God worthy of three of the greatest privileges, the rule of the nation, the office of high priest, and the gift of prophecy (ἀρχῆς τοῦ ἔθνους καὶ τῆς ἀρχιερατικῆς τιμῆς καὶ προφητείας).
The story of their downfall (τὴν καταστροφήν) is worth relating (ἄξιον ἀφηγήσασθαι), and will show how great was the decline from their father's good fortune (παρ' ὅσον τῆς πατρῴας εὐδαιμονίας ἀπέκλιναν).	And the story of their downfall (τὴν καταστροφήν) is worth relating (ἄξιον ἀφηγήσασθαι), to show how far they were from having their father's good fortune (ὅσον τῆς τοῦ πατρὸς ὑπέβησαν εὐτυχίας).

Note: [a] I have diverged here from the LCL translation in order to stress the identity between the passage in *Antiquities* and *War* 1.67.

It is obvious that, in *Antiquities*, Josephus repeats the sequence of events found in *War*, but inserts a new unit there: the story of the rupture with the Pharisees. Josephus creates a link to the preceding material by specifically identifying the opponents of John mentioned in the original narrative as the Pharisees (288).[36] He was also forced to delete the sentence describing the war started by these

[36] D. R. Schwartz ("Josephus and Nicolaus," 159) suggests reconstructing an opposite process. In the narrative (which, according to Schwartz and many others, has its source in Nicolaus of Damascus; see text near n. 40), which was hostile to the Pharisees, Hyrcanus's enemies were identified with the Pharisees. Josephus erased this identification in *War* but left it in *Antiquities*. I think it more likely, in the wake of Mason (*Josephus on the Pharisees*, 224–5) that this is a connective sentence added in *Antiquities* alone, whose purpose was to link the general description of an uprising against Hyrcanus to the story of the crisis in his relationship with the Pharisees. The statement regarding the power of the latter against the king or high priest, a general libel uttered against the Pharisees in the late Second Temple period (see below), was inserted here by Josephus for literary purposes.

opponents, because in the new context in *Antiquities* the envy of John's opponents led to the account of the feast and the rupture rather than to actual war.

Nonetheless, traces of the earlier version found in *War* can be discerned in the new blend in *Antiquities*. After the account of the rupture in *Antiquities*, Josephus notes that "Hyrcanus quieted the sedition" (στάσις, 299). But no sedition is mentioned in *Antiquities*, and Josephus here undoubtedly refers to what appeared in his first version, preserved only in *War*, that John's good fortune "provoked a sedition among his countrymen."[37]

As noted in the early twentieth century, Josephus's introductory paragraph fits neither the body of the story nor Josephus's day, because it separates the functions of king and high priest into two distinct spheres (288). During the Hasmonean age the rulers wore both crowns, and neither office existed separately at the time of the writing of *Antiquities*.[38]

The story also displays incongruent features as compared to its surrounding narrative framework. In the introduction Josephus states that the Pharisees envy John's successes (288), but in the body of the story he is portrayed as one of their beloved disciples. Another difference between the introduction and the rupture story inheres in the description of the cause of the rupture. In the introduction it is ascribed to jealousy of the Pharisees (ibid.) and their tendency to arouse the masses "against a king or high priest." However, in the body of the story the rupture is the result of intrigue by others and not the fault of the Pharisees, who are innocent victims of persecution. Moreover, if the introduction portrays John as a successful ruler who unwittingly arouses envy, the body of the story portrays John as making an error in judgment and being influenced by an instigator. Also, according to the introduction the Jews envy John his success; according to the body of the story their enmity is the outcome of the cancellation of the statutes of the Pharisees. Similarly, the idyllic description of John's life that follows the story is disharmonious with the harsh rupture between the ruler and the influential Pharisees and the hatred displayed toward him by the people in the body of the story. In general, the portrayal of John in the story is not consistent with the portrait drawn by Josephus elsewhere. Josephus admired John and viewed him as the last worthy ruler of the Hasmonean house and also as epitomizing the ideal ruler,[39] a description incongruent with that of the easily influenced, passive, impulsive ruler in the body of the story.

---

[37] According to D. R. Schwartz (*Reading the First Century*, 79–80), Josephus erased the description of open warfare for apologetic reasons, in order to obscure the existence of a civil war among the Jews. I view this as the result of the interpolation of the legend.

[38] See the reference in D. R. Schwartz, "Josephus' Source on Agrippa II," 244 n. 10. For another view, see Mason, *Josephus on the Pharisees*, 223.

[39] See Alon, "Attitude of the Pharisees," 26–8 n. 22; Mason, *Josephus on the Pharisees*, 225; Gray, *Prophetic Figures*, 16–23. The rabbis as well cast him in a positive light (see Chap. 2, section B: "Historical Background"). In this regard, the rabbinic attribution of the story to Janneus is more in harmony with their doctrine.

In light of these data it has been suggested in the scholarship that the frame of the Josephan narrative in *Ant.* 13.288, 299–300, which parallels *War* 1.67–9 and evidences hostility toward the Pharisees, has its source in Nicolaus of Damascus, whereas the story of the rupture has its origins in an internal Jewish source.[40] In Mason's opinion, Josephus himself wrote the introduction to the story (288).[41] In any event, there is scholarly consensus that the legend itself is contextually anomalous and was interpolated from another source.

Having been arbitrarily interpolated into a late halakhic discussion regarding the credibility of a single witness for testifying that a woman has committed adultery, the baraita is incongruous in the talmudic context as well. There is no connection between the political aspect of the story itself, grounded as it is in Second Temple-period reality, and the frame sugya: a fourth-century halakhic discussion in Babylonia to which the story can only make a forced contribution.[42]

D. HISTORY OF RESEARCH

Over the past 150 years this legend has broadly engaged scholarly discourse, both because of its ramifications for study of the sects in the Hasmonean era, their interaction and relationship with the regime, and because of the striking parallel between the Josephan version and the talmudic baraita. Earlier researchers sought the historical kernel of the legend in both versions;[43] in

---

[40] D. R. Schwartz, "Josephus' Source on Agrippa II," 244; idem, "Josephus and Nicolaus," 158–9. See also the literature cited by Mason, *Josephus on the Pharisees*, 222 n. 45. Regarding the assumed Jewish origin of the Hyrcanus legend, this is grounded in the amity toward the Pharisees in the story and in the existence of a talmudic parallel. To this Mason (*Josephus on the Pharisees*, 219–21) has added linguistic evidence.

[41] Mason, *Josephus on the Pharisees*, 222–7.

[42] See e.g. Baumgarten, "Rabbinic Literature," 37–8; Kalmin, *Jewish Babylonia*, 56. Indeed, the attempts by the anonymous editors of the sugya to create a link between the story and its frame are strikingly artificial. The sugya assumes that the rumor regarding Janneus's mother having been a captive: (1) came up in a halakhic-legal proceeding in some court; (2) was uttered by a single witness; (3) was denied by two witnesses; (4) arriving at the conclusion that the testimony of a single witness to a woman's promiscuity suffices for her to be forbidden to her husband, unless overturned by two witnesses. None of the above is attested in the body of the story. The tenuousness of the link is so glaring that it raises the possibility that Abaye, who tells the story, or the redactor of the sugya, sought an artificial excuse to cite the tradition of the rift with the Pharisees in the Talmud because of some inherent importance that he identified in the story, obscuring this desire in a forced halakhic association.

[43] The following does not propose to cover the extensive bibliography devoted to the two versions of the story, but only cites the main proponents of the different scholarly viewpoints. For historical reconstructions based on this tradition, see e.g. Schürer, *History*, 1:213–14, 223 n. 16; Derenbourg, *Essai*, 79–82; Aptowitzer, *Parteipolitik*, 13–17; Klausner, *Historiyah*, 3:136–9; Tcherikover, *Hellenistic Civilization and the Jews*, 254–61; Zeitlin, *Rise and Fall of the Judaean State*, 1:168–70. For more recent, refined efforts to draw limited historical conclusions from this legend, see Levine, "Political Struggle," 70–4; D. R. Schwartz, "Pharisaic Opposition," 48–9; Baumgarten, "Rabbinic Literature," 36–52; Goodblatt, "Priesthood and Kingship," 11–14; Main, "Sadducéens," 190–202; idem, "Les Sadducéens et l'origine des partis juifs," 399–496; Regev, *Sadducees*, 251–61, Rappaport, *House of the Hasmoneans*, 292–4.

recent decades scholars have questioned its historical value, shifting the focus to the unraveling of its aims, sources, and reworking.[44]

A prominent, exceptional characteristic of the rabbinic story, frequently noted in the scholarly literature, is its use of biblical style, syntax, and vocabulary rarely or never attested elsewhere in the rabbinic corpus. The *waw* consecutive, marking the past, which is totally absent from Rabbinic Hebrew except in the liturgy, appears here seven times (ויבוקש, ויבדלו, ויאמר [3 times], ויהרגו, ותתץ).[45] Words such as רמס, זעם, בליעל, and others are identifiably biblical vocabulary, as will be elaborated in section I. For some scholars, this further supports the antiquity and authenticity of the rabbinic version of the story,[46] identified as a leaf plucked from an ancient, now lost Hebrew book.[47] Thus, for example, Heinrich Graetz suggested that it is either a section of Josephus's early, Hebrew (according to Graetz) version of the *Jewish War*,[48] or a passage from the chronicle of John Hyrcanus mentioned in 1 Maccabees.[49] Israël Lévi proposed a lost chronicle of the Hasmonean dynasty, shaped in biblical patterns, as the source of the legend,[50] whereas Ben-Zion Dinur proposed as its source a chronicle of Janneus's reign that also included the episode of his being pelted with citrons and his instructions to his wife.[51] Others have compared its overall style to Ben Sira, the *Damascus Document*,[52] the Dead Sea Scrolls,[53] or to the Jewish literature of the Second Temple era in general.[54]

---

[44] Levine, "Political Struggle"; Efron, "Simeon Ben Shataḥ and Jannaeus," 161–5, 176–85; Neusner, "Josephus' Pharisees," 283–6; idem, *Rabbinic Traditions about the Pharisees*, 1:173–6; D. R. Schwartz, "Josephus and Nicolaus," 158–9; Mason, *Josephus on the Pharisees*, 213–45; Baumgarten, "Rabbinic Literature"; Main, "Sadducéens"; idem, "Les Sadducéens et l'origine des partis juifs," 399–496; Kalmin, *Jewish Babylonia*, 53–9; D. R. Schwartz, "Remembering the Second Temple Period," 70–1, 74–6.

[45] On *waw* consecutive, see Segal, *Grammar of Mishnaic Hebrew*, 72 (he elaborates in the later, Hebrew edition of this book, Segal, *Dikduk*, 124); Kutscher, *Isaiah Scroll*, 351–2; Mark S. Smith, *Waw Consecutive*. For additional references, see Bar-Asher, *Studies in Mishnaic Hebrew*, 1:111 and n. 8.

[46] See e.g. Zeitlin, *Rise and Fall of the Judaean State*; Friedlaender, "Rupture"; Geller, "Alexander Jannaeus," 202–11; Levine, "Political Struggle"; Baumgarten, "Rabbinic Literature."

[47] Segal, *Grammar of Mishnaic Hebrew*, 13; idem, *Dikduk*, 11–12.

[48] See *War* 1.3; Graetz, *Geschichte*, 3:688. Baumgarten rejects this idea ("Rabbinic Literature," 38). Apart from the fact that the first edition of *War* was probably written in Aramaic and not in Hebrew, I note that the rupture tradition is missing from the current *War* altogether, and that Josephus could hardly be the source of the rabbinic version of the story, which differs in many respects from his account in *Antiquities*. In any event, it seems that Graetz himself did not take his own theory too seriously, since he proposed a different work as the source of this legend in the same volume; see section D.

[49] 1 Macc 16:23–4. This possibility is only implicitly alluded to by Graetz (*Geschichte*, 3:82; see his reference in the footnote to Appendix 11, which is devoted to the rupture legend). See also Friedlaender, "Rupture," 448.

[50] Lévi, "Sources talmudiques," 222.

[51] Dinur, "Historiographical Fragments," 142–3. See Chaps. 4 and 5.

[52] Klausner, *Historiyah*, 3:137.   [53] Neusner, "Josephus' Pharisees," 285.

[54] Segal, *Grammar of Mishnaic Hebrew*, 13, 72.

Still others claim, however, that in the context of its composite biblical and mishnaic language, its biblical characteristics should be judged as purposeful, artificial archaisms deliberately employed by a later author that provide no clues as to dating.[55] Against this, one scholar who dates the story early argues that all the features of biblical language are concentrated in the middle section of the story: if the story was composed in artificial biblical language in order to make it seem early, its author would not have restricted his use of this tactic to a specific part of the text.[56] A third view assigns the heart of the story with its biblical characteristics to an early, authentic source, attributing its first part, written in typical Mishnaic Hebrew, which is also missing from Josephus, to a separate, later source.[57]

Many have compared the Josephan and the talmudic versions in an attempt to explain the differences between them.[58] Most scholars grant precedence to the historian's version over the talmudic one: the first was preserved in a historical book written toward the end of the first century CE; the second is found in the eclectic Babylonian Talmud, detached from any sequential historical narrative and at a geographical-temporal remove from the events. Therefore, in the scholarship the protagonist of the original story is usually identified as John Hyrcanus, as in Josephus, and not with Janneus, as in the baraita.[59] Various arguments are put forth for Hyrcanus as the protagonist. Thus, a claim is made that it is more reasonable to raise doubts regarding John's mother, the wife of Simeon the Hasmonean, who was taken captive during the Hasmonean revolt in Modi'in,[60]

---

[55] See Rabinowitz, *Liturgical Poetry of Yannai*, xxxv n. 25 (but cf. Baumgarten, "Rabbinic Literature," 38 n. 88); Efron, "Simeon Ben Shataḥ and Jannaeus," 183. Kalmin (*Jewish Babylonia*, 58–9) identifies disparate layers within the story. See the discussion below.

[56] Baumgarten, "Rabbinic Literature," 38 n. 88.   [57] Kalmin, *Jewish Babylonia*, 59.

[58] For a detailed comparison, see Main, "Sadducéens"; Kalmin, *Jewish Babylonia*, 53–9.

[59] Of the studies mentioned in nn. 48–9, see Derenbourg, *Essai*, 80–1 n. 1; Aptowitzer, *Parteipolitik*, 13–17; Tcherikover, *Hellenistic Civilization and the Jews*, 254–61; Neusner, *Rabbinic Traditions about the Pharisees*, 283–6; Efron, "Simeon Ben Shataḥ and Jannaeus." See also Rabin, "Jannaeus and the Pharisees," 8–9; Cohen, "Parallel Historical Tradition," 14; Stern, *Hasmonaean Judaea*, 188 n. 30, 199; Goodblatt, "Priesthood and Kingship," 13; Regev, *Sadducees*, 254–5. For more recent treatments, see also Rappaport, *House of the Hasmoneans*, 291–2; Regev, *Hasmoneans*, 156. See also the bibliographical references cited in Friedlaender, "Rupture," 443 n. 3; Geller, "Alexander Jannaeus," 203 n. 6; Efron, "Simeon Ben Shataḥ and Jannaeus," 178 n. 151. Graetz (*Geschichte*, 3:687–9) and Lévi ("Sources talmudiques") preferred, like their followers, the identification of the protagonist with John Hyrcanus, as in Josephus, over the talmudic one with Janneus. Nonetheless, both argued for the uniqueness and early date of the baraita in *Qiddushin*, viewing it as part of a lost Hasmonean chronicle. Klausner (*Historiyah*, 3:136–9) and Zeitlin (*Rise and Fall of the Judaean State*, 1:169) take a similar approach. Although they thought the baraita's version the more ancient one, they still proposed that the mention of Janneus was a corruption. See also Baumgarten ("Rabbinic Literature," 46 n. 116), who, although he assigns historical significance to the baraita, still prefers the Josephan dating.

[60] For details, see Goodblatt, "Priesthood and Kingship," 12 n. 20. Although Josephus indeed reports elsewhere that John's mother was taken captive, this took place decades after the Hasmonean revolt, when John had already reached adulthood (therefore this captivity could not affect his status as a priest). John's mother was held hostage, and was eventually murdered by her son-in-law Ptolemy, who sought to accede to the throne (*Ant.* 13.228–35).

than Janneus's mother, the wife of John Hyrcanus, who lived a generation later. It has also been suggested that the rabbis attributed a political volte-face to John Hyrcanus under Sadducean influence late in his life,[61] and that this fact is consonant with the Josephan version. Menahem Stern observed that the version in *War*, uninfluenced by our story, which is entirely absent there, contains a description of a popular rebellion against John Hyrcanus; accordingly, the beginning of the rupture with the Pharisees took place during his reign and not that of his son, in accord with the Josephan version of the story in *Antiquities*.[62]

Because the rabbis lacked detailed knowledge of the lives of the Hasmonean rulers, many scholars attribute the Hyrcanus–Janneus interchange to the rabbinic tendency to conflate historical figures and to assign traditions to archetypal heroes or villains at the expense of less-known figures.[63] Adherents of this view also cite the allegedly fixed rabbinic propensity for placing Janneus in a negative light, and their ascription to him of every mistake and every anti-rabbinic act. Explicit attestation to the proclivity of switching between the names of John and Janneus is cited elsewhere in the Talmud in Abaye's name: "Yohanan is the same as Yannai" (*b. Ber.* 29a).[64] Note that it was Abaye who transmitted the baraita from *Qiddushin* under discussion.[65] Some scholars have therefore suggested that, as the transmitter of the legend, it was Abaye who made the name-switch from John to Janneus, in line with his doctrine. Others maintain that the rabbis deleted John's name from the original story because of their fondness for this historical figure.[66] For his part, Graetz proposed

---

[61] *B. Ber.* 29a; see text near n. 64. See e.g. Klausner, *Historiyah*, 3:139; Stern, *Hasmonaean Judaea*, 199.

[62] Stern, *Hasmonaean Judaea*, 199.

[63] On this trend in and of itself, see Cohen, "Parallel Historical Tradition," 11. On "King Yannai" as a prototypical name, see the bibliographical references in Goodblatt, "Priesthood and Kingship," 13 n. 21. This was already noted by Derenbourg, *Essai*, 80–1 n. 1: "Ce nom est donné indistinctement à tous les princes de la famille asmonéene;" "C'est que pour lui le nom de Janée deviant un veritable collectif" and many others in his wake. But see recently Ilan, "King Jannaeus in the Babylonian Talmud," 289–91, who argues that this impression is incorrect, at least with regard to the BT.

[64] But, according to Raba (ad loc.), "Yohanan and Yannai" are different. Geller ("Alexander Jannaeus") suggests that the two amoraim were not divided regarding the identification of the two figures, but rather regarding the two versions of our story as found in *Antiquities* and *Qiddushin*: whether they were one story or two episodes that took place during the reign of John and Janneus respectively. This proposal seems forced. First of all, the dialogue between the two amoraim makes no reference to the story in *Qiddushin*. Second, there is no evidence that the rabbis had any awareness of the existence of two versions of the story in general, or of the Josephan version, in particular (see also Rappaport, *House of the Hasmoneans*, 292).

[65] This point was noted by Derenbourg, *Essai*, 80–1 n. 1. Baumgarten ("Rabbinic Literature," 38–9) suggests that the thrust of the story was to explain why Simeon ben Shatah had to renew Pharisaic authority in Alexandra's day; accordingly the name of the ruler was changed to Janneus, who preceded her on the throne. Goodblatt ("Priesthood and Kingship," 13) suggests that the author of the Hebrew version of the legend was interested in utilizing the phrases "crown of kingship" and "crown of priesthood," and Janneus, rather than John, fitted the bill.

[66] Efron, "Simeon Ben Shatah and Jannaeus," 176–7.

that the switch was simply the result of the similarity between the names Yoḥanan and Yonathan.[67]

Citing the centrality of the motif of the crown of kingship and the emphasis on the dual authority of kingship and high priesthood, a minority opinion among scholars ascribes the original story to Janneus, giving precedence to the talmudic version.[68] Because John Hyrcanus, unlike his son Janneus, did not yet bear the title king, the assumption that John was the original protagonist of the story is difficult.[69] Among the coins of Yonathan/Alexander, referred to by the rabbis as Yannai, there is a group first minted with the legend "YHWNTN HMLK" (Yonathan the king) that was later restruck with the legend "YNTN HKHN HGDWL WḤBR HYHWDYM" (Yonathan the high priest, head of the council of the Jews).[70] Some attribute the erasure of the title "king" to Pharisaic pressure, similar to the demand made in our story.[71] Nonetheless, it should be noted that in our story the demand is that Janneus cede the high priesthood, not the monarchy. Moreover, other coins of Janneus carrying the inscription "YHWNTN HMLK" continued to be minted until the end of his regime.

Others link our story to a group of five-to-eight unusual Jannean coins imprinted with the double title כהן-מלך "priest-king". Dan Barag postulates that this group was minted in order to reinforce Janneus's dual status, more specifically, to address the demand described in our story that he cede one of these posts.

---

[67] Graetz, *Geschichte*, 3:687. Nonetheless, such a switch could not have been made by the person citing the baraita in the Talmud, as Graetz suggests, but only by recounters during the Second Temple period, who would have been familiar with Janneus also as Yonathan, as found on his coins and in a Qumran document (see E. Eshel, H. Eshel, and Yardeni, "Scroll from Qumran," 295–324). The rabbis were not aware that the name Yannai was an abbreviation for Yonathan, nor did they ever name this king Yonathan.

[68] See Friedlaender, "Rupture"; Alon, "Attitude of the Pharisees," 26–8 and n. 22; Geller, "Alexander Jannaeus"; Main, "Sadducéens." See also the bibliographical references in Efron, "Simeon Ben Shataḥ and Jannaeus," 177 n. 150; Stern, *Hasmonaean Judaea*, 198–9 n. 9. Evidently, D. R. Schwartz's arguments ("Pharisaic Opposition," 48–9) depend on the version in the BT and on the identification of the ruler as Janneus. See Goodblatt, "Priesthood and Kingship," 12–13; Main, "Les Sadducéens et l'origine des partis juifs," 406.

[69] Geller ("Alexander Jannaeus," 208; see also Main, "Les Sadducéens et l'origine des partis juifs," 406) who notes that in the case of John Hyrcanus, ceding the high priesthood would in essence mean ceding the sole support of his authority as a ruler; to ask that he give up the priesthood and retain the monarchy is therefore illogical. But it can be applied to Janneus, who was a king who held secular power. But see Tcherikover (*Hellenistic Civilization and the Jews*, 259–61), who thought that ceding the priesthood would indeed have undermined the Hasmonean leader's power base. He, however, saw this as a foundational aspect of the original story and proof of Pharisaic guile: by asking the ruler to give up the priesthood they were in actuality undermining the regime.

[70] See Meshorer, *Treasury of Jewish Coins*, 211–12, 216–17, and for minor variations in the inscriptions there. For further information on Janneus/Yonathan coins, see ibid. 37–41, 209–18, 301–15.

[71] For this argument and counter-arguments, see the discussion and bibliographical references in Goodblatt, "Priesthood and Kingship," 9–10. See also Geller, "Alexander Jannaeus," 208–9, although his description of the numismatic phenomenon there is erroneous.

Barag assumes that, in the final analysis, the regime decided that these coins did not serve Hasmonean propaganda purposes and their minting ceased.[72]

As noted above, contradictions exist between the story and the narrative frame in *Antiquities*, where Josephus underscores John Hyrcanus's righteousness, success, and harmonious rule. Seen as incongruent with the ruler's intransigent behavior in the story and the hatred exhibited toward him by the influential Pharisees and the people in their wake, this constitutes proof, for this scholarly school, that the original story did not treat John. Further argued is that the portrait of the ruler in the story is inconsistent with the positive depiction of John in other rabbinic sources.[73] In contrast, the harsh descriptions of Janneus's murderous instincts and a popular uprising against him, in both Josephus and in the Qumranic *Pesher Nahum*,[74] as well as in talmudic literature, are consistent with Janneus's presence in this story.

Regarding the libelous accusation concerning the ruler's mother, this school of thought singles out testimony by Josephus himself, who relates elsewhere the spread of a rumor regarding Janneus's mother having been in captivity.[75] Indeed, Gedalyahu Alon suggests that both Josephus and the rabbinic sources reflect traces of contrary traditions with respect to when the rupture between the Hasmoneans and the Pharisees took place: in John Hyrcanus or Janneus's day. The sugya in *b. Ber.* 29a, which was mentioned above, states that the high priest John became a Sadducee late in life, an accusation similar to the one aimed at Janneus in our story in *Qiddushin*. Alon himself leaned toward the tradition that ascribes the rupture to the later ruler, based on the assumption that the Pharisees never quarreled with John, as emerges from the Josephan testimony that his reign ended peacefully. Also, Josephus and rabbinic literature alike suggest that Janneus's reign began with a correct relationship with the

---

[72] Barag, "Alexander Jannaeus," 1–5. Note that Barag accepts the Josephan version that attributes the episode to John Hyrcanus, arguing that the Pharisaic demand for ceding the high priesthood intensified during the reign of his son Janneus, as emerges from the aspersions cast on his lineage (*Ant.* 13.372–3; *War* 1.88; see Chap. 4). For a different view of the coinage, see Regev, *Hasmoneans*, 183 n. 22.

[73] The sources were noted and evaluated by Alon, "Attitude of the Pharisees," 26–8 n. 22. See also Chap. 2, section B: "Historical Background."

[74] See section F.

[75] *Ant.* 13.372. For a discussion of this episode, see Chap. 4. But Stern (*Hasmonaean Judaea*, 198 n. 7), and Goodblatt ("Priesthood and Kingship," 14), in his wake, maintain that *Ant.* 13.372 intended to convey that Janneus was of captive lineage but not that he was the son of a captive. For a proposal that ascribes the libel of captivity regarding Janneus to a late battle (135 BCE) that took place at Modi'in between John Hyrcanus and a general sent by Antiochus Sidetes (1 Macc 16:4), see Ilan and Noam, "Pharisaic Apologetic Source," 125. Intriguingly, Josephus attests that, like Hyrcanus's mother, John Hyrcanus's wife, who perhaps was Janneus's mother, was held captive by her son Aristobulus and died in captivity (*Ant.* 13.302). Geller ("Alexander Jannaeus," 209–10) links this event and the libel regarding Janneus's mother in the talmudic story. However, because this took place when Janneus was an adult, it could not have invalidated him from being a priest; there is therefore no link between this late confinement and the libel in our story. Be that as it may, the reiterative theme of captivity of women in the Hasmonean family might well explain the opacity regarding the identity of the ruler who was accused of possessing a flawed pedigree.

Pharisees: accordingly, the rupture did not take place prior to Janneus's day.[76] In Chapter 5 I argue that both our story and that of Janneus's deathbed instructions originally belonged to a single work or collection of sources that focused on the relationship between the Pharisees and this king. If this is the case, then, at least with regard to the version known to the rabbis, the legend dealt with Janneus from the outset. However, the main contribution of this story is not the long-debated identity of the protagonist, but rather its origins and thrust.

E. THE PURPOSE AND PROVENANCE OF THE LEGEND

In addressing this legend, the rich scholarly research has neglected two fundamental elements that have the ability to shed fresh light on its provenance and purpose: first, the biblical allusions scattered throughout the text of the story; second, specific expressions and language that are indicative of its date, origins, and thrust. Naturally, these elements are more visible in the Hebrew version of the story. Although traces have also been preserved in the Greek, Josephan, version, the following discussion focuses on the version found in the baraita.

Biblical Allusions

This legend clearly alludes to two biblical contexts: the book of Esther and Numbers 16–17. Of these, the allusions to Numbers have greater weight.

The Book of Esther

The first noteworthy allusion is the use of the expression כתר מלכות "royal crown," which appears in Yehudah ben Gudgeda's demand that Janneus content himself with the monarchy alone. Found only three times in the Bible, all of the occurrences of the word כתר "crown" appear in the book of Esther (1:11, 2:17, 6:8).[77] Another allusion to Esther is the phrase ויבוקש הדבר ולא נמצא, "the matter was investigated, but not sustained," a transparent paraphrase of ויבקש הדבר וימצא : "the matter was investigated and found to be so" (Esth 2:23), as

---

[76] Alon, "Attitude of the Pharisees," 26–8 n. 22.

[77] See Goodblatt, "Priesthood and Kingship," 13 n. 21, although he does not note this intentional allusion. The Hebrew word כתר is also unique to these three biblical occurrences. Interestingly, the only other rabbinic context that mentions swearing by the priestly golden plate which is placed "between the eyes" alludes to Esther as well. See *t. Ḥal.* 1:10: לבוש שלבש בו אבא וציץ שנתן בין עיניו ("[By] the clothes that father wore and the [gold] plate that he bore on his brow! I will make an example...."). Cf. Esth 6:8: וַאֲשֶׁר נִתַּן כֶּתֶר מַלְכוּת בְּרֹאשׁוֹ...לְבוּשׁ מַלְכוּת אֲשֶׁר לָבַשׁ-בּוֹ הַמֶּלֶךְ ("let royal garb which the king has worn be brought").

Israël Lévi recognized.[78] In Esther the context is the verification of Mordecai's discovery of a planned assassination plot by two of Ahasuerus's eunuchs. The associations between the Janneus tradition and the story of Esther are not surprising. The rabbinic story, like the biblical one, centers on a king who persecutes the innocent after receiving poor advice offered by a villain. In both, dramatic events take place during a royal feast or banquet,[79] and we also hear of two scoundrels who scheme against the king.

Numbers 16–17

The second biblical source of inspiration, the pericope which recounts the story of Korah's rebellion, is more significant. Korah and his faction accuse Moses and Aaron of unjustly elevating themselves above the congregation and of assuming both leadership and the priesthood. This insurrection is quashed through divine intervention, and the rebels are harshly punished.

Identification of the Korah story as the biblical underpinning of the baraita elucidates some of the unique expressions chosen by its author and, more importantly, his message. The phrase רב לך ("[let the royal crown] suffice thee"), which appears in Yehudah's demand of the king, is a transparent allusion to the Korah dispute, where it appears twice, in the rebels' claim and in Moses's reply (Num 16:3, 7: רב לכם). This expression is also recognizable in Josephus's Greek version: ἀρκείτω σοι (*Ant.* 13.291).[80] In addition, the noun כהונה (priesthood), found in the combination כתר כהונה (crown of priesthood) in the rabbinic story, is quite rare in the Pentateuch. Of its two occurrences there (Exod 29:9, Num 16:10), one is in the Korah story.

Another allusion to the Korah story relates to the motif of separation. The phrase, "and the Sages of Israel separated themselves (ויבדלו) in anger," clarifies neither who was angry with whom, nor from what the sages separated themselves and why.[81] The apparently arbitrary use of the verb ויבדלו can be attributed to its dominance in the Korah story, where it denotes both the separation of the privileged Levites from the multitude, and of Moses and Aaron from the wicked and their fate (Num 16:9, 21: הבדלו, הבדיל; see below). Moreover, an examination of the biblical story reveals that separation is a leading motif in

---

[78] Lévi, "Sources talmudiques," 222; Koller, *Esther in Ancient Jewish Thought*, 147–51.

[79] For this point, see Baumgarten, "Rabbinic Literature," 45; Koller, *Esther in Ancient Jewish Thought*, 147–51. On meals as sites that manifest hierarchic struggles in rabbinic literature, see R. Weiss, *Meal Tests*, 16–38, 320–5. I thank Inbar Raveh for this reference.

[80] Nonetheless, it appears that the Josephan version depends on some Hebrew version of our story and not directly on the biblical context of Korah, because in the LXX translation of the relevant verses in Num 16 we find the verbs ἐχέτω and ἱκανούσθω, not ἀρκείτω, which Josephus uses in *Antiquities*.

[81] See Baumgarten, "Rabbinic Literature," 37 and n. 86; Kalmin, *Jewish Babylonia*, 58, and the discussion of this expression in n. 100 below.

this pericope, as manifested in the frequent use of the Hebrew roots בד"ל (Num 16:9, 21), על"ה (Num 16:24, 27),[82] סו"ר (Num 16:26), and רו"ם (Num 17:10) as key words.[83] The same motifs, of authority and prestige on the one hand, and departure from malicious people or movements on the other, appear in the rabbinic story.

Finally, the exceptional use of the verb [הרעה] ותתצץ "[the evil] burst forth,"[84] is a wordplay on ציץ, the priestly golden plate mentioned earlier, which symbolizes the metaphorical "crown of priesthood." But the choice of this root also echoes the miraculous blossoming of Aaron's staff at the conclusion of the Korah story: "the staff of Aaron of the house of Levi had sprouted: it had brought forth sprouts, produced blossoms (וַיָּצֵץ צִיץ), and borne almonds" (Num 17:23).[85]

Further evidence for the covert rabbinic association between the Janneus legend and the Korah passage comes from a passage in *Sifre Numbers* that links central themes found in the Janneus legend with the aftermath of the Korah story. Focusing on the biblical laws of the priestly gifts in Numbers 18, which follow the Korah passage and the re-establishment of Aaron's status, the midrash explains the juxtaposition of these texts as confirming Aaron's rights in the wake of Korah's challenge. Following a series of midrashim in praise of the priests, *Sifre* sets out to prove the priority of Torah study over priestly status:

> *I am thy portion and thy inheritance.*
> Twenty-four priestly gifts were given to the priest, twelve in the Sanctuary and twelve outside of the Sanctuary... It was all to Aaron's good that Korah came and contested the priesthood against him. Therefore this section concerning the priestly dues comes close to the section about Korah....
> What love has God bestowed upon the <priests>,[86] that when he calls them by a pet name, He calls them "*ministering angels*," as it is said (Mal. ii. 7): "*For the lips of the priest keep knowledge...*" As long as teaching (torah) comes out of his mouth, he is like the ministering angels, but if not, he is like a wild animal and like a beast which does not recognize its owner.
> Beloved is the Torah, for when David, the King of Israel asked God (to give him something), it was the *Torah* that he desired... It turns out that there are three crowns: the crown of priesthood, and the crown of kingship, and the crown of Torah. Aaron merited the crown of priesthood and assumed it. David merited the crown of kingship and assumed it. Behold, the crown of Torah is lying

---

[82] See also Num 16:12–13 for a different use of the same verb, undoubtedly a play on words.

[83] See also Num 17:2; 18:8, 11, 19 for additional examples of the use of the same verb. Here too, there is a deliberate play on words.

[84] Of the variants and corruptions, the best reconstruction is ותתצץ, which means that the evil flourished. See n. 14.

[85] Rashi apparently intuited this link. See *Qidd.* 66a, s.v. ותתצץ הרעה.

[86] Should read כהנים. MS Vatican 32 has יש'. But Israel was mentioned in the previous section and from the context it is clear that the reference here is to the priests.

[unassigned] (הרי כתר תורה מונח) so as not to give an excuse to anyone in the world to say: If the crown of priesthood and the crown of kingship were available I would have merited and assumed them. Behold, the crown of Torah is an admonition to everyone in the world, so that anyone who merits it, I regard him as if all three of them were available and he merited all of them, and anyone who does not merit it, I regard him as if all three of them were available, and he did not merit a single one.[87]

This midrash evinces awareness of the link between the priestly gifts and the preceding Korah pericope ("for that reason it was adjacent to Korah"). It provides a series of homilies in praise of the priesthood, as would be expected from the biblical context of priestly gifts. Nonetheless, immediately following the citation of the scriptural proof-text for the comparison between priests and angels (Mal 2:7), the midrash makes a volte-face: it now seeks to prove the superiority of Torah over priesthood: a priest from whose mouth Torah does not emerge is "like a wild beast and an animal that knows not its creator." The presence of such anti-priestly comments embedded in a midrashic stratum entirely devoted to praise of the priesthood is surprising.

It is noteworthy that this anti-priestly midrash contains two motifs found in the Janneus narrative: the crowns of priesthood and kingship, and the theme of the Torah as "lying," available to all.[88] Evidently components of a tradition that was linked with the biblical Korah context, these two motifs can therefore serve as further proof for the association of the *Qiddushin* passage, which contains them as well, with the Korah narrative.[89]

The use of the Korah story as a paradigm for dangerous schisms in Jewish society, and of Korah as the archetypical representative of heresy, is widespread in Jewish tradition.[90] Moreover, there is a strong thematic link between the Korah pericope and the story of the rupture with the Pharisees. In both contexts

---

[87] *Sifre Num.* 119. I thank Yoni Pomeranz for his assistance in the translation of this passage. Part of the translation is cited from Levertoff, *Midrash Sifre on Numbers*, 125–9.

[88] On the "three crowns" motif, see section G. Kister ("Aggadic Traditions," 205 n. 65) maintains that the description of the Torah lying and waiting for those who merit it is a late addition to our story in the wake of midrashim like the one discussed here. In any event, the crowns of priesthood and kingship are certainly original in both contexts and both exhibit a link to the Korah pericope.

[89] Another intriguing link between the Korah story and the Hasmonean dynasty appears in midrashim on Deut 33:11. An ancient Aramaic midrash was embedded in *Tg. Ps.-J.*, ad loc., which expounds Moses's blessing to the tribe of Levi: "Smite the loins of his foes; Let his enemies rise no more," as referring to John Hyrcanus: "so that there will not be for the enemies of Johanan, the high priest, a foot to stand on" (*The Aramaic Bible*, vol. 5B). See Chap. 2. On the other hand, the tannaitic midrash identifies the "foes" in the biblical verse with Korah (*Sifre Deut.*, piska 352).

[90] For the rabbinic treatment of the story of Korah, see Urbach, "Ten Commandments," 304–7; Feldman, *Josephus' Rewritten Bible*, 94–7; and the bibliographical references compiled by Scott, "Korah and Qumran," 190 n. 35. See also Draper, "Korah," 74–150. Five different corpora attest to the centrality of this biblical story in pre-rabbinic times as well. Korah and his allies are mentioned in the section on Aaron in Ben Sira 45:18–19. As Feldman (*Josephus' Rewritten Bible*, 91–109) has shown, Philo's paraphrase of the Korah story (*Moses* 2.174–86, 275–87; *Rewards* 74–8) emphasizes

we find a revolt against the leadership; moreover, we also find a protest against a leadership that has assumed dual authority: governance and the priesthood. Indeed, I can think of no scriptural pericope more suited to the story of a political crisis and lack of belief in the leadership than that of Korah and his associates.

These strong links have thematic implications for our understanding of the narrator's aim and moral stance. Because Moses and Aaron were instructed to separate themselves (הבדלו מתוך העדה הזאת) from Korah's community (16:21), and the "sages of Israel" also "separated themselves" (ונבדלו חכמי ישראל בזעם),[91] we may infer that the sages of the legend are perceived as equivalent to Moses and Aaron. This is not surprising. The idea that the rabbis, and previously the Pharisees, were the successors of Moses and the carriers of his tradition is deeply rooted in rabbinic literature[92] and well known from pre-rabbinic times too.[93]

In the rabbinic story, Eleazar ben Po'irah seeks to undermine the sages' authority. As noted above, his remark "Behold, it is bound up and lying in the corner... whoever wishes to study, let him come and study!" evidently reflects a covert dispute with rabbinic authority that was grounded in their being the teachers of the Oral Law. Eleazar's derision for the sages' authority, which resembles the threat to the Mosaic-Aaronitic leadership in the Korah story,

---

its moral and theological lessons, whereas Josephus's lengthy account of this episode (*Ant.* 4.14–66) stresses its political import for Josephus's time and life circumstances. The story of Korah is also paraphrased in *L.A.B.* 16. Finally, Korah is mentioned in some Qumranic fragments as well. The words משפט קורח (the punishment of Korah) appear in 4Q423 5, line 1 (see the possible parallel in 4Q418a 3, line 3). Since the fragmentary text contains the words והשמר לך ("and take care"), נשיא עמכה ("leader of your people"), and כל מושלים ("all rulers"), it seems to be warning against opposing the leaders/rulers (of the sect?) and assuring that transgressors would receive "the punishment of Korah" (but cf. Elgvin, "4QInstruction⁸," 518–22). See also Strugnell and Harrington, "4QInstructionᵉ," 479–80. According to Scott ("Korah and Qumran," 182–202), in 4QInstruction the Korah affair is used as a paradigm of a schism that took place during the history of the *Yaḥad* sect. 4QWarScrollᵃ (4Q491 1–3, line 1) refers to קורח ועדתו...משפט ("Korah and his congregation...judgment"), probably in the context of eschatological judgment, but the text is highly fragmentary (see Baillet, *Qumran Grotte 4.III*, 13, 15–16). On a Josephan parallel to the expression משפט קורח, see Elgvin, "4QInstruction⁸," 520. According to Scott ("Korah and Qumran," 189 n. 34), this expression does not occur in rabbinic literature. However, tannaitic midrash (*Sifre Deut.*, piska 307) does mention Korah's punishment as one manifestation of God's judgment (משפט) as mentioned in Deut 32:4 (כל דרכיו משפט; lit.: "All His ways are [true] judgment"). A third Qumran reference to Korah in 4Q171 3–10 IV, 23 is merely a citation of Ps 45:1. Aharon Shemesh ("Scriptural Background," 212–16; Werman and Shemesh, *Revealing the Hidden*, 267) argues that the root לון (to grumble), denoting grumbling against the authority of the community—as mentioned in the penal code, 1QS VII, 17 and parallels, and in 1QHᵃ XIII, 25—alludes to the story of Korah at Num 16:11.

[91] Note the link between this emphasis and the very name Pharisees, which is synonymous with נבדלים ("those who separate themselves").

[92] I restrict myself to the best-known source, *m. 'Abot* 1:1. On the rabbinization of the figure of Moses, see Cohen, "Parallel Historical Tradition," 12.

[93] See e.g. Matt 23:2.

makes the inciter, Eleazar ben Po'irah—who is "frivolous, evil and a scoundrel"—Korah's counterpart. However, Yehudah ben Gudgeda, the slanderer, must also be identified with the "bad guys" of the biblical story: (a) like Korah he argues against the dual authority of the leader as king and high priest; (b) the sages "separate themselves" from him, similar to the separation by Moses and Aaron from Korah's faction; and (c) the "evil burst forth," according to the original story, through both Eleazar ben Po'irah and Yehudah ben Gudgeda, for the primary text witnesses read: ותוצץ הרעה על ידי אלעזר בן פועירא ועל ידי יהודה בן גודגדא. Yehudah is omitted from this sentence in the printed editions and therefore his role has not been discussed in the scholarship, but his name appears in all the other versions, as well as in medieval citations of the Talmud.[94] This fact is of significance for the reconstruction of this story's purpose and political stance. It means that, according to the authors, the disastrous results are equally the fault of those voicing objections to the Hasmonean ruler (Yehudah) and those who incite against the sages of Israel/Pharisees (Eleazar). In other words, the opponents of Hasmonean rule are no less hated by the author of the story than the opponents of the Pharisees.[95]

A negative depiction of the slanderer is also found in the Josephan version. We may therefore infer that, according to the talmudic storyteller, the Pharisees did not support Yehudah's demand that the king resign the high priesthood. In other words, in contrast to a widely held scholarly opinion,[96] our story cannot serve as proof of Pharisaic objections to the dual authority of the Hasmonean rulers. On the contrary, the advocates of this objection are considered the enemies of the sages, and one thrust of our story, in the Josephan as well as in the rabbinic version,[97] is that the sages disassociated themselves from this demand and from its proponents. This point will be further elaborated in section F (text near n. 100).

---

[94] See Friedlaender, "Rupture," 448 n. 24, and n. 15 above.

[95] See the identification suggested between this figure and what it represents and the "hypocrites who ape the Pharisees" treated in Chap. 5.

[96] See e.g. D. R. Schwartz, "Pharisaic Opposition" (for a disputation with his views, see Goodblatt, "Priesthood and Kingship"; Regev, *Hasmoneans*, 157–60). In light of the above, Yehudah is certainly not "a spokesman for the Pharisees" (as Schwartz, "Pharisaic Opposition," 48 and Regev, *Sadducees*, 256 argue; Schwartz, however, presents a different view in his later article, "Remembering the Second Temple Period," 75). According to the manuscript testimony, it is also not the case that Yehudah "is not described as wicked" (Kalmin, *Jewish Babylonia*, 57). Kalmin argues that Yehudah is defined as an elder and is, therefore, designated a sage, but the expression זקן אחד (an elder), is in certain cases applied to Sadducees and other adversaries of the rabbis (see *b. Sotah* 49b = *b. B. Qam.* 82b = *b. Menaḥ.* 64b; and Chap. 6; *b. B. Bat.* 115b; *b. Menaḥ.* 65a). Scholion P on *Megillat Ta'anit* mentions an ideological enemy of the sages on several occasions, using the designation אחד שהיה מפטפט כנגדו ("one who began to babble") whereas the hybrid version there reads זקן אחד (Noam, *Megillat Ta'anit*, 61, 86, 97, 108).

[97] Mason (*Josephus on the Pharisees*, 230) reached an identical conclusion regarding the Josephan version: "Indeed . . . the story seems to say that Jonathan's accusation of the Pharisees was a shrewd piece of 'disinformation', not an accurate statement of the facts."

F. THE JANNEUS LEGEND AS A POLITICAL MIDRASH

I suggest on this basis that the Janneus legend is actually a political midrash that projects biblical images and events onto the Hasmonean dynastic context. This midrash implicitly identifies two distinct political parties with Korah, the ultimate biblical rebel and villain: (a) those who oppose the Hasmonean rulers and demand that they abandon the high priesthood, represented by Yehudah; and (b) those who oppose the "sages of Israel" and claim that these sages are provokers of quarrels, and, furthermore, that their presence is not crucial to the study of Torah, represented by Eleazar. Although the talmudic version of the rupture tradition does not specify which of these factions advocated Eleazar's stance that there is no need for the Oral Torah, rabbinic literature usually attributes this argument to sects like the Sadducees or Boethusians.[98] Bearing in mind that the Josephan version explicitly identifies the inciter against the Pharisees as a Sadducee, we can therefore infer that this political midrash engages in sectarian polemic.[99]

In both the Josephan and talmudic versions of the story, one of the anti-heroes accuses the Pharisees/sages of backing the defamatory view of the Hasmonean ruler and the demand that he resign from the high priesthood. However, as shown above, the storyteller in both versions is determined to prove this accusation false. On the contrary, according to Josephus the sages "were very indignant (καὶ πάντες δ᾽ οἱ Φαρισαῖοι σφοδρῶς ἠγανάκτησαν)" (292), and the baraita states that they "separated themselves in anger (ויבדלו חכמי ישראל בזעם)."[100] The narrator wishes then to underscore that the sages distanced themselves from this slander, which was in any case incorrect, and from the demand that the king cede the high priesthood, in direct contradiction of Eleazar's claim.

It seems that what troubled the storyteller was a commonly held opinion that laid the blame for the breach with the Hasmonean dynasty at the Pharisees' door, the outcome of their impertinent demand that the Hasmonean ruler resign the high priesthood. Those who endorsed this opinion probably ascribed the rumor

---

[98] See Rivkin's conclusions based on a string of disputes between the sages/Pharisees and the Sadducees/Boethusians ("Defining the Pharisees," 217–18). See also Scholion O on *Meg. Ta'an.*, 4/10 Tammuz (Noam, *Megillat Ta'anit*, 78–9, 206, and the discussion on 206–16). The debate revolves about the need for "halakhot" in addition to "Torah."

[99] This conclusion was also reached by Rivkin ("Defining the Pharisees," 218–20) for additional reasons. Rappaport (*House of the Hasmoneans*, 293–4) maintains that the statement regarding the Torah in the legend preserves a historical kernel: John sought to assume the judicial and legislative powers of the Pharisees, and Eleazar's remarks reflect his new claim that "the law specific to Judea is the divine law in the Torah, but beyond that the king is the legislator."

[100] Rashi comments: "The king was angry at them." Baumgarten ("Rabbinic Literature," 37 and n. 86) also pursues this tack, translating the passage as follows: "and the Sages of Israel departed [with the king] angry [at them]." But according to the plain meaning of the passage, it is the sages, who are the grammatical subject of the sentence, who are angry, and not the king. This is also supported by the Josephan version, which indicates that the vague anger is not the king's anger at the sages, but rather the sages' anger at the slanderer (see also Neusner, *Rabbinic Traditions about the Pharisees*, 1:175). Likewise, from the Josephan parallel it is clear that the sages' "departure"

regarding the Hasmonean ruler's problematic pedigree to the Pharisees. A collective impression of the Pharisees as quarrel-mongers and rebels is well reflected in Josephus's introduction, which clearly contradicts the story itself: "when they speak against a king or high priest, they immediately gain credence" (*Ant.* 13.288).[101] Similar accusations against the Pharisees are found in *Pesher Nahum*, which depicts them as exercising great influence over the masses, including "kings, princes, priests, and populace" (מלכים, שרים, כוהנים ועם) and as causing "nobles and rulers" to "fall by the fury of their tongue" (נ]כ[בדים ומוש]לים [מז]עם לשונם [יפולו)."[102]

Through an apologetic tale, the author of our tradition sets out to refute this impression. His primary message is that the Pharisees/the sages never opposed the king, nor did they support the false, wicked defamation regarding his maternal descent. They are not pugnacious troublemakers, but rather, according to the baraita, "the sages of Israel," the exclusive teachers of the Torah and the true successors of Moses and Aaron, in whose absence "the world is desolate" and the Torah absent. The rupture with the Hasmoneans was neither their fault nor that of the Hasmonean ruler. Rather, the Pharisees' adversaries, villains and rebels like Korah, were the ones who "took pleasure in dissension" according to Josephus,[103] and who, according to the baraita, caused evil to "burst forth." They were the ones who spread the wicked rumor about the king, instigated the quarrel, and occasioned disaster.

G. THE TERMINOLOGY OF THE LEGEND

In addition to its already noted composite linguistic features, this text contains several terms charged with political meaning that impact the consideration of its dating and purpose.

Crowns

One dominant feature of its terminology is the notion of metaphorical "crowns." These crowns represent the political tensions at the heart of this story: the dual authority symbolized by the supreme privileges of kingship and the priesthood.

does not mean physically leaving the place, but rather separating themselves from this person and his words. A physical departure is not described in *Antiquities* either. Graetz (*Geschichte*, 3:688) also comments that such an understanding is incongruent with the ending of the story, according to which all the sages present were murdered.

[101] As explained above, this declaration comes from Josephus's introduction to our story (which was either penned by Nicolaus or Josephus himself) and is incontrovertibly not part of the story itself, which it contradicts in several respects.

[102] 4QpNah (4Q169) 3–4 II, 9–10. Translation according to Berrin, *Pesher Nahum*, 194. See also Horgan, *Pesharim*, 164. For bibliography, see Horgan, *Pesharim*, 158–9.

[103] According to the description of Eleazar in Josephus, *Ant.* 13.291: στάσει χαίρων.

Allusions to these two "crowns," plus the special privilege of the sages—the knowledge of Torah—recur throughout the narrative. In the opening section, Janneus functions as a victorious king (an allusion to the crown of kingship) and also symbolically re-establishes the temple after a fashion: "Our forefathers ate mallows when they were engaged in the building of the [second] temple; let us too eat mallows in memory of our forefathers" (which alludes to the crown of priesthood). The ultimate symbol of priesthood, the golden diadem of the high priest, appears at the core of the narrative as well. Later on, Eleazar mentions a Torah scroll "lying in a corner," and in the concluding sentence Simeon ben Shataḥ, the representative of the sages, reinstates the Torah.

The motif of "three crowns" is familiar from rabbinic sources like *m. 'Abot* 4:13 and *Sifre Num.* 119 (as cited above), among others.[104] Scholars consider this rabbinic formula a later version of an earlier theme of "three privileges/attributes" that appears in several pre-rabbinic sources, among them Josephus's narrative regarding John Hyrcanus, who merited "the three greatest privileges" ($\tau\rho\iota\hat{\omega}\nu\ \tau\hat{\omega}\nu\ \mu\epsilon\gamma\acute{\iota}\sigma\tau\omega\nu$); as named by Josephus (*Ant.* 13.299, *War* 1.68), they encompass: the rule of the nation, the office of high priest, and the gift of prophecy.[105] In essence the Second Temple-period manifestation of the three offices of biblical leadership,[106] the rabbis later exchanged prophecy for Torah in this triplet.[107]

I note here another pre-rabbinic occurrence of this triad. The same virtues— priesthood, government, and prophecy—are applied (if somewhat vaguely) to the tribe of Levi in the Greek *Testament of Levi*, and at least two of them appear in the earlier *Aramaic Levi Document*.[108] The latter work, which treats the life of Levi, recounts visions that he saw, his appointment to the priesthood, and his speech to his sons. Most scholars date *Aramaic Levi* to the late third or early second century BCE. Others assign it to the late second century BCE and identify

---

[104] All the occurrences of this motif were reviewed by Moshe Beer ("Crown of Torah," 397–417). Stuart A. Cohen dedicated an entire volume to this theme, which for him symbolizes a basic rabbinic agenda of "constitutional power-sharing in Jewish public life" (*Three Crowns*, 12).

[105] See Chap. 2. See also Flusser, "Jewish Messianism Reflected in the Early Church," 273–5; Kister, "Aggadic Traditions," 202–12; S.A. Cohen, *Three Crowns*, 18; H. Eshel, *Dead Sea Scrolls and the Hasmonean State*, 77 and n. 46.

[106] On this triad and its permutations in the Second Temple period, see the bibliographical references compiled by Mason, *Josephus on the Pharisees*, 223 n. 52.

[107] H. Eshel, *Dead Sea Scrolls and the Hasmonean State*, 77; see Urbach, "Matai paskah ha-nevu'ah," 9–49; Flusser, "Jewish Messianism Reflected in the Early Church," 275. Kister ("Aggadic Traditions," 205 and n. 65), however, concludes that the crown of the Torah was added to the list at an earlier period and was not a Pharisaic innovation, finding backing in Ben Sira. He suggests that the sentence ומונחת... כל הרוצה ללמוד יבוא וילמד in our story is an addition by a late redactor who relied on the late motif of the three crowns in rabbinic literature.

[108] I extend thanks to Esther Eshel for her assistance with the *Aramaic Levi Document*. On this work and the history of its discovery, see Greenfield, Stone, and E. Eshel, *Aramaic Levi Document*, 1–47. For a succinct, illuminating summary, see E. Eshel, "Biblical Apocrypha and Pseudepigrapha," 580–4. Recently, another fragment of this work from the Cairo Genizah was discovered. See Bohak, "New Genizah Fragment," 373–83. For further discussion, see Chap. 2.

in it allusions to the Hasmonean period.[109] The text underscores that Levi was deserving of both priesthood and monarchy.[110] In his vision, Levi receives an angelic message. Though fragmentary and difficult, the verse evidently mentions Levi's sons, the word "third" (תליתין), "the kingdom of priesthood" (מלכות כהנותא), and perhaps "the [Most H]igh G[o]d" (ל[א]ל[ע]ל[יון])(*ALD* 4:7).[111] As is well known, the *Aramaic Levi Document* was one of the main sources for the later Greek *Testament of Levi*, part of the *Testaments of the Twelve Patriarchs*, which contain Christian additions and reworking.[112] In the parallel passage there, Levi is told that his descendants will be divided into three "offices" (ἀρχὰς). The next lines mention belief, priesthood, and a king who will arise from Judah and found a new priesthood, after the fashion of the gentiles: the presence of this priest (from the new priesthood?) will be as marvelous as that of a high prophet (ὡς προφήτου ὑψίστου).[113] Evidently, the mention of the tribe of Judah, and perhaps also the virtue of belief, is the result of a late Christian reworking.[114] But beyond this reworking, *T. Levi* evidences the three features mentioned above: priesthood, kingship, and prophecy. Given the parallel between *T. Levi* and *Aramaic Levi* here it is also possible that the fragmentary verse in the early Aramaic document also mentioned prophecy to the High God.[115]

In any event, it is apparent that the motif of three merits enjoyed by the tribe of Levi—priesthood, kingship, and perhaps prophecy—was prevalent in the various streams of Second Temple literature.[116] The Janneus legend, with its two crowns and a Torah scroll "bound up and lying in the corner," seems to represent an intermediate stage between the early "three greatest privileges"—

[109] See Greenfield, Stone, and E. Eshel, *Aramaic Levi Document*, 19–22 and the references noted there. For the later dating of the text, see Kugel, "How Old Is the Aramaic Levi Document?" 291–312.

[110] See Greenfield, Stone, and E. Eshel, *Aramaic Levi Document*, 35–8.

[111] See ibid. 66 and the English translation, ibid. 67. See also ibid. 37 and n. 145 and the commentary on 4:7–8, at 139–41. Evidently, the phrase כהנותא רבא should not be understood as "high priesthood" (see ibid. 141), for if so it should read כהנותא רבתא. On the other hand, the phrase מלכות כהנותא is difficult: the editors link it to the biblical phrase ממלכת כהנים (Exod 19:6).

[112] For a summary and bibliography, see E. Eshel, "Biblical Apocrypha and Pseudepigrapha," 580–1.

[113] *T. Levi* 8:11–15; de Jonge, *Testaments*, 34, according to most of the manuscripts; see the variants for line 15. For the English translation, see Hollander and de Jonge, *Testaments: Commentary*, 149, 153–4. I thank Shlomi Efrati for his assistance with *T. Levi*.

[114] On the addition that mentions the tribe of Judah, see Greenfield, Stone, and E. Eshel, *Aramaic Levi Document*, 37.

[115] The expression אל עליון is largely reconstructed here. However, it does appear twice elsewhere in the *Aramaic Levi Document* (5:8, 8:6) and its presence here is supported by the late parallel in *T. Levi*.

[116] Cf. *Tg. Onq.* to Gen 49:3: Jacob's blessing of Reuben: לך הוה חזי למסב תלתה חולקין בכירותא כהונתא ומלכותא "For you it would have been fitting to take three parts—the birthright, the priesthood, and royalty." I thank Yoel Elitzur for this observation.

rule, priesthood, prophecy—and rabbinic literature's "three crowns"—Torah, priesthood, kingship.[117]

Frivolous, Evil, and a Scoundrel

Another noteworthy linguistic usage, also the first occurrence of biblical language and forms in the legend, is the description of Eleazar as לץ, רע ובליעל. The definitively biblical words לץ and בליעל *never* appear in rabbinic sources, apart from biblical citations.[118] But this does not just reflect use of early terms, but rather of loaded terms with political meaning: known from the Qumran corpus, they are part and parcel of its distinctive terminology for its enemies.[119]

Widespread in sectarian polemical contexts, the word לצון is used to designate both the leader of the sect's opponents—referred to as איש הלצון ("the man of mockery")[120]—and its opponents as a group—labeled אנשי הלצון ("the men of mockery"), as seen from the following example:

> These (are) the men of mockery (אנשי הלצון), who are in Jerusalem. They are the ones who 'rejected the Torah of the Lord, and the word of the Holy One of Israel they treated without respect' (Isa 5:24).[121]

Even the full expression איש לץ ("[a m]an who is a scorner"; 4Q426 [4QSap-Hymnic Work A] 8, line 4) occurs in a Qumran fragment, exactly as in our legend.[122] Note that the word איש in this phrase is also unusual in rabbinic literature:[123] as opposed to Biblical Hebrew, Rabbinic Hebrew always uses אדם as the indefinite pronoun ("someone").[124] In the Qumran scrolls we find both words; the biblical form איש is, however, more frequent.

---

[117] See nn. 105–7.

[118] Qimron and Strugnell, *MMT*, 84. They also note: "רע as an adjective is frequent in all phases of Hebrew" (ibid. 87).

[119] On conceptual clusters typical of Qumran sectarian terminology, see Dimant, "Qumran Manuscripts," 27–9. For a more recent piece, see Dimant, "Qumran Sectarian Texts," 49–86. On the typical use of בליעל in sectarian texts but also in the contemporary non-sectarian literature, see Dimant, "Qumran Sectarian Texts," 76; Qimron and Strugnell, *MMT*, 84.

[120] CD I, 14 (=4Q266 2 I, 18).

[121] 4QpIsa^b (4Q162 ii, 6). See also line 10 (Allegro, "Commentary on Isaiah (B)," 15–16; Charlesworth, *Dead Sea Scrolls*, 6B: 42–3). For the biblical citation, see Isa 5:24. Cf. CD XX, 11; 4Q433a 3, line 7; 4Q525 23, line 8.

[122] 4Q426 8, line 4. The text is too fragmentary to determine its content.

[123] The word איש appears in MS Oxford 367, and in the printed editions. It is missing in MS Munich 95 and has apparently been corrected in MS Vatican 111 to its more common synonym אדם.

[124] Sarfatti, "Inscriptions," 58–60.

As for "Belial," which appears more than eighty times in the DSS,[125] it sometimes denotes a personification of evil,[126] or the name of the leader of the forces
of darkness;[127] in other instances it is used as an adjective to describe a wicked
person or persons: as Qimron has observed, in *Hodayot* the words רוע, רע, and
בליעל are synonymous.[128] The sect's opponents are named עדת בליעל ("the congregation of Belial"),[129] and דורשי החלקות ("seekers of smooth things"); as the
derogatory name applied to the Pharisees, they are described as having thoughts
of מזמות בליעל ("plots of Belial").[130] As an adjectival modifier for individuals we
find in the DSS איש בלי[על] איש שוע שוע עינים ("a man of Belial, a man of smeared-over
eyes");[131] and ואנה [איש] ארור (אחד)[132]בליעל ("behold a cursed man, [a man of]
Belial").[133]

The last reference is especially instructive: note the strong resemblance between
the phrase ואנה איש ארור איש אחד בליעל and our talmudic source: והיה שם איש אחד לץ, רע
ובליעל ("now, there was a man there, frivolous, evil, and Belial"). Moreover, the
Qumranic text, 4QTestimonia, in which this phrase appears, shares additional
features with the Hyrcanus/Janneus tradition. As we have seen in the previous
chapter, this Belial, to whom the text applies Joshua's curse on the future build-
ers of Jericho (Josh 6:26), was identified in scholarship as John Hyrcanus.
Hanan Eshel also maintained that the preceding biblical passages in the
Qumran text, which treat an ideal prophet, a future victorious leader, and the
blessing of the priests, were all commonly applied to John Hyrcanus,[134] who
had merited, according to Josephus, the rule of the nation, the office of high
priest, and the gift of prophecy (see Chapter 2).[135]

If this is correct, 4QTestimonia and the Janneus/Hyrcanus legend not only
share terminology (איש אחד בליעל), but also a protagonist (Hyrcanus, according
to the Josephan version, or his son, according to the talmudic one) and a
theme—the privileges of leadership, priesthood, and prophecy hinted at in the
Qumranic text and the "crowns" of kingship and priesthood, combined with

---

[125] But only twenty-seven times in the Bible!

[126] E.g. CD IV, 13, 15–18; XIX, 14. For greater detail, see Dimant, "Qumran Sectarian
Texts," 76.

[127] CD V, 18.   [128] Qimron and Strugnell, *MMT*, 87.

[129] *Hodayot* (1QHᵃ) X, 24.   [130] *Hodayot* X, 18.

[131] 4Q425 1+3, line 7. The reconstruction is doubtful, however. See Steudel, "425. 4QSapiential-
Didactic Work B," 204–5.

[132] The word אחד has been partially erased and the supralinear emendation איש added.

[133] 4Q175 23 (DJD 5:57–8; Charlesworth, *Dead Sea Scrolls*, 6B:318–19). Cf. 4Q379
(ibid. 322).

[134] Indeed, one of the biblical pericopes in the Qumran fragment (Deut 33:11) was interpreted
as applying to John Hyrcanus, according to an ancient midrash embedded in *Tg. Ps.-J.* ad loc.
See n. 89.

[135] H. Eshel, *Dead Sea Scrolls and the Hasmonean State*, chap. 3. For other interpretations of the
Qumran text, see the discussion there and Chap. 2, n. 39.

the Torah scroll "lying [unassigned]" in the rabbinic text. Be that as it may, I posit, as an interim conclusion, that our legend uses terminology and motifs typical of the historical-political context of the Dead Sea Scrolls in general and of the reign of John Hyrcanus in particular.

In his description of Eleazar, Josephus also uses terminology similar to the terms לץ, רע ובליעל found in the baraita. The portrayal κακοήθης ὢν φύσει καὶ στάσει χαίρων ("who had an evil nature and took pleasure in dissension," *Ant.* 13.291) is not fully equivalent to the three adjectives in the rabbinic version. However, the word κακοήθης may reflect the Hebrew לץ, since this biblical word is occasionally rendered κακός in the LXX.[136] As for the expression στάσει χαίρων, it can best be reconstructed as שש לריב, since στάσις is the LXX's equivalent for ריב,[137] and χαίρειν frequently translates the root ש"שׂ.[138] Interestingly, this expression is also attested in the DSS as a derogatory name for the sect's opponents. In the section of CD mentioned above that deals with איש הלצון and דורשי החלקות, namely, the Pharisees, these opponents are also described as ויסיסו לריב עם ("joyful over dissension amidst the people").[139] In other words, Josephus's Hebrew source may have used inter-sectarian vocabulary, just like the rabbinic version.

Another dominant characteristic of sectarian discourse is recognizable in the *Qiddushin* baraita. As Aharon Shemesh has asserted: "If there is a single concept that characterizes the Qumran sect it is without a doubt the separatist world view to which they adhere and which—more than anything else—has shaped their way of life."[140] The sectarians portray themselves as a group that separated itself from the sinful multitude of Israel, and define this separation by the use of the Hebrew roots פר"ש,[141] סו"ר,[142] and especially בד"ל. The sectarians are commanded "to separate themselves (להבדל) from the sons of the pit,"[143] to "separate themselves (להבדל) from the congregation of the men of deceit,"[144] and they explain their departure to the desert as deriving from the same necessity: "they shall separate themselves (יבדלו) from the session of the men of deceit in order to depart into the wilderness."[145] The use of the same verb in the

---

[136] See e.g. the LXX of Prov 9:7, 8, 12.   [137] Prov 17:14.

[138] Isa 66:10, 14; Lam 1:21, 4:21.   [139] CD I, 21.

[140] Shemesh, "Origins of the Laws of Separatism," 224.

[141] MMT C, line 7 (DJD 10:58).

[142] CD VII, 12–13; VIII, 4, 16; XIV, 1; XIX, 17, 29; *Serek Hayahad* I, 2; *Melchizedek* (11Q13) II, 24.

[143] CD VI, 14–15. It is entirely possible that here too the author alludes to the Korah pericope. See the root בד"ל and the discussion above on its centrality to the Korah story, and the description of the wicked בני שחת, similar to the fate of the congregation of Korah.

[144] *Serek Hayahad* V, 1; see also line 10 (Charlesworth, *Dead Sea Scrolls*, 1:18–19, 22–3).

[145] *Serek Hayahad* VIII, 13. The root בד"ל is focal in sectarian works and carries additional meanings, such as the expulsion of a member from the sect, and halakhic distinctions between pure and impure, among others.

Janneus legend (ויבדלו),[146] this time with regard to the "sages of Israel," is probably not accidental.

Two additional roots in this tradition, both typical of biblical language but quite exceptional in the rabbinic corpus, are זע"ם and רמ"ס. Intriguingly, they both appear in the above-mentioned sectarian, polemical *Pesher Nahum*, where the root זע"ם describes the Pharisaic way of speech. The Pharisees, מתעי אפרים ("the misleaders of Ephraim"), are said to have caused "nobles and rulers" to fall בזעם לשונם ("by the fury of their tongue").[147] The root רמ"ס probably depicts the trampling of Jerusalem: אחר תרמס ("and afterwards it will be trampled").[148] This pesher engages themes strikingly similar to those addressed in the talmudic legend: King Janneus's military campaigns, his persecution of the Pharisees, the Pharisaic role in the breach between themselves and the king (the Pharisees being traitors and rebels, in the author's view), and harsh inter-sectarian polemic.[149] This comparison also shows that the talmudic legend uses terminology specific to the first-century BCE inter-sectarian polemic.

Another hint of the date of this story and its protagonist perhaps comes from the name of its anti-hero: Eleazar ben Po'ira. One possible identification is Eleazar ben Pachura, mentioned in the YT as a violent priest and a contemporary of John Hyrcanus,[150] as Graetz and others have noted.[151]

H. THE SOURCE OF THE LEGEND

Given the clearly pro-Pharisaic, anti-sectarian nature of the legend, how are we to account for its terminology, which reflects the archetypal discourse of sectarian polemic? In noting that "the sectarians were not alone in criticizing their opponents [and that] the rabbis were by no means indifferent to the 'exegetical methods' of their opponents," Aharon Shemesh and Cana Werman introduce several examples of the deliberate use of sectarian rhetoric by the rabbis. This explains the presence of some appellations and polemical key words in

---

[146] See above, text at n. 81.

[147] *Pesher Nahum*, 3–4 II, 9–10 (see text at n. 102). On the biblical source of this expression, see Kister, "Biblical Phrases," 32. Simcha Kogut suggests that the word בזעם alludes to Lam 2:6: וַיִּנְאַץ בְּזַעַם אַפּוֹ מֶלֶךְ וְכֹהֵן ("In His raging anger He has spurned King and priest"), and that the association of king and priest pointed to Janneus (oral communication).

[148] See Berrin, *Pesher Nahum*, 49 n. 47, 87, 120–2, 140–1.

[149] For a summation and detailed bibliography, see Horgan, *Pesharim*, 158–62. See also Berrin, *Pesher Nahum*, chaps. 4, 6, 8, and the appendix to chap. 5.

[150] Y. *Ma'as. Sh.* 5:9, 56d = y. *Sotah* 9:11, 24a. Intriguingly, there too he is accompanied by another protagonist—his brother?—named Yehudah ben Pachura (*Sotah*: פכורה; *Ma'as. Sh.*: פטירה [MS Leiden]; פחורה [Vatican 133]; פתירה [Venice printed edition]).

[151] Graetz, *Geschichte*, 3:688. See Lieberman, *Tosefta Ki-fshutah*, 8:748–9 and nn. 43–4; and the additional bibliographical references in Baumgarten, "Rabbinic Literature," 40 n. 94. This identification was apparently accepted by Gedalyahu Alon. See Alon, "Biqoret," 94–5.

sectarian works on the one hand, and in rabbinic sources on the other.[152] The same strategy is evident—but on a much larger scale—in our case too: the author deliberately used the rhetoric and derogatory language of his opponents. I do not suggest that he was necessarily aware of the Qumran literature specifically, but rather that he employed a shared network of vocabulary, arguments, strategies, and degrading nicknames that was current in the political disputes of Second Temple Jewish society. Their rivals named the Pharisees אנשי לצון, בליעל, עדת and the like, and our author used the very same insults to depict his Sadducean enemy: איש לץ רע ובליעל.

The Qumran sectarians considered themselves אנשי האמת עושי התורה ("the men of truth, those who observe the Torah"),[153] and the חכמי ("wise men") of Israel: "and he raised up from Aaron men of discernment (נבונים) and from Israel wise men (חכמים)."[154] Our author uses nearly the same terms to insist that the Pharisees were the real חכמי ישראל ("sages/wise men of Israel"). Whereas the sectarians boasted of their separation from Israel, our storyteller contends that the ones who separated themselves were the Pharisees, but that they, in contrast to their adversaries, did not depart from "the multitude of the people," but rather from the sinful minority groups, just as Moses and Aaron were instructed to separate themselves from the evil congregation of Korah.

But the author of the Janneus legend did not just borrow his opponents' terminology—he borrowed some features of their preferred genre too. As shown above, our legend is essentially a political, polemical midrash that projects biblical images and stories onto Second Temple events. It is, in this respect, strongly reminiscent of the pesher genre, in content if not in form. True, it does not contain explicit verse citations, nor does it use the terms typical of this genre, such as פשר הדבר and פשרו על ("its interpretation is").[155] It is a reasonable assumption that the Pharisees refrained from applying this exact style to their own writings. What I am suggesting is that the authors of this anti-sectarian, polemical piece deliberately imitated, perhaps parodied, features of their opponents' characteristic literary style.

As noted earlier, the legend aims to refute accusations directed at the Pharisees. Josephus's frame narrative and *Pesher Nahum* attest to the fact that the Pharisees were accused of inciting the masses against rulers and high priests, an accusation that resembles the deeds attributed to biblical Korah. As preserved in the Talmud, our legend responds by comparing the accusers to

---

[152] Shemesh and Werman, "Hidden Things," esp. 423–7. Citation at 423.

[153] *Pesher Habakkuk* VII, 10–11.   [154] CD VI, 2–3 (=4Q267 2, line 8; 4Q266 3 II, 10).

[155] Regarding the contradictory definitions of pesher and the scholarly debate on this issue, see Brooke, "Qumran Pesher," 483–503. It is not my intent to delve into this thorny issue but rather to note the general similarity between the rupture legend and Qumran pesher, just in terms of biblical allusions, political content, and exegetical nature; namely, the projection of the biblical story on actual events.

Korah and blaming *them* of incitement and instigation, both against the Hasmonean government and the Pharisees themselves.

I. THE LANGUAGE OF THE LEGEND

In order to substantiate my claim that the baraita has preserved a Pharisaic polemical piece, it is necessary to subject the language and terminology of the passage to closer examination. As mentioned earlier, alongside typical Rabbinic Hebrew, the baraita uses an exceptional, biblical style. Elsewhere I have categorized the linguistic phenomena in this legend according to Classical Biblical Hebrew (CBH), Late Biblical Hebrew (LBH), Qumran Hebrew (QH), and Mishnaic Hebrew (MH).[156] Discussed there in depth are the linguistic phenomena that support my contention; here I restrict myself to chosen linguistic phenomena and general conclusions.[157]

Essentially, our story can be defined as a linguistic hybrid. Classical biblical words, terms, and constructs are intermittently interwoven here into a post-biblical framework, replete with post-biblical, or at least post-exilic, words, phrases, ideas, and verbal forms, as well as some clearly MH forms.

The opening unit of the baraita (lines 1–5) displays the features of standard MH, with no biblical phenomena.[158] The six verbs found in this unit appear in normal past tense, without what is termed *waw* consecutive. Nonetheless, note that the *weqatal* form which recurs several times to denote a single action in the past (וכבש, וקרא, ואמר, והעלו, ואכלו) is post-classical, typical of LBH and QH, but not of MH, which uses the *qatal* form at the beginning of a sentence (as seen below: היה שם, הקים להם, אמר לו).

Only from line 6 do the above-mentioned biblical phenomena appear. This unit of the story opens with the string of descriptions of a biblical nature: איש לץ, רע ובליעל;[159] and its chain of *wayyiqtol* forms is unmatched in MH. On the other hand, alongside these verbs (ויהרגו, ותוצץ, ויבדלו, ויבוקש, ויאמר, ויאמר) we find verbs in regular past tense (אמר, החזיר, בא, היה, הקים). In juxtaposition to the biblical lexicon (רמסס, בזעם), we find some noteworthy phenomena that

---

[156] Noam, "Story of King Jannaeus," 54.
[157] I thank Yoel Elitzur, Noam Mizrahi, and Elisha Qimron for their generous assistance on linguistic matters.
[158] Most of the linguistic features in this section are also known from LBH and QH, but two phrases are unique to MH and are unknown earlier: (1) the opening…מעשה ב; (2) the root ח"ר, evidently an Aramaism, which, as opposed to the verb שב"ב, was common in MH but is never found in BH or QH. For greater detail and bibliography, see Noam, "Story of King Jannaeus," the section on "The Language of the Legend."
[159] For elaboration of the linguistic phenomena discussed below, see ibid.

are, on the one hand, later than CBH, but absent from MH; they are rather characteristic of LBH or QH. The formula והיה שם איש...ושמו... occurs in LBH and post-biblical works but is rare in MH. As used here, the verb הקם is totally absent from Scripture, but is found in Second Temple Hebrew and once or twice in MH.

Nonetheless, the baraita has later linguistic features characteristic of, and even unique to, MH: the phrases זקן אחד, ציץ בין עיניו/עיניך, כתר כהונה are typical of rabbinic literature. Nor does the Greek word הדיוט (ἰδιώτης) appear in pre-Mishnaic Hebrew. Also the use of the word כך, as opposed to biblical ככה, was renewed in MH. The combination of the participle with an auxiliary from the root היה to indicate past progressive (היו אומרים) typifies MH; it is, however, occasionally found in LBH and in the linguistic stratum of the temple period. Forms such as נשבית originated in MH and are unknown in earlier strata of Hebrew. The use of the active participle to note a future possibility in a conditional clause (אם אתה שומע) is also typical of MH. Interestingly, the dialogue ומה עשה? אמר לו: אם אתה שומע לעצתי רמסם is almost identical to the dialogue that appears in a different talmudic legend.[160] The expression מה י/תהא עליה/יו/יהם is frequent in rabbinic literature, especially the BT. The abbreviated future of הי"ה (יהא/תהא) was renewed in MH. The word הרי, the phrase קרן זוית, and the root חז"ר (החזיר את התורה) are unknown before MH. The word עולם functions in the legend in the meaning of "world", as in MH, and not as "eternity" in BH. The flowery phrase החזיר ליושנה is known from two additional contexts in rabbinic literature.

Scholarly attempts to divide the text into distinctive sections and to assign each section to a different period seem misdirected, since the allegedly "biblical" part of the text is also an inseparable mixture of early and late linguistic features. Many of these MH phenomena can be traced back into Second Temple times and also appear in LBH or in the DSS, whereas other occurrences are unique to LBH and are never found in MH. On the other hand, quite a few lexical and syntactical usages throughout the entire story are familiar only from rabbinic literature and never occur in any earlier extant context.

Clearly, the CBH forms do not reflect the authentic, natural style of the storyteller, who was unconsciously, but persistently, using late Hebrew. In other words, the language of the story clearly reflects an intentional, archaizing literary style, which employed classical biblical forms long after their use had ceased, as several scholars argue. Nonetheless, their argument that an archaizing style is a sign of deliberate rabbinic reworking is indefensible. The opposite is true. The rabbis purposely refrained from imitation of biblical language and attempted to make a clear stylistic distinction between the Written Law and the Oral Law as well: "The language of the Torah is distinct and so is the language

---

[160] מה אעשה? אמר לו, אם אתה שומע לעצתי גרשה (*b. Giṭ.* 58a; see Shoshany, "Carpenter's Apprentice," 92 n. 24).

of the Sages."[161] The total absence from the entire rabbinic corpus of *waw* consecutive and the CBH expressions and vocabulary that appear in our story well
illustrate this propensity. Moreover, even if we argue for its authenticity and
early date, namely, soon after the death of the historical King Janneus, we must
admit that the CBH features found in the story are an archaization, for CBH
was certainly not a living language during the first century BCE.

To which literary corpus, then, should we ascribe the linguistic mixture at
the core of this story? Until recently, the prevailing scholarly attitude characterized the Hebrew of the late biblical books and that of the DSS as reflecting a
transitional stage between CBH and MH. Therefore, most linguists regarded
the language of the scrolls as a mixture of these two types. The widely held
assumption was that the authors made a deliberate attempt to imitate CBH but
were unknowingly influenced by their own spoken language, probably an early
form of MH.[162] This impression has been gradually altered, enriched, and
refined, in line with a different approach that has emerged over the past two
decades. According to this approach, represented mainly by Elisha Qimron,
the Hebrew of the DSS should not be considered an artificial, transitional language, but rather a reflection of an independent spoken dialect of the Second
Temple period that contains features of both BH and MH, but also many
autonomous characteristics.[163]

Notwithstanding, these very same scholars still seem to argue that the linguistic register of the DSS is a literary one, leaning heavily on Scripture.[164]
Qimron describes "the clear influence of BH, expressed in the use of biblical
phraseology" and "elements that appear to be mechanical retroversions in BH,
or biblicizing forms of MH words and phrases." He recognizes a deliberate
"tendency of the Qumran texts to safeguard against vernacular features" and to
employ "another and higher genre," namely, "a biblicising [*sic*] jargon."[165] The

---

[161] B. *'Abod. Zar.* 58b according to MS New York, JTS, Rab. 15. Cf. *b. Ḥul.* 137b (MS Vatican
122): לשון תורה לעצמן, לשון חכמי' לעצמן ("The Torah uses its own language and the Sages their own").
Chaim Rabin ("Historical Background of Qumran Hebrew," 149–50) concluded: "The choice of
BH on the part of the Rabbis was, therefore, not a matter of necessity but an act of free will." On
possible reasons for the growth of MH, see e.g. Rabin, "Historical Background of Qumran
Hebrew"; idem, "Hebrew and Aramaic," 1015–18; Talshir, "Ha-Ivrit," 284–301, and the survey of
other opinions there. For another proposal for the origins of MH and a useful survey of earlier
approaches, see Rendsburg, "Galilean Background of Mishnaic Hebrew," 225–40.

[162] See e.g. the remarks by Moshe Bar-Asher (*Studies in Mishnaic Hebrew*, 1:126): "A language
that bridges Biblical Hebrew of the First Temple period and tannaitic Hebrew ... which is reflected
to some extent in late biblical books, Qumran scrolls, and early mishnayot." For a detailed review
of this position and its advocates, see Qimron, "Early Hebrew," 350–2.

[163] See Qimron, "Early Hebrew," 350–2; idem, "DSS Hebrew," 232–44. See also Muraoka,
"Hebrew," 1:344. For opposing positions, see Hurwitz, "Was QH a 'Spoken' Language?" 110–14;
Blau, "Conservative View," 20–5.

[164] See Muraoka, "Hebrew"; Qimron and Strugnell, *MMT*, 107.

[165] Qimron and Strugnell, *MMT*, 107. See also ibid. 73, 104, 108.

nature of LBH and Second Temple Hebrew has been described in scholarly literature as follows:

> Evidently late lexemes...occur side-by-side with their more ancient equivalents...and later syntax, such as the use of *we-qatal* to express single past actions, intermingles with earlier constructions (in this case *wayyiqtol*).[166] Such mixing may show that the authors were not dealing with one system of language, but with two: classical Hebrew as they knew it from the study of texts, and post-classical Hebrew, which was their natural medium of communication.[167]

This general description is eminently applicable to our source. This suggests that at the core of the Janneus legend in the Talmud there lies a passage of a Hebrew work characterized by the mixed nature of Second Temple Hebrew: a deliberate agglomerate of CBH on the one hand, and LBH on the other; early expressions alongside later ones; and even some linguistic features characteristic of the pre-Mishnaic Hebrew stratum. In fact, some very early scholarly opinions with regard to our text intuitively surmised the existence of such an intermediate, literary Hebrew and suggested a pre-rabbinic origin for the story, based specifically on its mixed, archaizing, and artificial style.[168]

However, this assumption does not fully account for the uniquely rabbinic features of the legend. One explanation for these features is perhaps the apparent Pharisaic provenance of this pro-Pharisaic tradition. As shown above, obviously this text did not emanate from a Qumranic context. It therefore might have used a dialect different than that of the DSS, one closer to the MH used in other contemporary Jewish circles.[169] Another likely explanation is that the text underwent some reworking by tannaitic transmitters,[170] while retaining its content and language. Thus, for example, it appears likely that the ending of the rabbinic legend ("All the Sages of Israel were massacred and the world was desolate until Simeon ben Shataḥ came and restored the Torah to its pristine [glory]"), which inserts the name of a known scholar into the political story, and uses mishnaic language,[171] belongs to a rabbinic reworking intended to underscore the king's cruelty.

---

[166] The reference is to the biblical book of Daniel, where *wayyiqtol* is used.

[167] Joosten, "Pseudo-Classicisms," 148–9.

[168] See the history of research above. The most prominent are Segal, *Dikduk*, 11–12; Rabin, "Historical Background of Qumran Hebrew," 371–3. Neusner ("Josephus' Pharisees," 285) surmised: "The Talmudic story is written in biblical, not mishnaic or rabbinic, Hebrew. In this respect one recalls the anachronistic, pseudo-archaic language of the Dead Sea Scrolls."

[169] See Qimron's postulation that the Pharisees living at the time of MMT, "apparently spoke a kind of MH" (*MMT*, 104).

[170] I tend to ascribe this reworking to the phase during which the Hebrew version was created, *before* the citation of the tradition in the talmudic sugya. In contrast to Kalmin (*Jewish Babylonia*, 58), I do not find any traces of Babylonian intervention in this text, except perhaps for the dialogue אם אתה שומע בעצתי...ומה אעשה, which, as noted, has a talmudic parallel. See n. 160.

[171] This sentence contains the word עולם in its post-biblical geographical meaning ('world'), not in its temporal biblical meaning "eternity". On the shift in meaning from Biblical Hebrew to

J. CONCLUSION

The legend of the rupture between the Pharisees and the Hasmonean regime has in all probability preserved a rare piece of a Pharisaic polemical work, as evidenced both by its style and content. The Hebrew version of the episode as preserved in the baraita is characterized by a unique mixed Hebrew, a random, artificial mosaic of biblical vocabulary and syntax in a later linguistic substratum typical of Second Commonwealth Jewish literature, which is unattested in later rabbinic literature.

Its literary and topical features are similarly incongruent in the context of rabbinic legend. This relates to the very appearance of the theme of the relationship between the Hasmonean dynasty and the Pharisees, the direct description of the nature of one of the protagonists, of emotions accompanying deeds, knowledge of Modiʿin as the place where the Hasmonean revolt started, the motif of "two crowns" as distinguished from that of "three crowns" that is developed in rabbinic literature, and the more positive portrayal of Janneus as opposed to rabbinic literature in general. Above all, the terminology used by the author, as well as the skillful integration of biblical allusions into the narrative to refer to current political situations, is typical of the inter-sectarian disputes familiar to us from the Dead Sea Scrolls.

In its Greek version as well, the legend is anomalous in the Josephan corpus. The figure of John Hyrcanus receives a much more negative portrayal than usual, the Pharisees a more positive portrayal, and different elements of the story contradict the surrounding sequential narrative.

Its major themes in both versions—namely, the image and status of the Pharisees, their relationship with the Hasmonean rulers, and the sectarian dispute—are shared by sectarian polemical works, placing the origins of the legend in the late Second Temple period. Its thrust is clearly pro-Pharisaic, aimed at refuting anti-Pharisaic rumors and arguments familiar to us from Second Temple literature, Josephus, and the Dead Sea Scrolls.

Various aspects of the story link it more directly to John Hyrcanus's or Janneus's day. The motif of the types of authority at the heart of the story (kingship,

Mishnaic Hebrew, see Friedman, "Transformation of עולם," 272–85; idem, "From Here to Eternity," 77–97. Friedman argues that there is no real precedent for the rabbinic use of עולם in the later sense (see "Transformation of עולם," 273). As opposed to biblical שו"ב, the root חז"ר was common in MH but is never found in BH or the DSS. See Segal, *Grammar of Mishnaic Hebrew*, 50 (§94.5); Bendavid, *Biblical Hebrew and Mishnaic Hebrew*, 131, 240, 364; Qimron and Strugnell, *MMT*, 87. The flowery phrase החזיר...ליושנה ("restored to its former status") is known from two other contexts in rabbinic literature: *y. Ber.* 7:3, 11c = *y. Meg.* 3:8, 74c; *b. Yoma* 69b, all parallels of the same tradition. See also *b. Ketub.* 8b.

priesthood, [Torah]) is characteristic of the political discourse in the context of John Hyrcanus's rule, and was used both by his supporters (Josephus) and his adversaries (4QTestimonia). Also the epithet איש אחד בליעל is known from his period and may refer to Hyrcanus in a Qumran document. To this we can perhaps add the possible identity of the name of the protagonist in the baraita and a figure with the same name from Hyrcanus's day, mentioned in an obscure tradition in the YT.[172]

All our knowledge of the Pharisees is second-hand, drawn from testimony by other, sometimes hostile, groups and from later sources in rabbinic literature.[173] If we found a fragment of an authentic Pharisaic document in some cave, this would constitute an invaluable, exciting discovery. The story of the rupture between the Pharisees and the Hasmoneans is precisely such a source.[174] It was, however, not preserved in a cave but in two distinct literary corpora.

One is an early historical narrative; the other, a late reservoir of miscellaneous Jewish sources. The advantages of the first, Josephan corpus inhere in its earlier date, greater historical proximity to the circumstances, and the realism, accuracy, and historical awareness of its account. On the other hand, the ancient source was here preserved in a foreign language, thereby erasing its unique linguistic features and the biblical allusions that shed light on its date and purpose. As for the second corpus, the Babylonian Talmud, this source is there inserted arbitrarily, almost incidentally, into a clearly ahistorical context. Nonetheless, its great advantage is that, as preserved there, this gem miraculously remained close to its conjectured original form, in spite of the slight adaptations intended to underscore Janneus's cruelty. However, the two contexts in which this document is implanted are less essential for its comprehension than we might expect. They are the equivalents of the metaphorical silent cave in which an ancient Pharisaic text could have been discovered. Like the Dead Sea Scrolls, both versions of this text reflect the turbulent social climate of the closing centuries of the Second Temple period, but provide a genuine glimpse of the missing Pharisaic perspective.

The episode considered in the next chapter is in many respects the continuation of the present story. Following the description of the moment of the

---

[172] See above, text at n. 150. I find it difficult to accept Efron's proposal ("Simeon Ben Shatah and Jannaeus," 179–80) that the author of this legend knew this unique, obscure legend in the YT and deliberately altered the protagonist's name and inserted it here.

[173] See Rivkin, "Defining the Pharisees," 205.

[174] Along with the story of Janneus's instructions to his wife, according to my supposition (see Chap. 5).

rupture between the Hasmoneans and the Pharisees—and the people in their wake—we move to a stage of open hostility toward the Hasmonean ruler on the people's part. In this story as well we meet different versions and different protagonists: Josephus recounts a story involving Janneus; the rabbis a story involving an unnamed priest.[175]

---

[175] A previous version of this chapter appeared in Vered Noam, "The Story of King Jannaeus (*b. Qiddushin* 66a): A Pharisaic Reply to Sectarian Polemic," *Harvard Theological Review* 107 (2014): 31–58.

4

Alexander Janneus/The Priest Who Was
Pelted with Citrons

The two traditions treated in this chapter recount the story of a priest who was pelted with citrons in the temple on the festival of Sukkot. They differ, however, as to the identity of the priest and what sparked the citron-throwers' anger. In Josephus we find a known historical figure, Janneus, and the backdrop is a political rebellion. In the rabbinic corpus the priest is an anonymous Boethusian/Sadducee, and the backdrop is halakhic.

In the contemporary literature—the Dead Sea Scrolls, Josephus, and the rabbinic corpus—the figure of Janneus is enmeshed in a web of conflict. Janneus, whose leading role in the rabbinic version of the rupture legend was treated in the previous chapter, is featured in the Josephan version in this chapter and again in both the Josephan and the rabbinic versions of the episode examined in the next chapter.

Consideration of the Josephan account of the citron-pelting incident deconstructs the prima facie impression of a single, homogenous tradition. It appears that here, as in other instances discussed in this book, Josephus adroitly interwove several "Jewish" traditions into his narrative. One of these traditions ostensibly has a parallel in rabbinic literature; however, the relationship between the stories is not clear. In examining the relationship between these two narratives, this chapter explores not only its ramifications for the Josephan appraisal of the figure of Janneus, but also uses it as a test case for evaluating the overall phenomenon of Josephan–rabbinic parallels.

A. THE SOURCES

Antiquities 13.372–4; *m. Sukkah* 4:9; *t. Sukkah* 3:16 (=*b. Sukkah* 48b)

Josephus, *Antiquities* 13.372–4

(372) As for Alexander, his own people revolted (στασιασάντων) against him—for the nation was aroused against him—at the celebration of the festival

($\tau\hat{\eta}s$ $\dot{\epsilon}o\rho\tau\hat{\eta}s$),[1] and as he stood beside the altar and was about to sacrifice, they pelted him with citrons, it being a custom among the Jews that at the festival of Tabernacles everyone holds wands made of palm branches and citrons— these we have described elsewhere ($\delta\epsilon\delta\eta\lambda\dot{\omega}\kappa\alpha\mu\epsilon\nu$ $\delta\dot{\epsilon}$ $\kappa\alpha\dot{\iota}$ $\tau\alpha\hat{\upsilon}\tau\alpha$ $\dot{\epsilon}\nu$ $\ddot{\alpha}\lambda\lambda o\iota s$); and they added insult to injury by saying that he was descended from captives ($\dot{\epsilon}\xi$ $\alpha\dot{\iota}\chi\mu\alpha\lambda\dot{\omega}\tau\omega\nu$)[2] and was unfit to hold office and to sacrifice ($\tau o\hat{\upsilon}$ $\theta\dot{\upsilon}\epsilon\iota\nu$); (373) and being enraged at this ($\dot{o}\rho\gamma\iota\sigma\theta\epsilon\dot{\iota}s$), he killed some six thousand of them, and also placed a wooden barrier about the altar and the temple as far as the coping (of the court) which the priests alone were permitted to enter, and by this means blocked the people's way to him. (374) He also maintained foreign troops of Pisidians and Cilicians, for he could not use Syrians, being at war with them.

Rabbinic Sources

M. Sukkah 4:8[3]

ניסוך המים שבעה כיצד [...] ולמנסך אומרין לו הגבה את ידך שפעם אחת ניסך על רגליו ורגמוהו כל העם באתרוגיהם.

The water libation, seven days: how so? [...] And to the one who pours out the water libation they say, "Lift up your hand!" For one time [one priest] poured out the water on his feet, and all the people pelted him with their citrons.

T. Sukkah 3:16[4]

... שכבר היה מעשה בביתסי[5] אחד[6] שניסך על רגליו ורגמוהו כל העם באתרוגיהן, ונפגמה קרנו של מזבח ובטלה עבודה בו ביום, עד שהביאו גוש אחד של מלח ונתנו עליו, כדי שלא יראה מזבח פגום, שכל מזבח שאין לו לא קרן, ולא כבש, ולא יסוד, פסול. ר' יוסה בי ר' יהודה אומ' אף הסובב.

---

[1] The manuscripts read "the festival" $\tau\hat{\eta}s$ $\dot{\epsilon}o\rho\tau\hat{\eta}s$ (P, E "festival": $\dot{\epsilon}o\rho\tau\hat{\eta}s$), without specifying its name. See Marcus, *Jewish Antiquities* (LCL), 7:413, note *d*, where he notes that the term " '*the* festival' would correspond exactly to the rabbinic Heb. term *he-ḥag*, indicating the festival of Tabernacles as *the* festival *par excellence*." See also Rubenstein, *Sukkot*, 82. The Latin specifies the name of the festival: "*festivitas tabernaculorum*."

[2] Literally, "from captives": the word $\alpha\dot{\iota}\chi\mu\alpha\lambda\dot{\omega}\tau\omega\nu$ can be either masc. or fem. plural. VFP $\alpha\dot{\iota}\chi\mu\dot{\alpha}\lambda\omega\tau o\nu$ ("born...a captive"—evidently a mistake, since Janneus was not born a captive). Latin: *de captiva* (fem., i.e. "from a female captive").

[3] According to MS Kaufmann A 50.

[4] This story from the Tosefta is quoted, with minor variations, in *b. Sukkah* 48b, and alluded to in *y. Sukkah* 4:8, 54d = *y. Yoma* 1:5, 39a, which also contains a parallel to the ending of the toseftan halakhah, though the anecdote of the pelting with citrons is not cited. I note only one major textual variant in the BT version, which is pertinent to the discussion below.

[5] בביתסי] thus MS Vienna (ONB, Cod. Hebr. 20); Erfurt, Evangelisches Ministerium, Or. 2° 1220; בביתוסי London, BL, Add. 27296; *editio princeps*.

[6] שכבר היה מעשה בביתסי אחד] "It once happened that one Boethusian." *B. Sukkah* 48b: ת"ר מעשה בצדוקי אחד ("Our rabbis taught, it once happened that one Sadducee...").

...For there already was the case of one Boethusian who poured out the water on his feet, and all the people pelted him with their citrons, and the horn of the altar was damaged, so the sacred service was cancelled for that day, until they brought a lump of salt and put it on it, so that the altar should not appear to be damaged. For any altar lacking a horn, ramp, or foundation is invalid. R. Yosé b. R. Yehudah says, "Also the rim."

B. HISTORICAL BACKGROUND

Alexander Janneus, son of John Hyrcanus I and grandson of Simeon the Hasmonean, ruled Hasmonean Judea from 103 to 76 BCE. Known in Hebrew as Yehonathan/Yonathan (as seen from the coins he minted, and a Qumran document), the name Yannai found in the rabbinic corpus is the Aramaic, or abbreviated, form of this name. Janneus acceded to the throne in 103 BCE (*Ant.* 13.320–3; *War* 1.85) following the death of his older brother, Aristobulus I, who ruled for only a year (*Ant.* 13.301–19; *War* 1.70–84). Taking advantage of internal dissension in the Seleucid kingdom on the one hand, and in Egypt on the other, Janneus engaged in wars of conquest, and it was during his reign that the Hasmonean kingdom reached its greatest territorial extent (*Ant.* 13.395–7).

Janneus undertook a long campaign against Ptolemy IX Lathyros, the son and enemy of Cleopatra III of Egypt, to whom the residents of Acre (Ptolemais) turned for assistance when Janneus threatened to capture the city. Following successful campaigns in Transjordan, Janneus completed the Hasmonean conquest of the coastal region, from the Carmel to the Egyptian border, with the exception of Ascalon (Ashkelon) (*Ant.* 13.324–64; *War* 1.86–7).

The late nineties and eighties of the first century BCE saw Janneus entangled in both internal and external conflicts. Internally, Janneus faced widespread rebellion by broad sectors of the Jewish public. According to the Josephan account, in the course of quashing the revolt with the assistance of mercenaries from Asia Minor, Janneus killed 6,000 of his opponents (*Ant.* 13.372–4; *War* 1.88–9). It is this event that forms the backdrop to the episode analyzed in this chapter. Externally, Janneus was at this time also involved in conflict with the neighboring powers to the east and to the north.

In 94/93 BCE Janneus attacked the Nabateans, but lost his entire army to an ambush in the Golan. This defeat brought renewed internal opposition in its wake, and Janneus murdered many of his opponents during a six-year period of unrest. They in turn requested assistance from the Seleucid ruler Demetrius III, who ruled from Damascus. Demetrius brought forces to the Shechem region, and civil war ensued between Janneus and his Jewish supporters, aided by foreign mercenaries, and the Jewish rebels backed by Demetrius's army. Although Demetrius scored a victory, threats to the stability of his rule in Syria made him leave the area; subsequently, many of Janneus's former enemies rejoined his ranks. Others, who continued to oppose him, were subjected to the cruel punishment of death by crucifixion (*Ant.* 13.374–83; *War* 1.90–8).

After overcoming this internal crisis, Janneus set off on a new campaign of conquest in the final years of his reign (79–76 BCE), defeating the Nabateans and their king Aretas III in East Transjordan and penetrating the cities of the Decapolis in Transjordan and the Golan. He died of illness in 76 BCE, while besieging the Ragaba fort in Transjordan (*Ant.* 13.392–4, 398–404; *War* 1.103–6), and was succeeded by his wife Alexandra (Shelamzion).[7]

The stormy events of Janneus's reign are reflected in Second Temple literature. *Pesher Nahum* terms King Janneus כפיר החרון ("lion of wrath") and describes his great cruelty toward, and persecution of, דורשי החלקות, namely the Pharisees, who invited "[Deme]trius, King of Greece" to oppose him. Like Josephus, this text mentions Janneus's vengeful actions: "he would hang men up alive [on a tree]."[8] Additional Qumran pesharim perhaps also refer to Janneus's behavior: כפיר החרון appears in *Hosea Pesher 2* (4Q167=4QpHos^b), and it too describes the smiting of the Pharisees, there termed Ephraim, by the כהן אחרון ("last priest"), namely, Janneus.[9] *Isaiah Pesher A* (4Q161=4QpIsa^a) has preserved a pericope that interprets Isaiah 10:28–34, the description of Sennacherib's Judean campaign,[10] regarding an enemy "who goes up from the Valley of Acco to fight against Phil[istia...]"; some interpret this as Ptolemy Lathyros coming to engage Janneus in battle.[11]

Apart from *Pesher Nahum*, which attests to harsh criticism of Janneus by the sectarians, a text sympathetic to this king was also found at Qumran. A fragment of a leather scroll from Cave 4 contains passages from a prayer for the welfare of "King Yonathan," and with him, the people of Israel. The scroll may allude to a campaign in which King Yonathan received divine aid, but this interpretation depends on doubtful readings and reconstructions. The editors of the fragment note that in content, which is favorable to Janneus and the Hasmonean kingdom, and in language too, this text does not display the typical hostility of the Qumran sectarians toward the Hasmonean regime and the high priesthood; this suggests that this text originated in circles outside the Qumran sect and found its way to Qumran.[12]

---

[7] See Chap. 5.

[8] *Pesher Nahum*, 3–4 I, 1–8. See Flusser, "Pesher Nahum," 214–57. For a critical edition of, and commentary on, this work, see Berrin, *Pesher Nahum*. For a topical summary and bibliography, see Horgan, *Pesharim*, 158–62. For more comprehensive consideration of the historical allusions in the pesher and earlier scholarship, see H. Eshel, *Dead Sea Scrolls and the Hasmonean State*, 117–31.

[9] H. Eshel, *Dead Sea Scrolls and the Hasmonean State*, 130–1 and the bibliography cited there.

[10] For a discussion of this chapter from Isaiah and its application to Second Temple-period events, see Chap. 1, section C.

[11] See the discussion in H. Eshel, *Dead Sea Scrolls and the Hasmonean State*, 97–100.

[12] For a more comprehensive treatment, see ibid. 101–15.

Additional evidence regarding Alexander Janneus's reign comes from his coins, the most numerous of all extant Second Temple Jewish coins. Imprinted with different inscriptions—in Hebrew, Aramaic, and Greek—and varied devices, some bear the Greek inscription *ΒΑΣΙΛΕΩΣ ΑΛΕΞΑΝΔΡΟΥ* on one side and יהונתן המלך on the other. Many are imprinted with the symbol of a star inside a diadem with the legend יהונתן המלך placed between the rays. A special group of coins is imprinted with the legend ינתן הכהן הגדל וחבר יהדם ("Yonathan the high priest and the *ḥbr* of the Jews"); underneath it traces of an erased legend are visible: יהונתן המלך. Some maintain that Janneus erased the title "king" from his coins for a certain time under Pharisaic pressure.[13] Nahman Avigad has published two bullae that mention Janneus: one bears the legend יהונתן מלך; the other 'ינתן כהן גדל ירשלם מ.[14]

An allusion to an event related to Janneus's day also appears in *Megillat Ta'anit*. Listed among the festive days is "On the fourteenth of Sivan, Sher Tower [= Straton's Tower, later Caesarea] was captured."[15] According to *Ant.* 13.324, 335, Janneus annexed this city to the Hasmonean kingdom. It is noteworthy that, as opposed to later, classical rabbinic sources, this allusion to Janneus's deeds in *Megillat Ta'anit* has a positive tenor. Elsewhere in *Megillat Ta'anit* we find a less favorable, albeit conjectural reference: "On the twenty-third of Marheshvan the *soreg* (latticed partition) was torn down from the [temple's] courtyard."[16] Uzi Leibner has suggested that this description of what was seen as a happy event refers to the supposed destruction of the barrier erected by Janneus, following his death.[17]

As opposed to the vague allusion in the Scroll itself, and in contradistinction to its positive bent, Janneus receives explicit—and denunciative—mention in the Scholion, the later commentary on *Megillat Ta'anit*. Another event mentioned there is: "the gentiles rose up against the remnant of the scribes in the city of Chalcis in the House of Zabdi, and a salvation occurred."[18] Scholion O identifies the protagonists of this story as individuals who fled to "Syria" because of persecution by Janneus.[19] Another event from the scroll: "the 'Kenishta' took its seat for judgment," is explained in both Scholia as a Pharisaic victory over the Sadducees in the Sanhedrin; according to Scholion O this took

---

[13] For more on Janneus's coins, see Meshorer, *Treasury of Jewish Coins*, 37–41, 209–18, 301–15. See Chap. 3, text at n. 70.

[14] See Avigad, "Bulla of Jonathan the High Priest," 8–12; idem, "Bulla of King Jonathan," 245–6.

[15] Noam, *Megillat Ta'anit*, 44, 68, 193–5.

[16] See ibid. 45 (and the variants cited in the apparatus), 95–6, 239–42. For another textual variant of the event and its scholion in a recently discovered manuscript, see Rosenthal, "Newly Discovered Leaf," 362, 366, 389–92. Translations of the text cited from Noam, "Scroll of Fasting," 343.

[17] Leibner, "23rd Day of Heshvan," 5–17.

[18] Translation cited from Noam, "Scroll of Fasting," 344, here and below.

[19] Noam, *Megillat Ta'anit*, 122–3, 306–8.

place "in the days of King Janneus and Queen Shalzion (*sic*)."[20] The date 2 Shevat, not explained in the scroll itself, is attributed by both Scholia to the death of Janneus. Scholion P here cites a legend regarding a plot by Janneus to have the elders killed following his death, an episode related by Josephus in connection with Herod.[21]

Note the discrepancy between the ancient work and the later Scholion here. The only event almost definitely related to Janneus in *Megillat Ta'anit* is the conquest of Strato's Tower; thus, Janneus's victory and the territorial expansion of his kingdom are viewed positively and even declared a half-holiday. But, in the Scholion, the references to Janneus are always couched in negative terms: as the ally of the Sadducees in the Sanhedrin, as persecuting the righteous who were miraculously saved in Lebanon, and as plotting to murder the sages, to the extent that a holiday was declared in honor of this evil person's death. This difference between *Megillat Ta'anit*, whose origins lie in temple times, and its commentary, which represents the world of the rabbis, typifies the negative downturn in Janneus's image in Pharisaic/rabbinic circles.[22] Earlier, in Chapter 3, we saw a disparity between the more favorable portrayal of Janneus in the story of the rupture between Janneus and the Pharisees—an ancient story that originated in temple times—and its adaptation in classic rabbinic literature.

Janneus receives fairly frequent mention in the rabbinic corpus, in amoraic literature and the BT in particular.[23] In his rabbinic version he is often portrayed as an enemy, and even a murderer, of the sages.[24] Thus, as mentioned above, according to Scholion P on 2 Shevat he conspires to have "the elders of Israel" executed following his death, a scheme eventually thwarted by his wife Shelamzion (Josephus relates the same tale of Herod and his sister Salome), and his persecutions force other elders to flee to Lebanon.[25] Other legends tend to place his wife at his side, opposing the royal pair to the leader of the rabbis, Simeon ben Shataḥ, who is identified as the king's brother-in-law, namely, his wife's brother, in some of the stories. One series of legends recounts amusing anecdotes regarding clashes between the king and Simeon ben Shataḥ, in which the rabbi always has the upper hand; in others, the sage acts against the backdrop of the king's activities, without engaging him in direct conflict. Thus,

---

[20] Ibid. 107–9, 277–9.

[21] Ibid. 109–10, 280–2. See Ilan and Noam, "The Plot and Death of Herod/Jannaeus," 429–50.

[22] Although Tal Ilan's study has shown that this negative image, at least in the BT, is less sweeping than generally presumed in the scholarship. See Ilan, "King Jannaeus in the Babylonian Talmud."

[23] For a detailed analysis of these traditions, see Efron, "Simeon Ben Shataḥ and Jannaeus," 143–218; Noam, "Agrippa/Jannaeus and the Nazirites' Offerings," 493–507. My viewpoint is not always in agreement with that of Efron; see each individual chapter.

[24] See Chap. 3.

[25] See Ilan and Noam, "The Plot and Death of Herod/Jannaeus"; Scholion O, 17 Adar. See also *b. Sotah* 47a (=*b. Sanh.* 107b).

Simeon ben Shataḥ deviously makes Janneus contribute toward the sacrificial offerings of poor Nazirites; wins a verbal contest at a shared meal; eats against Janneus's will or drinks from his cup (*y. Ber.* 7:2, 11b = *y. Naz.* 8:3, 54b, and parallels in aggadic midrash; cf. *b. Ber.* 48a); judges Janneus in his court, and acts fearlessly and without bias (*b. Sanh.* 19a). It was Simeon ben Shataḥ who established Pharisaic hegemony in the Sanhedrin and ousted the Sadducees during Janneus's reign (both Scholia to *Meg. Ta'an.*, 28 Tevet)[26]; who restored the Torah after Janneus killed the sages of Israel (see Chapter. 3); and who called for Yehoshua ben Peraḥiah to return to Jerusalem after the latter fled to Alexandria for fear of Janneus (*b. Sotah* 47a; *b. Sanh.* 107b).[27] The presence of some of these traditions in Josephus, albeit with regard to other historical figures and in different circumstances,[28] indicates that most of them derive from the Second Temple period.

In addition to the above-mentioned group of stories, various strange traditions were appended to Janneus, some of which are incongruent with the historical biography of this figure.[29] One tale has Janneus appointing Yehoshua ben Gamala, who lived at the time of the destruction of the temple (!) as high priest in exchange for a bribe (*b. Yoma* 18a=*b. Yeb.* 61a), and supposedly living in Jesus's day (*b. Sotah* 47a; *b. Sanh.* 107b).[30] Similarly, the BT provides in one tradition hyperbolic descriptions of the fertility and population of the "sixty thousand cities," and in another, of one city, or one tree, that King Janneus possessed in the "king's mountain" (*b. Ber.* 44a; *b. Git.* 57a).[31] The vagueness of this Hasmonean king's personality and era for the rabbis is evident in the dispute between Abaye and Raba as to whether "Yoḥanan is the same as Yannai" or perhaps "Yoḥanan and Yannai are different persons" (*b. Ber.* 29a).

It appears, then, that we can chart a three-stage process in the shifting attitude toward Janneus in Pharisaic-rabbinic circles: in stage one *Megillat Ta'anit*

[26] The same episode is cited in both Scholia and Simeon ben Shataḥ is the hero of both, but only Scholion O explicitly mentions Janneus and his wife.

[27] On this episode, into which the figure of Jesus is anachronistically inserted, see Schäfer, *Jesus in the Talmud*, 34–40. For the parallel in the YT, which does not mention Janneus, see Efron, "Simeon Ben Shataḥ and Jannaeus," 154–61, and below.

[28] For a possible parallel to the Nazirites' story, see the story of Agrippa and the Nazirites (*Ant.* 19:294; 330–4). For a parallel to the trial of Janneus, see Herod's trial in *War* 1.203–5, 208–11; *Ant.* 14.158–60, 163–84; and Ilan "The Trial of Herod/Jannaeus," 349–72; Noam, "Agrippa/Jannaeus and the Nazirites' Offerings."

[29] For indirect allusions to Janneus, see the anecdotes "the daughter of King Yannai's wreathmaker" (*b. B. Bat.* 133b), "palace of King Yannai" (*b. 'Abod. Zar.* 50a).

[30] To this list we must ostensibly add the tradition of Janneus cutting off the hands of a high priest named Issachar of Kefar Barkai, who gave what was regarded as an inappropriate reply to Janneus and his wife (*b. Ker.* 28b); see Fisch, "The Brazenness of the High Priests," 526–43. However, Tal Ilan has shown that Janneus's name is a late addition to this tradition (see "King Jannaeus in the Babylonian Talmud").

[31] On a parallel to this tradition in the YT, that does not explicitly mention Janneus, and a hypothesis regarding its development, see Efron, "Simeon Ben Shataḥ and Jannaeus," 203–6. On the nature and origins of these traditions, see Shahar, "*Har Hamelekh*," 275–306.

still celebrates the victory of a successful, admired Hasmonean king, who enlarges the kingdom's territorial borders. In stage two, despite the fact that the Janneus legends studied in this book (as quoted in Josephus and rabbinic literature) describe the deterioration of the relationship between Janneus and the Pharisees from the Pharisaic perspective, nonetheless they still try to frame him positively, assigning responsibility for the rupture to a third party (see Chaps. 3 and 5). Rabbinic literature, the Talmud, but mainly the Scholion, represents the third stage, in which Janneus is transformed into an archetypically evil king. Evidently, the disputed evaluation of Janneus's figure was not just diachronic, as evidenced by these three stages within a distinct Jewish coterie, but also synchronic, across the various Second Temple-period circles as attested by *Pesher Nahum* on the one hand, and the prayer for King Yonathan's welfare on the other.

C. THE TRADITION IN THE JOSEPHAN CONTEXT

In *Antiquities*, Josephus integrates the story of Alexander Janneus being pelted by citrons into his account of this king's reign. This particular story (along with some other units found in this account) is missing, however, from the parallel narrative in *War*. Table 4.1 compares the relevant units in the two narratives.

This comparison of *War* and *Antiquities* reveals an essentially identical narrative sequence: Janneus's Transjordanian conquests; the taking of the coastal cities of Raphia, Anthedon, and Gaza; the Jewish rebellion and the killing of 6,000 Jews in response; the existence of a mercenary army; and the subduing of the residents of Gilead and Moab. In addition to topical similarity, the accounts share close language. There are, however, several main differences between the accounts. These include, first of all, the length of the description of the conquest of Gaza. Briefly narrated in *War* 1.87, in *Ant.* 13.358–64 it is described over seven sections, and Josephus notes that the campaign lasted a year (364).[32] A second significant difference between the accounts is the addition of a seven-section-long passage (365–71) in *Antiquities* that describes the fratricidal wars, and changes of regime, in the contemporary Seleucid kingdom. The scholarship has long noted that this unit, which does not mention Judea and breaks the sequence of events concerning Janneus, was taken from a Hellenistic source—most probably Strabo—and interpolated here. Two characteristic features of interpolation are found here: the unit opens with "about

---

[32] Menahem Stern ("Nicolaus of Damascus," 461–2) has suggested that this expansive description, which is biased in favor of the Gazans, was drawn from Nicolaus of Damascus. D. R. Schwartz ("Josephus' Source on Agrippa II," 250 n. 31) proposed that, when writing *War*, Josephus distilled Nicolaus's account, whereas in *Antiquities* he copied it out at length.

Table 4.1. Comparison of *War* and *Antiquities*

	War 1		*Antiquities* 13
86	The conquest of Gadara and Amathus in Transjordan.	356	The conquest of Gadara and Amathus in Transjordan.
87	Theodorus, son of Zenon, keeps the treasures of Amathus; he kills 10,000 Jews and plunders Alexander's baggage.		Theodorus, son of Zenon, keeps the treasures of Amathus; he kills 10,000 Jews and plunders Alexander's baggage.
	Janneus takes Gaza, Raphia, and Anthedon.	357	Janneus takes Raphia and Anthedon.
		358–64	Detailed description of the year-long conquest of Gaza.
		365–71	Seleucid fratricidal wars.
88	"... *the Jewish populace rose in revolt against him at one of the festivals;* (ἐπανίσταται τὸ Ἰουδαϊκὸν ἐν ἑορτῇ)	372	"... his own people revolted against him —the nation was aroused against him—at the celebration of the festival," (ἐπανέστη γὰρ αὐτῷ τὸ ἔθνος τῆς ἑορτῆς ἀγομένης)
	For it is on these festive occasions that sedition is most apt to break out"		
			the pelting with citrons when he was about to sacrifice;
			they also said that he was descended from captives and unfit to sacrifice.
		373	"and being enraged at this, he killed some six thousand of them
			and also placed a wooden barrier about the altar and the temple..."
	Janneus quells the uprising with his mercenaries, natives of Pisidia and Cilicia (but not of Syria).	374	Janneus maintains foreign troops of Pisidians and Cilicians (but does not use Syrians).
89	Janneus kills some 6,000 of the insurgents.		
	Janneus subdues the people of Galaad and Moab; imposes tribute on them and razes Amathus.		He subdues the Arabs of Moab and Galaaditis, forcing them to pay tribute and demolishes Amathus.

this same time" (365), and ends with an unrealized reference: "as has been related elsewhere" (371).[33] The third difference pertains to our story. *War* 1.88–9 describes a Jewish uprising against Janneus during the festival and its suppression by mercenaries. The hostile comment regarding the Jews—"for it is on

[33] On unrealized references as signifying interpolations in Josephus, see D. R. Schwartz, "Josephus' Source on Agrippa II," 249–50 and the bibliographical references to earlier literature in n. 30 there. Another reference in our unit is the one regarding the Jewish custom of taking lulavim and ethrogim on Sukkot (372), but this one is realized elsewhere; see *Ant.* 3.245 and below.

these festive occasions that sedition is most apt to break out" (*War* 1.88)—probably indicates a non-Jewish source for this section, most likely Nicolaus of Damascus,[34] which served as Josephus's main source for the history of the Hasmonean kingdom.[35] But in the parallel in *Antiquities* (13.372–4), this comment has been omitted, and the story of the pelting of Janneus with citrons on the festival and his defamation as the descendant of captives has been juxtaposed to the description of the uprising. The structure of the unit in *Antiquities* can be outlined as follows:

1. An uprising against Janneus takes place on the festival.

2. Janneus is pelted with citrons while sacrificing in the temple.

3. Insulting remarks are made regarding Janneus's ancestry and fitness for the priesthood.

4. Janneus kills 6,000 Jews.

5. Janneus erects a wooden barrier in the temple.

6. Janneus retains a mercenary army.

The units of the story shift between political-military events: the uprising, its suppression, and the formation of a mercenary force (1, 4, 6)—and internal Jewish temple anecdotes:[36] sacrifice in the temple, the throwing of citrons, the questioning of Janneus's qualifications for the priesthood, and the building of a barrier in the temple (2, 3, 5). Only the "military" units have parallels in the earlier narrative in *War*. Whereas in *War* it is the mercenaries who suppress the revolt, in *Antiquities* no reference is made to their involvement in quashing the revolt; nor do the mercenaries take any other actions.

Structurally, this indicates that, in *Antiquities*, Josephus integrated "temple" units from internal Jewish stories into a narrative drawn from Nicolaus. The artificial combination of the uprising that took place on the festival (described in *War* 1.88 using the verb ἐπανίστημι and the noun στάσις; cf. *Ant.* 13.372) with the somewhat ridiculous event of citron-throwing in the temple—the "Jewish" addition in *Antiquities*—transformed the uprising from a violent event into an amusing anecdote, making the involvement of the mercenary forces superfluous and the killing of 6,000 Jews incomprehensible.[37] Accordingly, in *Antiquities* Josephus was forced to detach the mercenaries from the story of the uprising

---

[34] See Efron, "Simeon Ben Shataḥ and Jannaeus," 167–70.

[35] See "Introduction," n. 9 and section D: "Approaches to Josephus and His Sources."

[36] For the halakhic ramifications of this description regarding the use of the four species, see Rubenstein, *Sukkot*, 82.

[37] Halevy (*Dorot ha-rishonim*, vol. 1, pt. 3, p. 481) postulates that the version in *Antiquities* is the correct one, and that the people did not rebel but engaged in a harmless, spontaneous uprising in response to Janneus's provocative actions in the temple, whereas the version in *War* was written from a hostile Sadducean perspective and libelously accused the people of starting a rebellion that never took place in order to justify Janneus's subsequent cruelty.

and to treat them separately, and to preface the killing of the Jews with the unconvincing explanation that Janneus was "enraged" (ὀργισθείς, 373) because of the insults uttered in the temple. Once again, I note the existence in this instance as well of signs indicating the Josephan interpolation of internal Jewish traditions found only in *Antiquities*, but not in *War*.

The manner in which these units were interpolated into the narrative here and its outcome are very similar to what we saw for *Antiquities* 13.288–99, the rupture with the Pharisees. As demonstrated in Chapter 3, that Josephan passage also treats a rebellion (στάσις—see *War* 1.67; cf. *Ant.* 13.288). There too Josephus interpolates a Jewish legend dealing with insults and misunderstandings (*Ant.* 13.288–96). But, because no violent steps were taken, there too Josephus was forced to omit the sentence describing the war instigated by these opponents ("until the smouldering flames burst out into open war [φανερὸν πόλεμον] and the rebels were defeated," *War* 1.67) from the original narrative. In *Antiquities* the opponents' zeal led to the events at the feast and the rupture with the Pharisees, but not to open war.[38]

As preserved in *Antiquities*, the Josephan sequence conveys the impression that Janneus was pelted with citrons because the crowd questioned his ancestry ("they pelted him with citrons... and added insult to injury by saying that he was descended from captives," 372).[39] However, a closer look at the text shows this impression to be mistaken. This text actually contains a double interpolation, of two different traditions. One recounts the episode of the citrons and ends with the reference (δεδηλώκαμεν δὲ καὶ ταῦτα ἐν ἄλλοις, "these we have described elsewhere," 372), which signals the ending of an interpolation in Josephus.[40] The other, which opens with the words "and they added" recounts the questioning of Janneus's lineage and qualifications for the priesthood. Indeed, the story of the possible captivity of a ruler's mother or a ruler's descent from captives is an independent Jewish tradition, separate and apart from the story of the citrons. In recounting the rupture with Pharisees both Josephus and the baraita in *b. Qidd.* 66a describe an identical accusation thrust at Janneus or his father, John Hyrcanus.[41] Perhaps the use of the words καὶ τοῦ θύειν ("[and was unfit to hold office] *and to sacrifice*"), in the current tradition of the defamation,

---

[38] For greater detail, see Chap. 3. [39] See e.g. Rubenstein, *Sukkot*, 121.

[40] On the possibility that even realized cross-references sometimes indicate interpolations, see "Introduction," n. 87.

[41] Various scholars have addressed the existence of both stories of defamation, here regarding Janneus and in *Ant.* 13:292 regarding Hyrcanus (Chap. 3), and their relationship. Gedalyahu Alon ("Attitude of the Pharisees," 26–8 n. 22) noted that alternating traditions on John and Janneus left traces in the Josephan and rabbinic corpora alike. For his part, Joshua Efron ("Simeon Ben Shataḥ and Jannaeus," 168–9) doubts the trustworthiness of the tradition of captivity because of the duplication with that episode. According to Menahem Stern (*Hasmonaean Judaea*, 198 n. 7), Josephus does not have a double tradition. The accusation against Janneus in our story is that he is "descended from captives," not that his mother was a captive. This is therefore not a repetition, but rather corroboration of the accusation made against Hyrcanus, Janneus's father (above, *Ant.* 13.292) that his mother, namely Janneus's grandmother, was in captivity. Whatever the case may be,

was meant to link this tradition with that of the citrons, which describes a sacrificial scene (also using θύειν). Evidently, the detail regarding the erection of a barrier in the temple by Janneus originally belonged to the first Jewish tradition of the citrons. Josephus here detaches it from its source, placing it after the libelous accusation that Janneus was descended from captives and the account of the killing of 6,000 Jews which was grounded in the underlying Nicolean base narrative. Let us now turn to the first Josephan insertion, the episode of the citrons, and examine its alleged parallel in rabbinic literature.

D. THE RABBINIC TRADITION

In enumerating the commandments related to Sukkot, the Mishnah (*m. Sukkah* 4:1) refers to the water libation that accompanied the daily sacrifice (*tamid*) on that festival. It provides a detailed description of the ceremony: the drawing of the water from the Siloam pool, the festive procession to the temple, the features of the libation as carried out on weekdays and the Sabbath respectively (*m. Sukkah* 4:9–10).[42] The rejoicing of *bet ha-sho'evah* (Water-Drawing Festival) on Sukkot was also related to the water libation.[43] A more extensive description of the water libation appears in the Tosefta, alongside statements regarding its symbolic meaning. Linked to the water that will emerge from the temple in the future and the well that accompanied the Israelites in the wilderness, the purpose of the libation is, according to the Tosefta, "so that the rain will be blessed on its account" (*t. Sukkah* 3:3–18), as Rabbi Akiba taught (ibid. 3:18), for it is on the festival of Sukkot that the world is "judged in regard to water" (*m. Rosh Hash.* 1:2). The water libation has no pentateuchal source,[44] and the rabbis viewed it as "law given to Moses at Sinai,"[45] although attempts were also made to find scriptural allusions to this practice.[46] Evidently, this was an ancient custom linked to the hope for a rainy winter, as Sukkot marks the beginning of the

the story of the possible captivity of a ruler's mother or a ruler's descent from captives is an independent Jewish tradition.

[42] See also *m. Zebaḥ.* 6:2.

[43] See primarily *m. Sukkah* 5:1–4; *t. Sukkah* 4:1–10. For an alternative etymology of *sho'evah/she'uvah* and scholarly suggestions regarding the development of the custom, see Fox, "'The Joy of the Place of Drawing,'" 173–216; Benovitz, *BT Sukkah*, 487–92.

[44] Even though the custom of drawing water and pouring it out before God is mentioned in Scripture (1 Sam 7:6; 2 Sam 23:16), and the YT identifies the second reference as the Sukkot water libation (*y. Sanh.* 2:5, 20c). The link between Sukkot and rain is already alluded to in Scripture, in Zech 14:17. See also the NT, John 7:38.

[45] *Y. Sukkah* 4:1, 54b and parallels; *b. Sukkah* 34a and parallels.

[46] *Sifre Num.* 143, 150; *b. Ta'an.* 2b–3a and parallels; see also *b. Sukkah* 48b, which supports the custom with a proof-text from Prophets. See Rubenstein, "Water Libation," 427–9.

rainy season.[47] Scholars conjecturally attribute the origins of the water libation to a ritual act found in many cultures, which is underpinned by the magical notion that pouring water on the ground inspires rain from the heavens. Another facet of this ritual is a mythical notion, traces of which are found in rabbinic sources, that views the temple as the center of the cosmos, a conduit linking the primeval waters with the earth and a locus where the waters of Creation flow. According to this scholarly supposition, only at a later date did the water libation receive the theurgic explanation put forth by Rabbi Akiba, which attributes the divine blessing of rain to the performance of the commandment, rather than to the ritual act's influence on the universe.[48]

The mishnah ascribes one of the laws mandated for the libation—that the person performing the libation lift up his hand—to an event that took place in the past: an anonymous priest's pouring of the libation on his feet instead of on the altar. In the Tosefta (*t. Sukkah* 3:16) the priest is identified as a Boethusian,[49] and additional information is provided: that the pelting with citrons led to the debasement of the temple, because the horn of the altar was damaged.[50] As cited in the BT, the priest is denoted a Sadducee, not a Boethusian. This exchange is typical, as Yaakov Sussmann has shown.[51]

Exegetes and scholars of rabbinic texts pinpoint the event described in the Mishnah and the Tosefta in a sectarian dispute regarding the water libation. They adduce that the Sadducees/Boethusians objected to the water libation because it lacked a pentateuchal source,[52] citing that as the reason why the

[47] See Urbach, *Halakhah*, 34–5, where he ascribes the custom to the early Second Temple period. Alexander Rofé ("Sects," 14–15) dates the water libation controversy very early, as he does the sectarian disputes, according to the LXX reading of 1 Sam 7:6, in which Rofé identifies a "Sadducean" addition opposing the water libation in the biblical text available to the translator. For an archeological finding that perhaps alludes to the water libation ritual in Iron Age Palestine, see the recent article by Arav, "Water Rituals," 357–69.

[48] For a more comprehensive treatment of the water libation, its origins and meanings, see Rubenstein, *Sukkot*, 117–31, and the bibliographical references there; Tabory, *Jewish Festivals*, 198–200; Halbertal and Naeh, "Ma'ayane ha-yeshu'ah," 182–4.

[49] *Tosefta*: *Mo'ed* (Lieberman ed.), 270, note on line 63 (and Lieberman, *Tosefta Ki-fshutah*, 4:881). Lieberman comments that "the baraita elaborates on our mishnah (4:9) ולמנסך אומרים לו הגבה ידך." On the form ביתסי rather than ביתוסי found in most of the good manuscripts of rabbinic sources, see Sussmann, "History of *Halakha*," 42 n. 137. This is not the appropriate forum for a discussion of the identity of the Boethusians. For a consideration of this question and a survey of the research, see Schremer, "Name of the Boethusians," 290–9.

[50] On the disparity implied by a comparison of the Tosefta and the BT regarding the question of whether the repair to the altar with salt sanctioned the rituals performed there or was just for show, see Lieberman, *Tosefta Ki-fshutah*, 4:882.

[51] "The Tosefta tends to use Boethusians…whereas we find Sadducee in other parallel sources. On the other hand, the BT tends to relatively frequent use of Sadducee" (Sussmann, "History of *Halakha*," 48–9 n. 166. See also ibid. 51–2 n. 171). For a general discussion of the use of these names in tannaitic literature, see ibid. 48–53.

[52] See e.g. Regev, *Sadducees*, 159–60 and the bibliographical references there. According to this interpretation, the Boethusians applied the same rationale to their objections to the custom of placing willow branches around the altar (*m. Sukkah* 4:5), which was also defined as "a law revealed to Moses at Sinai" (*t. Sukkah* 3:1 and elsewhere), "a usage of the prophets," or "an institution of the

priest in question poured the water on his feet. Others attribute the opposition to the ritual to its popular, public nature, which undermined the aristocratic underpinnings of the priesthood,[53] or to its presumed pagan-gentile origins.[54] Israel Knohl proposes that, because they did not believe in personal divine providence or reward for divine worship, the Sadducees opposed rainmaking rituals.[55] The people, who supported Pharisaic halakhah, pelted the priest with citrons, which led the mishnaic regulation that the priest pouring out the libation should raise his hand in order to demonstrate that he is offering the water libation in line with Pharisaic halakhah. Many associate the following mishnah in *Sanhedrin* with these events: "If a man stole the *kasvah* [the vessel used for libation],[56] or cursed by the *kosem* [some form of magic], or had sexual relations with an Aramean woman, zealots may fall upon him" (9:6).[57] The anti-Pharisaic sects were suspected of stealing the libation vessel in order to prevent the performance of the water libation on Sukkot, in line with their approach. The stringency of the law in this ancient mishnah is ascribed in the scholarship to the loaded sectarian debate on this matter.[58]

Against this prevailing view, Jeffrey L. Rubenstein argues that there is no firm evidence in the sources that the Sadducees, among whose number he includes the priest in our story, opposed the water libation because it lacked pentateuchal roots. First of all, he claims, the supposition that the Sadducees opposed extra-pentateuchal halakhic traditions is incorrect, because they too possessed oral traditions. Moreover, the event related in the mishnah, in which neither the priest's affiliation nor motives are identified, cannot be explained as a sectarian dispute. As for the Tosefta, on which the Talmuds rely, it interprets the mishnah independently. Although it relates that the priest was a Boethusian, it does not explain whether he spilled the water on his feet because of principled opposition to the libation itself, or just to the manner or moment of its pouring. Rubinstein proposes that a minor technical dispute over the manner in which the libation was to be poured, or over license to perform it on the Sabbath, was in rabbinic awareness linked in some version or other to the pelting of Janneus known from the Josephan narrative, and that the combination of these two separate traditions created the impression of a harsh, principled polemic.[59] Nonetheless, in

---

prophets" (*b. Sukkah* 44a). The sources attest to Boethusian opposition to carrying out the custom of beating the willow branches on the Sabbath (*t. Sukkah* 3:1; *b. Sukkah* 43b).

[53] Urbach, *Halakhah*, 34–5. For a similar view, see Stemberger, *Jewish Contemporaries of Jesus*, 59.

[54] Hallewy [Halevi], *Ha-aggadah*, 58–60.

[55] Knohl, "Ancient Israelite Priesthood," 216–17. For other, somewhat far-fetched explanations, see Finkelstein, *Pharisees*, 105–10.

[56] Num 4:7. See *b. Sukkah* 48b.   [57] Translation cited from Urbach, *Halakhah*, 34.

[58] See e.g. Albeck, *Mishnah: Seder Neziqin*, 454. Urbach (*Halakhah*, 34–5) suggests that the opponents alluded to in *m. Sanhedrin* are Hellenizers. See his arguments (ibid.) for the early date of the mishnah in question and of the water libation custom.

[59] Rubenstein, *Sukkot*, 121 n. 67; idem, "Water Libation."

my opinion, the extra-biblical, mythical, and popular nature of water libation, alongside the "publicization" of the ritual by the rabbis,[60] and in concert with the sources cited above, give greater weight to the generally accepted scholarly approach. The water libation itself was a disputed matter, and there is no need for recourse to conjectural disputes regarding halakhic details not mentioned in any known source.[61]

The YT alludes to our episode but does not cite it explicitly. According to *y. Yoma* 1:5, 39a,[62] a certain high priest followed the doctrines of the Sadducees/ Boethusians on three separate occasions, each described independently in the Tosefta: one is our episode, in which "a Boethusian" poured out the water libation on his feet and was pelted with citrons. The second, related in *t. Yoma* [*Kippurim*] 1:8, mentions "a Boethusian" who offered the Day of Atonement incense outside the holy of holies, in opposition to the rabbinic doctrine that it had to be offered within. According to the tosefta, "not three days passed before they put him into his grave."[63] The third episode, found in *t. Parah* 3:8, recounts how "a certain Sadducee" waited until sunset to ritually immerse before burning the red heifer, as opposed to the rabbinic view that immersion during the day suffices. There also the priest was swiftly punished—he too was buried within three days.[64]

In *y. Yoma* (1:5, 39a) the discussion continues by noting Rabbi Simon's opposing view according to which, the priest from the Day of Atonement died immediately, as did the priest from Sukkot; they were therefore two separate individuals. Thus, the protagonist of the rabbinic story died shortly after, or even in the course of, being pelted with citrons. This conclusion has bearing on the question of the relationship between the Josephan Janneus story and the rabbinic baraita, to be discussed in section E. However, the connection drawn by the YT between the three episodes is a homiletical step that is not in line with the plain meaning of the toseftan stories; moreover, no tannaitic sources allude to the death of the priest as a result of his being pelted with citrons.[65]

---

[60] *Y. Sukkah* 4:6, 54c. See Sussmann, "History of *Halakha*," 67 n. 220.

[61] See also Knohl, "Ancient Israelite Priesthood," 216–17.

[62] See also *y. Sukkah* 4:8, 54d, where the discussion was partly copied.

[63] *Tosefta: Mo'ed* (Lieberman ed.), 222–3. See *y. Yoma* 1:5, 39a; *b. Yoma* 19b.

[64] *Tosefta* (Zuckermandel ed.), 632.

[65] Lieberman (*Tosefta Ki-fshutah,* 4:881) notes that, according to the YT, the priest was killed: therefore they must not have just pelted him with citrons but also with rocks, linking this supposition with Rashi's assumption that the horn of the altar was chipped by a rock (Rashi, *Sukkah* 48b, s.v. נפגמה). Nonetheless, he also cites other explanations, according to which citrons could have damaged the horn of the altar (*Tosefta Ki-fshutah,* 4:882), making reference to the legend in *Lev. Rab.* 25:5 (Margalioth [Margulies] ed., 579) which teaches that citrons have the potential to harm those pelted with them. In any event, Lieberman also states that "here [namely in the Tosefta] and in our mishnah and in the BT no mention is made of his being killed."

E. THE RELATIONSHIP BETWEEN THE JOSEPHAN
AND THE RABBINIC TRADITIONS

One scholarly approach, popular from the nineteenth century on, views the two traditions—the Josephan one with its known historical figure and the rabbinic one with its anonymous Boethusian/Sadducee—as descriptions of the same incident, and conflates the information recounted in both, arriving at the following approximation of events. By acting in opposition to the Pharisaic tradition regarding the water libation, Janneus aroused the anger of the people, who also questioned his lineage and suitability for the priesthood. On that occasion Janneus was pelted with citrons; in response, assisted by mercenaries, he killed thousands of his opponents.[66] Some saw the omission of Janneus's name in rabbinic sources as a deliberate attempt to "conceal the shame of the Hasmonean dynasty."[67]

Other scholars take a different approach and regard these accounts as two separate stories, stressing that the rabbinic traditions attribute the pelting solely to the water libation and in no way allude to Janneus's day or person. On the other hand, according to Josephus the rift between Janneus and the Pharisees was political, not religious, in nature. Moreover, in *War* Josephus attributes the uprising to a general tendency on the part of the Jews to rebel on the holidays, and not to any action taken by Janneus.[68] Nor does the motif of pelting with citrons suffice, in Gedalyahu Alon's opinion, to regard the stories as identical; rather, he argues: "It appears that it was a daily occurrence for the people to pelt with citrons anyone whom they wished to insult," and cites the talmudic anecdote of the pelting of Rabbi Zera for teaching a halakhah of which his audience did not approve.[69] He also notes that, according to the Josephan description in *Antiquities*, Janneus was pelted as he was about to sacrifice, and not afterwards; namely, the time for the water libation had not yet arrived and therefore it was not the libation that sparked the pelting with citrons.

---

[66] See e.g. Graetz, *History of the Jews*, 2:42–3; Schürer, *History*, 1:222–3 and n. 16; Weiss, *Dor dor ve-dorshav*, 1:129; Halevy, *Dorot ha-rishonim*, vol. 1, pt. 3, pp. 480–3; Derenbourg, *Essai*, 98; Finkelstein, *Pharisees*, 110; Klausner, *Historiyah*, 3:149–50; Luria, *Mi-yannai ad hordus*, 120–5 (see also the additional halakhic tinge he imagined he found in the story); Hallewy [Halevi], *Ha-aggadah*, 58–60. Lieberman (*Tosefta Ki-fshutah*, 4:881) also accepts this identification. See also Regev, *Sadducees*, 158, who sees in the libation an "obscure echo" of the pelting of Janneus, and more recently, Rappaport, *House of the Hasmoneans*, 318.

[67] Hallewy [Halevi], *Ha-aggadah*, 58–60. See also Churgin, *Studies*, 180; Finkelstein, *Pharisees*, 110.

[68] Alon, "Attitude of the Pharisees," 33–4 n. 34; Efron, "Simeon Ben Shataḥ and Jannaeus," 169; Safrai, *Pilgrimage*, 213 n. 178; Stemberger, "Narrative Baraitot," 75; idem, *Jewish Contemporaries of Jesus*, 109 and n. 139.

[69] B. *Qidd.* 73a. To this one can add the midrashic account of a person pelted with figs whose wife notes that, to his good fortune, he was not pelted with citrons (*Lev. Rab.* 25:5 [Margalioth (Margulies) ed., 579; see n. 65 above]). Rubenstein (*Sukkot*, 121 n. 67) mentions a late parallel of this story found in *Tanḥuma*.

Some scholars have commented that, because the above-mentioned story in the YT relates that the priest died, just like the priest involved in the red cow and Day of Atonement episodes, this makes it impossible to link the Josephan and rabbinic versions. Janneus certainly did not meet his death in the citron-pelting episode during the Sukkot festival. Moreover, one of the opinions in the YT identifies the high priest of the red cow as the high priest of the Sukkot incident. As the priest who deviated from the practice regarding the red cow was active in Rabban Yoḥanan ben Zakkai's day, he could certainly not have lived in Janneus's day. But, as I have already noted, the late identification of the three priests is a homily grounded in literary similarity between the stories.

Shaye J. D. Cohen and Jeffrey Rubenstein represent a third approach. For Cohen, the rabbinic version of the story exemplifies the "rabbinization" of an early Jewish story. He argues that the original version of the story, as found in Josephus, is a secular political tradition regarding Janneus, who was pelted with citrons because of the people's hatred for his regime. Cohen maintains that it was the rabbis who erased the historical character of the story and endowed it with halakhic content in line with their ideology, transforming Janneus into an anonymous Sadducean/Boethusian priest and replacing the rationale for his being pelted with citrons with a halakhic one: his refusal to adhere to the rabbinic directives governing the ritual. After this reshaping, the story was added to a series of stories aimed at proving that the Sadducees must follow the rabbinic practice even in cases where they disagree with the rabbinic halakhah.[70] Rubinstein follows Cohen's approach, even using this reconstruction to cast doubt on the very existence of a halakhic dispute regarding the water libation, as we saw in section D. He maintains that the motif of citron-pelting, which originated in the political story of Janneus, was incorporated into an obscure tradition regarding a minor halakhic dispute, unjustifiably endowing it with a loaded, principled character.[71]

As seen in the Introduction, the scholarly approaches to this story as outlined here can be applied to the wider phenomenon examined in this book. To recall, they are: the harmonistic approach that joins the traditions to create a historical reconstruction; the critical approach that views the stories as two independent sources; and the diachronic approach that identifies one version as the other's source. The first approach is somewhat naive; after all, the equation of the two stories on citron-pelting is not self-evident and, even if they derive from a single source, this is a literary source and not a definite historical event. In addition, we must take into account possible political biases or corruptions that shaped the uniqueness of one or the other tradition, or both, and avoid creating a solid, uniform narrative from the two.

---

[70] Cohen, "Parallel Historical Tradition," 12. See also idem, "Significance of Yavneh," 37 n. 23.
[71] Rubenstein, *Sukkot*, 121 n. 67; idem, "Water Libation."

On the other hand, the conclusion reached by the second school of thought—that there was no contact between the stories—is not inevitable. Perhaps an ancient tradition did link the uprising against Janneus to a halakhic tradition, and separate elements of this tradition survived, either fortuitously or purposefully, in Josephus, on the one hand, and in rabbinic literature, on the other. Various scholars have argued that, given rabbinic familiarity with Janneus, the absence of his name from the Mishnah and the Tosefta indicates that it was either deliberately erased or not part of the original tradition. However, here we must consider the different strata of rabbinic literature. It is noteworthy that notwithstanding the multiple mentions of Janneus's name in rabbinic literature at large, he appears nowhere in any of the tannaitic genres, except for one doubtful mention in the tannaitic work *Sifre Zuta on Deuteronomy*, as preserved in a Karaite commentary on the Pentateuch.[72] Indeed, the scholarship has not noted that the traditions concerning Janneus are concentrated in amoraic literature, primarily in the BT and the Scholion, with one tradition also found in the YT and aggadic midrash.[73] Therefore, no special significance inheres in the fact that his name is not mentioned in either the mishnah or tosefta treating this story. On the other hand, the fact that Janneus's name does not appear in the Babylonian Talmud's version, in spite of the BT's acquaintance with him elsewhere, indicates that the authors of the sugya were not familiar with the Josephan story.

Of the three above-noted approaches, it is the third, more recent, sophisticated one that requires further discussion. With respect to its identification of Josephus as the source and the rabbinic version as a manipulative reworking, I make two observations. First, as Albert Baumgarten has shown, in many cases rabbinic sources on sectarian disputes preserve trustworthy memories of the Second Temple-period milieu.[74] Further evidence that there was a significant historical dispute surrounding the Sukkot water libation comes from the distinctly public nature of this ritual, as already noted by the amoraim. The procession, the shofar-blowing, the rejoicing of *bet ha-sho'evah*, and the performance of the libation on the Sabbath are all definitive elements of "publicized" customs that were part and parcel of the sectarian debate.[75] Thus, caution should be exercised before offhandedly characterizing the halakhic dispute regarding the water libation as a late literary reworking of a secular, political source: the tradition regarding the halakhic disagreement has an independent existence.

---

[72] See Ilan, "The Trial of Herod/Jannaeus."

[73] See Noam, "Agrippa/Jannaeus and the Nazirites' Offerings."

[74] Baumgarten, "Rabbinic Literature." For example, the dispute regarding the red cow (*m. Parah* 3:7 and elsewhere), seen in the YT as a twin to our dispute over the water libation, was with the publication of 4QMMT revealed to be an actual historical issue. Its discussion, however, exceeds the scope of this book.

[75] See text at n. 60.

Second, I question the intuitive assumption by many scholars that the "original" facts should be sought in the earlier, "historical" Josephan context, because the rabbinic sources, being later, and more biased and ahistorical in nature, contain the reworked legend. Time and again, our study has shown this assumption to be incorrect.[76] In many instances, it is obvious that the story is "foreign" in the Josephan context also and was secondarily and artificially inserted into the narrative. What we have here is not a piece of "Josephan history" but rather a Jewish legend whose origins lie in a hidden treasury of Jewish traditions that preceded Josephus just as it preceded rabbinic literature. Here too, as discussed above, we saw that the internal Jewish tradition of the citrons was secondarily incorporated by Josephus into his narrative. This counters the automatic assumption that the rabbis borrowed, and reworked, the Josephan tradition.

As seen above, it is not difficult to extract the "Jewish" elements which have been interpolated here and there in the narrative sequence in *Antiquities*, a narrative also known from *War*. They include: the pelting with citrons; the libel concerning Janneus's lineage; and the building of a wooden barrier in the temple. In section C I showed that the libel concerning his lineage derives from a separate source; thus, the early Jewish source cited by Josephus recounted the pelting of Janneus with citrons and the erection of a barrier in the temple. In other words, this was an etiological story that explained the circumstances underlying Janneus's erection of a wooden barrier in the temple, which forms the focus of the story. No such story is found in rabbinic literature. On the other hand, the version found in the tosefta/baraita is independent and stresses the damage to the altar and its temporary repair with a lump of salt. This tradition also concerns the history of the temple and its laws, but from a different direction. This leads to the conclusion that, as opposed to other episodes treated in this book, such as that of Hyrcanus and the heavenly voice, this is not a case of a single literary source cited in both corpora, but a source that reached Josephus but was not preserved in rabbinic literature, and vice versa.

Perhaps the distant, lost source for the rabbinic traditions treated Janneus, and recounted the story of the pelting of the Hasmonean king, similar to the Josephan narrative. But the opposite may also be true: the distant source for the Josephan narrative may have dealt with an anonymous Sadducean priest. In any event, in their present form the tale of the conflict over the water libation was not in Josephus's literary source; nor was the Josephan story of Janneus being pelted with citrons available to the rabbis, as the matter of the wooden barrier indicates. Briefly, we have two early traditions that made their way separately to Josephus and to the rabbis. Perhaps they possessed some distant generic connection in the past, but, as preserved in the Josephan and the rabbinic

---

[76] See especially the larger study by Ilan and Noam, *Josephus and the Rabbis.*

context, the two stories are not based on a single text, nor do they show signs of being a source and its reworking.

With respect to the image of the Hasmoneans in the Second Temple period and afterwards, we can therefore in this instance rely only on the Josephan version, for it alone definitely involves a Hasmonean ruler. Like the story of the rupture with the Pharisees in the previous chapter, this is an etiological legend marking a turning-point in the Hasmonean history. But whereas the story of the rupture sought to describe the underlying cause of a psychological-political phenomenon—the roots of the hostility between the Pharisees and the Hasmoneans—our legend attempts to explain the circumstances that led to the erection of a physical object: a barrier erected in the temple. The legend ascribes its erection to the need to protect the king and high priest Janneus from the hostility demonstrated by the populace, whom he was supposed to represent before God. This hostility is the opposite of the harmony described in the story of John Hyrcanus and the voice in the temple. In that story the temple symbolizes the unity of a national victory, exalted priestly mediation, and revelation (a prophetic *bat kol*). If the Hyrcanus legend reflects the unification of God with his people through the mediation of the high priest, our story, which treats Hyrcanus's son Janneus, reflects the creation of a physical—as well as a symbolic—barrier in the temple that represents dispute, hostility, and the beginning of a decline. In the following chapter we will again encounter tension between Janneus and the Pharisees, albeit in a muted, more ambivalent form. Once again, the precise relationship between the tradition as found in Josephus and in rabbinic literature will turn out to be elusive.

5

Alexander Janneus's Instructions to His Wife

Chapter 3 ("The Rupture with the Pharisees") considered a legend that explicated the circumstances underlying the Hasmonean political shift from
endorsement of the Pharisees to support for the Sadducees. One version attributed this volte-face to the reign of John Hyrcanus; the other to that of his son
Janneus. The legend examined in this chapter explains the opposite process,
which took place after Janneus's death: namely, the Pharisees' return to power
with the accession of Janneus's widow Alexandra (Shelamzion). Not only are
these two stories closely linked in both the Josephan and the rabbinic versions
but, as shown here, both originated in a unique source or pool of sources that
articulated the Pharisaic perspective on events and sought to defend the
Pharisees.[1] Given the absence of any extant, definitively Pharisaic documents,
and because all our data on this Jewish group derive from secondary witnesses,
this source from a lost Pharisaic apologetic work has even greater value. In
these two legends we hear, for the first time, the voices of the Pharisees themselves, their self-perception and reading of the contemporary political map.

A. THE SOURCES

Antiquities 13.398–404; *b. Sotah* 22b

Josephus, *Antiquities* 13.398–404

(398) But after these conquests King Alexander fell ill from heavy drinking,
and for three years he was afflicted with a quartan fever, but still he did not give
up campaigning until, being exhausted from his labours, he met death in the

---

[1] This conclusion has been enunciated by Tal Ilan and Vered Noam in the past. See Noam,
"Introduction," 44–6, 67–70; Ilan and Noam, "Pharisaic Apologetic Source." The bulk of this chapter is a fresh analysis and presents new conclusions not found in the previous contexts.

territory of the Gerasenes while besieging Ragaba, a fortress across the Jordan. (399) And when the queen saw that he was on the point of death and no longer held to any hope of recovery, she wept and beat her breast, lamenting the bereavement that was about to befall her and her children, and said to him, "To whom are you thus leaving me and your children, who are in need of help from others, especially when you know how hostile the nation feels toward you!" (400) Thereupon he advised her to follow his suggestions for keeping the throne secure for herself and her children and to conceal his death from the soldiers until she had captured the fortress. (401) And then, he said, on her return to Jerusalem as from a splendid victory, she should yield a certain amount of power to the Pharisees, for if they praised her in return for this sign of regard, they would dispose the nation favourably toward her. These men, he assured her, had so much influence with their fellow-Jews that they could injure those whom they hated and help those to whom they were friendly; (402) for they had the complete confidence of the masses when they spoke harshly of any person, even when they did so out of envy; and he himself, he added, had come into conflict with the nation because these men had been badly treated by him. (403) "And so," he said, "when you come to Jerusalem, send for their partisans, and showing them my dead body, permit them, with every sign of sincerity, to treat me as they please, whether they wish to dishonour my corpse by leaving it unburied because of the many injuries they have suffered at my hands, or in their anger wish to offer my dead body any other form of indignity. Promise them also that you will not take any action, while you are on the throne, without their consent. (404) If you speak to them in this manner, I shall receive from them a more splendid burial than I should from you; for once they have the power to do so, they will not choose to treat my corpse badly, and at the same time you will reign securely." With this exhortation to his wife he died, after reigning twenty-seven years, at the age of forty-nine.

Rabbinic Sources

B. Sotah 22b[2]

א"ל ינאי מלכא לדביתהו: 1

אל תתיראי לא מן הפרושין ולא מי שאינן פרושין   2

אלא מן הצבועין[3] הדומין לפרושין.   3

שמעשיהם מעשי זמרי ומבקשין שכר כפינחס.   4

---

[2] Base text: Genizah fragment, Oxford 2675.
[3] Vatican 110: הצנועין, apparently an error.

King Yannai said to his wife, "Fear not the Pharisees nor the non-Pharisees but the hypocrites who ape the Pharisees; because their deeds are the deeds of Zimri but they expect a reward like Phinehas."

B. HISTORICAL BACKGROUND

The events described here took place in 76 BCE, the year of Alexander Janneus's death. Following Janneus's death, his wife Alexandra (Shelamzion) acceded to the throne;[4] she ruled for nine years, until 67 BCE. On her death, a war of succession ensued between her sons (see Chapter 6). In his description of her reign (*War* 1.107–19; *Ant.* 13:398–432), Josephus underscores the power and hegemony she granted to the Pharisees, whom he portrays as steering Queen Alexandra's actions and relentlessly pursuing their opponents (*War* 1.110–13; *Ant.* 13.408–10), in essence styling them the actual rulers of the kingdom.

In Qumran literature, Shelamzion is explicitly mentioned twice, in two fragmentary chronistic texts (4Q 331 1 II, 7; 4Q332 2, line 4).[5] Tal Ilan has also tentatively identified the presence of negative allusions to her in *Pesher Nahum* and *Pesher Hosea*.[6]

Aside from the source examined in this chapter, the Hasmonean queen appears in additional rabbinic sources. One example comes from the tannaitic midrash *Sifre Deuteronomy* (piska 42), which relates that in her day the promise in the verse "I will grant the rain for your land in season" (Deut 11:14) was fulfilled.[7] Some talmudic legends and Scholion O on *Megillat Ta'anit* describe her seated beside Janneus.[8] The BT transmits a halakhic tradition regarding Alexandra's attempt to purify utensils that had been defiled at a banquet she made for her son (*b. Shabb.* 16b). Finally, a pseudo-historical legend found in Scholion P (2 Shevat; Noam, *Megillat Ta'anit*, 110) attributes to Alexandra the cancellation

---

[4] On Alexandra, see the comprehensive treatment by Ilan, *Silencing the Queen*; idem, *Integrating Women*, 21–3, 100–5, 127–53.

[5] See H. Eshel, *Dead Sea Scrolls and the Hasmonean State*, 136–7.

[6] Ilan, *Silencing the Queen*, 63–72.

[7] See also *Sifra: Behuqotei* 1:1 (110b) and a parallel in *b. Ta'an.* 23a that does not mention the queen's name. An additional tradition concerning the miracle of rain during Herod's day, which has a Josephan parallel, was appended to both sources (*Ant.* 15.425).

[8] The Scholion on *Meg. Ta'an.*, 28 Tevet (Noam, *Megillat Ta'anit*, 107); another legend appears in *y. Ber.* 7:2, 11b = *y. Nazir* 5:5, 54b, without the queen's name. For parallels to this legend, see *Gen. Rab.* 91:4; *Qoh. Rab.* 7:24; cf. *b. Ber.* 48a. The queen's name, Shelamzu, appears only in *Qohelet Rabbah*. For a discussion of this source, see Noam, "Agrippa/Jannaeus and the Nazirites' Offerings." For yet another story ostensibly concerning King Janneus and his queen, see *b. Ker.* 28b (=*b. Pesah.* 57a); this story, however, involves the late Second Temple period, and scholars have correctly asserted that it refers to Agrippa II and Berenice and not Janneus and Alexandra (D. R. Schwartz, "Josephus' Source on Agrippa II," 267). Indeed, Tal Ilan has noted ("King Jannaeus in the Babylonian Talmud") that Janneus's name is missing from the parallel in *Pesahim*, and even from one of the manuscripts of the legend in *Keritot*.

of a cruel murder verdict issued by Janneus after his death; Josephus, however, attributes this tradition to Herod and his sister Salome (*War* 1.659–60, 666; *Ant.* 17.173–81, 193).[9] No non-Jewish source refers to Queen Alexandra (Shelamzion) or to her reign.

C. THE TRADITION ACCORDING TO JOSEPHUS

As recounted by Josephus in both *Antiquities* 13.398–404 and *War* 1.105–6, the events in Janneus's campaign in Transjordan and his death in its midst follow a similar sequence. Conspicuously absent from the parallel account in *War*, however, is the anecdote of Janneus's deathbed instructions to his wife. As noted in the Introduction, this applies to each of the Jewish traditions examined here: without exception, all were integrated into Josephus's later work, *Antiquities*. Also evident here, as elsewhere, is how the interpolated story in *Antiquities* interrupts, generates contradictions, and disrupts the smoother narrative sequence found in Josephus's earlier work, *War*. In this instance, the disruption takes the form of the repetition of the report of the king's death, first noted in section 398. Because of the subsequent insertion of the story of his deathbed instructions, the king's death was repeated in section 404. As the sequence in *War* is uninterrupted, no such repetition appears there.

The scholarly treatment of the Josephan testimony ranges from acceptance as historical fact to doubts regarding its veracity. Those scholars who treat the Josephan account of Janneus's deathbed instructions as historical fact propose various rationales for his change of heart. Janneus had tired of the conflict with the Pharisees; or, as he neared death, he saw his hostility toward them as a political mistake; or, he himself had drawn closer to the Pharisees late in life and only charged his wife with completing this process; or, in the spirit of the talmudic tradition, he understood that it was not the "real" Pharisees who had persecuted him but rather the hypocrites among them.[10] Some scholars inserted elements from the talmudic parallel into their historical reconstructions of this episode.[11]

Others cast doubt on the trustworthiness of the story,[12] viewing it as a tendentious insertion. The actual nature of this bias is, however, a debated matter.

---

[9] For a discussion of this source, see Ilan and Noam, "The Plot and Death of Herod/Jannaeus." For a survey and analysis of all the sources on Alexandra in rabbinic literature, see Ilan, *Silencing the Queen*, 35–42.

[10] Graetz, *History of the Jews*, 2:47; Derenbourg, *Essai*, 101; Klausner, *Historiyah*, 3:157–8; Schalit, "Domestic Politics and Political Institutions," 296–7. In recent years this assumption has been backed by Regev (*Sadducees*, 270–1 and n. 32). For a detailed survey of the scholarship, see Ilan, "Jannaeus's Deathbed Instructions," 308–17.

[11] See Graetz, *History of the Jews*, 2:47; Derenbourg, *Essai*, 101; Klausner, *Historiyah*, 3:157–8.

[12] See e.g. Schürer (*History*, 1:230).

Some discern a fundamentally pro-Pharisaic bias in the story. Aimed at legitimating Pharisaic acquisition of power following Janneus's death, the story attributes this turning-point on the verge of death to the king's regret for his earlier persecution of the Pharisees ("because these men had been badly treated by him," 402; "because of the many injuries they have suffered at my hands," 403). Others identify the story as harshly critical of the Pharisees, noting their caustic portrayal as power-hungry, influential schemers who speak disparagingly of others—"even when they did so out of envy"—and incite the masses (402). They observe that, according to our story, Janneus's planned reconciliation with the Pharisees is grounded neither in respect, nor regret, for his past treatment of them, but is rather portrayed as a cynical political ploy fueled by their abundant power. For their part, the Pharisees' willingness to reach reconciliation with the Hasmoneans is governed not by pursuit of peace but by pursuit of honor ("for if they praised her in return *for this sign of regard*," 401).

The foundations of the first of these two approaches were laid by Morton Smith, who views the tale of the deathbed instructions as a pro-Pharisaic, Josephan addition, aimed at painting the Pharisees as power-holders for his Roman readers. According to Smith, a shift took place in Josephus's attitude toward the Pharisees between the composition of *War* immediately following the First Jewish Revolt and the writing of *Antiquities* two decades later; thus, in his later work, he advocated for the Pharisees by attributing to Janneus death-bed instructions in their favor.[13] Daniel R. Schwartz takes an opposite view. He argues that many of the Josephan descriptions of the Pharisees originated in the works of Nicolaus of Damascus, Herod's court historian, who displayed antagonism toward the Pharisees, and that these derived, inherently anti-Pharisaic comments do not represent Josephus's own political stance in either *War* or *Antiquities*. Schwartz notes the striking similarity, to be discussed below, between the negative descriptions of the Pharisees' wiliness and great power over the masses in sections 401–2 of our story, and in *Antiquities* 13.288, which precedes the story of the rupture with the Pharisees treated in Chapter 3 of this book. He further identifies Nicolaus as the source of *Antiquities* 13.288.[14] Schwartz's discussion implies that he regards our entire story as anti-Pharisaic in tone, and therefore derived from Nicolaus.[15]

---

[13] Morton Smith, "Palestinian Judaism," esp. 75–6. For references to studies that accepted his general approach to Josephus and the Pharisees, see D. R. Schwartz, "Josephus and Nicolaus," 164 n. 23.

[14] On this section and its incongruity with respect to the story of the rupture that follows, see Chap. 3.

[15] D. R. Schwartz, "Josephus and Nicolaus," esp. 159. Even earlier, Efron ("Simeon Ben Shataḥ and Jannaeus," 172–5) argued that the story was essentially anti-Pharisaic and was drawn from Nicolaus's writings, in line with his opinion that the rivalry between Janneus and the Pharisees was none other than an invention by this hostile non-Jewish author. Given the description of Janneus's persecution of the Pharisees in *Pesher Nahum* from Qumran (see n. 21 and Chap. 3; see also Regev,

Steve Mason takes a similar stance, maintaining that this story describes the Pharisees negatively. Like Smith, however, he adduces that this description, similar to others in *Antiquities*, was a Josephan invention, who then espoused a pro-Hasmonean, anti-Pharisaic stance.[16] Based on its absence from *War*, Eyal Regev concurs with the premise that this section is not derived from Nicolaus's works and, given the existence of its talmudic parallel, suggests that it originated in a Jewish source and was not written by Josephus himself.[17] Similar to Mason, Tal Ilan also identifies the deathbed instructions as a tendentious Josephan interpolation; she views it as fueled, however, not by Josephus's attitude toward the Pharisees but by the needs of the portrait he wished to draw of Queen Alexandra, who sought to pursue a new pro-Pharisaic policy as opposed to her late husband's path. Seeking to detract from her independence and judgment, Josephus ascribed the shift to her husband's wishes. Ilan too argues that Josephus did not invent this episode but interpolated it from another source or some similar work, which was also available to the redactor of the sugya in the BT.[18] Thus, scholarly opinion is divided regarding three issues related to this episode: (1) historical veracity; (2) source—Nicolaus, Josephus, or a third source; and (3) political thrust—for or against the Pharisees.

The following discussion addresses the latter two questions, based on my understanding that correct identification of the story's thrust can also reveal its source. Closer examination discloses what underlies the two scholarly extremes regarding the question of whether the story is pro- or anti-Pharisaic. It shows the defamation of the Pharisees to be restricted to a single, parenthetical, explanatory comment inserted by the narrator, which is not integral to the events recounted:

> These men, he assured her, had so much influence with their fellow-Jews that they could injure those whom they hated and help those to whom they were friendly; for they had the complete confidence of the masses when they spoke harshly of any person, even when they did so out of envy. (*Ant.* 401–2)

Removal of this explanatory comment from the passage leaves a text that is not critical of, but rather displays sympathy toward, the Pharisees. Several fundamental messages are conveyed in this passage: first of all, not just the Pharisees but the entire nation is unkindly disposed to Janneus (section 399), because he persecuted the Pharisees whom the people championed. By instituting conciliatory steps toward the Pharisees, this would incline the people more favorably toward Alexandra (401), whereas Janneus's ruthless treatment of the Pharisees had brought him into conflict with the nation (402). Second, Pharisaic

---

Sadducees, 270–1 n. 32), this approach no longer seems tenable and is not currently espoused in the scholarship.

[16] Mason, *Josephus on the Pharisees*, 249–50.

[17] Regev, *Sadducees*, 270–1 n. 32.

[18] Ilan, *Silencing the Queen*, 76–7. See also idem, "Jannaeus's Deathbed Instructions."

hostility toward the Hasmoneans was the outcome of their persecution by Janneus; namely, responsibility for the conflict lay with the king, not the Pharisees (402, 403). Third, the Pharisees would generously accede to a conciliatory gesture (401, 404). Thus, as Morton Smith notes, the story appears to have a pro-Pharisaic bent. But, to this narrative Josephus added a derogatory remark, either borrowed or of his own invention.

A similar picture emerged from the analysis of the rupture with the Pharisees in Chapter 3. To recall, the body of the story there is well disposed to the Pharisees, whereas the narrational framework evidences hostility toward them. Moreover, comparison of the two episodes shows them, on the one hand, to bear very similar messages; on the other hand, the anti-Pharisaic additions to each also display similar content and language, as Schwartz and Mason have shown.[19] Table 5.1 demonstrates the topical similarities between the two. (Where there are also linguistic similarities I have cited the Greek in parentheses.)

It appears, then, that Josephus was familiar with at least two stories concerning the relationship between the Pharisees and the Hasmonean dynasty. Drawn from an earlier source, both endeavored to come to the defense of the Pharisees and to exculpate them from charges of rebellion against the regime. One describes how and why the Hasmoneans turned their backs on the Pharisees; the other recounts the rapprochement between the Pharisees and the Hasmoneans that took place during Queen Alexandra's reign. The first story claims that the Pharisees were loyal, even sympathetic, to the Hasmonean ruler and that he was misled by a conniving Sadducee, who instigated persecution of the Pharisees and fomented the rift between them and the king. The second claims that, toward the end of his life, the same Hasmonean ruler from the first story (talmudic version), or his son (Josephan version), regretted his persecution of the Pharisees and perceived them as amenable to rapprochement. Both stories assert that the masses sympathized with the Pharisees and attribute public resentment of the Hasmonean regime to its persecution of this sector. And, in both instances, the stories were juxtaposed to an anti-Pharisaic comment or framework, which presents, in almost identical language, an opposing view that portrays the Pharisees as an influential, power-hungry, contentious group that, grounded in envy of their rivals' successes, arbitrarily incited the masses against various individuals.

Based on the conclusion that the story of the deathbed instructions is indeed a Pharisaic-Jewish tradition, as evidenced by its partial talmudic parallel and mainly by the affinity between its message and that of the rupture tradition, we can now answer the questions posed in the opening of this section. The story is neither from Nicolaus's work as Schwartz maintains, nor Josephus's own invention as Mason suggests, but rather an earlier Jewish-Pharisaic tale. Therefore,

---

[19] See text at nn. 14–16.

Table 5.1. The Rupture and the Deathbed Instructions Stories: A Thematic Comparison

Theme	*Ant.* 13.288–98: The Rupture	*Ant.* 13.398–404: Deathbed Instructions
The pro-Pharisaic stance as cited in the narrative:		
The Pharisees are loyal to the Hasmonean ruler and are prepared to be reconciled with him.	(289) Hyrcanus too was a disciple of theirs, and was greatly loved by them...But they testified to his being altogether virtuous, and he was delighted with their praise (τοῖς ἐπαίνοις) (292) while all the Pharisees were very indignant [regarding the libel against the ruler]	(401) For if they praised (ἐπαινοῦντας) her in return for this sign of regard, they would dispose the nation favourably toward her. (404) for once they have the power to do so, they will not choose to treat my corpse badly.
The Hasmonean ruler injured the Pharisees.	(296)...brought him to join the Sadducaean party and desert the Pharisees, and to abrogate the regulations which they had established for the people, and punish those who observed them.	(402)...because these men [the Pharisees] had been badly treated by him (403) because of the many injuries they have suffered at my hands.
The people as a whole hated the ruler because of his negative attitude toward the Pharisees.	(296) Out of this, of course, grew the hatred of the masses to him and his sons.	(402) He himself...had come into conflict with the nation because these men [the Pharisees] had been badly treated by him.
The anti-Pharisaic stance as cited in the frame narrative or in parenthetical remarks:		
Pharisaic envy of others' success.	(288) As for Hyrcanus, the envy (φθόνον) of the Jews was aroused against him by his own successes...particularly hostile to him were the Pharisees, who are one of the Jewish schools.	(402)...when they spoke harshly of any person, even when they did so out of envy (φθονοῦντες).
Their great influence on the masses.	(288) And so great is their influence with the masses (τῷ πλήθει)...	(401)...These men...had so much influence with their fellow-Jews (402) for they had the complete confidence of the masses (παρὰ τῷ πλήθει)
Successful Pharisaic incitement against their rivals.	(288) even when they speak against a king or a high priest, they immediately gain credence (πιστεύεσθαι).	(401) they could injure those whom they hated and help those to whom they were friendly. (402) for they had the complete confidence (πιστεύεσθαι) of the masses when they spoke harshly of any person.

it does not reflect a Josephan pro-Pharisaic bias, and certainly not an anti-Pharisaic one, but rather its own message and concerns. Moreover, because Nicolaus would not have been exposed to internal Jewish stories, the inevitable conclusion is that Josephus himself inserted the story into his narrative. It follows that Josephus is also responsible for the criticism of the Pharisees implanted in the heart of the story (13.401–2).[20] Josephus's political tendentiousness should then be considered not through the message of the story itself, but rather in light of two contradictory facts regarding its Josephan reception. Josephus incorporated unmistakably Pharisaic traditions into his book on the one hand, but implanted hostile statements into, or before, these traditions on the other. The wider implications of this finding on the overall question of Josephus's attitude to both the Pharisees and the Hasmoneans will be discussed in the concluding chapter. Let us now return to the provenance of the story itself, through consideration of the rabbinic parallel.

D. THE TRADITION IN RABBINIC LITERATURE

The Antiquity of the Story

As found in the Talmud, the story of Janneus and his wife is not formulated as a tannaitic source: its opening, א"ל ינאי מלכא לדביתהו, lacks the usual introductory formula for a baraita and is furthermore worded in the Babylonian Aramaic typical of the BT. Nonetheless, a number of features support the presumption that this is a much earlier source than the surrounding sugya and that only its opening exposition underwent rewording in the style of the BT. First of all, the topic addressed in the story, namely, the Hasmonean attitude toward the Pharisees, of Janneus in particular, is characteristic of Second Temple-period political discourse. This is exemplified both by *Pesher Nahum*, which describes the persecution of the Pharisees by the "Lion of Wrath," namely Janneus,[21] and by the ancient legend concerning the rupture between John Hyrcanus/Janneus and the Pharisees discussed in Chapter 3. That the Babylonian amoraim would have invented a legend concerning a Palestinian political dispute that took place centuries earlier, regarding which they possessed but limited knowledge, seems unlikely. Second, as many scholars have shown, the term "Pharisees" is typical neither of amoraic terminology nor of rabbinic terminology in general, but is always placed in the mouths of anti-Pharisaic elements in legends that are

---

[20] The possibility that Josephus borrowed the *wording* of this critical comment from Nicolaus is discussed in Chap. 7, section C, subsection "Josephus and the Pharisees."

[21] 4Q169 (4QpNah) 3–4 I, 2–8. For a discussion and survey of previous scholarship, see H. Eshel, *Dead Sea Scrolls and the Hasmonean State*, 117–31.

rooted in the Second Temple period.[22] Third, rabbinic literature tends to exegesis of scriptural verses, rather than to direct comparisons between biblical scenes and actual political situations as found in our story, which compares the episode of Zimri and Phinehas to political events in Janneus's day. On the other hand, this literary phenomenon is characteristic of Second Temple-period discourse.[23] Fourth, the words placed in Janneus's mouth, whose purpose is to reveal that it is not the Pharisees who are hypocritical but rather another group that apes the Pharisees, support the legend's authenticity; namely, the narrator is defending the Pharisees against the claim of hypocrisy.[24] Familiar from Qumran literature and the New Testament,[25] there is no doubt that a story aware of, and troubled by, this accusation must have originated in the stormy Second Temple arena in Palestine. Finally, because the nuclear tradition of Janneus's instructions to his wife regarding the Pharisees was known to Josephus, this means that, despite the differences between the Josephan and the talmudic versions, this was an early, non-Babylonian tradition. On the other hand, given the significant differences in detail between the Josephan and talmudic stories, and the incongruity of the story in the Josephan narrative, the BT could not have borrowed from Josephus. The parallel stories rather exemplify use of individual variants of an early source by both corpora.

If this is indeed an early tradition from a source close to the events in question, what are its origins and thrust? According to the talmudic version, Janneus sought to assuage his wife's fear of the Pharisees: it is not they who endanger her, but others, termed "hypocrites who ape the Pharisees" in a pithy aphorism that compares them to the protagonists of the biblical drama in Numbers 25:1–15. In the biblical story Midianite women entice the Israelites to engage in prostitution and idol worship, whereupon Phinehas son of Eleazar son of Aaron takes a spear and stabs Zimri son of Salu, the sinful chieftain of the tribe of Simeon, along with his Midianite partner. Phinehas merits an impressive reward for this act: he is blessed with a covenant of peace and another everlasting one

---

[22] See Chap. 3, n. 20.

[23] The word צבועים in this sense is a *hapax legomenon*. Other occurrences of the root צבע in rabbinic literature refer to painting (e.g. *m. Shevi'it* 7:1; *m. B. Qam.* 9:4) or catching and holding (e.g. *m. Kelim* 25:7). However, the context here clearly points to the common interpretation—hypocrites—probably borrowed from the pristine sense of painting; namely, one who colors himself, pretending to be different from what he really is. For a comparison of scriptural interpretation at Qumran to rabbinic midrash aggadah, including extensive bibliographical references, see Fraade, "Legal Midrash at Qumran," 169–92. Fraade contends: "Qumran…interpretation was more intent on defining and justifying the present…" (192).

[24] As opposed to Finkelstein's understanding (*Pharisees*, xxiii) who finds criticism of the Pharisees in the story, based on the "Talmud" itself.

[25] See the designation of the Pharisees as דורשי החלקות ("Seekers-after-Smooth-Things"), which is close in meaning to hypocrisy (*Pesher Nahum* [4Q169], 2–3 II, 10; 3–4 I, 2; II, 2, 4; 3–4 III, 3, 6–7; *Hodayot* (1QH^a) X, 17, 34; 4QCat^a (4Q177) 9, line 4). See also Matt 23. For further discussion, see Flusser, "Pesher Nahum," 218–19.

of priesthood because "he took impassioned action for his God, thus making expiation for the Israelites" (Num 25:12–13). The key to decoding the message of the talmudic tradition is certainly the Hebrew aphorism that links the situation in Janneus's day to the biblical story of Zimri and Phinehas. What does the aspiration to resemble Phinehas signify and to whom can it be appropriately applied in the first century BCE?

Phinehas in Post-biblical Literature

Post-biblical literature highlights two facets of the figure of Phinehas: his zealotry and the divine promise of the high priesthood.[26] We tend to underscore the first, in large part because of this figure's well-known role in 1 Maccabees, in the description of Matthias's zealous act that opened the Maccabean revolt (1 Macc 2:24–7), and in Matthias's parting words to his sons (vv. 51–4). In many other contexts, however, this figure functions to confirm the eternal right to the high priesthood, which is grounded in the divine promise to Phinehas. Psalm 106:30–1 downplays Phinehas's zealotry, stressing his righteousness and the everlasting pact of priesthood: "Phinehas stepped forth and intervened, and the plague ceased. It was reckoned to his merit for all generations, to eternity." Ben Sira (45:24) as well provides no explicit description of Zimri's sin and death at Phinehas's hands, but rather underscores his atoning for Israel, and mainly "that he and his descendants should have the dignity of the priesthood forever." The emphasis on Phinehas in Ben Sira's "Praise of the Fathers" (chaps. 44–50) is intended as an introduction to Ben Sira's tribute to the Zadokite priestly dynasty, and primarily to the radiant figure of Simeon son of Onias: "the leader of his brothers and the pride of his people was the high priest…" (50:1–2). In other words, the attribution of their lineage to Phinehas serves as divine authorization of the Zadokite dynasty's everlasting right to officiate in the high priesthood.

Whereas Philo, who makes reference to Phinehas in no less than eight of his works,[27] did underscore and praise his zeal, Pseudo-Philo, by contrast, concealed his fanatical act, using this figure as "a kind of leitmotif, a symbol of the work of priesthood," as Louis Feldman has observed.[28] Regarding the Josephan description of the biblical episode of Phinehas's fanaticism (*Ant.* 4.152–3), Feldman notes that Josephus mentions neither the biblical Phinehas's zealotry nor his divine reward, attributing this to Josephus's desire to tone down the

---

[26] For a survey of the attitude toward Phinehas in post-biblical literature, see e.g. Feldman, "Portrayal of Phinehas," 315–45; Batsch, "Priests in Warfare," 173; and more recently B. Elitzur, "Zeal of Pinhas," 9–39.

[27] For bibliographical references and further details, see Feldman, "Portrayal of Phinehas," 316 and passim.

[28] Ibid. 316; see also 324.

impetuous, autonomous aspects of Phinehas's act because it served as a model for the zealots in Josephus's day, whom the historian opposed strongly.[29]

Intriguingly, only one definite (and perhaps one doubtful) reference to Phinehas has survived in Qumran literature and that only with respect to the priestly lineage.[30] He is cited as one of the forefathers of Jeshua son of Jozadak, a priest who was among the leaders of the restoration period: [   ] ישוע[בן יוצדק אשר]   מבני פינחס וש ("from the sons of Phinehas, and ... [Jeshua] son of Jozadak who").[31] Similar to what we saw in Ben Sira, the purpose of this genealogical fragment was apparently to convey that the eternal priesthood promised to Phinehas had been bestowed on the Zadokites. The other, doubtful, reference, from *The Apocryphon of Joshua* (4Q522 9 II, 7), depends on the reconstruction of the text.[32]

Traces of the use of the figure of Phinehas in order to glorify the name and lineage of high priests can perhaps also be identified in a polemical tannaitic midrash. In its exposition of the pentateuchal verse promising Phinehas a pact of peace, *Sifre Numbers* 131 notes that during the Second Temple period there were forty priests descended from Phinehas (as opposed to eighteen in the First Temple period), whom it censures for having purchased their posts with gold and silver.[33]

We can then conclude that someone who "expect[s] a reward like Phinehas" is a claimant to the high priesthood either for himself or his cronies, and questions the right of the current officiant in the post, in this instance, the Hasmonean dynasty.[34] Supporting this claim is the demand that the Hasmonean ruler

---

[29] Ibid.; see also Batsch, "Priests in Warfare," 172–3.

[30] Christophe Batsch ("Priests in Warfare") suggests that the Qumran sect opposed the notion of fighting-priests like Phinehas because of the fear of defilement, as found in the *War Scroll*, and promoted a different model of priestly leadership that mediated between humans and God and did not serve as a military leadership. However, the short review above shows that the sect was not the sole group that chose to highlight the promise of the priesthood to Phinehas over his zealous act.

[31] *6QPriestly Prophecy* (6Q13), lines 4–5 (DJD 3:127). English translation cited from Martinez and Tigchelaar, *Dead Sea Scrolls Study Edition*, 2:1153.

[32] As reconstructed by Emile Puech, the text's original editor, lines 6–7 read as follows: [(?)ואהרון] חס] בני פינ] יכהן שם ראישׁוֹ֗ נ֗ מ הואה יבננו תצדוק הכוהן [ובנו הקטן ("And his younger son [shall build (the temple) and Zadok the priest] shall serve as priest there first from [the children of Pin]chas [and Aaron (?)]") (Puech, *Qumran Grotte 4.XVIII: Textes Hebreux*, DJD 25:55. English trans. cited from Parry and Tov, *Dead Sea Scrolls Reader: Parabiblical Texts*, 339, slightly revised. See also Qimron "Joshua Cycles," 503–8). If this reconstruction is correct, then Phinehas is mentioned here for the sole purpose of establishing the priestly lineage. Note that, according to the more recent reconstructions proposed by Elisha Qimron (*Dead Sea Scrolls: Hebrew Writings*, 2:76) and A. Feldman (*Rewritten Joshua Scrolls*, 142), Phinehas receives no mention in this fragment. Below I present a singular restoration of Phinehas's name in 4Q372 3. However, this is only a supposition, for no letters or any other hints of the name פינחס have survived.

[33] Kahana, *Sifre on Numbers: The Edition*, 2:437.

[34] In Ilan and Noam, "Pharisaic Apologetic Source," a different stance was taken, attributing the zeal to the Pharisees who are compared to Phinehas in our story. I have now changed my mind.

relinquish the high priesthood, put forth by one of the scoundrels from the story of the rupture with the Pharisees (Chap. 3).

Zimri in Post-biblical Literature

The contrast between Phinehas as the positive protagonist and Zimri as the embodiment of evil found in the BT is also attested at Qumran. Fragment 4Q372 3 is part of a text that defies classification: it contains both poetry and prose,[35] and incorporates a description of the Israelites' war against their enemies alongside prayers and words of praise planted in the mouths of Joseph and Moses.[36] At the end of the fragment in question (lines 10–12), the author praises God for avenging the Israelites against their enemies, mentioning in that context the bitter end of Midian, specifying Zimri son of Salu and the five kings of Midian:

...כל הנגעים בנחל]תו   [ ] [....ואת דמם ידרוש מידם ראו מה עשה למדין א]   [אחד הוא
זמרי בן סלוא וחמשת מלכי מדין נהרגו]   .(

All those who harm [his] inheritance[ ]

[ ]....And their blood he will demand from their hand. See what he did to 'Midian' [ ]

One, namely Zimri son of Salu. And the five kings of Midian were slain [][37]

According to the editors of the text, the unmentioned figure of Phinehas links the two biblical stories: the war against Midian (Num 31) and the killing of Zimri (Num 25:7–13).[38]

To return to the story as found in the BT: what does "deeds of Zimri" signify there? As was the case with Phinehas, there are two possible explanations. One is that the "deeds" are the biblical sins of consorting with foreign women or idolatry. Such a context, however, does not fit our story, which treats the political fears of the Hasmonean dynasty, not a polemic against intermarriage

---

[35] See Bernstein, "4Q371–373," 33.

[36] Qimron (*Dead Sea Scrolls: Hebrew Writings*, 2:77) called this fragment "Divre Yosef u-Moshe."

[37] Schuller and Bernstein, "372. 4QNarrative and Poetic Compositionᵇ," 181. Qimron (*Dead Sea Scrolls: Hebrew Writings*, 2:82) supplies a very similar reading with additional reconstructions not cited here because they are not focal to the discussion.

[38] Schuller and Bernstein, "372. 4QNarrative and Poetic Compositionᵇ," 184. In a separate publication, Bernstein suggested reconstructing the name of Phinehas: ראו מה עשה למדין א]רצם אבדה...
הרג פינחס מהם] אחד הוא זמרי בן סלוא...." ("See what he did to Midian; [their] l[and is lost...Phinehas killed] one [of them], Zimri son of Salu...") (Bernstein, "4Q371–373," 25). Lacking a textual basis, this supposition has not been accepted in later scholarship and has apparently even been abandoned by Bernstein. See Schuller and Bernstein, "372. 4QNarrative and Poetic Compositionᵇ," 181; Qimron, *Dead Sea Scrolls: Hebrew Writings*, 2:82.

or idolatry.[39] A second possibility emerges from the Second Temple-period exegesis of the biblical pericope, which perceives Zimri as rebelling against Mosaic authority, similar to the episode of Korah recounted earlier in Numbers.[40] Although the biblical text simply describes the fact of Zimri's sin with the Midianite woman, Josephus creates an entire speech for Zimri (whom he calls Zambrias), whose axis is a harsh attack on Mosaic leadership, the laws taught by Moses, and his tyrannical rule:

> (145) "Nay, do *thou*, Moses, keep these laws on which thou has bestowed thy pains, having secured confirmation for them only through these men's simplicity; for, were they not men of that character, thou wouldest often ere now have learnt through chastisement that Hebrews are not duped so easily. (146) But *me* thou shalt not get to follow thy tyrannical orders ($\tau\upsilon\rho\alpha\nu\nu\iota\kappa\hat{\omega}s$); for thou hast done nought else until now save [to contrive] by wicked artifice ($\kappa\alpha\kappa\sigma\upsilon\rho\gamma\epsilon\hat{\iota}s$), under the pretext of 'laws' and 'God,' ($\pi\rho\sigma\sigma\chi\acute{\eta}\mu\alpha\tau\iota\ \nu\acute{\sigma}\mu\omega\nu\ \kappa\alpha\grave{\iota}\ \tau\sigma\hat{\upsilon}\ \theta\epsilon\sigma\hat{\upsilon}$) ... servitude for us and sovereignty for thyself, robbing us of life's sweets and of that liberty of action, which belongs to free men who own no master. (147) By such means thou wouldest prove more oppressive to the Hebrews than were the Egyptians, in claiming to punish in the name of these laws the intention of each individual to please himself. Nay, far rather is it thyself who deserves punishment ($\tau\iota\mu\omega\rho\acute{\iota}\alpha\nu$), for having purposed to abolish things which all the world has unanimously admitted to be excellent and for having set up, over against universal opinion, thine own extravagances. (148) ... I have married, as thou sayest, a foreign wife ... (149) and I sacrifice to gods to whom I hold sacrifice to be due, deeming it right to get at the truth for myself from many persons, and not to live as under a tyranny ($\ddot{\omega}\sigma\pi\epsilon\rho\ \dot{\epsilon}\nu\ \tau\upsilon\rho\alpha\nu\nu\acute{\iota}\delta\iota$), hanging all my hopes for my whole life upon one." (*Ant.* 4.145–9)

Intriguingly, Josephus has Korah voice similar arguments, using close or identical expressions:

> (15) So he proceeded to denounce him [Moses] among the Levites ... declaring that it was monstrous to look on at Moses hunting round to create glory for himself and mischievously working ($\kappa\alpha\kappa\sigma\upsilon\rho\gamma\sigma\hat{\upsilon}\nu\tau\alpha$) to attain this in the pretended name of God ($\dot{\epsilon}\pi\grave{\iota}\ \pi\rho\sigma\phi\acute{\alpha}\sigma\epsilon\iota\ \tau\sigma\hat{\upsilon}\ \theta\epsilon\sigma\hat{\upsilon}$) ... in despotic fashion ($\tau\upsilon\rho\acute{\alpha}\nu\nu\omega\nu$[41] $\tau\rho\acute{\sigma}\pi\omega$) ... (17) ... but those who are incapable of obtaining honours by just means ... scheme by wicked artifice ($\tau\acute{\epsilon}\chi\nu\eta\ ...\ \kappa\alpha\kappa\sigma\upsilon\rho\gamma\sigma\hat{\upsilon}\sigma\iota$) to attain to power. (18) It was expedient for the people, he continued, to punish ($\kappa\sigma\lambda\acute{\alpha}\zeta\epsilon\iota\nu$) such persons ... (*Ant.* 4.15, 17, 18).[42]

---

[39] In general, inveighing against intermarriage is not widespread in texts from the Hasmonean period. See M. Himmelfarb, "Intermarriage," 21.

[40] The two stories of these negative heroes are already combined in Ps 106:17–18, 28–9 without mentioning their names.

[41] This is Niese's emendation; the MSS read: $\tau\upsilon\rho\acute{\alpha}\nu\nu\omega$ or $\tau\upsilon\rho\acute{\alpha}\nu\nu\sigma\upsilon$. See Thackeray, *Josephus* (LCL), 4:482 n. 2.

[42] Note that an argument similar to that voiced by Korah, in both the Josephan and rabbinic versions, was incorporated in a rabbinic midrash on the biblical pericope of Zimri and Phinehas. Korah claims that the tribe of Reuben is more worthy of greatness than the tribe of Levi because Reuben is the eldest (*Ant.* 4.19; see also the late midrash in *Tanḥuma* [Buber ed.], *Koraḥ* 3 and the

In addition, according to a rabbinic midrash in the BT (*b. Sanh.* 82a–b), Zimri rebuked Moses, using accusations similar to those of Korah: "He then seized her by her coiffure and brought her before Moses. 'Son of Amram,' exclaimed he, 'is this woman forbidden or permitted? And should you say "She is forbidden", who permitted thee Jethro's daughter'?"

The Signification of the Allusion to the Episode of Phinehas and Zimri in the Janneus Legend

Both the Josephan paraphrase of the biblical pericopes and the rabbinic midrash portray Zimri, like Korah, as rebelling against Mosaic rule. The various midrashic interpretations of these episodes have the protagonists voicing similar arguments. If Zimri is perceived as an archetypical rebel, in contrast, Phinehas is the progenitor of a worthy line of high priests who officiate by dint of divine mandate. It turns out that Second Temple-period exegesis compared the claimants to the high priesthood, or those who disputed the claims of the regnant dynasty, to rebels of Zimri's type, designating them those "who expect a reward like Phinehas."

That links were drawn between the sectarian arena of the Hasmonean period and the biblical drama of Phinehas and Zimri receives further affirmation from an unexpected direction. A tannaitic midrash relates:

אמרו לו פינחס להיכן אתה הולך. אמר להן . . . אמרו, הניחו לו ויכנס והיתירו פרושין את הדבר

They said to him, Phinehas, where are you going? He replied. . . .[43] They said, let him go in, the Pharisees must have permitted (והיתירו פרושין) his action [of entering the chamber where Cozbi was]. (*Sifre Num.* 131; Kahana, *Sifre on Numbers: The Edition*, 2:434)

The exegete imaginatively elaborates on the biblical scene. While entering the tent to exact revenge on Zimri and the Midianite, Phinehas pretends that his entry, like that of all the leaders of the people before him, is for the purpose of sexual intercourse with the Midianite. Accordingly, the sinners gathered around

---

parallels). In the midrash on the episode of Zimri and Phinehas in *Sifre* 131 (Kahana, *Sifre on Numbers: The Edition*, 2:434; see also *b. Sanh.* 82b), Phinehas argues, while pretending to go into the chamber to be with the Midianite woman: Levi is not greater than Simeon; everywhere we find Simeon is greater than Levi. Namely, if the prince of Simeon allows himself to have sexual relations with the foreign woman, then I, whose tribe is younger, can surely do the same. Cf. the argument tendered by Zimri himself in *b. Sanh.* 82a, that he is greater than Moses: "I too," he replied, "am the prince of a tribe; moreover, my tribe is greater than his [Moses], for mine is second in birth, whilst his is third." (The same argument appears in *Sifre* [Kahana, *Sifre on Numbers: The Edition*, 2:434, lines 60–2], but the editor thinks it is an insertion imported from the Talmud; see Kahana, *Sifre on Numbers: Part IV: Commentary*, 1104.)

[43] Phinehas's reply: "Levi is not greater than Simeon; everywhere we find Simeon is greater than Levi," was treated in the previous note.

the entrance allow him to enter. On seeing him approach, they assume that "the Pharisees" must have permitted this act.

Rashi, in his commentary on the parallel in the BT (*b. Sanh.* 82a–b), explains: " 'It is certainly permissible to do so (= to have intercourse with the Midianite), for Phinehas acted as we did,' thus said those standing there when they saw him enter." These outside observers assumed that if Phinehas went into the tent where the Midianite woman had been, this was a sign that the halakhists, here unusually designated פרושים, had already given permission for him to do so.[44] The expected designation חכמים ("sages") does not appear here; rather, this story terms the Teachers of Halakhah associated with Phinehas's deeds פרושים. As noted above, in rabbinic sources the term Pharisees is always placed in the mouths of external observers, usually their opponents.[45] This indicates that this legend identified the righteous protagonist of the biblical story, Phinehas, with the Pharisees, and the sinful, ignorant followers of Zimri with other factions, perhaps the Sadducees. The surprising appearance of the designation "Pharisees" in the tannaitic depiction of the biblical scene suggests that this tradition has preserved traces of a pre-rabbinic Pharisaic aggadah, which applied the biblical story to the circumstances of its day.

Decoding Janneus's Deathbed Story

Based on the discussion above, I infer that the legend embedded in the BT represents the Pharisaic viewpoint, which is voiced by implanting the following insights into Janneus's instructions: the Pharisees are not dangerous, nor do they rebel against the monarchy. It is not the real Pharisees who are to be feared but rather pretenders. Moreover, the accusations of subversion and hypocrisy tendered against the Pharisees are incorrect. These attributes typify the pretenders, not the actual Pharisees. The negative attributes by which the Pharisees are usually—and unjustly—designated in fact characterize other people, who purport to be Pharisees. It is this group of imitators, rather than the "real" Pharisees, which objects to the Hasmonean high priesthood, seeking it for itself or its cohorts. Although it aspires to perpetual priesthood per Phinehas's reward, in reality, its members are rebels and scandalmongers in the image of Zimri who question the authority of the leader of the generation.

Striking similarities exist between the strategy and message of this story and those found in the talmudic version of the rupture with the Pharisees. In both we find definitively Second Temple terminology: פרושים וצבועים ("Pharisees and

---

[44] Or possibly: The Pharisees would in the future make such harlotry permissible to the entire people, since Phinehas had now joined the transgressors. In the talmudic parallels and most witnesses of *Sifre*: התירו פרושים. However, the superior text of MS Vatican 32 reads והיתירו. Kahana (*Sifre on Numbers: Part IV: Commentary*, 1107 n. 215) suggests that the *waw* is predicative (see Epstein, *Introduction to the Mishnaic Text*, 1076–86), and also raises the possibility that והיתיר is equivalent to יתירו, in the future tense (i.e. as an imperfect form), and that the *heh* serves as a *mater lectionis* for *schwa*.

[45] See Chap. 3, n. 20.

hypocrites") in our story; ליץ, בליעל, זעם ("frivolous," "scoundrel," "rage"), among others, in the story of the rupture. Both depict an ambivalent relationship between Janneus and the Pharisees. Moreover, the casting of Janneus in a tolerant light diverges from his usual depiction in rabbinic literature. The storyteller rejects the existence of any real rivalry between the ruler and the Pharisees; it is other groups that mislead the ruler and foster dissension. Each story uses a biblical model—from the book of Numbers specifically—of individuals who rebel against the divinely chosen leadership, and these figures receive similar treatment in post-biblical exegesis. In both stories the author comes to the defense of the Pharisees, to whom low acts or despicable opinions are unjustifiably attributed, which were actually espoused by groups with external resemblance to the Pharisees only: thus, the elder in the story of the rift from whom the sages swiftly "separated"; thus, the "hypocrites who ape the Pharisees" in our story. Evidently, apart from the Pharisees, various groups used an apologetic argument to clear themselves of charges of anti-Hasmonean rebellion during this period.[46]

This suggests that the BT has either preserved two fragments from a single source, or two sources from a single collection of Pharisaic apologetics. One—the story of the rupture between Janneus and the Pharisees—retained its original language; the other—Janneus's instructions to his wife—underwent partial reworking. Within the broad context of rabbinic literature both were miraculously embedded, and survived, in the BT alone, and both retained authentic motifs and language that reflect the political-sectarian arena of the Hasmonean period. Supporting the conjecture that both originated in a single source or collection is the fact that, as opposed to most of the parallels to Josephus in the BT, these two legends reached Babylonia without the mediation of a tannaitic source.[47] This suggests that the BT here retained extra- or pre-tannaitic traditions that were not preserved in the official collections of tannaitic literature.

E. JOSEPHUS AND THE RABBIS

Here too, as in other instances studied in this book, the early scholarship conflates the Josephan and the talmudic testimony into a single historical reconstruction,[48] whereas later scholars question the historicity of the event

---

[46] Thus, the statement made by the sectarian author of 4QMMT— ואתם י]ודעים שלוא י[מצא בידנו [נפשנו] מעל ושקר ורעה כי על [אלה א[נחנו נותנים א[ת נפשנו] ("And you k[now that there is not] to be found in our actions deceit or betrayal or evil, for concerning these things we give [our lives]"), as restored and interpreted by Menahem Kister, belongs to this genre and was a claim that the sect did not rebel against the regime (4QMMT C 7–9) (Kister, "4QMiqsat Ma'ase Ha-Torah," 321).

[47] See Ilan and Noam, "Pharisaic Apologetic Source," 114–15.

[48] First by Rashi, *b. Sotah* 22b, s.v. אל תתיראי מן הפרושים, who introduced to his commentary information that had its source in Josephus ("when he died his wife was fearful of them, that they not divest her sons of the monarchy"), evidently through the mediation of *Josippon*.

described in each.[49] In line with his approach which views the Josephan source as derived from an invention by Nicolaus of Damascus, Joshua Efron assumes that the BT relied on Josephus or a close parallel.[50] As we have seen in this chapter, the incongruous, early features of the talmudic source (the attribution of hypocrisy to the Pharisees; the comparison to the biblical pericope of Zimri and Phinehas) do not appear in Josephus; and other, significant differences divide the two versions. Moreover, the episode's incongruity in the narrative sequence in *Antiquities* is salient. Taken in conjunction, this indicates that the Talmud did not draw on Josephus for its version of the episode, but rather that both corpora were informed by unknown, earlier Jewish sources.[51]

Nonetheless, as Tal Ilan has observed, this is not a case in which an identical source has been embedded in two contexts. The detailed Josephan story of the deathbed instructions is totally missing from the minimalistic talmudic anecdote, which recalls a pithy saying regarding Phinehas and Zimri—not necessarily deathbed instructions—which is not found in the Josephan account. Perhaps this epigram, known to us from the BT, appeared in the Hebrew original available to Josephus and he chose to omit it, as was the case elsewhere with respect to biblical allusions.[52] But this does not explain the additional differences between the stories. The story available to Josephus attributes the conflict to the king's mistreatment of the Pharisees, whereas the talmudic version blames unknown "hypocrites" who ape the Pharisees. This suggests that Josephus, and centuries later, the Talmud, were from the start familiar with two different variants of an apologetic Pharisaic story that attributed to Janneus a temperate statement to his wife regarding the Pharisees,[53] which cleared them of accusations of subverting Hasmonean rule. Heightening the distance between the two versions was Josephus's decision to insert a statement, similar to others found in *Antiquities*, that displays hostility toward the Pharisees, which perhaps originated in the works of Nicolaus of Damascus.

F. CONCLUSION

The legend on which this chapter has focused, in conjunction with the rupture tradition studied in Chapter 3, discloses not just a lost literary source but a vibrant historical reality. As preserved in Josephus and the BT, both traditions are in actuality variants of apologetic Pharisaic sources that addressed the

---

[49] For both opinions, see text at nn. 11–18.
[50] Efron, "Simeon Ben Shaṭaḥ and Jannaeus," 186–90.
[51] See Regev, *Sadducees*, 270–1 n. 32; Ilan, "Jannaeus's Deathbed Instructions."
[52] See Chap. 1.
[53] This differs somewhat from the conclusion found in Ilan and Noam, "Pharisaic Apologetic Source."

Pharisaic–Hasmonean relationship. These sources faithfully reflect Pharisaic self-perception and propaganda. The Pharisees viewed themselves as a group eminently loyal to the Hasmonean rulers, as endowed with generosity and willingness to compromise. Moreover, they attributed the conflict with the Hasmoneans to others: quarrel-mongering Sadducees; hypocrites who ape the Pharisees; and even the ruler himself. Nonetheless, the storytellers do not seek to totally blacken the reputation of the Hasmonean rulers, and an ambivalent stance toward them emerges from both stories. In one, the ruler was misled by a third party; in the other, he recanted his negative attitude toward the Pharisees. Moreover, in their Josephan version, both stories share the claim that the masses are loyal to the Pharisees and that their hatred of the Hasmonean ruler stemmed from his attitude toward this sector.

In their talmudic versions, both stories share the comparison of the political situation to a biblical pericope from the book of Numbers. In both, the Pharisees are identified with a positive biblical protagonist—Moses and Aaron or Phinehas—and their rivals with a scheming rebel—Korah or Zimri, two figures that were linked in post-biblical exegesis. In Josephus, both stories were juxtaposed to contexts hostile to the Pharisees: one is found in the frame narrative; the other appears as a comment in the body of the story. These hostile comments, which contradict the spirit of the stories themselves, are of great significance. They reflect the aspersions cast on the Pharisees by their opponents, thereby revealing the backdrop to, and motivation for, the creation of a Pharisaic apologetic. Also known from other contemporary sources,[54] these shared accusations portray the Pharisees as a hypocritical, scheming, influential, power-hungry group that incites the masses against various figures, at times simply from envy, and in this spirit striving to undermine the Hasmonean dynasty. The insertion by Josephus of these contentious observations into the original traditions has ramifications for understanding Josephus's own outlook.

Who, then, were the "real" Pharisees? Given the distance between their era and ours, it is difficult to reach a definitive conclusion regarding this political dispute. One fact, however, is of interest: both parties to the dispute acknowledge the tremendous influence of the Pharisees on the masses, which is interpreted positively in the original Pharisaic stories and negatively in the appended hostile remarks in the Josephan context. This, then, reflects a historical reality: the Pharisees indeed exercised great influence on the broad public, as attested by the Dead Sea Scrolls, Josephus, and the New Testament.[55] This conclusion affects a longstanding scholarly debate.[56] Going further, this analysis of the

[54] See n. 25.

[55] For the DSS, see *Pesher Nahum*, 3–4 II, 9–10 (Charlesworth, *Dead Sea Scrolls*, 6B:150); for Josephus, in addition to the sections discussed above (*Ant.* 13.288, 296, 298, 401–2), see also *War* 2.162; *Ant.* 17.41, 18.15; for the NT, see Matt 23:2.

[56] See Goodblatt, "Place of the Pharisees," 12–30. For an instructive, up-to-date survey of the research on this question, see D. R. Schwartz, "Introduction: Was 70 CE a Watershed in Jewish

brief anecdote of Janneus's instructions to his wife has brought to life a two-millennium-old stormy political debate.

This story, which describes the beginning of the reconciliation between the Pharisees and the Hasmonean dynasty during the golden period of Shelamzion's reign, is the last tradition that provides an optimistic portrayal of the Hasmonean dynasty. The following chapter, which is devoted to the internecine struggles of the following—and final—Hasmonean generation, has tragic aspects. It marks the end of the Hasmonean dynasty and harbingers the future destruction of the temple.

History?" 1–19, esp. 6–11. Until the mid-twentieth century the scholarship (among whose representatives Schwartz notes Emil Schürer, George Foote Moore, and Gedalyahu Alon) accepted the testimony of the ancient sources regarding the primacy of the Pharisees. From the 1950s the scholarly trend was to doubt Pharisaic supremacy. The turning-point was Morton Smith's "Palestinian Judaism." The 1970s saw the entrenchment of this viewpoint in the works of Neusner, Sanders, and others, and later in the article by David Goodblatt cited at the beginning of this note.

6

The Fratricidal Hasmonean Conflict and the Murder of Onias

The final episode treated in this book touches on events from the waning days of the Hasmonean dynasty. At center stage is an internecine struggle between two Hasmonean brothers. The plot revolves around broken agreements, incitement, murder, and, above all, the danger to the ongoing cult at the invisible epicenter: the Jerusalem temple.

This tradition is unique because of its multiple variants and adaptations, not only in the different corpora, but even within a single rabbinic sugya. In the Josephan version, and only there, is the story of the murder of a righteous man juxtaposed to the central siege tradition belonging to the internecine struggle between the Hasmonean brothers. This story constitutes an example of the Josephan transmission of a source that, by virtue of its features, obviously belonged to a pre-rabbinic Jewish collection of stories of the type often cited in rabbinic literature, but which was in this case not preserved there. This is also an instance in which, despite the BT's geographical and temporal distance from events, the traditions preserved there were found to be superior to, and earlier than, the parallels in the YT. It is even possible that the BT has here preserved original features of the ancient tradition deliberately obscured by Josephus. Beyond their diverse details, the versions in both Josephus and the Babylonian Talmud transmit the same message as to the moral roots underpinning the calamity that befell the Jewish people with the Hasmonean downfall. The tradition underlying both in fact reflects a facet of Jewish, probably Pharisaic, theodicy, which ascribed the loss of independence to the breach of Jewish unity. The polemical nature of this political-historiosophical stance is elaborated in Chapter 7.

A. THE SOURCES

Antiquities 14.19–28; *y. Berakhot* 4:1, 7b; *y. Ta'anit* 4:8, 68c; *b. Sotah* 49b;
b. Baba Qamma 82b; *b. Menaḥot* 64b; [*m. Ta'anit* 3:8]

Josephus, *Antiquities* 14.19–28[1]

(19) Because of these promises which were made to him, Aretas marched against Aristobulus with an army of fifty thousand horsemen and footsoldiers as well, and defeated him in battle. After his victory many deserted to Hyrcanus, and Aristobulus, being left alone, fled to Jerusalem. (20) Thereupon the Arab king took his whole army and attacked the temple, where he besieged Aristobulus; and the citizens, joining Hyrcanus' side, assisted him in the siege, while only the priests remained loyal to Aristobulus. (21) And so Aretas placed the camps of the Arabs and Jews[2] next to one another, and pressed the siege vigorously. But as this action took place at the time of observing the festival of Unleavened Bread, which we call *Phaska*, the Jews of best repute left the country and fled to Egypt. (22) Now there was a certain Onias, who, being a righteous man and dear to God (δίκαιος ἀνὴρ καὶ θεοφιλής), had once in a rainless period prayed to God to end the drought, and God had heard his prayer and sent rain; this man hid himself when he saw that the civil war continued to rage, but he was taken to the camp of the Jews and was asked to place a curse on Aristobulus and his fellow-rebels,[3] just as he had, by his prayers, put an end to the rainless period. (23) But when in spite of his refusals and excuses he was forced to speak by the mob, he stood up in their midst and said, (24) "Oh God, king of the universe (ὦ θεὲ βασιλεῦ τῶν ὅλων), since these men standing by me are Thy people, and those who are besieged are Thy priests, I beseech you not to hearken to them against these men nor to bring to pass what these men ask Thee to do to those others." And when he had prayed in this manner the villains among the Jews who stood round him stoned him to death.

(25) But God straightaway punished them for this savagery, and exacted satisfaction for the murder of Onias in the following manner. While the priests and Aristobulus were being besieged, there happened to come round the festival called *Phaska*, at which it is our custom to offer numerous sacrifices to God. (26) But as Aristobulus and those with him lacked victims, they asked their countrymen to furnish them with these, and take as much money for the victims as they wished. And when these others demanded that they pay a thousand

---

[1] For a better understanding of the context, the citation from Josephus extends beyond the parallel itself.

[2] Camp of the Jews: Ἰουδαίων] Ἰδουμαίων (Idumeans) P.

[3] Rebels: συστασιωτῶν E; his soldiers: στρατιωτῶν WMAL.

drachmas for each animal they wished to get, Aristobulus and the priests will-ingly accepted this price and gave them the money, which they let down from the walls by a rope (διὰ τῶν τειχῶν καθιμήσαντες). (27) Their countrymen, however, after receiving the money did not deliver the victims, but went to such lengths of villainy that they violated their pledges and acted impiously toward God by not furnishing the sacrificial victims to those who were in need of them (τοῖς δεομένοις). (28) But the priests, on suffering this breach of faith, prayed to God to exact satisfaction on their behalf from their countrymen; and He did not delay their punishment, but sent a mighty and violent wind to destroy the crops of the entire country, so that the people at that time had to pay eleven drachmas for a *modius* of wheat.

Rabbinic Sources

Y. Ta'anit 4:8, 68c = *y. Berakhot* 4:1, 7b[4]

1. *And the daily whole offering was canceled:*	'ובטל התמיד'
2. R. Simeon in the name of R. Yehoshua ben Levi:	ר' סימון בשם ר' יהושע בן לוי
3. "In the days of the Greek kingdom, they would let down two baskets containing gold, and they [the besiegers] would send up two sheep [for the daily offering].	בימי מלכות יוון היו משלשלין להם שתי קופות שלזהב והיו מעלין שני כבשים
4. "One time they let down to them two baskets of gold, and they sent up to them two kid goats [which are not suitable for a daily offering].	פעם אחת שילשלו להם שתי קופות שלזהב והעלו להן שני גדיים
5. "At that time the Holy One, blessed be he, opened their eyes and they found two lambs in the chamber of the lambs [which were suitable].	באותה השעה האיר הקב'ה את עיניהם ומצאו שני טלאים בלישכת הטלאים
6. "It was concerning this time that R. Yehudah ben Aba gave testimony concerning the daily whole offering brought in the morning, that it was offered at the fourth hour."	על אותה השעה העיד ר' יהודה בן אבא על תמיד שלשחר שקרב בארבע שעות
7. Said R. Levi,	ואמ' ר' לוי
8. "Also in the time of this evil kingdom [the Romans, presently ruling] they would let down to them two baskets of gold, and they would send up to them two <sheep>.	אף בימי מלכות הרשעה הזאת היו משלשלין להן שתי קופות שלזהב והיו מעלין להן שני <כבשים>
9. "Finally they let down to them two baskets of gold, and they sent up to them two pigs.	ובסוף שילשלו להם שתי קופות שלזהב והעלו להם שני חזירים
10. "The basket had not gotten halfway up the wall, before the pig shrieked[5] and forty *parasangs* of the land of Israel shook [in an earthquake].	לא הספיקו להגיע למחצית החומה עד שנ(א)[ע]ץ החזיר וקפץ מארץ-יש' ארבעים פרסה

---

[4] The base text is cited from *y. Ta'anit* (MS Leiden), which was apparently the legend's initial location in the YT.

[5] See Lieberman, *Studies*, 489.

[6] Following the reading of Saul Lieberman (ibid.). The letter is a doubtful *taf* according to the Academy of the Hebrew Language edition of the Jerusalem Talmud.

11. "At that time the sins [of Israel] brought it about   באותה השעה גרמו העוונות ובטל התמיד וחרב הבית
that the daily offering was canceled, and the
house [the temple] was laid to waste."

B. Menaḥot 64b[7] (= b. Sotah 49b; b. B. Qamma 82b)

Our Rabbis taught:	תנו רבנן

1. When the kings of the Hasmonean house besieged   כשצרו מלכי בית חשמוניי זה על זה היה הורקנוס
one another, Hyrcanus was outside and Aristobulus   מבחוץ ואריסטובלוס מבפנים
within [the city wall][8]

2. Each day [those that were within] used to let down   בכל יום ויום היו משלשלין להם דינר' בקופה ומעלין
[to the other party] *denars* in a basket, and haul up   להם תמידין
[in return] animals for the daily offerings.

3. There was an old man there, who was learned in   היה שם זקן אחד שהיה מכיר בחכמת יוונית
Greek wisdom.[9]

4. [He said to them:][10] "As long as they carry on the   <אמ' להן:> כל זמן שעסוקין בעבודה אין
temple service they will never be delivered into your   נמסרין בידכם
hands."

5. On the morrow they let down *denars* in a basket and   למחר שילשלו להם דינר' בקופה והעלו להן חזיר
hauled up a pig.

6. When it reached halfway up the wall, it stuck its   כיון שהגיע לחצי חומה נעץ ציפרניו בחומה
claws into the wall,[11]

7. and the land of Israel was shaken over a distance of   ונזדעזעה ארץ ישר' ארבע מאות פרסה על ארבע
four hundred *parasangs* by four hundred *parasangs*.   מאות פרסה

8. At that time they declared, "Cursed be the man who   באותה שעה אמרו ארור ארור אדם שיגדל חזירים וארור
rears pigs and cursed be the man who teaches his   אדם שילמד את בנו חכמת יוונית
son Greek wisdom!"

9. It was concerning this time [of siege] that we   על אותה שעה שנינו מעשה שבא העומר מגגות
learnt: It once happened that the '*Omer* was   צריפין ושתי הלחם מבקעת בית סוכר
brought from Gaggoth[12] Ẓerifin and the two
loaves from the valley of Bet Sokher.

---

[7] The base text is cited from *b. Menaḥot*, which was apparently the legend's initial location in
the BT, according to MS Paris, AIU, H147A.

[8] In some witnesses, the order has been corrupted and is reversed: הורקנוס מבפנים ואריסטובלוס מבחוץ
("Hyrcanus was inside and Aristobulus outside"), but it is obvious that the text cited above was
the original version. See Wiesenberg, "Related Prohibitions," 215 n. 11 and the bibliographical
references there.

[9] Many manuscripts of the three *sugyot* add here: לעז להם בחכמת יוונית ("he communicated with
them in [the language of] Greek wisdom").

[10] Thus in most versions, though not in MS Paris, AIU, H147A of *Menaḥot*.

[11] The words "its claws into the wall," or the word "wall" alone, are missing in some versions. In
other versions, the verbs צווח/זעק/צעק are added here. These versions attest to the veracity of
Lieberman's reconstruction (*Studies*, 489) of the original version: נאק alone (see the Yerushalmi
above), meaning "shrieked," rather than נעץ, meaning "stuck." The words "its claws into the wall"
are a later, erroneous addition.

[12] In the Palestinian versions of the mishnah cited here (*Menaḥ*. 10:2), as well as in some BT
versions: גנות.

M. Taʿanit 3:8[13]

על כל צרה שתבוא על הציבור מתריעים עליה חוץ מרוב גשמים. מעשה שאמרו לחוני המעגל. התפלל
שירדו גשמים. אמ' להם. צאו והכניסו תנורי פסחים בשביל שלא ימקו. ו(ני)[ה]תפלל ולא ירדו גשמים.
עג עוגה ועמד בתוכה ואמ'. רבונ(י)[ו] שלעולם]. בניך שמו פניהם עלי שני כבן בית לפניך. נשבע אני
בשמך הגדול שאיני זז מיכן על שתרחם על בניך. התחילו הגשמים מנטפים. אמ'. לא כך שאלתי אלא
גשמי בורות שיחים ומערות. ירדו בזעף. אמ'. לא כך שאלתי אלא גשמי רצון ברכה ונדבה. ירדו כתיקנן עד
שעלו ישרא' מירוש' להר-הבית מפני הגשמים. אמ' לו. כשם שהתפללתה עליהם שירדו כך היתפלל
שילכו להם. אמ' להם. צאו וראו אם נימחת אבן [ה]טועים. שלח לו שמעון בן שטח. אמ' לו. צריך אתה
ל(ו)[נד]ות. אבל מה אעשה ל(ו)[ך] ואתה מתחטא לפני המקום כבן שהוא מתחטא לאביו ועושה לו
רצונו. ועליך הכתוב אומ' "ישמח אביך ואמך ותגל יולדתך".

On account of every sort of public trouble do they blow [the *shofar* and fast],
except for an excess of rain. It once happened that they said to Ḥoni, the circle
drawer, "Pray for rain." He said to them, "Go and take in the clay ovens used for
Passover, so that they not soften [in the rain which is coming]. He prayed, but it
did not rain. What did he do? He drew a circle and stood in the middle of it and
said before Him, "Lord of the world! Your children have turned to me, for before
you I am like a chief steward. I swear by your great name—I'm simply not moving
from here until you take pity on your children!" It began to rain drop by drop. He
said, "This is not what I wanted, but rain for filling up cisterns, pits, and caverns."
It began to rain violently. He said, "This is not what I wanted, but rain of good will,
blessing, and graciousness." Now it rained the right way, until Israelites had to flee
from Jerusalem up to the Temple Mount because of the rain. Now they came and
said to him, "Just as you prayed for it to rain, now pray for it to go away." He said to
them, "Go and see whether the stone of the strayers is disappeared." Simeon ben
Shataḥ said to him, "If you were not Ḥoni, I should decree a ban of excommunica-
tion against you. But what am I going to do to you? For you importune before the
Omnipresent, so he does what you want, like a son who importunes his father, so
he does what he wants. Concerning you Scripture says, *Let your father and your
mother be glad, and let her that bore you rejoice* (Prov. 23:25)."

B. HISTORICAL BACKGROUND

Following the death in 67 BCE of Queen Alexandra (Shelamzion), Alexander
Janneus's wife and successor, the friction between her sons erupted into civil
war. Her firstborn son, Hyrcanus II, who had earlier been appointed high priest,

---

[13] This mishnah, which treats Ḥoni/Onias the rainmaker, is not an actual parallel to the
Josephan story and is therefore quoted last. Nor are the other rabbinic sources or legends on Ḥoni
and his miraculous rainmaking, which are scattered throughout rabbinic literature, cited here.
See, in addition to the mishnah, esp. *t. Ta'an.* 2:13; *y. Ta'an.* 3:10–11, 66d; *b. Ta'an.* 23a; Scholion P
on *Meg. Ta'an.*, 20 Adar. See also *b. Ber.* 10a; *Tanḥuma* (Buber ed.), *Va-era* 22, *Ki tavo* 4. Some of
the sources incorporate the story of Ḥoni's seventy-year-long sleep. Because the matter of rainmaking is not developed in Josephus, these sources are not cited here. Nor do I treat the scholarship on these stories, except where it touches on the parallels to the story of Onias in Josephus.

acceded to the throne, whereas his younger brother Aristobulus II aspired to the monarchy. During the ensuing conflict, Aristobulus prevailed. Following a reconciliation between the two, Hyrcanus abdicated in favor of Aristobulus, who now became king and high priest (*War* 1.109, 117–22; *Ant.* 13.408, 422–30; 14.4–7).

Advised and assisted by Antipater the Idumaean, Hyrcanus regretted having ceded the throne and drafted the Nabatean king, Aretas, to his side in his renewed campaign against Aristobulus. Unable to withstand their collective might, Aristobulus was driven into Jerusalem, where he was besieged by the combined forces of Hyrcanus and the Nabateans. It is this siege (64 BCE) that forms the backdrop for the stories examined below (*War* 1.123–6; *Ant.* 14.8–28).

A new turn of events came with the arrival in Syria of Pompey the Great's emissary, the Roman general Aemilius Scaurus. Each Hasmonean brother dispatched a deputation to Scaurus, offering a bribe in return for Roman assistance. Having decided in Aristobulus's favor, Scaurus employed threats to force Hyrcanus and the Nabateans to drop their siege. The fratricidal conflict continued, as did the lobbying of Pompey by both parties. In the final analysis, this Roman intervention paved the way for the Pompeian conquest of Jerusalem and the commonwealth, as Josephus writes: "For this misfortune which befell Jerusalem Hyrcanus and Aristobulus were responsible, because of their dissension. For we lost our freedom and became subject to the Romans..." (*Ant.* 14.77; see *War* 1.127–58; *Ant.* 13.29–79).

Allusions to these events also appear in Qumran texts. *Pesher Nahum* and the fragmentary text 4Q471a evidently refer to Pompey's conquest of Judea.[14] Yohanan, Shelamzion, Hyrcanus, "Aemilius" (Scaurus, Pompey's emissary), and even the "Ara[bs]" receive mention in an annalistic text discovered in three Cave 4 documents (4Q331–4Q333).[15] Various scholars link the famine described in the Qumran pesharim on Hosea, Isaiah, and Psalms with the famine described in the story of the sacrifices in the Josephan and rabbinic versions, and even with the drought in Honi's day known from the rabbinic corpus, also mentioned by Josephus in his account of the fratricidal Hasmonean conflict.[16]

C. THE TRADITION IN THE JOSEPHAN CONTEXT

As was the case for other episodes in this book, this story appears only in *Antiquities* and not in the parallel in *War* 1.126–8.[17] Table 6.1 compares the

---

[14] See Chap. 7, section C, subsection ("The Fourth Generation: Hyrcanus II and Aristobulus II"), and H. Eshel, *Dead Sea Scrolls and the Hasmonean State*, 133–7, and the references to earlier scholarship there.

[15] H. Eshel, *Dead Sea Scrolls and the Hasmonean State*, 136–42.

[16] See ibid. 143–50 and the bibliographical references there.

[17] This study has repeatedly shown the existence of Jewish sources not found in *War* but which are interpolated into *Antiquities* (see Introduction, section E), of which some of the parallels in

Table 6.1. *War* 1/*Antiquities* 14: The Interpolations

War 1; *Ant.* 14	*Ant.* 14
Hyrcanus marches into battle against his brother Aristobulus, aided by the Nabatean king Aretas and his army. After suffering defeat at their hands, Aristobulus is pushed back to Jerusalem, where he is besieged by Hyrcanus and his allies. (*War* 1.126; *Ant.* 14.19a–20)	
	The people join Hyrcanus and the priests side with Aristobulus. (20b)
	Siege camps are set up by Arabs and Jews at Aretas's direction. (21a)
	The event took place on Passover; therefore the Jewish leaders fled to Egypt to celebrate the holiday there. (21b)
	The episode of the righteous man Onias, which ends in his murder. (22–4)
	The episode of the sacrificial animals and the breaking of the agreement. (25–8)
Ptolemy's emissary Scaurus intervenes and the siege of Aristobulus is lifted. (*War* 1.127–9; *Ant.* 14.29–32)	

events as recounted in these works, and the right-hand column highlights the interpolated units in *Antiquities* 14.

The table indicates the interpolation of a long unit in *Antiquities* 14.20–8,[18] which describes events and details not recounted in *War*: (1) the setting up of siege camps; (2) the internal division between the people, who supported Hyrcanus, and the priests, who backed Aristobulus; (3) the comment regarding the Passover festival and the notables' flight to Egypt; (4) the murder of Onias (22–4); and (5) the episode of the sacrifices and the breaking of the agreement (25–8).

The last two units of the long interpolation in *Antiquities*—the murder of Onias and the episode of the sacrifices—are the focus of the discussion here. As outlined in the Introduction, these units display all the features of the Jewish traditions incorporated by Josephus into his later book, *Antiquities*, and it is clearly apparent that they derive from Jewish legends available to Josephus,[19]

rabbinic literature are found in the BT (Introduction, section C). I take issue with Wilk's statement: "The presence of a parallel in the BT to information recounted in Josephus does not provide sufficient backing for the conjectured direct derivation from an internal Jewish source, *especially when the information is not found in* War *and in Palestinian rabbinic sources*" ("When Hyrcanus Was Besieging Aristobulus," 99). Rather, the absence of material from *War* on the one hand, and often from Palestinian sources on the other, is a definitive feature of these Jewish traditions.

[18] See Colautti, *Passover in Josephus*, 88 and the literature cited there.

[19] This is the consensus in the scholarship as noted already by Hölscher, *Quellen des Josephus*, 20; idem, "Josephus," 1973–4; Laqueur, *Jüdische Historiker Flavius Josephus*, 142; Cohen, "Parallel Historical Tradition," 13.

which he interpolated into the narrative sequence of the events previously recounted in *War*. They are "closed" units with an identifiable beginning and end that stand out in the narrative sequence;[20] can be easily "lifted" from the narrative without impairing the flow of the surrounding text; are anecdotal in nature in contrast to the sequential account of broader military-political events; and treat internal Jewish matters, often linked to the temple and the temple service, which diverge from the surrounding wider geographical and human contexts. Further evidence that these are autonomous units comes from the fortunate fact that rabbinic literature has preserved a parallel to the second story of the sacrificial animals.[21] However, notwithstanding the fact that he was a well-known figure in rabbinic literature, the episode of Onias is not paralleled there. The rabbinic recounters and redactors of the story of the sacrifices were either unfamiliar with the story of Onias's murder or failed to connect it to the fratricidal Hasmonean conflict.

The Structure of the Josephan Passage

The story of Onias and the story of the siege appear to have been two independent legends regarding the siege of Jerusalem during the fratricidal Hasmonean war. At their center is tension between insiders and outsiders, which serves as the backdrop for the emergence of sinful behavior. The two legends place the blame on the besiegers, though each provides a different rationale for the downfall: the sin of Onias's murder or the sin associated with the sacrificial animals. Both also conclude with a prayer to God, though the prayers are inversions of each other. Whereas the story of Onias holds up Onias's appeal to God as exemplary, so that "what these men ask Thee to do to those others" will not come to pass (24), the story of the sacrifices teaches, uncritically, that "the priests...prayed to God to exact satisfaction on their behalf from their countrymen; and He did not delay their punishment" (28).

Before examining these two main traditions more closely, I first analyze the complex structure of the Josephan passage. The stories of the murder of Onias

---

[20] Many have noted the traces of the interpolation of different sources in this unit. See e.g. Marcus, *Jewish Antiquities* (LCL), 7:460–1 note *a*; Betz, "Choni-Onias," 89; S. Schwartz, *Josephus and Judaean Politics*, 183 and n. 141; Colautti, *Passover in Josephus*, 93, 95. See text near n. 22.

[21] This parallel's existence, in addition to the criteria listed above, led to a scholarly consensus that this is an internal Jewish source. One exception is the proposal by Hengel (*Judaism and Hellenism*, 2:53 n. 153) that the source originated in Nicolaus. Wilk ("When Hyrcanus Was Besieging Aristobulus") regards the story as a Jewish source hostile to Hyrcanus and the Romans, a product of Antigonus's court, which reached Josephus via Nicolaus of Damascus. However, given its legendary, internal-Jewish nature, its absence from *War*, the existence of the talmudic version, and Nicolaus's sparse knowledge of Antigonus (I thank Matan Orian for the final observation), among other factors, it is unlikely that the source originated in Nicolaus.

and of the sacrificial animals are not the only sources that were interpolated into this Josephan passage. Evidence of Josephus's interpolation of several sources to his account comes from the repetitions in the text: the repeated mention of Passover (21, 25) and the two different rationales offered for the divine punishment in response to the Jews' actions (25, 28),[22] which, according to Marcus, reflect Josephus's carelessness in combining his sources.[23] Colautti notes that the repetition of the siege (25) also indicates an interpolation.[24] Let us consider the structure and composition of the Josephan passage in light of these repetitions. The structure of the unit in *Antiquities* can be outlined as follows:

A. Aretas besieges Aristobulus (20a);

B. The people support Hyrcanus; the priests back Aristobulus (20b);

C. Aretas sets up camp with the Arab and Jewish forces side by side (21a);

D. These events took place on Passover; the flight of Jews to Egypt (21b);

E. Murder of Onias (22–4);

F. God punishes them for the murder of Onias (25a);

G. The episode of the siege and sacrificial animals, which occurred on Passover (25b–28);

H. God punishes them for the breach of faith (28).

I begin with the repetition of the rationales for the divine punishment inflicted on the Jews. In section F (25a) Josephus informs us that he will now recount the punishment God inflicted on the Jews for Onias's murder: however, he does not then describe a punishment but rather goes on to relate the second story, that of the sacrificial offerings, which focuses on the description of a different sinful incident (G, 25b–28). It is to this second episode that the punishment of a crop-destroying wind is attached, with Josephus explicitly stating that this was the punishment for the breach of faith regarding the agreement on the sacrificial animals (H, 28). Undoubtedly, this punishment was originally part of the second incident and a direct continuation of the priestly prayers to God that he exact satisfaction from their countrymen on their behalf. Moreover, a natural disaster—an earthquake—also concludes the rabbinic parallel. Additionally, rabbinic literature alludes to the destruction of the crops in this context too, for the story is prominently juxtaposed to the testimony in *m. Menaḥot* regarding a period when there was a scarcity of crops in the vicinity of Jerusalem, which made it necessary to bring the *omer* from afar.[25]

---

[22] See also Betz, "Choni-Onias," 89; Colautti, *Passover in Josephus*, 93.

[23] Marcus, *Jewish Antiquities* (LCL), 7:460–1 note *a*.   [24] Colautti, *Passover in Josephus*, 93.

[25] See Wiesenberg, "Related Prohibitions," 215–16; Colautti, *Passover in Josephus*, 94 n. 25. See also section D, text near n. 81.

Accordingly, the punishment originally belonged to the second episode of the sacrificial animals, and the first episode concluded with no punitive consequences. Rather, Josephus's statement: "but God straightaway punished them... for the murder of Onias in the following manner" (25) is a clumsy attempt to link the two stories and to frame the story of the sacrifices as the outcome of Onias's murder.[26] I conclude, then, that units E and G–H are both insertions of Jewish traditions, whereas unit F is a Josephan editorial addition.

With respect to Josephus's double mention of the Passover holiday (D, G), this detail appears in section 25b as the backdrop to the episode of the sacrifices (G), to explain the need for many sacrifices.[27] Some view this mention of Passover as an independent Josephan addition.[28] I suggest, however, that it was an integral part of the story of the sacrifices in the source available to him. Even though the talmudic parallel mentions the daily *tamid* rather than the Passover sacrifice, traces of a connection to Passover have survived there as well. As we have seen, the story in the BT is prominently connected to *m. Menaḥot* and the bringing of the *omer*, which is offered on the morrow of the first day of the Passover holiday.[29]

In unit D (21b), however, the topic of Passover stands alone, as part of a comment on the flight of the Jewish notables to Egypt. Identified as a Josephan addition by Colautti, he notes that the difficult nature of the events described here—a fratricidal conflict that led to the loss of independence and the deliberate cessation of temple worship—is heightened by the fact that this took place during the Passover holiday, which symbolizes freedom, unity, and divine sovereignty. In his opinion, the story of the Jewish notables who fled to Egypt (21) places events in an ironic light: the notables returned to Egypt on Passover, the very holiday that celebrates the exodus from that land. He further claims that Josephus's use of the verb ἐκλείπω confirms the innate anti-exodus thrust, for it is often used by Josephus to describe the exodus from Egypt.[30]

However, both this tradition and the story of the sacrificial animals during the siege underscore the fact that the events took place on Passover: both cite interference with divine worship and the temple service because of a fratricidal conflict, for the siege and the flight to Egypt alike did not permit the offering of

---

[26] See D. R. Schwartz, "Josephus on Hyrcanus II," 225 n. 16.

[27] Like Josephus, the tannaitic sources emphasize the great number of Passover sacrifices offered under normal circumstances (*m. Pesaḥ* 5:5; *t. Pesaḥ* 4:15; see *War* 6.420–7). However, this comment may also refer to the public sacrifices offered during the seven days of the festival and not to the paschal lamb offered on 14 Nisan.

[28] Colautti, *Passover in Josephus*, 95.

[29] See the discussion of the rabbinic sources below. Colautti (ibid. 94 and n. 25) notes this fact, even though it contradicts his opinion that Josephus interpolated the mention of Passover into this story.

[30] Ibid. 90 and n. 11.

the Passover sacrifice in the Jerusalem temple.[31] Based on these two topical links to the story of the sacrifices, I suggest that this is not an insertion by Josephus, who usually only adds background information or connective sentences to his Jewish sources, but rather an autonomous tradition of distinctly Jewish content.

As for the duplication of the siege (A, G), it appears that its second mention— "while the priests and Aristobulus were being besieged" (G, 25b)—opened the story of the sacrifices, and that a superfluous repetition was created when it was interpolated into the Josephan historical narrative, which described the siege earlier (A, 20–1). An identical opening has been preserved in the talmudic parallel: "when the kings of the Hasmonean house besieged one another, Hyrcanus was outside and Aristobulus within."

Apart from the three "Jewish" traditions surveyed above (D, E, G–H) and the sentence that links the episode of Onias to the story of the sacrifices (F), the pericope in *Antiquities* includes some additional details not found in *War*: the start of the siege (A, 20a), which receives only indirect mention in *War* 1.127–8;[32] the statement that the people supported Hyrcanus and the priests Aristobulus (B, 20b), added in order to provide the background to Onias's prayer that will appear in the continuation: "since these men standing by me are Thy people, and those who are besieged are Thy priests" (24);[33] and the setting up of the siege camps (C, 21a), meant to anticipate Onias's subsequent presence in the Jewish camp that was besieging the city (22).[34]

In sum, this passage includes three Jewish traditions (D, E, G–H: the flight to Egypt; the murder of Onias; the sacrificial animals) and four Josephan additions. One of them supplements the events described in the original narrative, evidently derived from Nicolaus (A: Aretas besieges Aristobulus). The other three are connective passages that anticipate the Onias story (B, C: the people support Hyrcanus and the priests remain with Aristobulus; Aretas sets up camp with the Arab and Jewish forces side by side) or link the distinct traditions (F: God punishes the Jews for the murder of Onias). Table 6.2 summarizes the complex structure of this passage.

---

[31] Colautti (ibid. 90–1) suggests that the notables went to sacrifice in the temple of Onias and that Josephus took a positive view of this act. This proposal is, however, unsubstantiated.

[32] Note that the anticipatory remark in *War* 1.127 regarding the lifting of the siege, a fact that appears also in section 128, creates duplication (see the comment by Israel Shatzman in the Hebrew translation of *War* by Lisa Ullman, 110, on section 128. See also Colautti, *Passover in Josephus*, 89 and the reference to Laqueur in n. 9 there). It appears that this remark was added by Josephus to compensate for the omission of any explicit mention of the siege having previously been set in place, an omission that probably stems from Josephus's source, Nicolaus. In *Ant.* 14 (19, 29), this prefatory remark is missing from the narrative sequence, because here Josephus adds a sentence explicitly noting that Aretas besieged Aristobulus (A, 20a).

[33] Laqueur, *Jüdische Historiker Flavius Josephus*, 143.

[34] Orian, "Hyrcanus versus Aristobulus," 209.

Table 6.2. The Structure of *Antiquities* 14.20–8

A	20a	Aretas besieges Aristobulus.	Josephan addition: supplementation of an event which receives only indirect mention in the original narrative in *War* (evidently derived from Nicolaus).
B	20b	The people support Hyrcanus; the priests back Aristobulus.	Josephan addition: anticipates Onias's prayer: "these men standing by me are Thy people, and those who are besieged are Thy priests." (24)
C	21a	Aretas sets up camp with the Arab and Jewish forces side by side.	Josephan addition: anticipates Onias's presence in the Jewish camp that was besieging the city. (22)
D	21b	These events took place on Passover; the flight of Jews to Egypt.	*First Jewish tradition*
E	22–4	Murder of Onias.	*Second Jewish tradition*
F	25a	God punishes them for the murder of Onias.	Josephan addition: connective link between the second and third Jewish traditions.
G	25b–28	The episode of the siege and sacrificial animals, which occurred on Passover.	*Third Jewish tradition*
H	28	God punishes them for the breach of faith.	

The Onias Tradition

As noted, one of the two main interpolated traditions in Josephus is the story of Onias. Even though the story of his murder is nowhere found in rabbinic litera-ture, the shared Josephan and rabbinic emphasis on his rainmaking ability clearly indicates a Jewish source for this legend.[35]

Otto Betz assumes that the tradition found in the Mishnah formed the basis for the Josephan attestation to Onias's rainmaking ability, even though it may not as yet have been recorded at that juncture.[36] For his part, Moshe Simon-Shoshan argues that Josephus was familiar only with an initial kernel of the rainmaking tradition and reported everything at his disposal.[37] In Tal Ilan's opinion, the

---

[35] See the mishnah above and the sources cited in n. 13. On a possible relationship between these sources, see Simon-Shoshan, *Stories of the Law*, 157–66. In the nineteenth century Jacob Brüll (*Einleitung in die Mischnah*, 1:25) suggested identifying Josephus's Onias with Ḥanan ha-Neḥba, Onias's grandson who is mentioned in *b. Ta'an.* 23b. On a forgotten scholarly proposal that identified Onias with the Qumran Teacher of Righteousness, see Schürer, *History*, 1:235 n. 6. On attempts to identify him as a member of the Essene sect, and a counter-argument, see Safrai, *In Times of Temple and Mishnah*, 2:502–4.

[36] Betz, "Choni-Onias," 88.

[37] Simon-Shoshan, *Stories of the Law*, 156–7. In light of his remarks (ibid. 152) that the lengthy, rich legend of Ḥoni was not born in the framework of the Mishnah simply to support a halakhic determination, but existed independently even earlier, it seems more likely that this ancient legend was also available to Josephus in some form or other. However, this is not the place for a detailed discussion.

original story is the shorter, anonymous one in the Tosefta, regarding a nameless "certain pious man" (חסיד אחד) who refused to pray for the rains to cease. It was the editor of the Mishnah, according to Ilan, who inserted the figure of Onias the rainmaker, known to him from a laconic, vague tradition similar to the one cited by Josephus, into the kernel story preserved in the Tosefta.[38]

Also reinforcing this tradition's origins as a Jewish legend are the motifs and language shared by the Josephan story and the legends of rainmaking by Onias in the rabbinic corpus.[39] As outlined by Betz, a chronological match is the first among these features. According to Josephus, Onias was an old man in 64 BCE, during the fratricidal conflict between the two sons of Janneus and Alexandra (Shelamzion). The Mishnah (*Ta'an.* 3:8) places a younger Onias in the generation of Simeon ben Shatah, whom rabbinic tradition sees as contemporary with the same king and queen. Second, there is the description of Onias's special relationship with God. Josephus describes Onias as θεοφιλής, "dear to God."[40] In *m. Ta'anit* Onias portrays his relationship to God as a *ben bayit* ("like a chief steward"),[41] and Simeon ben Shatah describes him as "a son who importunes his father, so he does what he wants." Note also the similarity between the Josephan opening: Ὀνίας δέ τις ὄνομα δίκαιος ἀνήρ... (lit. "One, named Onias, who was righteous," section 22) and the toseftan version that opens the parallel to the episode of Onias with the words: מעשה בחסיד אחד ("A story concerning a certain pious man").[42] Moreover, both stories link Onias to Passover. In Josephus the story takes place on Passover; the mishnah mentions clay ovens used on Passover; and the talmudic baraita opens with: "once it happened that the greater part of the month Adar had gone and yet no rain had fallen."[43] And

---

[38] Ilan, *Massekhet Ta'anit*, 44.

[39] See Betz, "Choni-Onias," 84–97. On the other hand, note Schürer's intriguing comment (*History*, 1:235 n. 6) regarding the critical rabbinic attitude toward Onias, which is totally missing from the Josephan description. See also Vermes, *Jesus the Jew*, 71–2. This criticism was apparently a layer added by the rabbis to the wonder-working legends from the Second Temple period, as Safrai (*In Times of Temple and Mishnah*, 2:504, and see the entire chapter, 501–17) has noted: "The sages denoted pietists are not fully identical with the world of the sages." See also Urbach, "Talmudic Sage," 409–10; Green, "Palestinian Holy Men," 619–47; Rubenstein, *Rabbinic Stories*, 128–9; the literature cited by Ilan, *Massekhet Ta'anit*, 44 n. 17; Simon-Shoshan, *Stories of the Law*, 151–5 and his interesting comment that the redactors of the Mishnah evoked the figures of the pietists mainly in the context of prayer. This feature, of a prayer cited in its entirety, is also found in the Josephan story.

[40] On the general use of *theophiles* in Josephus, see Gray, *Prophetic Figures*, 145–7. Nonetheless, given the obvious mishnaic parallels, I suggest that in this case the appellation applied to Onias was part of the original story and not a Josephan addition. Betz ("Choni-Onias," 86 n. 7) even suggests that underlying this appellation is a Hebrew homily that understands the name Honi as deriving from the Hebrew word חן.

[41] See Samet, "The Administrative Term *ben bayit*," 283–93, esp. 289.

[42] *T. Ta'an.* 2:13, pp. 334–5 (Lieberman ed.). On the characterization of Onias as a pietiest, see Safrai, *In Times of Temple and Mishnah*, 2:501–17; Sarfatti, "Pious Men," 126–30; Simon-Shoshan, *Stories of the Law*, 151–2 (for a different viewpoint, see Green, "Palestinian Holy Men," 631–2).

[43] *B. Ta'an.* 23a. Scholion P on *Megillat Ta'anit* and the YT (*y. Ta'an.* 3:10, 66d) link the episode of Onias to the date mentioned in *Meg. Ta'an.*, 20 Adar, shortly before Passover (Noam, *Megillat Ta'anit*, 309). See Sarfatti, "Pious Men," 126 n. 1.

in both stories Onias refuses to utter what he views as an unsuitable prayer. In the mishnah and its parallels he refuses to pray that the rain cease, for it is improper to pray for abundant rainfall or a good wind to cease;[44] in Josephus he refuses to pray for the defeat of one Jewish camp. Also, in both stories those who turn to Onias rely on his proven ability for prayer. In Josephus: he "was asked to place a curse on Aristobulus and his fellow-rebels, just as he had, by his prayers, put an end to the rainless period" (22). In the mishnah: "Just as you prayed for it to rain, now pray for it to go away." Finally, there is an affinity between the expression רבונו של עולם in Onias's prayer in the mishnah and in the baraita in the BT and the language of his prayer in Josephus βασιλεῦ τῶν ὅλων ("king of the universe," section 23), as Betz briefly notes.[45]

The prayers of Onias, as cited in both corpora, also exhibit structural, linguistic, and topical similarities. Table 6.3 compares the Josephan and rabbinic versions of the prayer.

In both prayers Onias appeals directly to God, using a similar divine appellation. In both, Onias goes on to describe the situation, portraying the people of Israel as belonging to God: your people, your priests, your children. The prayers also depict a dialectic that hampers acceptance of the prayer: different groups making opposing demands (Josephus), or the same group of people

---

[44] The entire story is related in *m. Taʿan.* 3:8 in support of the statement: "On account of every sort of public trouble do they sound the *shofar*, except for an excess of rain." See Betz, "Choni-Onias," 88; Simon-Shoshan, *Stories of the Law*, 151 (but see also his reservations, ibid. 152). In the mishnah Ḥoni jestingly refers to "the stone of the strayers," stating that as long as this well-known large stone in Jerusalem has not melted because of the rains he will not pray for them to stop. Cf. a similar hyperbolic statement in *t. Taʿan.* 2:13, and the explanation in *y. Taʿan.* 3:11, 66d: "Just as it is not possible for this stone to be blotted out of the world, so it is not possible to pray that rain will go away."

[45] See Betz, "Choni-Onias," 84–9 (esp. 87). This last expression is of particular interest. There are two possible reconstructions of the original Hebrew of Josephus's source. One is that what underlies the Josephan version is some variation of רבונו של עולם. Betz was unaware that the Palestinian version of the mishnah is רבוני and not רבונו של עולם. In MSS Kaufmann, Parma, and Paris of the Mishnah the reading is רבוני, which has been corrected to רבונו שלעולם by another hand. (See Yalon, *Vocalization of the Mishna*, 29; Kutscher, *Hebrew and Aramaic Studies*, 95–8. The question of the vocalization of this word, widely treated in the scholarship, is beyond the scope of this study. For bibliographical references, see Eldar, *Hebrew Language Tradition*, 275. I thank Yoel Elitzur for his assistance.) Nonetheless, in all extant versions of the BT (*Taʿan.* 23a) the baraita reads רבונו של עולם in slight variations, which ostensibly indicates that רבונו של עולם is a Babylonian usage. It appears, nonetheless, that the Hebrew expression underlying the Josephan phrase was closer to רבונו של עולם, making this another instance of a seemingly Babylonian version in the BT that is grounded in a Palestinian dialect. (On early Palestinian language traditions preserved in the Babylonian branch, see e.g. Bar-Asher, *Studies in Mishnaic Hebrew*, esp. 95–108.) Alternatively, if we underscore the mention of the divine name in Onias's prayer (ὦ θεὲ βασιλεῦ τῶν ὅλων) we may reconstruct a Hebrew phrase with the divine name and kingship—מלך הכל/העולם ה׳. If this is correct, this is an intriguing phenomenon from the perspective of the development of blessing formulas and the liturgy, because this then is one of the earliest examples of the motif of divine kingship in the Jewish liturgy. (See Kimelman, "Blessing Formulae," 12; for similar combinations of the divine name and divine sovereignty in Second Temple sources, see ibid. 7. I thank Uri Ehrlich and Uzi Fuchs for the reference.)

Table 6.3. Onias's Prayers

Josephus	Rabbinic Sources
Oh God, king of the universe (*Ant.* 14.24)	Lord of the world (*m. Ta'an.* 3:8; *b. Ta'an.* 23a)
since these men standing by me are Thy people, and those who are besieged are Thy priests	Your children have turned to me[a] (*m. Ta'an.* 3:8; *b. Ta'an.* 23a)
I beseech you not to hearken to them against these men nor to bring to pass what these men ask Thee to do to those others.	You have brought evil upon your children, and they could not endure it. You brought good upon your children, and they could not endure it. "But may it be pleasing to you…" (*y. Ta'an.* 3:11, 66d; cf. *b. Ta'an.* 23a)
But God straightaway punished them for this savagery…but sent a mighty and violent wind to destroy the crops of the entire country.	Forthwith the wind blew, the clouds were scattered, the sun shone, and the earth dried out. (*y. Ta'an.* 3:11; *b. Ta'an.* 23a)

Note: [a] See also Jawitz, *Toledot yisrael*, 4:212 n. 4; Betz, "Choni-Onias," 87–8 and n. 10.

making conflicting demands at different times (YT, BT). This leads to an unusual request of God: not to heed the prayers of the rivals; not to continue the blessed rainfall. God responds immediately in both cases, through the agency of a "wind," but with inverse results. In the rabbinic tradition, the skies clear after the blessed rainfall; in the Josephan one, the wind brings drought.[46] To conclude, the two stories about Onias—the story of rainmaking and of his murder—obviously belonged to a single collection of Jewish stories treating that figure,[47] which utilized the same literary and linguistic patterns.

D. THE RABBINIC TRADITIONS AND THEIR INTERRELATIONSHIP

Due to the complex interrelationship between its variants in the BT and the YT, the rabbinic parallel to the story of the sacrificial animals in Josephus warrants separate consideration. This consideration exemplifies the multifaceted nature of rabbinic literature, its creativity and fluidity, which has the ability to puzzle historians and scholars of the text alike.

---

[46] Moreover, the tripartite pattern noted by Joseph Heinemann (*Prayer in the Talmud*, 193–208) for talmudic prayers recited by individuals appears in full in both the Josephan and the mishnaic versions. These individual prayers follow a typical pattern, that of the lawcourt. Their parts include: (1) direct address to God using the language of "Master of the Universe"; (2) a plea, a statement of the facts, a complaint or an accusation, which is not found in the statutory prayers; and (3) a petition. For objections to this observation, see Green, "Palestinian Holy Men," 629–30 n. 52.

[47] Accordingly, it is very difficult to accept the proposition that this was a source reworked by Nicolaus (see Luria, *Mi-yannai ad hordus*, 207–8; Wilk, "When Hyrcanus Was Besieging Aristobulus," 100–1). Nor is Colautti's second suggestion (*Passover in Josephus*, 92), that this unit was composed by Josephus, tenable; his first suggestion that this comes from a lost source seems more plausible.

The BT Tradition

In rabbinic literature the story of the sacrificial animals appears in three versions, of which one is found in the BT and two in the YT. Of these versions, it is the one in the BT, which is repeated in three different treatises (*Sotah, Baba Qamma*, and *Menaḥot*), that displays the greatest affinity to the Josephan account. According to the BT, the story took place "when the kings of the Hasmonean house besieged one another," and the names—Hyrcanus and Aristobulus—and positions of the warring parties are explicitly noted. This appearance of the foreign names of Hasmonean leaders is unique in rabbinic literature,[48] as is the very reference made to these figures and to the Hasmonean fratricidal conflict in the tannaitic and amoraic corpora.[49] As we have seen elsewhere in this book, incongruent and unique phenomena, which are not characteristic of rabbinic literature as a whole, can indicate the preservation of extra- and pre-rabbinic traditions in this corpus.[50]

The affinities between the versions in Josephus and the BT inhere both in their specification of the historical circumstances, and in the episode's sequence and details: the besiegers and the besieged reach a cooperative agreement concerning provision of sacrificial animals in exchange for payment; the money (and the animals, in the rabbinic version) is lowered via a basket (the Josephan version is very close to that of the BT: διὰ τῶν τειχῶν καθιμήσαντες, 26); the agreement is broken and disaster ensues.

Nonetheless, the BT version differs from the Josephan one in a number of respects. In Josephus, the setting of the story is Passover and the paschal sacrifices, whereas the BT mentions the daily sacrifice. Also, the BT contains an anti-hero who is missing from the Josephan version, namely, the Greek-speaking elder whose malevolent advice upsets the balance and cooperation between the two camps with respect to the consolidating principle of the temple cult. Additional differences relate to the sacrificial animals: according to Josephus, the besiegers never provided the besieged with animals, whereas they did so in the BT version until they stopped at the elder's instigation; nor does Josephus contain any hints of the motif of the besiegers supplying a pig instead of sheep. A detail that appears in Josephus and not in the BT is how the besieged priests prayed to be avenged on the agreement-breaking besiegers. The punishments also differ: in Josephus we find crop blight, whereas the BT describes an earthquake. Finally, in the BT the episode is linked to halakhic matters mentioned in three different mishnayot: the prohibitions against teaching Greek wisdom to children (cf. *m. Sotah* 9:14; this matter will be treated below) and against raising

[48] Tal Ilan ("Names of the Hasmoneans") has shown that rabbinic literature generally refrains from use of the Hasmoneans' foreign names.

[49] Efron, "Psalms of Solomon," 230 n. 41. This fact, however, does not undermine the trustworthiness of the tradition, as he states there. The opposite is the case.

[50] See Introduction, sections E and F.

pigs (cf. *m. B. Qam.* 7:7) are attributed to "that time" ("at that time they declared…"), and an event mentioned in *m. Menaḥ.* 10:2 is framed as the outcome of this episode ("it was concerning this time [of siege] that we learnt"): "The requirement of the *omer* is to bring it from [barley growing] nearby. [If] it [the crop] did not ripen near Jerusalem [in time for use on Nisan 16] [however,] they bring it from any place. It once happened that it was brought from Gannot Ṣerifin, and [the grain] for the two loaves [Lev. 23:17] from the valley of En Sokher." That is, the narrator in the BT linked the disaster that ensued from the sin in the story to the event described in *m. Menaḥot*: the inability to glean barley for the *omer* offering and wheat for the first-breads near Jerusalem and the need to bring it from afar. It is because of the link to these three mishnayot that this story appears in the BT three times, in the context of the sugyot in which each is discussed.

Many scholars view the talmudic version as devoid of historical value, as directly or indirectly dependent on *Antiquities*.[51] Others base their historical reconstructions on a conflation of the talmudic testimony with the narratives found in the parallel stories, interweaving the story of the pig from the YT version into Josephus's description,[52] along with the Greek-speaking elder from the BT, and also fusing the accounts of the earthquake (YT; BT) and the crop blight (Josephus).[53] There are those who, because of the related halakhic prohibition, accept the talmudic version regarding the Greek-speaking elder and seek historical circumstances in line with this detail.[54] Others note the

---

[51] See the bibliography cited in Wiesenberg, "Related Prohibitions," 217 n. 17; Efron, "Psalms of Solomon," 230 n. 41; idem, "Bar-Kokhva," 70 nn. 110–11; Wilk, "When Hyrcanus Was Besieging Aristobulus," 102. A sole exceptional view identifies the BT story as the reworking of historical elements from the time of the decrees of Antiochus IV (Hengel, *Judaism and Hellenism*, 1:76).

[52] See Graetz, *History of the Jews*, 2:60. For a more comprehensive treatment, see idem, *Geschichte*, vol. 3, appendix 15, pp. 710–11. He suggests that Josephus omitted the episode of the pig because of his non-Jewish audience, but alluded to it nevertheless in his harsh judgment of the besiegers' acts. A similar view was expressed by Luria, *Mi-yannai ad hordus*, 207–8. See also Amusin, "Reflection of Historical Events," 148–9 n. 49, who suggests that the pig was an integral part of the original story and was omitted by Josephus. Rosenblum ("Jews, Food, and Identity," 103–5) makes a similar assumption, viewing the pig as symbolizing Roman intervention in the fratricidal conflict (see also below, n. 72). For an opposing view, see Wiesenberg, "Related Prohibitions," 217.

[53] Graetz, *History of the Jews*, 2:61. See also Weiss, *Dor dor ve-dorshav*, 1:146–7. In addition to all the elements from Josephus and the BT—tamid and paschal sacrifices, the pig and the Greek-speaking elder, the earthquake and crop blight, the prohibitions against pig husbandry and teaching Greek—he added to the story the testimony from one of the YT versions (see below) regarding the offering of the tamid sacrifice in the fourth hour. See also the bibliography cited by Wiesenberg, "Related Prohibitions," 217 and n. 18.

[54] Graetz (*History of the Jews*, 2:59–60), for example, identifies the elder as Antipater the Idumean, who incited Hyrcanus to rebel against his brother. See also Jawitz, *Toledot yisrael*, 4:213. However, according to Rashi's understanding that the elder was with the besieged and sent coded messages to the besiegers, namely, that he betrayed his own party and advised the besiegers not to assist with the sacrifices (*b. Sotah* 49b, s.v. היה שם זקן אחד לעז להם; *b. Menaḥ.* 64b, s.v. חכמת יוונית...והיה שם זקן אחד), this figure belonged to the party of Aristobulus, not Hyrcanus. See Derenbourg, *Essai*, 114 n. 2. Elimelech Hallewy [Halevi] (*Ha-aggadah*, 62–5) thought that Hyrcanus's Nabataean allies were

contradiction between ascription of the prohibition of teaching Greek to the circumstances of our story and its ascription to the "war of Quietus," namely, Trajan's day,[55] in *m. Sotah* 9:14.[56] Regarding some details, Wiesenberg awards precedence to the talmudic version (the siege did not take place on Passover; the price of a sacrifice was a specific amount of "dinars" as in the talmudic version, as opposed to the astronomical sum named by Josephus). For others, he assigns precedence to the Josephan version: the pig scene in the talmudic version is unlikely; the murder of someone like Onias is eminently possible.[57]

The YT Tradition

We now move from the single version of this story found in the BT (though repeated three times) to the more complex state of affairs in the YT, where we find two similar versions of an event involving a siege, an agreement regarding sacrificial animals for the daily tamid sacrifice, and the callous breaking of this agreement. Each, however, attributes the circumstances to a different time frame. The first is dated to the "days of the Greek empire." This version relates that, in contradistinction to their usual practice of sending up two sheep in exchange for gold, the besiegers suddenly sent two goats, which are unsuitable

the addressees of the messages delivered in Greek. See also Wilk, "When Hyrcanus Was Besieging Aristobulus," 101 n. 8. Wilk claims that the elder delivered "the secret of the city in a language ostensibly understood only by the besiegers."

[55] "Titus" in the printed editions. However, MSS Kaufmann, Parma, and Cambridge read קיטוס and this has been universally accepted as the correct version. Most scholars think that this refers to Lusius Quietus, who governed Judea during Trajan's reign. See Albeck, *Mishnah: Nashim*, 393; Schäfer, *History*, 141–2; Hadas-Lebel, *Jerusalem*, 164–6. For another proposal, see Rokeah, "Kitos," 79–84. Wiesenberg's proposal ("Related Prohibitions," 221 n. 34, 227) that gives preference to the version in the printed editions is untenable not only because of the evidence from other versions but also because the First Jewish Revolt is termed "the war of Vespasian" in the very same mishnah.

[56] Thus, as early as the *Tosafot* on *b. B. Qam.* 82b, s.v. ואסור לאדם. See Wiesenberg, "Related Prohibitions," 219–20; and in his wake Hirshman, *Torah*, 143, who also comments on typical Babylonian locutions in the episode of the elder and Greek. See also Efron, "Bar-Kokhva," 70 n. 111. Graetz (*Geschichte*, 3:711) explains that, like the above-mentioned sugyot in the BT, the prohibition ad loc. is not identical to the prohibition against studying the Greek language mentioned in the mishnah, which was issued later, but a prohibition against Greek wisdom, which he understands here as meaning a diplomatic ruse. For similar proposals, see Derenbourg, *Essai*, 114 n. 2; Rappel, "Hokhmat Yevanit," 321. For an opposing view see Weiss, *Dor dor ve-dorshav*, 1:146–7 n. 1. Weiss himself explains that the prohibition was either forgotten or not accepted, and then reinstated. A similar distinction between Greek wisdom and Greek language is made by Lieberman, *Hellenism in Jewish Palestine*, 100–1. Hallewy [Halevi] ("Greek Wisdom," 270–1) thought that Greek wisdom and language were the same, and that the prohibition was renewed from time to time because it was not implemented by the public. S. Stern (*Jewish Identity*, 177) follows in the wake of Tosafot and assumes that this was at first only a curse and only later became a prohibition. Regarding the expression חכמת יוונית, see n. 94 below.

[57] Wiesenberg, "Related Prohibitions," 218–22. Also, many view the motif of the pig in the talmudic legend as an addition to the original story; see text near n. 76.

for the daily offering,[58] leaving the besieged with no animals for the daily sacrifice. However, with the discovery of two lambs in the chamber of lambs, the story ends happily. Although nowhere stated explicitly, it appears that this story belongs to the Hasmonean revolt.[59] Not only is its opening phrase typical of legends on this revolt,[60] the episode itself is structured according to a fixed pattern of the purification of the temple by the Hasmoneans. It belongs to a series of legends, whose existence I have noted elsewhere. They concern the Maccabees who, on coming to renew the temple service after their victory, are confronted by the absence of some element vital for the service (oil, a candelabrum, an altar, sacrificial animals), whose lack is overcome through their initiative (rebuilding of the altar,[61] making the candelabrum out of spits[62]), or by finding the item: "they found the altar torn down and repaired it."[63] The well-known legend of the cruse of oil also belongs to this genre[64]—"they found pure oil in it"[65]/found only one cruse of oil"[66]—as does our episode: "they found two lambs."

In response to this version of the story, Rabbi Levi relates that a similar episode took place under Roman rule ("this evil kingdom"). In this instance, instead of sheep the besiegers sent up pigs. The pig shrieked[67] while being hoisted up the wall. This evidently caused an earthquake,[68] and ultimately, the sins of the people brought the cancellation of the tamid offering and the destruction of the temple.[69]

---

[58] See Ginzberg, *Commentary on the Palestinian Talmud*, 3:37–8.

[59] As opposed to Ginzberg (ibid. 3:37), Wiesenberg ("Related Prohibitions," 223–5); and Kalmin ("Portrayals of Kings," 325; idem, *The Sage*, 64), who understand the formula בימי מלכות יון as alluding to the conflict between Hyrcanus and Aristobulus and identify the episode in the YT with the version found in the BT. According to Kalmin (*The Sage*, 64) the YT erased the names of the Hasmonean brothers and the main elements of the story so as not to damage their reputations. Catherine Hezser ("[In]significance of Jerusalem," 16) suggests that the story concerns the siege of Jerusalem by Antiochus VII Sidetes in John Hyrcanus I's day.

[60] Of Scholion O on *Megillat Ta'anit* in particular. See Scholion O, 27 Iyyar (Noam, *Megillat Ta'anit*, 67); 24 Av (ibid. 86); 17 Elul (ibid. 90); 3 Tishri (ibid. 94); 3 Kislev (ibid. 98); 28 Adar (ibid. 128). See also Scholion P, 25 Kislev (ibid. 105): בימי נכנסו בני חשמונאי להר הבית; Scholia O and P, 13 Adar: מלכי יון/ומלכותא דיונאי. On this phenomenon, see Kister, "Scholia on Megillat Ta'anit," 461; Rosenthal, "Newly Discovered Leaf," 375, 382 n. 132.

[61] See Scholion O on *Meg. Ta'an.*, 25 Kislev (Noam, *Megillat Ta'anit*, 105, 272–3).

[62] *B. Rosh Hash.* 24b; *b. 'Abod. Zar.* 43a; *b. Menah.* 28b; *Pesiq. Rab.* 2:5a; Scholia O and P, 25 Kislev (Noam, *Megillat Ta'anit*, 105, 270–2. See also Rosenthal, "Newly Discovered Leaf," 364, 397–401).

[63] Scholion O, 25 Kislev (Noam, *Megillat Ta'anit*, 105). The wording may be a scribal emendation. See Noam, "Cruse of Oil," 214–15 and the version found in the new manuscript of Scholion O: אלא שסתרו את המזבח ובנאוהו (Rosenthal, "Newly Discovered Leaf," 364, 398).

[64] Even though as found in the BT it attests to secondary development. See Noam, "Cruse of Oil," esp. 218–26.

[65] Scholion P, 25 Kislev (Noam, *Megillat Ta'anit*, 103).

[66] *B. Shabb.* 21b.   [67] Lieberman, *Studies*, 489–90. See n. 11 above.

[68] That is what emerges from the wording וקפץ מארץ-יש' ארבעים פרסה and from the parallel in the BT. Lieberman (*Studies*, 489 n. 30) suggests that perhaps it was half of the wall that moved (קפץ) due to the earthquake rather than the land, which explains the masculine form of the verb.

[69] For an analysis of the story in the context of the destruction of the temple, see Ben Shahar, "Biblical and Post-biblical History," 154–5.

Intriguingly, the YT also links the two episodes to two mishnayot, using the same collocations found in the BT: על אותה שעה, באותה שעה ("at that time;" "concerning this time"), even though the mishnayot are not the same as the ones alluded to in the BT. The first episode is linked to the opinion of Rabbi Yehudah ben Abba[70] in *m. 'Ed.* 6:1: "Rabbi Yehudah ben Abba gave testimony concerning five matters... and concerning the morning daily whole offering that it may be offered at the fourth hour." The narrator assumes here that the lack of an animal for the tamid offering and its subsequent location in the chamber of lambs caused a delay, and this is what underlies the "testimony" of that tanna regarding the permission to delay the offering of the sacrifice until the fourth hour. This matter is addressed apropos the discussion of *m. Ber.* 4:1 in the YT, as one of two explanations for Rabbi Yehudah's doctrine in that mishnah, that the morning prayer can be recited until the fourth hour, since "the obligation to recite the Morning Prayer was derived from the daily morning sacrifice."[71]

The second episode, with its unhappy conclusion, is allusively linked to another mishnah, *m. Ta'an.* 4:6, which lists the cancellation of the tamid sacrifice among the sad events that took place on 17 Tammuz. The two versions of our story also appear in the discussion of this mishnah in the YT. The wording of the narrator—"at that time the sins [of Israel] brought it about that the daily whole offering was canceled, and the house [the temple] was laid to waste"— implies that he dated the second version of the episode to the cancellation of the tamid sacrifice, shortly before the destruction of the Second Temple.[72]

Given its many versions, in what historical circumstances was this story of the sacrificial animals first related? Although in most instances the fluidity of folktales makes it impossible to establish their chronology, here the answer seems obvious: the story was born in the context of the fratricidal Hasmonean conflict, as in the BT, and not in that of the Hasmonean revolt or the First Jewish Revolt, per the YT. First of all, the existence of a parallel in Josephus attests to the antiquity of the version that links the episode of the sacrifices to the conflict between Hyrcanus and Aristobulus. Second, the uniqueness of this episode in the context of rabbinic literature confirms this dating's authenticity. This is not the case for the legends of the Hasmonean revolt and of the destruction of the temple, which have fixed topoi (see above for a discussion of the Hasmonean model) and whose coordinates "automatically" attract various events.[73] Moreover,

---

[70] In *b. Ber.* 27a the reading is R. Yehudah ben Baba, but the Palestinian version of *m. 'Eduyot* has Yehudah ben Abba, as do all the versions of the YT, and this is the correct reading. See the discussion by Ginzberg, *Commentary on the Palestinian Talmud*, 3:38–9.

[71] *Y. Ber.* 4:1, 7b. *B. Ber.* 27a also links Rabbi Yehudah's opinion in *m. Berakhot* to *m. 'Eduyot*.

[72] See Wiesenberg, "Related Prohibitions," 225–9. Rosenblum ("Jews, Food, and Identity," 104) argues that this episode treats the fratricidal Hasmonean conflict, as in the BT, but stresses the role of Rome and the destruction wrought by Rome at the time of the Pompeian conquest. It seems to me incorrect to impose the circumstances found in the BT on the YT.

[73] Churgin (*Studies*, 65) thought that the transfer of the story to the destruction period was impelled by a desire to conceal the shame of the Hasmoneans. In my opinion, we should rather seek literary, not political, motives here.

the BT's precise noting of the names of the antagonists and their location during the siege also supports the trustworthiness of its tradition, as opposed to the conventional openings found in the YT. In addition, the story is consistent with the backdrop of civil strife, and with the conceptual tension between political–military rivalry and the principle of unity symbolized by the temple and the temple cult. The contexts suggested in the YT—a siege by foreign forces, either Greek or Roman—attenuate this tension. It is less reasonable that the enemy—be it the Greeks or the Romans—would provide animals for sacrifices, and it is less tragic when this enemy breaches his word, whereas such a breach on the part of a Jewish party is the shocking acme of the story in its Josephan-BT setting.

This exceptional case impacts our understanding of the broader relationship between the two Talmuds. As opposed to a common scholarly claim, automatic preference should not be awarded to the traditions in the YT over those found in the BT, just because of the dating and location of the final, overall redaction of each.[74] Although it is true that the YT was redacted at a closer geographical-temporal locus to the events related, both Talmuds are receptacles for innumerable fluctuating variants of stories, data, and traditions that circulated in the rabbinic world. Different metamorphoses were preserved in one Talmud or the other, sometimes due solely to the vagaries of chance. The traditions examined in this book support this claim: of the stories whose antiquity is attested by the parallels in Josephus, most were preserved in the BT, not the YT, making independent examination of each source a desideratum. In this instance, the more original form of the story was preserved in the BT, with the secondary versions making their way to the YT.

Thus, the main motif of cooperation between besiegers and besieged on the sacrificial rites, and its surprising breach, was born in the context of the siege during the internecine Hasmonean conflict, and was later borrowed and pasted into more familiar, prevalent contexts.[75] This also led to the reworking of the end of the tale: the topos of legend of the destruction usually concludes with "the sins [of Israel] brought it about that…the temple was laid to waste;" the Hasmonean legend ends with a joyful "find" that enables restoration of the temple service. Note that in both cases, as well as in the third, original setting of this legend, the hidden protagonist of the story is the Jerusalem temple and its cult.

---

[74] This is especially prominent in Joshua Efron's studies and the scholarly school of thought that he founded. See e.g. Efron, "Simeon Ben Shataḥ and Jannaeus," 143–7; idem, "Bar-Kokhva," esp. 47–51, 102–5. For his predecessors on this path, even if not as an explicit doctrine, see the rich bibliographical references, ibid. 50 n. 15. See also Stemberger, "Narrative Baraitot," 80 and n. 22.

[75] Wiesenberg ("Related Prohibitions") suggests that the story of the pig be viewed as an actual historical event that took place during the First Jewish Revolt. See also Wilk ("When Hyrcanus Was Besieging Aristobulus"), who maintains that the legends of the destruction are "a most appropriate framework for the logic and historical reality" of the episode. To my mind, there is no need for this assumption. This is probably a literary adaptation that dragged a tradition from a Hasmonean historical context to the more common one of the destruction; therefore it also added motifs typical of the latter context, such as the pig.

This reconstruction holds the key to understanding the YT's interpolation of the tamid-sacrifice motif, in its mishnaic contexts, into the story. Whoever planted the story in the arena of the destruction of the temple sought to link a specific story regarding the failure to provide a sacrificial animal with known traditions of the destruction, and located a solution in *m. Ta'anit* 4:6, which recounted the halting of the tamid sacrifice at that time. The transformation of the sacrifice from the paschal to the tamid offering made it possible to identify the one-time halting of a sacrifice with the cessation of the tamid sacrifice on the eve of the destruction of the temple and to thereby place the story in the desired context. As some scholars have noted, it appears that the motif of the pig, the symbol of the Tenth Legion and of Rome in general, and a known motif in some traditions of the destruction,[76] was added to the story in its "Roman" stage.[77] After all, as Wiesenberg points out, it is difficult to attribute such an act to Hyrcanus, himself a Jew and a high priest.[78] Perhaps the earthquake as well, which resulted from the pig's shriek, was part of this reworking of the episode, even though Graetz, and many others in his wake, link it to Dio Cassius's testimony (*History* 37.11.4) regarding a similar event that occurred in Asia in 64 BCE.[79] If the two are indeed related, the earthquake was perhaps an authentic element of the original story.

As for the "Hasmonean" version, this reworking appears to have been an outgrowth of the "Roman" one. The link between the Hasmonean version and the halakhah in *m. 'Eduyot* that the morning tamid sacrifice may be offered until the fourth hour is less natural than the one that explains the halting of the tamid sacrifice in *m. Ta'anit*. It appears that, in order to add this story to the collection of Hasmonean legends, another redactor looked for a mishnah that

---

[76] On additional motifs that associate the destruction of the First and Second Temples with the bringing of a pig to the temple, see Kister, "Legends of the Destruction," 502–3, and Ilan, "Titus's War Council," 731–40. See also Ginzberg, *Legends of the Jews*, 1:284 n. 162; 2:1076–7 n. 29; Wiesenberg, "Related Prohibitions," 227–8; Efron, "Bar-Kokhva," 69 and nn. 106–7; Wilk, "When Hyrcanus Was Besieging Aristobulus," 104 nn. 19–20; and more recently, Rosenblum, "Jews, Food, and Identity."

[77] According to Ginzberg (*Commentary on the Palestinian Talmud*, 3:36–7) the process proceeded in the opposite direction. It was not the Roman dating that attracted the pig to the story, but rather the pig that brought mention of the Roman period in its wake. In his opinion, the pig was first added to the Babylonian legend as a rationale for the earthquake that struck the land of Israel that year, whereas Rabbi Levi, who already knew this baraita, placed it in the First Jewish Revolt because of the motif of the pig. For Rosenblum ("Jews, Food, and Identity," 104–5) the pig belongs to the original story of the fratricidal conflict, for it symbolizes the Roman intervention in this war, and the parallel in the YT only added that this intervention eventually brought the destruction of the temple.

[78] See Wiesenberg, "Related Prohibitions," 219–20. Throughout this article he attempts to demonstrate that the related prohibitions against pig husbandry and studying Greek, which are juxtaposed to the story in the BT, had their source in an episode of the sacrificial offering of a pig that occurred while the Romans were besieging Jerusalem. See also Rosenblum, "Jews, Food, and Identity."

[79] Graetz, *Geschichte*, 3:711.

mentions the tamid sacrifice. The typical ending with a "find" in the legends of the purification of the temple enabled him to posit a delay in the offering and to juxtapose his story to a mishnah that treats such a delay.

In contrast, the legend as found in the BT preserved the original time frame: the Hasmonean fratricidal conflict. However, two motifs—the tamid sacrifice and the pig that caused an earthquake—entered the story *ex post facto* from the "Roman" version that was embedded in the YT.[80] Their secondary nature is obvious not just from their absence in Josephus, but from the story itself. The link to the event of the bringing of the *omer* offering (a sheaf of barley) from afar in the BT relays two facts: first, the story occurred on Passover, because the *omer* is brought on the morrow of the first day of the festival; this suggests that in its original form the legend dealt with the paschal sacrifice and not the tamid, just as in the Josephan version. Second, the punishment for the Jews' sin was crop blight as in Josephus, and not an earthquake, since according to the BT, the dramatic event at the heart of the legend destroyed all the barley and wheat near Jerusalem.[81] Moreover, the absence of the crops described in *m. Menaḥot* is elsewhere connected in rabbinic tradition to crop blight.[82] Thus, the link between the episode and *m. Menaḥot* created by the BT was born when the story still contained a description of crop blight, not an earthquake; that is, before the penetration of the motifs from the reworked "Yerushalmi" story. Matan Orian suggests that the link to *m. Menaḥot* belongs to the original rabbinic story, since its wording is unique: ועל אותה שעה שנינו—"it was concerning this time that we learnt"—as opposed to the later links to the prohibition against raising pigs and teaching Greek which say באותה שעה—"at that time."[83] It was this initial link that structured the legend as a foundation for a halakhic statement and led the way for later redactors in both Talmuds to seek additional

---

[80] As Efron ("Bar-Kokhva," 69–70) also assumes; see also Wilk, "When Hyrcanus Was Besieging Aristobulus," 103–4. I, however, do not share his approach, which views the story in the BT as a late composite text that relies on Josephus. See n. 17 above. Wiesenberg ("Related Prohibitions") also thought that the episode of the pig entered the BT from the YT's version and that its context lies in the First Jewish Revolt. Furthermore, he sought not just a literary tradition, but an actual historical event in the story of the pig.

[81] See Ginzberg, *Commentary on the Palestinian Talmud*, 3:35–40. Another intriguing link between famine and drought and the bringing of the *omer* offering to the temple is found in *Ant.* 3.320–1, with reference to the reign of Claudius (I thank Meir Ben Shahar for this reference).

[82] *Y. Sheqal.* 5:1, 48d: "One time there was a drought in the land of Israel [and they found grain at Gaggot Serifin]…one time there was a blight in the whole world…is there a place called Ein Sokher." See Halevy, *Dorot ha-rishonim*, 1/5, 96–106; Wiesenberg, "Related Prohibitions," 215–16. Halevy (*Dorot ha-rishonim*, 1/5, 101–2) attempted to show that there was no contradiction between the YT's testimony regarding blight in *Sheqalim* and the story of the fratricidal Hasmonean conflict in the BT. On the other hand, Safrai (*Pilgrimage*, 45, 99–100) thinks there is no reason to connect the two episodes and that each tradition is independent. Indeed, there may be no conscious connection between the traditions; for our purposes it is sufficient that *m. Menaḥot* was associated with crop blight, making it likely that whoever linked it to the Hasmonean fratricidal conflict knew a version in which the story included blight and not an earthquake.

[83] Orian, "Hyrcanus versus Aristobulus," 284 and n. 82.

connections that would harmonize with the later versions of the legend, ending with links to no less than *four* additional mishnayot: *Ta'anit* (the halting of the tamid sacrifice); *'Eduyot* (the delayed offering of the tamid); *Baba Qamma* (the prohibition against pig husbandry); and *Sotah* (the prohibition against studying Greek).

In summation, I reconstruct the stages of the development of the story as follows:

a. A legend from the Second Temple period related what happened to the paschal sacrifice during the fratricidal conflict between Hyrcanus and Aristobulus. The story concluded with a punishment—crop blight. This is the story cited by Josephus.

b. In the rabbinic world the legend was later linked to *m. Menaḥot*, which mentions a unique case in which it was necessary, as opposed to the usual custom, to bring grain from a distance for the *omer* offering on Passover.

c. An anonymous redactor adjusted the core of the legend to fit the style of the legends of the destruction. Thus, the tamid offering replaced the paschal sacrifice, and a link to *m. Ta'anit*, which recounts the halting of the tamid when the temple was destroyed, replaced the link to *m. Menaḥot*. This also promoted the integration of the theme of the pig so typical of stories of Rome/the Romans. The frightening picture of a pig that breaches the walls of Jerusalem and unsettles all of the land of Israel, a clear-cut symbol of the destruction wrought by the Romans, replaced the punishment of crop blight. It was this version that was fixed in the YT.

d. An additional redactor adapted the kernel of the story to the topos of the legends of the purification of the temple by the Hasmoneans. In this version the ending was changed to a more typical one of a "find" and the renewal of the cult, and a link to *m. 'Eduyot* that mentions a delay in the offering of the tamid was substituted for the link to *m. Ta'anit*. This version too was fixed in the YT.

e. Motifs from the reworked version known to us from the YT (c)—the tamid sacrifice, the pig, and the earthquake—penetrated the original legend (b). It appears that the link to *m. Baba Qamma*, which forbids pig husbandry, took place at this stage, after the introduction of the pig to the story. This version was at some point fixed in the BT, perhaps even before the introduction of these motifs. Therefore, no historical weight can be assigned to the statement that pig husbandry was forbidden during the conflict between Hyrcanus and Aristobulus.[84]

---

[84] Several scholars have noted the problematic nature of this dating, for it seems that the ban on pig husbandry by Jews was much earlier. See Efron, "Bar-Kokhva," 70 n. 111; Urbach, *Halakhah*, 28–9 (even though he attempts to verify the testimony in our story and assumes that the prohi-bition had to be renewed due to circumstances).

Tal Ilan proposes a different path of development. She maintains that the version in the YT is not a parallel to the Josephan story, that from the start it treated Rome and events related to the destruction. In her view, the coincidental similarity between the lowering of money for sacrificial animals in the two stories led the redactor of the BT to graft the two—the story on the internecine struggle between the Hasmonean brothers, which was available to him (and to Josephus centuries earlier), and the story on the First Jewish Revolt in the YT—which he perceived as one story. Preserving the literary framework of the YT on the First Jewish Revolt, he corrected its chronology in line with the story of the fratricidal conflict.[85] I think, however, given the resemblance in the central motif of an agreement between besiegers and besieged, the hoisting up of sacrificial animals, and the breach of the agreement, alongside the existence of two versions in the YT itself, it is difficult to posit that these are autonomous stories that were only later conflated by a redactor.

In any event, the penetration of motifs from the YT version, whether their source is independent or secondary, explains most of the elements that distinguish the legend in the BT from its Josephan parallel: the tamid sacrifice, the pig, and the earthquake. However, the origins of one BT motif remain mysterious. This is the inciting elder,[86] who is familiar with Greek wisdom, and the associated prohibition against teaching Greek. Unknown from the Josephan version, its origins do not lie in the reworkings found in the YT. Nonetheless, some have tried to link it to the "Roman" version of the episode,[87] and identify the elder as one of the leaders of the First Jewish Revolt, perhaps even Josephus himself.[88] In my opinion, however, we cannot rule out the possibility that this element in the BT does not belong to a rabbinic reworking of the story but is rather a unit from the original story. To that end I now reconsider the relationship between the legend in the BT and the episode of the sacrifices as related by Josephus.

E. THE JOSEPHAN VERSION AND THE SACRIFICIAL ANIMAL TRADITION IN THE BT

Yonah Fraenkel has demonstrated how the structure and wording of the legend in the BT were drafted to a didactic message regarding the necessity for, and dangers of breaching, unity. His analysis shows how the lack of a clear victory by either party, as embodied in the unusual phrase צרו...זה על זה ("besieged one

---

[85] Oral communication.

[86] On "an elder" as a negative figure in rabbinic legends, see Chap. 3, n. 96.

[87] Wiesenberg, "Related Prohibitions," 215–16; Hirshman, *Torah*, 143–4.

[88] See Wiesenberg, "Related Prohibitions," 230–1. See also the caveats regarding this suggestion.

another"[89]) was linked to the mutuality of the ritual cooperation: היו משלשלים להם ("they would let down to them") as opposed to היו מעלים להם ("they would send up to them"). He also shows how the breaking of this balance wreaked havoc on the entire land of Israel and not just the parties involved. According to Fraenkel, the inciting elder who causes disaster serves as a foil for the viewpoint the author seeks to impart to the reader. Whereas the narrator views the maintenance of the temple cult as a shared interest for both parties, "the elder is convinced that the 'cult' is pertinent only to the besieged and saves only them, whereas, by helping the besieged, the besiegers spoil their chances of victory."[90] According to this analysis, the narrator prefers the balance between the parties described in the opening of the story to the decisive act that brings disaster in its wake. The value of unity promoted by the narrator is portrayed as both an internal Jewish interest and as the divine will, whereas the conflict-promoting elder is characterized by "Greek wisdom," namely, the author identifies his separatist tendencies with the threat of the external gentile world.[91]

Interestingly, elsewhere Josephus also identifies the breach of unity as the main cause of the fall of the Hasmonean dynasty. Moreover, he offers this observation as a Jewish tradition transmitted throughout previous generations: "But they lost their royal power through internal strife…Such, then, is the account we have received of the end of the Asamonaean line" (*Ant.* 14.490–1).

However, this particularistic content is entirely absent in the Josephan version of our story. His version imparts a simple, universal message: the besiegers' sin lies in their breaching of the agreement, not the breaching of Jewish unity. As opposed to the talmudic narrator, Josephus sees the sacrificial rites not as a national interest but as the interest of the besieged priests: the besiegers did not furnish "the sacrificial victims to *those who were in need* of them (τοῖς δεομένοις)." Failure to provide the sacrificial animal was therefore not a crime against the shared Jewish commitment to God and his temple, but against the private need of a particular sector and a promised agreement. Accordingly, the punishment is defined as the outcome of the request for vengeance by the besieged, not as a national punishment. Josephus's view is identical to the simplistic, technical explanation that the talmudic narrator engages polemically, the one voiced there by the dastardly elder.[92] Obviously, there is no room for condemnation of Greek-speakers in the Josephan version.

---

[89] For a parallel to this wording in Josephus, see Chap. 7, text at n. 28.

[90] Fraenkel, *Darkhei ha-aggadah ve-ha-midrash*, 236–9. Citation from p. 239 (translation by author).

[91] According to S. Schwartz (*Josephus and Judaean Politics*, 91 n. 126), a polemic against the study of Greek wisdom lies at the core of the rabbinic version. However, the central lesson of this story is undoubtedly the tension between unity and divisiveness to which the link on the prohibition against studying Greek was appended, as were the links to various mishnayot.

[92] S. Schwartz (ibid.) notes among the aims of the Josephan story the message that the cult must continue under all circumstances, that priestly prayers are accepted, and that God swiftly punishes sinners. To my mind, Josephus indeed underscores the sin as he understands it. The

I argue that, with respect to the story's deeper message, it is the talmudic version that reflects the original tradition and Josephus the secondary adaptation which omitted the inciting elder. This conclusion is supported by elements found in the Josephan narrative itself. The story of Onias, which was not preserved in rabbinic literature, clearly reflects a theme similar to that found in the talmudic version of the episode of the sacrificial animals. Even through Josephan mediation, the story of Onias provides a clear-cut message that those who seek to acquire victory over their brethren through Onias's prayers are wicked, whereas the righteous person, who is beloved by God, staunchly refuses to favor one Jewish camp over the other and believes that God will never assist one of the warring parties, because the divine election of Israel requires their unity ("thy people...thy priests").

In other words, the two stories—that of the sacrificial animals in the talmudic version and that of Onias in the Josephan one—preach unity and impart the notion that neither sacrifice nor prayer is efficacious in promoting the cause of one Jewish camp over the other. Moreover, the stories have an inverse, mirror-image relationship. An elder appears in both: one is a righteous man, beloved by God; the other, a despicable person who represents foreign culture. In the first, the warring forces make a demand of the elder; in the second, the elder turns to them with advice. The elder in the first story, Onias, attempts to prevent a decisive outcome and to maintain the status quo; the elder in the second story works toward breaching the status quo. The first elder is put to death by those around him; the second brings disaster on others.

These two independent stories, the murder of Onias found only in Josephus, and the episode of the sacrificial animals as found in its talmudic version in particular, therefore belong to the same unique historical context, share the same message, and their literary shaping takes the form of an inverted mirror-image. This suggests that both coexisted in an early context and that explains their juxtaposition by Josephus.[93] Going one step further, this also suggests that the features of the talmudic version that are equivalent to the Onias story (which was unknown to the Talmud!)—the message of unity and the figure of the inciting elder—are not the result of later talmudic redaction but rather belonged to the original story. These elements—namely, the internal Jewish perspective and the basic hostility toward Hellenistic-Roman culture—necessarily underwent censorship by Josephus when he interpolated them into his narrative. Nonetheless, it appears that, like the links to various mishnayot in the talmudic versions of the story in both the BT and the YT, the link to the prohibition against

---

attempt to maintain the cult and the punishment that closes the story were already in the version transmitted to Josephus, as seen from the talmudic parallel, and were not a Josephan innovation.

[93] There is apparently no basis for Wiesenberg's conjectural reconstruction ("Related Prohibitions," 229–30) of the existence of a narrative sequence that contained the episode of the sacrificial animals as per the BT version, the episode of Onias, and another episode structured like the "Roman" version in the YT.

teaching Greek wisdom and the very appearance of the phrase חכמת יוונית in the BT[94] are a late addition, the result of redaction.[95]

The Josephan story, however, is superior to the talmudic parallel in several respects. It alone has preserved the tradition of the murder of Onias, which is missing from the rabbinic sources. Moreover, in rabbinic literature the episode of the sacrificial animals gave rise to new versions, distant from the original; even the version closest to the source underwent redaction and additions. Nonetheless, the talmudic version appears to have better preserved the original spirit and meaning of the episode, alongside significant details omitted by Josephus, because the aims and substance of his writing did not allow their preservation.

F. CONCLUSION

Josephus was familiar with two Jewish traditions that treated the fratricidal Hasmonean conflict, which ultimately led to the loss of Jewish independence and subjugation to Roman rule. These traditions—the murder of Onias and the episode of the sacrificial animals—and perhaps an additional one—the flight to Egypt—underscored the sinfulness, and the dangers, of breaching Jewish unity, which is equated with denial of the exclusive divine election of Israel, the cessation of worship in God's sole temple, and exposure to the dangers of external gentile influence. In these stories, it is Onias who exemplifies the principle of Jewish unity. Josephus preserved both stories, but only one reached rabbinic literature. Even this single story, concerning the sacrificial animals, was not uniformly preserved in rabbinic literature. It gave rise to new, more distant versions in the YT, and its early version, found in the BT, underwent reworking

---

[94] The expression חכמת יוונית is unique to the BT and does not appear in Palestinian rabbinic literature. See Hallewy [Halevi], "Greek Wisdom," 273; Hirshman, *Torah*, 143. For the meaning of the expression, its unusual construct form, and a bibliographical survey, see n. 56 above; Rokeah, *Jews, Pagans and Christians*, 202–4, 215; Werblowsky, "Greek Wisdom," 55–60; and Vidas, "Greek Wisdom in Babylonia," 287–305. According to Vidas, this expression was interpolated into the baraitot by the redactors of the sugya, whose tannaitic versions read יוונית only. See his intriguing, convincing argument that this is in fact a Syriac term, the product of the Babylonian context, which was borrowed from the discourse of the Eastern Church.

[95] Indeed, as shown above, in other sources the prohibition against teaching Greek is attributed to other historical contexts. See e.g. *m. Sotah* 9:14, which dates the prohibition to a later period. See also the attribution of the prohibition to the "eighteen regulations" evidently promulgated shortly before the destruction of the temple (*y. Shabb.* 1:4, 3c): יעל לשונן. This is not the appropriate place for a discussion of the nature and dating of the prohibition against teaching Greek/Greek wisdom in rabbinic literature. For bibliographical references, see Efron, "Bar-Kokhva," 70 n. 111, and the summary in Herr, *History of Eretz Israel*, 193–4. See also the classic dispute between Saul Lieberman (*Hellenism in Jewish Palestine*, 100–14) and Alon ("Ha-yevanit," 248–77); and Hallewy [Halevi], "Greek Wisdom"; Rokeah, *Jews, Pagans and Christians*, 200–5; Hirshman, *Torah*, 134–46; Vidas, "Greek Wisdom in Babylonia." See n. 56 above.

and was revised in line with those secondary traditions. Nevertheless, the BT retained the subtext of the story—Jewish unity against external dangers—which was deliberately obscured by Josephus in favor of a superficial, obvious lesson—the prohibition against reneging on an obligation. With this shift, other original elements of the story were lost, among them presumably the incendiary Greek-speaking elder, who represented divisiveness and the dangers of non-Jewish culture.

Examination of these phenomena led to a number of overall conclusions. First of all, despite the BT's relative geographical-temporal distance from Second Temple-period Palestinian traditions, and in contrast to the premises held in other scholarly approaches, there are instances in which the traditions preserved in the BT are superior to, and earlier than, their parallels in the YT. Second, notwithstanding the fluidity of rabbinic literature as orally transmitted folk literature that lacks commitment to historicity, it may at times preserve original features of ancient traditions deliberately obscured by Josephus. Third, in this case, clearly the recounters and redactors of the talmudic parallel did not depend on, or know, the text in *Antiquities*, for if they had they would not have refrained from including the episode of Onias, a known figure in their literature.[96] Finally, not all of the traditions available to Josephus from the pool of early Jewish traditions were available to the rabbis. Although the presence of a parallel in rabbinic literature confirms our identification of a Josephan unit as an early Jewish folk tradition, the case in question demonstrates that the existence of such a parallel is not a necessary condition for such identification. Namely, the traces of the hidden pool of Jewish traditions in Josephus are not limited to those instances in which the story also appears in rabbinic literature.

In conjunction with these general insights, the story of the downfall of the Hasmonean dynasty paves the way for an overarching characterization of the "Hasmonean legends" reviewed throughout this book. The comparative analysis of their various versions not only sheds light on the complex history of their reception and reworking in the Josephan and the rabbinic corpora, but also reveals shifts in the image of the Hasmonean dynasty. The final chapter of the book is devoted to a consideration of these broader issues.

---

[96] This appears to be decisive proof against the assumption made by Efron and his students that the BT here relies, directly or indirectly, on *Antiquities*. See Efron, "Bar-Kokhva," 70 nn. 110–11; Wilk, "When Hyrcanus Was Besieging Aristobulus," 102.

7

The Image of the Hasmoneans:
A New Perspective

A. THE LOST LEGENDS FROM THE SECOND TEMPLE PERIOD: A CHARACTERIZATION

Based on the individual treatment of each legend in the previous chapters, I now propose to more broadly characterize the Second Temple legends of the Hasmoneans, to unveil their origins and their political and religious messages. I will then examine, by generation, how Josephus on the one hand, and the rabbis on the other, reworked these embedded stories and attempt to identify the aims that fueled their redaction in each corpus. In the course of the discussion I will present new ramifications from this study for the much-studied question of Josephus's attitude toward, and affiliation with, the Pharisees.

The six episodes touching on the Hasmoneans set the stage for an attempted characterization of the "lost Atlantis" of Jewish legends that preceded both Josephus and the rabbis. Although arriving at a precise classification of these by no means homogeneous stories is difficult, it is nevertheless possible to detect several defined genres, each with its own distinctive content, style, and thrust, and to conjecture their origins. They include, in chronological order, fragments from Aramaic chronicles, priestly temple legends, Pharisaic legends, and theodicean legends explaining the fall of the Hasmonean dynasty. In what follows I survey how each of these genres is exemplified by the stories examined in this book.

Genres

Fragments from Aramaic Chronicles

In their rabbinic versions some of the stories considered here exhibit traces of an earlier stratum, whose language was typical Second Temple-period Middle Aramaic. Its vestiges were later fragmentarily preserved and embedded in a layer of amplified Hebrew stories, with which Josephus was familiar. If this stratum was known and cited in the late first century CE, then its roots and flowering must be identified as relatively early, in the heart of the Second Temple period.

The scant evidence for these sources places their origins in an Aramaic chronicle (or chronicles). The chronicle genre, with its laconic, uniformly patterned descriptions of historical events, such as Hasmonean victories or the later annulment of Caligula's decree,[1] served the formulator of *Megillat Ta'anit* and the raconteur of the temple legends concerning John Hyrcanus and Simeon the Righteous, which were worded in Hebrew and later incorporated into the Tosefta (*t. Sotah* 13:5–6 and parallels).[2] Although in most cases the later tendency to translate Aramaic into Hebrew has almost completely eradicated their original form,[3] the redactors who integrated these early Aramaic traditions into a Hebrew framework were inclined to preserve the original Aramaic in dramatic key sentences that encapsulated, or embellished, the heart of the story.[4] As seen in Chapter 2, Josephus was acquainted with one of these stories, not with its Aramaic nucleus but with its more developed Hebrew form, and interpolated it in his narrative (*Ant.* 13.282–3). Whereas the story in *Antiquities* is largely a free paraphrase, this is not the case for the sentence that was originally in Aramaic. Here Josephus chose to provide a literal version, evidently because this sentence stood out in the Hebrew story, both as a closely worded, concise version of the story's climax, and as an Aramaic source whose ancient, festive linguistic register differed from the surrounding text.[5]

---

[1] The reconstruction of these ancient chronicles strongly links our discoveries, which are grounded in a comparison of Josephus and the rabbis, to John Collins's above-mentioned hypothesis grounded in Qumran literature (see Introduction, section F, and Chap. 2). However, the Qumran texts consulted by Collins, which he views as archetypal, were composed in Hebrew and are therefore not identical to the Aramaic genre that I postulate underlies *Megillat Ta'anit* and other isolated embedded texts. Nonetheless, it appears that both reconstructions testify to the existence of various genres of brief Hebrew and Aramaic historical chronicles, whose use apparently crossed sectarian lines.

[2] For further detail, see Chap. 2. The incongruity of the two early stories in the toseftan chapter is discussed there.

[3] On this phenomenon, see also Noam, "New Leaf of *Megillat Ta'anit*," 416–18.

[4] These processes are not surprising when we recall the ancient, exceptional Aramaic mishnayot that appear in the Hebrew mishnaic orders (e.g. *m. 'Avot* 1:13; *m. 'Ed.* 8:4); the frozen, conservative Aramaic wording of legal documents (see e.g. *m. Ketub.* 4:12; *m. Git.* 9:3); and the Aramaic *Megillat Ta'anit* whose exegetical scholia were written in Hebrew.

[5] Further examples of close resemblances are found in Josephus. In some cases these similarities are not necessarily of key Aramaic sentences; in others, we cannot establish an Aramaic source as the basis for the resemblance. See e.g. the literary resemblance between the Hebrew and Greek versions of the climax of the story of the high priest and Alexander the Great (Ben Shahar, "The High Priest and Alexander the Great," 127–8): בדמותו של זה / ἐν τῷ νῦν σχήματι (lit. " in his current image"; *Ant.* 11.334; Scholion P, 21 Kislev) (Noam, *Megillat Ta'anit*, 102, lines 45–6).

Priestly Temple Legends

Temple- and priesthood-oriented stories comprise another identifiable genre of early legends.[6] Although these stories have shared motifs, not every legend belonging to this genre necessarily contains them all. Of these motifs, the most conspicuous include: a threat to the temple; an esteemed high priest who steps into the breach at moments of national crisis; and finally, divine salvation. Two spheres collide in these stories: an external military-political sphere that poses a threat to Jewish life, and an internal, metaphysical sphere that revolves about the divine–Israelite relationship. Symbolized by the temple, the latter also comprises the locus of events. As the divine–Israelite mediator in the temple sphere, and as a figure also involved, directly or indirectly, in the political or military events recounted, the high priest bridges these two loci. Similarly, as the focus of the external threat and also as the *mise en scène* for the divine–Israelite drama, the temple unites these planes.

These stories convey the message that history is not determined by world leaders and their emissaries, but rather by the God of Israel who resides in his temple. Hence, the genuine drama takes place in the temple, not on the battlefield, and the hero is not the famed conqueror or military leader but the high priest: the servant of God and the representative of the chosen people. Essentially a direct continuation of biblical theology, this message frames history in terms of the divine–Israelite relationship.[7]

A definitive example of this genre is the famous legend that essentially opens the Josephan account of post-biblical history, namely, the story of the encounter between Alexander the Great and the high priest (*Ant.* 11.302–47; Scholia O and P, 21 Kislev [=*b. Yoma* 69a], among others). Although not covered in this volume, it can serve as a prototype for some of the traditions that are included in the discussion. This tradition interweaves an aggressive Samaritan threat to the temple with Alexander's conquests. Garbed in priestly robes, the legendary high priest Jadus/Simeon the Righteous goes out to meet the conqueror, and the latter bows to him, for it is this man's image that guides him in battle. According to Josephus, Alexander also visits the temple and offers sacrifices there. What the storyteller wishes to underscore is that the celebrated conqueror's successes on the battlefield were actually contingent on the dictates of the God of Israel, who resides in the Jerusalem temple. The high priest plays a

---

[6] Cf. Rappaport's observation: "It appears that the fragmentary recollections [of the Hasmoneans] in rabbinic literature were mainly preserved in priestly circles, for they are almost without exception linked to the priests or the temple" (*First Book of Maccabees*, 73).

[7] One of the early, outstanding enunciators of this notion in biblical research was Gerhard von Rad. See e.g. von Rad, *Old Testament Theology*. For more recent observations see e.g. Y. Elitzur, "Tefisat ha-historiyah ba-miqra," 253–60; Amit, "Dual Causality," 106–21. For a similar religious perception in Josephus, see D. R. Schwartz, "Josephus on Albinus." Schwartz suggests that, in *Antiquities*, Josephus also views the Romans as a divine rod in the drama taking place between God and his sinful people.

striking dual role in this legend, as both a religious and political leader.[8] An event that occurred some four centuries later was also recounted in line with the unwritten rules of this genre. Another legendary "Simeon the Righteous" takes action during the national crisis engendered by Caligula's decree mandating that his statue be displayed in the temple, and eventually hears a heavenly voice emanating from the holy of holies that announces the murder of the wicked emperor.[9]

One representative of this genre is the story of Nicanor's defeat, with which this volume opened. Uniquely among the traditions considered here, this story is also known from earlier versions because of its inclusion in the books of Maccabees. In all its versions this story highlights a strong threat to the temple exemplified by Nicanor's actions: "he would raise his hand against Jerusalem and against the temple" (Scholion P, and similarly in the parallels), "and threatened that…he would pull down the temple when he returned" (*Ant.* 12.406). With the exception of the censored Josephan version, all the variants reflect measure-for-measure punishments of Nicanor: his head and his hand which he raised against the temple/Jerusalem, were hung "opposite the temple"/"from the gates of Jerusalem." The rabbinic version has no identifiable priestly figure as its protagonist, because the historical hero Judas Maccabeus is not mentioned by name and is simply depicted as a warrior. On the other hand, in 1 Maccabees, and in Josephus in its wake, we find descriptions of priestly prayer and of priestly efforts to placate Nicanor. In other words, here too we find the priests playing a dual role: as the representatives of the people vis-à-vis God in the temple and also vis-à-vis the foreign military leader. Moreover, this tradition contains not a miraculous deliverance but rather a natural victory, and makes no explicit reference to divine providence as guiding the victory. However, the marked allusions to the biblical account of the miraculous defeat of the Assyrian king Sennacherib in the days of King Hezekiah, and the descriptions of the priests praying and the prayer of Judas Maccabeus in 1 Maccabees, certainly allude to this viewpoint.

Another definitive example of the priestly genre is the tradition regarding the prediction of victory heard by the high priest John Hyrcanus in the temple (Chapter 2). Its backdrop is a military campaign being waged by John Hyrcanus's sons in Samaria. But, as we have seen, even though the story involves a military event outside of Jerusalem, it actually focuses on a religious event that takes place in the depths of the temple, and its protagonist is a high priest, not a military

---

[8] Massive scholarship has been devoted to this tradition, from the historical and literary perspectives. For an updated summary, including references to earlier scholarship, and many novel observations, see Ben Shahar, "The High Priest and Alexander the Great," 91–144. For another review and a slightly different take on the purpose of the legend, see Tropper, *Simeon the Righteous*, chap. 5.

[9] *T. Sotah* 13:6 and parallels; Scholia O and P on *Megillat Ta'anit* (Noam, *Megillat Ta'anit*, 112–14). On Caligula's decree, see Noam, "Statue in the Temple."

figure. This story as well indicates that the main drama inheres not in the arena of Israel and its enemies, but in the divine–Israelite relationship: accordingly, the true protagonist of the story is the religious, not the secular, leader. Nonetheless, the high priest is not isolated from the external military events, for, according to Josephus at least, it was his sons who were engaged in the military action.

It appears that another genre of putative Aramaic sources, namely lost Aramaic temple legends, underlies these Hebrew temple legends. Like the Aramaic chronicles discussed above, they did not survive, but their vestiges make sporadic appearances within their Hebrew successors. In Scholion O's version of the story of the annulment of Caligula's decree we encounter two Aramaic sentences in the Hebrew account.[10] Another Aramaic clause, perhaps a fragment of the lost Aramaic infrastructure of the full legend, also appears in a Palestinian midrash recounting the story of Alexander the Great and the high priest.[11] At a later stage, these traditions tended to be translated into Hebrew or integrated into Hebrew narratives, essentially nearly eradicating their original Aramaic form.

Finally, I note the anomalous nature of these temple legends as compared to the bulk of rabbinic narrative. Because sages are generally the protagonists of rabbinic legends, this genre has been awarded the scholarly appellation "tales of the sages."[12] In the genre of early priestly stories, however, the protagonists are priests. Also setting these types apart is the venue where the events take place. Rabbinic stories are typically set in the home, the marketplace, or places where sages gather, such as the upper chamber and the study house, whereas the more ancient stories always have a temple setting. Classic rabbinic stories usually focus on personal anecdotes, not broad epic events, whereas the priestly temple legends involve dramatic political-military events such as Alexander the Great's conquest, the Hasmonean wars, or Caligula's murder. In this respect they more closely resemble the Bible than the genre of the tales of the sages, which would succeed them. Their singularity and early date are also evidenced by their terminology: the phenomenon termed "a heavenly voice" in classic rabbinic literature is here still "a word," and, as noted above, fragments of Aramaic phrasing from a lost literary stratum have occasionally survived in these stories.[13]

Another issue to be considered is what the presence of this priestly genre in rabbinic literature signifies. Scholars tend to make a dichotomic division

---

[10] Scholion O (22 Shevat; Noam, *Megillat Ta'anit*, 112–14). See Noam, "Statue in the Temple," 470–2, 482.

[11] *Pesiq. Rab Kah.* 4:9. See Noam, *Megillat Ta'anit*, 265, 284; Ben Shahar, "The High Priest and Alexander the Great," 121, 128. For a detailed discussion of the phenomenon of lost Aramaic early texts, see Noam, "New Leaf of Megillat Ta'anit," 416–18; and Noam, "Introduction," 41.

[12] See e.g. Fraenkel, *Darkhei ha-aggadah ve-ha-midrash*, 235–85.

[13] As shown in Chapter 2 in this volume. These differences are readily apparent from a comparison of John Hyrcanus's and Simeon the Righteous's heavenly voices to the later stories from the rabbinic milieu appended to them in the Tosefta.

between the sources that display priestly trends, to which Sadducean affinities are ascribed, and those that represent the rabbinic anti-priestly attitude, viewed as reflecting the rabbis' desire to assume the mantle of leadership.[14] Although this distinction is fundamentally correct, nonetheless, as seen here, the rabbis lovingly adopted, and embedded in their literature, several definitively priestly stories that reflect no rabbinic presence or leadership. This suggests a more permeable barrier between the two worlds than what at first glance may appear to have been the case.

Pharisaic Legends

Other stories examined in this volume were identified, based on analogy and indirect evidence, as having originated in Pharisaic circles. Two, attested only in the BT, have a definitive Pharisaic imprint and clearly contain Pharisaic polemic. They are also the sole stories in the corpus examined here in which the rabbis explicitly refer to the Pharisees by this name. However, as in all other cases, here too this designation appears in a polemical context. Placed in the mouths of figures hostile or semi-hostile toward the Pharisees, it is voiced neither by the narrator nor the Pharisees themselves.[15]

My study of the rupture between John Hyrcanus/Janneus and the Pharisees (Chapter 3) revealed features of a sectarian dispute. Its Hebrew, talmudic version contains vocabulary, argumentation, strategies, and derogatory terms that were part and parcel of the political debate in Second Temple Jewish society. One such strategy was the creation of a political "midrash" that drew associations between biblical figures and events and the circumstances of the Hasmonean state. In addition, this story's exceptional, artificial interweaving of biblical

---

[14] This sharp distinction is already found in Geiger, *Urschrift*, esp. 101–58 and passim, and many have followed in his wake. Regarding the premise that the Pharisees sought to succeed to the priesthood, including a survey of the nineteenth- and early-twentieth-century scholarship and exposure of its political bias, see D. R. Schwartz, " 'Kingdom of Priests,' " 57–80. For a later, more moderate viewpoint regarding the relationship between priests and rabbis after the destruction, see D. R. Schwartz, "From Priests at Their Right," 21–41, and the additional bibliography cited there, p. 21 n. 1. For another version of this outlook, see Herr, "Continuum," 43–56. For a survey of the literature in support of, and dissenting from, the thesis that the Pharisees and the rabbis struggled against the priests, see Rosen-Zvi, "Bodies and Temple," 65–7 and nn. 65–71. On the priestly nature of Qumran halakhah, see D. R. Schwartz, "Law and Truth," 229 and the bibliographical references there, and more recently, Shemesh, *Halakhah in the Making*, 15–19. For an up-to-date survey of the sources and scholarship on the priesthood and its status, see Irshai, "Priesthood," 75–82. See also the discussion in Chapter 3 in this volume.

[15] This phenomenon has been observed in the scholarship in different contexts and indicates that this designation originated with the Pharisees' opponents and bore negative connotations from the start. Rivkin ("Defining the Pharisees," 213–17, 231–2, 247–8) has shown that tannaitic sources alternate between the attributions "Pharisees" and "sages," and that the first designation appears only in disputational contexts. See also Cohen, "Significance of Yavneh," 41 and n. 39; Flusser, "4QMMT," 97–103.

words and syntax into a later linguistic stratum typified Second Temple Jewish, not classic rabbinic, literature.

The passage in question aims to overturn a prevailing opinion regarding the Pharisees, also familiar from other contexts: Qumran literature, the NT, and the Josephan account. In line with this outlook, they are portrayed as a powerful, influential circle that can garner public support, but also as a quarrelsome, hypocritical group that possesses the ability to undermine kings and high priests. In response to the claim that they bear responsibility for the rupture with the Hasmoneans, the narrator puts forth the following counterclaim: the Pharisees/rabbis never opposed the Hasmonean ruler, nor did they espouse the defamatory libel regarding his lineage. The rupture was neither their fault, nor the fault of the ruler. Rather, it was the enemies of the Pharisees who created dissension and wreaked disaster by disseminating a wicked, libelous rumor.

Two scoundrels appear in the context of this story. One undermines the authority of the Hasmonean leader; the other incites this ruler against the Pharisees. However, these two are not identified with the Pharisees, whom the narrator clears of any blame, noting that they "separated themselves in anger" from the slanderer. In other words, the story aims to make a distinction between the purported Pharisees, who libel the ruler, and the "real" Pharisees, who detach themselves from this instigator. By so doing, the narrator diverts the accusations of subversion made against the Pharisees to others mistakenly identified with them.

A very similar tactic is employed in the story of Janneus's instructions to his wife (Chapter 5). Each of its versions conveys Janneus's advice to the queen to effectively change the royal treatment of the Pharisees. In the talmudic story his general instructions are worded as an aphorism: "Fear not the Pharisees and the non-Pharisees but the hypocrites who ape the Pharisees; because their deeds are the deeds of Zimri but they expect a reward like Phinehas." This well-attested accusation of hypocrisy tendered toward the Pharisees or those who resemble them is indicative of the story's authenticity.

These two stories—the story of the rupture with the Pharisees and of Janneus's instructions—treat the attitude of the Pharisees toward a Hasmonean ruler. Both display ambivalence: although there is attestation to underlying hostility, some of the protagonists aim for conciliation. Both stories also allude to biblical contexts from the book of Numbers: the rupture story alludes to Korah's rebellion, and that of Janneus's instructions to Zimri's provocative sin. Note that neither story employs the classic rabbinic form of verse citation followed by explicit midrash; rather, each draws implicit comparisons between a biblical situation and the circumstances of the story. But their political message is of greater interest. The claim put forth in the rabbinic version of Janneus's instructions is that it is not the Pharisees who seek to destabilize his reign, but "hypocrites who ape" them. The same argument is found in the rupture story.

This strongly suggests that both stories are fragments of apologetic Pharisaic literature, which sought to respond to widespread accusations that the Pharisees were subverting the Hasmonean regime. Their origins evidently lie in moderate Pharisaic circles, which tried to avert an irreparable rift with the Hasmonean dynasty and isolated themselves from the more extreme oppositional wings. The narrators of these stories claim that, because the latter are not "true" Pharisees, therefore "we" should not be accused of their acts. Notwithstanding the similarities between both stories with respect to political arena, arguments, and strategies, they differ stylistically. The story of the rupture preserves Second Temple syntax and idioms. This is not the case for the instructions story (with the exception of the term "hypocrite"), which opens in Babylonian Aramaic. As opposed to other ancient stories surveyed here that survived in the BT (Nicanor's defeat, whose source is the Scholion on *Megillat Ta'anit*; John Hyrcanus and a heavenly voice and the story of pelting with citrons that are known from the Tosefta), these stories did not reach the BT through the conduit of Palestinian rabbinic literature, but independently, and have no parallels in any other extant rabbinic source. This strengthens the surmise that they all came from a single work, collection, or pool of very specific Pharisaic traditions also available to Josephus, that made its way to Babylonia during the talmudic period.

Although these stories are the only rabbinic ones that mention the Pharisees explicitly, other parallels in Josephus and the rabbinic corpus concerning the entire Second Temple era, including the Hasmonean period, also appear to have Pharisaic origins. This observation, already noted in early Josephan studies,[16] emerges from their features. Aside from the two definitively Pharisaic stories treated here, the features that arouse suspicion that other Jewish traditions in Josephus had Pharisaic origins are an anti-priestly bent—the exact opposite of the message of the "temple legends" described above[17]—Pharisaic figures at the center of the story,[18] and in one instance, an explicit reference by

---

[16] Hölscher, *Quellen des Josephus*, 81–5.

[17] Some of these tales are almost grotesqueries. See e.g. the two Josephan stories concerning the late Persian period regarding a priest who murdered his brother in the temple and the son of a high priest who married a gentile woman and was involved in founding the rival Samaritan temple (*Ant.* 11.306–12; cf. the rabbinic tradition on Onias's temple, *y. Yoma* 6:3, 43c–d, *b. Menaḥ.* 109b), and the story of the pelting of Janneus/an anonymous priest with citrons in the temple. The parallel rabbinic story, according to which the corner of the altar was broken off as a result of a similar episode, is even more telling (Chap. 4 above). Other examples are the episode of Joseph son of Ellemus, a scheming priest who attempted to employ unusual circumstances in order to assume the high priesthood (*Ant.* 17.165–6; cf. *t. Yoma* [*Kippurim*] 1:4 and parallels); and the thieving priests in the late Second Temple period (*Ant.* 20.179–81, 205–7, 213–21; cf. *t. Menaḥ.* 13:18–21; *t. Zebaḥ.* 11:16, *b. Pesaḥ.* 57a, *b. Ker.* 28a–b).

[18] See the figures of the sages Pollion and Samaias (*Ant.* 14.172–6; 15.3–4, 370; cf. *b. Sanh.* 19a) and of Matthias the son of Margalothus and Judas the son of Sariphaeus (*War* 1.648–55; *Ant.* 17.149–63) in Herod's day; and Simon who was reputed for religious scrupulousness in Agrippa's day (*Ant.* 19.332–4; cf. the rabbinic traditions regarding conflict between Janneus and Simeon ben Shataḥ, which perhaps echo this story). The story of the conversion of the house of Adiabene (*Ant.* 20.34–5, 38–45) also highlights the role of Jewish sages, who teach the members of the family

Josephus to a Pharisaic source. In relating the miracle of the rainfall that took place during the construction of the Herodian temple, Josephus announces that its source is an oral ancestral tradition: καὶ τοῦτον τὸν λόγον οἱ πατέρες ἡμῖν παρέδωκαν ("and this story... our fathers have handed down to us," *Ant.* 15.425). This tradition was indeed transmitted in tannaitic literature in almost identical language (*Sifra: Beḥuqotei* 1:1, and parallels). Moreover, the terms used here display close affinity to the famous Josephan description of the Pharisees, who in addition to the Written Law passed on (παρέδοσαν) regulations (νόμιμα) handed down by former generations (ἐκ πατέρων διαδοχῆς) (*Ant.* 13.297). This is a clear Josephan allusion to the Pharisaic origins of the tradition of the miracle of the rainfall. Regarding other Jewish stories, Josephus employs verbs that explicitly indicate that they were transmitted orally and belong to ancestral tradition: λέγεται—"it is told";[19] παρειλήφαμεν—"we have received";[20] φασί[21]— "they say."[22] In each of these cases, these verbs introduce a source with a parallel in rabbinic literature. Note that two of these "transmitted" sources appear in the closing sections of books in *Antiquities*: "Such then is the account we have received of the end of the Asamonaean line," which ends book 14,[23] and "this story, which our fathers have handed down to us ..." that ends book 15.[24] This placement is indicative of their importance in Josephus's eyes.

Theodicean Legends Regarding the Fall of the Hasmonean Dynasty

The genres of the legends surveyed thus far relate to two distinct periods in Hasmonean history: the golden age of the first and second generations and the less rosy period of internal tension with the Pharisees in Janneus's day, or perhaps even at the end of John Hyrcanus's reign. The final period—of traumatic fratricidal warfare and Hasmonean loss of independence—was addressed in the last legend considered in this book.

As we saw in Chapter 6, the main message of this legend of the siege and the sacrificial animals, like its twin on the death of Onias that was preserved only

---

Jewish law and persuade Izates to undergo circumcision. This phenomenon is even more prominent in rabbinic literature. Herod murders the rabbis but in the end accepts advice from a sage, Baba ben Buta (*b. B. Bat.* 3b–4a). Simeon ben Shataḥ bravely confronts Janneus in the Sanhedrin (*b. Sanh.* 19a–b). The story of Janneus's plot to kill the rabbis (Scholion P, 2 Shevat), which relies on a parallel story told of Herod (*War* 1.659–60, 666; *Ant.* 17.173–81, 193), underscores that the victims of the planned plot were the "elders" and "rabbis" of Israel. In this instance it appears that the original story was related regarding notable Jews, as in the Josephan version, whereas during the process of transmission and revision the subjects of persecution were transformed into the rabbis.

[19] See John Hyrcanus and the heavenly voice (*Ant.* 13.282); the miracle of the rainfall in Herod's day (*Ant.* 15.425); a golden vine/garden in the temple (*Ant.* 14.36).
[20] *Ant.* 14.491.   [21] *Ant.* 15.367.   [22] See Chap. 2 (*Ant.* 13.282).
[23] *Ant.* 14.491. See Ilan, "Herod's Deeds," 373–408.   [24] *Ant.* 15.425.

by Josephus, is the need for unity and the grave danger inherent in its breach. The temple and its cult symbolize Jewish unity, which is under threat from internal strife. Well preserved in the rabbinic version of the story of the siege,[25] this message was obscured in the Josephan one. Yet even in Josephus this lesson is strongly proclaimed in the second episode, the story of Onias, in which the elderly man, who is beloved of God, asks that God not show greater favor to one side over the other.

In addition, elsewhere Josephus indicates that Jerusalem's misfortune, the loss of territory and of Jewish freedom, all resulted from the dissension between the Hasmonean brothers (*Ant.* 14.77–8). Daniel R. Schwartz has demonstrated that this unit shows definitive signs of interpolation into a sequence that originated in Nicolaus.[26] However, as opposed to Schwartz's contention that this reflects Josephus's personal viewpoint,[27] I have no doubt that this is a deeply rooted, pre-existing Jewish tradition that Josephus incorporated in his narrative. Even though in this case no exact parallel has been preserved in rabbinic literature, it displays all the features of the interpolated Jewish traditions surveyed in the Introduction to this volume. It appears only in *Antiquities* (and not in *War*), it breaks the sequence of the narrative into which it has been inserted, represents a Jewish viewpoint, and concludes with a Josephan reference to a discussion elsewhere in his work. Proof of my claim comes from the repetition of this unit at the end of book 14 (490–1), using similar wording, primarily the expression διὰ τὴν πρὸς ἀλλήλους στάσιν (lit.: "through strife with one another," 491; cf. 77: πρὸς ἀλλήλους στασιάσαντες) and the verb used to describe the loss of freedom or royal power: ἀπέβαλον (491) as compared to ἀπεβάλομεν (77). Both passages underscore the Hasmonean dynasty's priestly origins and the assumption, "to our misfortune," of the crown by a commoner. Moreover, in the second passage Josephus informs us that his account of the brothers' responsibility for the collapse of the Hasmonean commonwealth is not based on his own thoughts but is rather an "account we have received" (παρειλήφαμεν), namely, an ancestral, probably Pharisaic, tradition. We can thus conclude that the two legends of fratricidal dissension—the siege and the Onias stories—have preserved an authentic moral-historiosophical lesson which originated in Second Temple Jewish society: it was their forfeiture of internal unity that brought the end of the Hasmonean dynasty and the concomitant loss of freedom. It is even possible that the talmudic story's unusual reciprocal wording—צרו זה על זה [28] ("besieged one another")—echoes a Hebrew source that was also available to Josephus, giving rise to his repeated use of πρὸς ἀλλήλους.[29]

[25] See Fraenkel, *Darkhei ha-aggadah ve-ha-midrash*, 236–9.

[26] D. R. Schwartz, "Josephus on Hyrcanus II," 217–18.

[27] Ibid. 219–20.   [28] See Fraenkel, *Darkhei ha-aggadah ve-ha-midrash*, 236–9.

[29] Josephus himself used this Jewish convention in his remarks on the rebels during the First Jewish Revolt: "Whence did our servitude arise? Was it not from party strife among our forefathers,

Linguistic Features

The original language of the ancient legends cannot be reconstructed from their Greek, Josephan rendering. Nor can their original nature be elicited from rabbinic literature, because they were in many instances reworked to fit the language of the works in which they were embedded. Surprisingly, however, many of the stories were found to have faithfully preserved ancient features. As opposed to the prevailing view in the scholarship, rabbinic literature can in these cases serve as an excellent control for the Josephan version, because it not only reflects the topical contents preserved by the historian but also elements of the original stories' language and style.

As noted above, the various stories considered here reflect different styles and did not originate in a single work or collection. Yet many contain linguistic-stylistic phenomena that are anomalous in rabbinic literature and display authentic features of the earlier stratum whose traces we are exploring. Thus, for example, fragments from an above-mentioned Aramaic chronicle of events were later incorporated in Hebrew temple legends to mark the high point of the story (see Chapter 2). For the story of the rupture with the Pharisees I documented a mixed style that combined biblical language with a later linguistic stratum, which was typical of Second Temple literature (Chapter 3). An outstanding feature of some of the stories is their reliance on the Bible, albeit in a style not typical of classic rabbinic literature. Instead of an explicit biblical citation followed by a homily, these stories masterfully combine biblical expressions—the account of Nicanor's defeat in 1 Maccabees and rabbinic sources (Chapter 1); the rupture with the Pharisees (Chapter 3), or explicitly draw a comparison between the present and a parallel biblical situation: Janneus's instructions (Chapter 5).[30] In one of the stories treated in this volume a pithy aphorism comprises the climax of the story (Chapter 5), and this phenomenon is also characteristic of other early stories not treated in this volume.[31]

---

when the madness of Aristobulus and Hyrcanus and their mutual dissensions brought Pompey against the city...?" (*War* 5.395–6).

[30] Cf. the story of the appointment of the high priest Pinhas of Habbata, which the rabbinic version compares to the appointment of Elisha by Elijah (*t. Yoma* [*Kippurim*] 1:6 and parallels; cf. *War* 4.152–7).

[31] The aphorism בדמותו של זה אני רואה כשארד למלחמה ונצח featured in the tale of the high priest and Alexander the Great has a parallel in Josephus (Scholion P, 21 Kislev [Noam, *Megillat Taʿanit*, 102] and parallels; cf. *Ant.* 11.334). In the story of Caligula's plot to introduce an idol into the temple, the climax is the cry of the Jews: נמות ולא תהא זו (Scholion P, 22 Shevat; see also Scholion O [Noam, *Megillat Taʿanit*, 113, lines 32–3]; cf. *Ant.* 18.271). Another stylistic feature of some of the ancient legends (not studied in this volume) is their taking the form of short poems (the stories of the corrupt high priests [*t. Menaḥ.* 13:21; *b. Pesaḥ.* 57a; *b. Ker.* 28a–b; cf. *Ant.* 20.179–81, 205–7, 213–21]. Note that the version in *Antiquities* is in prose).

B. THE HASMONEANS AS MIRRORED IN JOSEPHUS AND RABBINIC LITERATURE

The Josephan Attitude toward the Hasmoneans

The Josephan attitude toward the Hasmonean dynasty has already been described from various perspectives. I now briefly review the main scholarly conclusions concerning the historical episodes tangential to the Jewish legends discussed throughout this study. Scholars have noted Josephus's positive attitude toward the first generation, and the pride he took in his Hasmonean lineage (*Life* 2–7; *Ant.* 16.187) and in the first members of the dynasty: Mattathias, his sons, and John Hyrcanus I.[32] They have also surveyed the reworking of 1 Maccabees in *Ant.* 12.246–13.212, both with respect to style and content. From a literary perspective, we find a Josephan tendency to stylistic simplification, omission of poetic passages, and use of indirect speech to relay the contents of speeches, alongside the invention of new speeches. With respect to content, Josephus censored sections that displayed animosity toward non-Jews, and also invented facts or added them based on his own knowledge. In addition, Josephus transformed the theocentric orientation of 1 Maccabees into an anthropocentric one that centers on human ability; accordingly, the praise heaped on Mattathias and Judas goes beyond that found in 1 Maccabees and stresses their loyalty to ancestral law and the rectitude of the goals for which they fought.[33] As for the Hasmonean dynasty as a whole, the scholarship has noted the Josephan tendency to moderate the dynastic trend emphasized by 1 Maccabees on the one hand,[34] and to underscore Hasmonean royal authority and loyalty to their Syrian–Seleucid allies on the other.[35]

For Josephus, the second-generation figure of John Hyrcanus was the last worthy Hasmonean ruler, an admired leader who reigned long and happily and merited the three greatest gifts: leadership, prophecy, and the high priesthood.[36] According to Mason, John Hyrcanus was Josephus's personal hero. Like John, Josephus himself took pride in the Hasmonean attributes of priesthood, prophecy, and royal descent, and he even named his son Hyrcanus.[37]

[32] See e.g. Goldstein, *I Maccabees*, 56; Mason, *Josephus on the Pharisees*, 83, 213–30, 246–59; Cohen, *Josephus in Galilee and Rome*, 44–7; Regev, "Hasmoneans' Self Image," 19–20.

[33] For a survey of, and bibliography on, this topic, see Gafni, "Josephus and I Maccabees"; Bar-Kochva, *Judas Maccabaeus*, 186–93; Feldman, "Josephus' Portrayal of the Hasmoneans"; Sievers, "Josephus, First Maccabees, Sparta," esp. 246; Rappaport, *First Book of Maccabees*, 10–12, 69–70. Tuval (*Jerusalem Priest to Roman Jew*, 194–201) views the emphasis in *Antiquities* on observance of the law as the goal of the Hasmonean struggle as additional proof of Josephus's later tendency to ground his Jewish identity in the Torah and not in territory or the temple.

[34] Cohen, *Josephus in Galilee and Rome*, 44–7; Goldstein, *I Maccabees*, 74.

[35] Feldman, "Josephus' Portrayal of the Hasmoneans."

[36] See Thoma, "John Hyrcanus I," 127.

[37] Mason, *Josephus on the Pharisees*, 225. See also Thoma, "John Hyrcanus I," 130–1. According to Fuks ("Josephus and the Hasmoneans") the biography of John in *Antiquities* places greater

As for Janneus's generation, in his two works Josephus underscores the cruelty of, and internal conflict sparked by, this Hasmonean king. Nonetheless, the scholarship has shown that Josephus evinces a slightly more forgiving attitude toward Janneus in the more expansive version in *Antiquities*, where he takes the trouble to describe the difficult circumstances that led Janneus to harshly suppress the rebellion against him,[38] than in the shorter version in *War*, which was based on Nicolaus.

As for the downfall of the dynasty in the fourth generation, as seen in Chapter 6 Second Temple Jewish theodicy ascribed the loss of independence to the breach of Jewish unity by the warring brothers, Hyrcanus II and Aristobulus II. Twice explicitly cited by Josephus, evidently he accepted this theological-historical interpretation.

In attempting to uncover the Josephan attitude toward the Hasmoneans, scholars have compared the references in *War* and *Antiquities*. They proceed based mainly on the assumption that the additions and changes found in the broader descriptions in *Antiquities* either reveal use of another source, or the Josephan outlook itself. They further maintain that in *Antiquities* Josephus reshaped the basic materials he inherited from Nicolaus, whether in the original, or in the secondary form embedded in his earlier work *War*. The scholarship has shown Josephus to exhibit a more favorable attitude toward the Hasmoneans in *Antiquities*, as compared to the hostile literary infrastructure reaped from Nicolaus, as preserved in *War*.[39]

Yet regarding the folk traditions on the Hasmoneans considered here, no systematic comparison of the Josephan sources to his reworking has been undertaken. Unlike 1 Maccabees and Nicolaus, these traditions were not definitively or universally recognized by scholars as a source external to, and earlier

emphasis on national-religious elements. In Tuval's opinion (*Jerusalem Priest to Roman Jew*, 201–3), Josephus glorifies the figure of John Hyrcanus in order to portray him as an exemplary leader who obeys the laws of the Torah and as a result merits happiness and all the virtues.

[38] See e.g. *Ant.* 13.375–6, 381–2. See Efron, "Simeon Ben Shataḥ and Jannaeus," 168–71; Fuks, "Josephus and the Hasmoneans," 169–71; Mason, *Josephus on the Pharisees*, 246–8. However, most scholars do not differentiate between the Jewish tradition on the citrons and the libel and the Josephan narrative framework; see the following discussion.

[39] This has been a prevailing approach in the scholarship, starting with Laqueur, *Jüdische Historiker Flavius Josephus*. See e.g. Stern, *Greek and Latin Authors*, 1:230; Fuks, "Josephus and the Hasmoneans"; Mason, *Josephus on the Pharisees*, chaps. 9 and 10; Thoma, "John Hyrcanus I," 130; D. R. Schwartz, "Josephus on Hyrcanus II." Nonetheless, Schwartz notes additional trends in Josephus that at times exhibit hostility toward certain Hasmonean rulers, in *Antiquities* in particular. The figure of Alexandra-Shelamzion is a striking example: she is described much more negatively in *Antiquities* (13.405–33) than in *War* (1.107–19). For a discussion of the relationship between the descriptions, see Mason, *Josephus on the Pharisees*, 82–115, 246–59; Ilan, *Integrating Women*, 21–3; Tuval, *Jerusalem Priest to Roman Jew*, 206–7. In any event, with the exception of the story of Janneus's instructions, these descriptions do not rely on Jewish legends and were therefore not treated here. In contrast to the previously mentioned scholars, there is the minority opinion of Efron ("Simeon Ben Shataḥ and Jannaeus," 161–75) who identifies a fundamentally hostile attitude toward the Hasmoneans, with minor variations, in both *War* and *Antiquities*, which he views as grounded in Nicolaus.

than, Josephus. On the contrary, these Jewish legends, interpolated only in *Antiquities*, were often identified in the scholarship as Josephan additions to the nuclear narrative that originated in Nicolaus or in *War*, and served as a tool for scholarly reconstruction of the historian's own viewpoint.[40] The isolation of the Jewish legends inserted into *Antiquities* 12–14 from the surrounding narrative and from the Josephan comments is instructive and reveals his attitude toward his sources and toward his Hasmonean protagonists. This distinction between the deliberate Josephan reworking and the underlying literary tradition is made possible, as we have seen, through examination of internal features of the text and comparison to close versions of the same legends that were embedded in rabbinic literature. Following an overview of the rabbinic attitude toward the Hasmoneans, I will embark on a comparison of the Josephan and rabbinic treatments of each Hasmonean generation.

The Rabbinic Attitude toward the Hasmoneans

The scholarly study of the rabbinic attitude toward the Hasmoneans has known sharp fluctuations over the past two centuries and the different trends evidenced there were no little influenced by the contemporary political-religious atmosphere. Thus, the pioneering nineteenth-century scholars assumed that the pietists and scribes mentioned in 1 Maccabees 7:12–17 who, as opposed to Judas Maccabeus, agreed to meet with, and were eventually murdered by, the Hellenizing high priest Alcimus, were the predecessors of the Pharisees. They further argued that, seeking only religious freedom and opposing national independence, the pietists left Judas's party.[41] Influenced by the European zeitgeist,[42] this hypothesis, which places the roots of the future rift between the Pharisees and the Hasmoneans in a reconstructed dispute between the Maccabees, who sought political independence, and religious figures, who sought theocracy and spirituality,[43] long dominated the scholarship.[44] Other

---

[40] See Introduction, p. 3, par. 2. See also D. R. Schwartz, "Josephus on Hyrcanus II," 217–18, where he reconstructs Josephus's historiographical principles according to the interpolations in *Ant.* 14.77–8, 490–1, which are missing from the parallel in *War*. However, as we saw above, both of these passages are a Pharisaic legacy that Josephus cites as is without adding any personal insights.

[41] See already Wellhausen, *Pharisees and Sadducees*, 17–19, 68–106; Graetz, *History of the Jews*, 2:16–34; Schürer, *History*, 1:212–13.

[42] Efron, "Hasmonean Revolt," 5–14.

[43] On the rupture between the Pharisees and the Hasmoneans, which different sources attribute to the end of John Hyrcanus's reign or to that of his son Janneus, see Chap. 3 (and Chap. 2 in part).

[44] For a review of additional literature and counter-arguments, see Efron, "Hasmonean Revolt," 3–14; and also Bar-Kochva, *Judas Maccabaeus*, 59 n. 101; Goodblatt, *Ancient Jewish Nationalism*, 89 n. 32. A moderate version of this viewpoint was voiced by Rappaport, *First Book of Maccabees*, 210–12.

scholars ascribed the subsequent Pharisaic hostility toward the Hasmoneans to opposition to the third generation's assumption of royalty, or to the common-wealth's political-military policies.[45] This approach relies heavily on the rupture legend treated in Chapter 3, identifying the demand made of the Hasmonean ruler to abandon the "crown of priesthood" with the Pharisaic, and later, the rabbinic stance. Many scholars drew a straight line from the Pharisees to the conjectured hostility toward the memory of the Hasmoneans on the part of their successors, the rabbis of the Mishnah and the Talmud. As proof of rab-binic literature's condemnation or removal of the Hasmoneans from its pages, these scholars cite the exclusion of the books of Maccabees from the canon and from Jewish collective memory; the absence of any mention of the Maccabees and their bravery in rabbinic literature; statements negating the appointment of king-priests or non-Davidic kings; the lack of a mishnaic tractate devoted to Hanukkah; the naive question in the BT (*Shabb.* 21b): "What is Hanukkah?"; and the sugya's choice to put forward the miracle of the cruse of oil as the rationale for the holiday instead of the story of the Hasmonean battles and victories.[46]

Starting in the 1930s, different voices, mainly among Jewish and Israeli scholars, first and foremost among them Gedalyahu Alon, began to question this historical reconstruction. They argued that the sources contain no real evi-dence of a rift in Judas's ranks or of a connection between the episode of nego-tiations with Alcimus and the Pharisaic conflict with the Hasmoneans decades later; nor is there any foundation for the reconstruction of an anti-common-wealth or anti-national ideology among the Pharisees or their successors, the rabbis. Those who espoused this viewpoint also sought to reject the proofs of anti-Hasmoneanism in rabbinic literature in one fell swoop. They claimed that, because rabbinic literature is by its very nature not historiographical, no argu-ment can be made based on its silence on historical matters, and they compiled rabbinic statements praising the Hasmonean dynasty and its members, and the holiday of Hanukkah and its commandments. In response to the argument that no mishnaic tractate is devoted to Hanukkah, they note that not every halakhic issue has a tractate or even a chapter in the Mishnah. Regarding the language of the question "What is Hanukkah?" and the story of the cruse of oil, they put forth various literary-exegetical rationales rather than a claim of deliberate censorship.[47]

---

[45] See e.g. Schalit, "Domestic Politics and Political Institutions," 277–97; D. R. Schwartz, "Pharisaic Opposition"; and more recently, Rappaport, *House of the Hasmoneans*, 317–18.

[46] Thus already Geiger, *Urschrift*, 200–31, esp. 202–6. For a detailed exposition of the argu-ments of this school of thought, see Alon, "Did the Jewish People and Its Sages Cause the Hasmoneans to Be Forgotten?" 1–8; Efron, "Hasmonean Revolt," 29–30. Aptowitzer (*Parteipolitik der Hasmonaeerzeit*) took this view to an extreme, identifying anti-Hasmonean propaganda in all corners of rabbinic literature.

[47] The chief proponent of this approach was Alon ("Did the Jewish People and Its Sages Cause the Hasmoneans to Be Forgotten?" 1–17). See also Rabin, "Jannaeus and the Pharisees"; Efron,

The voice of the initial approach remained quiescent for several decades, until Daniel R. Schwartz revived the argument regarding Pharisaic opposition to the Hasmonean assumption of monarchy. Schwartz too did not distinguish between Second Temple period and tannaitic evidence on the Pharisees, compiling anti-monarchic statements found in 1 Maccabees and Second Temple literature, numismatic evidence from Hasmonean coins, the demand that the ruler forgo the high priesthood in the rupture legend, and a tannaitic saying, alongside exegesis of *Megillat Ta'anit* that could be interpreted as anti-Hasmonean. Schwartz correctly notes the ideological-Zionist bias underlying the ascription of support of Hasmonean national aims to the Pharisees and the rabbis.[48]

It is thus the case that, in the scholarship, the Second Temple Pharisaic outlook has been inextricably entwined with that of the rabbis of the BT and the redactors of late midrashim, both by the scholars who argue for their favorable attitude toward the Hasmoneans and those who reconstruct hostility toward this dynasty.[49] Only a minority made the necessary distinction between sources and eras.[50] The next section will examine the reworking of the legends of the Hasmoneans in both corpora—Josephus's works and rabbinic literature—and its implications for our assessment of each one's overall attitude toward the Hasmoneans.

"Hasmonean Revolt," 29–32. On the sweeping rejection of Aptowitzer's doctrine in subsequent scholarship, see the bibliographical references in D. R. Schwartz, "Pharisaic Opposition," 44–5. On the miracle of the cruse of oil as a Babylonian anecdote only, which was born out of literary considerations, see Noam, "Cruse of Oil."

[48] D. R. Schwartz, "Pharisaic Opposition," 55–6. For other rationales that tipped the balance toward the viewpoint that the Pharisees and rabbis were not hostile toward the Hasmoneans, see ibid. 44–5.

[49] See the literature cited by D. R. Schwartz, ibid. 44 n. 1. Thus, for example, Alon ("Did the Jewish People and Its Sages Cause the Hasmoneans to Be Forgotten?" 1–2) surveys the arguments presented by the opposing school, namely the lack of a separate mishnaic tractate devoted to Hanukkah, and the Talmud's surprising inquiry about the essence of Hanukkah, and this state of affairs is attributed to "the struggle of Pharisees (and the masses) against the Hasmoneans" some half a millennium earlier. In the continuation, Alon himself extrapolates the Pharisaic stance based on amoraic statements in the YT (4–5) and on evidence from third-century CE Babylonia (17 n. 17). D. R. Schwartz opens the Hebrew version of his article ("Opposition of the Pharisees," 442) with the statement: "Did the Sages of Israel, *the Pharisees*, oppose the Hasmoneans' kingship? Did the *Sages*, or some of them, oppose the constitutional innovation … ?" (translation and emphasis mine, VN). This was corrected in the English version ("Pharisaic Opposition").

[50] This chronological leap, also made by Aptowitzer (see n. 46), was criticized by his opponents. Joseph Heinemann, in response, sought to somewhat defend Aptowitzer's approach by pointing at the earlier materials embedded in rabbinic literature (*Aggadah and Its Development*, 88–9). My argument here is that precisely because of the preservation of early material in rabbinic literature it is necessary to make a distinction between the early traditions embedded there and later stances that characterize tannaim, amoraim, and redactors. See also the methodological comments in Gafni, "Ha-ḥashmonaim be-sifrut ḥazal," 261. For my treatment, which is partially parallel to the current chapter, see Noam, "Did the Rabbis Cause the Hasmoneans to Be Forgotten? A Reconsideration," 295–333.

C. REWORKING OF THE HASMONEAN STORIES

As seen from the chapters of this book, both Josephus and rabbinic literature fundamentally accept the narrative of the Second Temple legends that praise the first two Hasmonean generations, criticize the cruelty of the third-generation figure of Janneus, and assign the blame for the fall of the dynasty to the fourth-generation internecine struggle. On the other hand, each corpus strongly imposes its own specific outlook on these ancient stories. For a comparative summary of the treatment of the Hasmoneans in the two corpora, see Table 7.1 at the end of the discussion of the generations.

The First Generation: Judas Maccabeus

The typical Josephan treatment of 1 Maccabees is exemplified in the opening chapter of this book, in the threefold comparison of Nicanor's defeat in 1 Maccabees, rabbinic literature, and Josephus. There I noted the Josephan deletion of many biblical allusions, the sidestepping of Judas's prayer, and the censoring of the abuse of Nicanor's corpse. Most noteworthy was the accentuation of the figure of Judas Maccabeus and his role in combat. As opposed to his source, 1 Maccabees, Josephus describes Judas alone as being pursued by Nicanor, who seeks his capture; as leading the army to battle on his own; singlehandedly chasing Nicanor's forces; and personally overcoming and killing many of the enemy troops.[51]

The rabbinic treatment of the same tradition is strikingly different. As early as the nineteenth century scholars noted the contrast between rabbinic literature, where the names and deeds of the Maccabees do not appear in any work, stratum, or genre,[52] and Josephus, who devotes nearly 400 sections to them in his account, including Judas Maccabeus, the hero of the revolt and of the first two books of Maccabees.[53] Some view this fact as additional evidence of the deliberate rabbinic obscuring of the Hasmoneans; others argue that: "whoever is conversant with rabbinic literature...may justifiably inquire if every silence necessarily indicates suppression, or ignorance...they [the rabbis] related only to those aspects that they saw as relevant to their tasks and daily round as teachers and moral-religious preachers."[54]

---

[51] See also Feldman, "Josephus' Portrayal of the Hasmoneans," 53–4. On the tendency to aggrandize the figure of Judas, see Cohen, *Josephus in Galilee and Rome*, 44–7; Regev, "Hasmoneans' Self Image," 19–20.

[52] "Judas the eldest" of the "four sons of the Hasmoneans" is mentioned in the post-rabbinic treatise *Baraita de-lamed bet middot* appended to the beginning of Rabbi Eliezer's Mishnah (*Mishnah of Rabbi Eliezer: Parashah 5* [Enelow ed.], 103), which provides further evidence of its provenance in the geonic period. See Zucker, "Le-fitron," 1–39.

[53] See already Derenbourg, *Essai*, 3. For more-contemporary literature, see e.g. Stemberger, "The Maccabees in Rabbinic Tradition," 201–2; Gafni, "Ha-ḥashmonaim be-sifrut ḥazal," 262, 269; Ilan, "Names of the Hasmoneans," 240, 241 n. 27.

[54] Gafni, "Ha-ḥashmonaim be-sifrut ḥazal," 265. See also Yerushalmi, *Zakhor*, 24–6.

The story of Judas's most brilliant victory, treated in Chapter 1 of this volume, can perhaps make a decisive contribution to this debate. As noted there, Nicanor's defeat was commemorated by a holiday that was accepted in the rabbinic world and whose observance continued into the geonic era.[55] There we saw that the early sources, the books of Maccabees and even more so the Josephan reworking of 1 Maccabees, underscore Judas's bravery and focal role in leading the army to victory and his encouraging words or prayers. A close version of the ancient story was also preserved in rabbinic literature; the trends evidenced there, however, are the opposite of the historian's account. If Josephus erased the biblical allusions, the rabbis highlighted them. If Josephus censored the description of the abuse of Nicanor's corpse, in rabbinic sources the story climaxes with the "measure for measure" punishment of his corpse. Conspicuously, as opposed to the glorification of Judas in the Josephan paraphrase, Judas is blatantly absent from the four rabbinic sources—the two Scholia and the two Talmuds—that recount this episode.

Instead, the victory is ascribed to an amorphous entity: "the Hasmonean dynasty." This is even more telling when contrasted with the dominance of the foreign general Nicanor, who is mentioned by name in the rabbinic versions as well, and whose invective and personal fate form the heart of this episode. The deliberate nature of the erasure of Judas's name emerges most strongly in the rabbinic version recognized as closest to the lost Hebrew original of 1 Maccabees—the YT—and in Scholion O. These works attribute the victory over the enemy to an enigmatic figure: אחד מבית חשמונאי/אחד משלבית חשמונאי ("a member of the Hasmonean dynasty"), a unique phrase not found elsewhere in rabbinic literature. This unusual expression evidently reflects the deliberate erasure of the name that appeared in the ancient text cited in these works, undoubtedly that of Judas Maccabeus. The reworking of this ancient tradition thus illustrates a wider phenomenon in rabbinic literature—the absence of references to the Maccabean generation—and indicates that it is not coincidental. Underscoring this lack of references is the widespread use of Hasmonean names in the Second Temple period, for, as Tal Ilan has shown, every third man-in-the-street was given one of six names: that of Mattathias or of his five sons. Ilan concluded: "The entire population identified with the Hasmonean rebels...the first Hasmoneans became a myth. The successors of the Hasmoneans, both physical and spiritual, but also their opponents, regarded the first Hasmoneans as a source of inspiration...in the Second Temple period the people and their sages certainly did not cause the Hasmoneans to be forgotten."[56]

---

[55] See Noam, *Megillat Ta'anit*, 298–302. The starting-point for the rabbinic sources that recount the episode of Nicanor's defeat is the holiday set for 13 Adar, which was treated in Chap. 1 of this volume.

[56] See Ilan, "Names of the Hasmoneans." The citation is from p. 240 (translated by author).

However, the callous erasure of the names of historical figures from rabbinic literature shows this conclusion to be invalid with regard to the later sages.

On the other hand, as often noted, the rabbis frequently praise the Hasmonean dynasty and its victory over the Greeks, and make reference to the holiday of Hanukkah in various contexts: candle-lighting, the prohibition against fasting, the pentateuchal readings, and the liturgy. It thus appears that the rabbis attributed great importance to the Maccabean victory and to the institutionalization of its memory through religious means, but also made certain to ascribe the victory to a collective, not an individual. I thus return to the oft-asked question: did the sages cause the Hasmoneans to be forgotten? Certainly not, if we speak of the Hasmonean dynasty as a whole; but, with respect to the Maccabees themselves—the individual figures from the first generation—the rabbis indeed sought to erase their memory, even going so far as to deliberately omit Judas's name from the ancient source on which they relied. For the moment, I content myself with simply mentioning this phenomenon. I will return to the possible reasons for it later in the discussion.

The Second Generation: John Hyrcanus

Like other testimony from Second Temple times, the story of the heavenly voice that John Hyrcanus heard in the temple (Chapter 2) attributes to this ruler and high priest the reception of a semi-prophetic message in the depths of the temple. Taking its rendering into Greek and the penning of connective sentences to the surrounding historical narrative into account, we can nevertheless say that this tradition was not reworked by Josephus but was rather cited in its original form. Josephus's willingness to adopt this Jewish legend unchanged is consistent with the very positive portrait he painted of Hyrcanus, as noted above.

This Josephan attitude vis-à-vis John Hyrcanus comes to the fore even more strongly when he cites a source that takes an opposite stance. To recall, in Josephus the episode of the rupture with the Pharisees is associated with John Hyrcanus. As we saw in Chapter 3, this is a Pharisaic tradition that seeks to speak positively of the Pharisees who are being libelously persecuted, and criticizes—albeit temperately—the ruler who was misled by evil advice. Josephus, however, implants this tradition in a narrative that praises John and attributes the blame to the Pharisees, deemed contentious by nature.[57]

---

[57] Mason, *Josephus on the Pharisees*, 215–30. Tuval (*Jerusalem Priest to Roman Jew*, 202) notes that the comment that precedes the rupture tradition is a Josephan attempt to soften the episode by praising John Hyrcanus. Later I will discuss the scholarly debate between the prevailing opinion that ascribes section 288, which praises Hyrcanus and denigrates the Pharisees, to Nicolaus, and Mason's opinion that ascribes its authorship to Josephus.

Although also largely positive, the rabbinic attitude toward John Hyrcanus manifests a quite different approach. The rabbis indeed incorporated the story of John and the heavenly voice into their literature but, on the other hand, quickly created mirror images of prophetic powers exercised by *rabbis* in the attics where they gathered. Thus, the ancient traditions of a "word" heard by temple priests appear in a string of stories on heavenly voices heard by rabbis. The message concerning the rabbis reflects an intriguing phenomenon: although individual rabbis merited the gift of prophecy, their generation was unworthy of this gift. Namely, the recounters of these stories implanted an opposite message into these "prophecies," essentially making them reveal the end of the age of prophecy. Thus, the context into which the story of John Hyrcanus was implanted undermines the message of the story itself. If the ancient story portrays a leader and high priest as the successor to the biblical prophets, the rabbinic context announces the shifting of the scepter from the priest to the rabbis, from prophecy to wisdom and, last but not least, transforms John into a rabbi among rabbis.

This finding is in marked harmony with the treatment of John Hyrcanus elsewhere in rabbinic literature.[58] Here too, as was the case for Nicanor, the rabbinic orientation is the reverse of the Josephan one. Whereas Josephus attempts to construct a link between the legend and the historical figure of John, the rabbis excise John's military and political roles, placing him in a religious context alone, as "Yoḥanan the high priest." The same phenomenon is also apparent in the shift between *Megillat Ta'anit*, a Second Temple-period document that preceded, and was adopted by, rabbinic literature, and the Scholion, which originated in the rabbinic world. *Megillat Ta'anit* evidently lists three of John's victories, but the later Scholion connects none of these commemorative days to John.[59] Rabbinic literature in general is aware of his activity as a high priest, but not as a military and political leader. In the Mishnah, John serves as an example of an honored man (*m. Yad.* 4:6), an illustrious high priest (*m. Parah* 3:5), and a sage who sets halakhic regulations (*m. Ma'as. Sh.* 5:15 = *m. Sotah* 9:10). Indeed, a tradition embedded in the Scholion and also cited in the BT mentions the practice of citing the number of years to John's reign in the date formulas on official documents: "In the year So-and-so of Yoḥanan, High Priest to the Most High God," and its annulment because of halakhic considerations.[60] Nonetheless, it seems that there is historical evidence for the use of this date formula, and that it was

---

[58] For surveys of references to this figure, see e.g. Alon, "Attitude of the Pharisees," 26 n. 22; Efron, "Hasmonean Revolt," 30–1; Gafni, "Ha-ḥashmonaim be-sifrut ḥazal," 270–1; and see Chap. 2.

[59] The exile of "the people of Beth Shean and the Valley," the conquest of the city of Samaria, and "the day of Mount Gerizim." See Noam, *Megillat Ta'anit*, 44–6, 196, 243–9, 262–5. It appears that the origins of the ancient exegesis of Deut 33:11 found in *Targum Pseudo-Jonathan*, which ascribes Moses's blessing of Levi to Yoḥanan the high priest, portraying him as battling those who hate him, also lie in the Second Temple period, as early scholars suggested.

[60] Scholion P on *Meg. Ta'an.*, 3 Tishri; *b. Rosh Hash.* 18b. See Noam, *Megillat Ta'anit*, 94, 235–8.

the rabbis who diverted this evidence from the political to the halakhic realm.[61] Later sources contain sporadic reservations regarding John Hyrcanus's personality and deeds.[62]

In summation, whereas Second Temple sources—Josephus, the Dead Sea Scrolls, *Megillat Ta'anit*, and even a legend embedded in the Tosefta—convey an image of John Hyrcanus as a general, a prophet, and a high priest,[63] rabbinic literature appropriates him for its world.[64] It is silent regarding his secular leadership, conquests, and military accomplishments, drawing instead a portrait of an admired high priest, and mainly of an early sage who issues regulations, incorporating his figure into a series of stories of early rabbis whose powers equaled his.

The Third Generation: Janneus

The legends of the third Hasmonean generation invite an encounter with the complex figure of Janneus. The original tales of Janneus do not belong to the genre I have defined as temple legends, but rather to Pharisaic apologetics. As we have seen, these stories describe the conflict between the Hasmonean king and the Pharisees and even his cruelty toward them. Yet they treat him with moderation, and also mention his merits. According to the rabbinic version of the story of the rupture with the Pharisees, of which Janneus is the protagonist (Chapter 3), the Hasmonean ruler enjoyed a good relationship with, and favored, the Pharisees. The shift came with the evil advice tendered by an unreliable individual and third-party incitement that wrongly attributed a malicious libel of the king to the Pharisees. According to the story of Janneus's instructions to his wife (Chapter 5), the king instructed her not to fear the Pharisees

---

[61] See *Ant.* 16.163. For additional external attestation to this formula, see D. R. Schwartz, "Pharisaic Opposition," 47–8. Schwartz suggests that the halakhic rationale for the commemoration of the erasure of John's name from the deeds is a smokescreen for Pharisaic political opposition to this figure. However, we must also consider the fact that this opposition is not explicit in the source. See also Gafni, "Ha-ḥashmonaim be-sifrut ḥazal," 270.

[62] In the YT some of his regulations received a negative interpretation (*y. Ma'as. Sh.* 5:9, 56d; *y. Sotah* 9:11, 24a), but this was not the case in the BT (*b. Sotah* 47b–48a). Elsewhere in the BT a baraita recounts that "Yoḥanan the High Priest officiated as high priest for eighty years and in the end he became a Sadducee" (*b. Ber.* 29a). According to Alon ("Attitude of the Pharisees," 26 n. 22) this is a late post-tannaitic baraita. On the question of the identities of Janneus and John in this sugya, see Chap. 3. Another tradition in the BT also attributes to John an eighty-year tenure as high priest (*b. Yoma* 9a), albeit its tone is positive. For further discussion of this tradition, see Ben Shahar, "Biblical and Post-biblical History," 238.

[63] See the survey in Chap. 2.

[64] This phenomenon is termed "rabbinization" in the scholarship. On rabbinization of the biblical past, see I. Heinemann, *Darkhei ha-aggadah*, 35–9, and the discussion by Gafni, "Rabbinic Historiography," 295–312. On rabbinization of the post-biblical period, see Cohen, "Parallel Historical Tradition," 11–12; Kalmin, *Jewish Babylonia*, 61–85; D. R. Schwartz, "Remembering the Second Temple Period."

(talmudic version), or to effect a reconciliation with them (Josephus). Similar to the rupture tradition, the talmudic version of Janneus's instructions also indicates that it is not the "true" Pharisees who are Janneus's enemies but rather "pretenders." Here too the legend has a two-pronged message: to clear the king of unequivocal hatred of the Pharisees and the Pharisees of the charge of rebellion against the king.

In Chapter 4 we saw how, in *Antiquities*, Josephus first separated the strands of another Jewish tradition on Janneus and then interwove them into a political-military sequence that recounts the story of a rebellion quashed by Janneus, which has a parallel in *War*.[65] This tradition told the tale of the pelting of Janneus with citrons and the wooden barrier he erected in the temple in its wake, and a second tradition related the libel that ascribed his lineage to a captive and thereby sought to disqualify him for the priesthood. Apart from the literary strategies employed by Josephus in interpolating this material, it displays no signs of topical intervention or any alteration of its political ramifications. Evidently, the thrust of the story, which recounted popular hostility toward Janneus and its detrimental influence on the temple, was consistent with Josephus's own above-mentioned inclination to accentuate the internal strife generated by Janneus's brutality.

However, Josephus's greater clemency toward Janneus in *Antiquities*, as described by various scholars, is apparent in his treatment of the story of Janneus's instructions to his wife. This apologetic Pharisaic propaganda assigns responsibility for the dispute to the king, whose unwarranted persecution of the Pharisees caused the entire nation to hate him, as he admits on his deathbed. Yet, at the end of his life the king expresses regret for his actions and instructs his wife to attempt a reconciliation, which he predicts that the Pharisees will graciously accept. As noted above, Josephus interpolated a sentence that condemns the Pharisees—and by implication defends Janneus—using language very similar to that found in the preface to the rupture episode.[66]

As opposed to the minor Josephan interventions in the Janneus traditions that censure the Pharisees, in the rabbinic corpus we find a conspicuous gap between the worldview of the rabbis and that of the Second Temple legends embedded in their literature. As compared to the story's conciliatory message, rabbinic literature paints a much harsher picture. The rabbis magnify Janneus's wickedness, both in the rupture legend itself and elsewhere. If, according to the Josephan version, the ruler (Hyrcanus, according to Josephus) is content with

---

[65] Josephus's treatment of Aristobulus I will not be discussed here; Josephus's description of his brief reign does not enable identification of definitively Jewish sources with rabbinic parallels. On the negative Josephan portrayal of this king (*War* 1.70–87; *Ant.* 13.301–19), and the more positive evaluation that emerges from Josephus's citation of Strabo based on Timagenes (*Ant.* 13.318–19), see Tuval, *Jerusalem Priest to Roman Jew*, 203–4.

[66] On the question of whether this sentence was penned by Josephus, or by Nicolaus and inserted here by Josephus, see below.

rescinding the laws of the Pharisees, in the talmudic version he massacres "all the sages of Israel," and "the world was desolate until Simeon son of Shataḥ came and restored the Torah to its pristine [glory]." It appears likely that this ending, which inserts the name of a known scholar into the political story, and uses mishnaic language[67] as opposed to the earlier linguistic stratum of most of the passage, belongs to a rabbinic reworking intended to underscore the king's cruelty. In this instance as well, the tendentious treatment of one Second Temple legend illustrates the rabbinic propensity, especially in the BT, to attribute negative traditions to Janneus, even some originally ascribed to other figures, and to highlight his cruelty, as demonstrated in Chapter 4.[68]

A similar gap is apparent between the Second Temple-period work *Megillat Ta'anit* and its commentary, the Scholion, which represents the rabbinic world. Among its commemorative dates, the text of *Megillat Ta'anit* mentions the conquest of "Sher Tower" (Strato's tower, later Caesarea),[69] which was annexed to the Hasmonean kingdom by Janneus.[70] Thus, the territorial expansion of the kingdom at Janneus's hands is seen as praiseworthy and merits a commemorative day. The Scholion, on the other hand, knows nothing of this individual's involvement, and vaguely attributes the conquest of the tower to "Hasmonean hands" (יד חשמונאי; Scholion O) or to some unspecified collective (כבשוהו; Scholion P). Moreover, Janneus receives unfavorable mention in the Scholion on several occasions: he is the ally of the Sadducees in the Sanhedrin (Scholion O, 28 Tevet),[71] a persecutor of the righteous who merited a miraculous rescue in Lebanon (Scholion O, 17 Adar),[72] and evilly plots to kill the sages. This plot, attributed by Josephus to Herod, underpins the Scholion's statement regarding the setting of a holiday to commemorate Janneus's death. In comparing Janneus to Herod, it judges him the worse of the two (Scholia O and P, 2 Shevat).[73] This distinction between *Megillat Ta'anit* and the Scholion is typical of the more negative image of Janneus in the rabbinic world as compared to his portrayal in Second Temple Pharisaic literature.

To sum up this survey, the Pharisaic stories of Janneus evidence a moderate approach, speak favorably of the Pharisees and of Janneus, and attribute the Pharisaic–Hasmonean rupture to third-party intrigue. Josephus somewhat shifts this balance: he defames the Pharisees in two stories thereby defending their Hasmonean antagonist. For their part, the BT and the Scholion completely

---

[67] See Chap. 3, n. 171.

[68] *B. Sotah* 47a (=*b. Sanh.* 107b. On this episode, into which the figure of Jesus is anachronistically interpolated, see Schäfer, *Jesus in the Talmud*, 34–40. For the parallel in the YT, which does not mention Janneus, see Efron, "Simeon Ben Shataḥ and Jannaeus," 154–61); *b. Sanh.* 19a. The traditions in the Scholia for 2 Shevat and in Scholion O for 17 Adar also represent this topos. On the legends concerning Janneus and Simeon ben Shataḥ, and other legends linked to Janneus, see Chap. 4.

[69] Noam, *Megillat Ta'anit*, 14 Sivan, pp. 44, 68, 193–5.   [70] *Ant.* 13.324, 335.

[71] Noam, *Megillat Ta'anit*, 107, 277–9.   [72] Ibid. 122, 306–8.

[73] Ibid. 109–10, 280–2.

turn their backs on this complexity. They portray the sages/Pharisees as the persecuted, righteous teachers of the Torah, and situate Janneus as their antithesis and enemy. If the father, John Hyrcanus, was transformed into the archetypical figure of an early sage among the rabbis' spiritual ancestors, the son, Janneus, was portrayed as their ruthless foe.

The Fourth Generation: Hyrcanus II and Aristobulus II

In the story of the siege and the sacrificial animals (Chapter 6), we encountered Second Temple Jewish theodicy, which ascribed the loss of political independence to the warring brothers. This probably Pharisaic historiosophical explanation for the downfall of the Hasmoneans is in fact polemical. It represents one side of a political debate, whose opposite stance we are fortunate enough to be able to reconstruct. A small fragment from Qumran Cave 4 (4Q471a) accuses the sect's opponents of violating the divine covenant. The scroll cites these adversaries as saying: "We shall fight His battles, because He redeemed us," and describes them as becoming "mighty for battle" and arrogant. The author, however, prophesies that they "will be brought low" because God despises them. The editors, Esther Eshel and Menahem Kister, plausibly conjecture that the foes in question are the Hasmoneans and their supporters, "with the redemption mentioned by the opponents in line 3 referring to the establishment of the Hasmonaean state and the political successes of the first Hasmonaeans. Lines 4–6 describe the subsequent downfall of these circles (under Alexander Jannaeus or during the Pompeian conquest)."[74] Indeed, the joyous reaction of the sect to the Hasmonean defeat is well documented in the pesharim as well.[75] The *Yaḥad* interpreted the Roman occupation as proof of the sinfulness of the Hasmonean state from its very inception, as they had argued all along. With the collapse of the Hasmonean state, the sect could claim that, in inflicting punishment on the Hasmonean state, which it deemed guilty for its fundamental religious choices, the Romans were acting as the divine rod of wrath. The Pharisees, on the other hand, believed that the Hasmoneans' previous victories represented divine redemption, and that their eventual downfall was due only to "internal strife" which caused the last generation to lose "their royal power" (*Ant.* 14. 490–1). Both Josephus and the rabbis appear to have adopted this basic narrative. As noted above, Josephus twice mentions the theological-historical interpretation that attributed the destruction of the Hasmonean dynasty to the fratricidal war between Hyrcanus II and Aristobulus II, and its spirit is preserved in the Josephan account of the tradition of the murder of Onias. Nonetheless, certain features of the national-particularistic message and the fundamental enmity toward Greco-Roman

---

[74] Eshel and Kister, "471a. 4QPolemical Text," 446–9, citation from 447.
[75] 4QpNah 3–4 I, 9–II, 4; 1QpHab IV, 8–9.

culture displayed in the legend of the siege were deliberately obscured by Josephus,[76] who replaced them with an ordinary universal message condemning the breaching of agreements in general.

In contradistinction to Josephan censorship, the rabbinic version of the siege tradition preserves the original message regarding the merits of Jewish unity and underscores the devastating results of its breach. There are two facets to the rabbinic reworking of this tradition. One is the garbing of the episode in a halakhic frame. Using the phrase באותה שעה/על אותה שעה ("at that time"; "concerning this time"), the BT creates links in the body of the story to three halakhic issues mentioned in three separate mishnayot. It identifies the consequences of our episode with what is related regarding the *omer* offering in *m. Menahot*, and portrays the two prohibitions mentioned in *m. Sotah* and *m. Baba Qamma*—on teaching Greek and rearing pigs—as derivative lessons. The YT versions of the story also connect two mishnayot to the episode: the delayed offering of the tamid sacrifice is linked there to *m. 'Eduyot*, and its cancellation just prior to the destruction of the temple as recounted in *m. Ta'anit* is also presented as a consequence of this event. Similar to the "dressing up" of the protagonist as a sage in the case of John Hyrcanus, here too the legend assumes a halakhic guise.

A second facet of the rabbinic reworking of this story inheres in another, already noted phenomenon: the migration of the tradition to distant historical contexts. This phenomenon is characteristic of orally transmitted collective memory, as Funkenstein notes in his analysis of Halbwachs:

> Collective memory, by contrast, is completely insensitive to the differences between periods and "qualities of time"; its time is monochromatic; its interests are thoroughly topocentric. People, events, and historic institutions of the past serve as prototypes for the collective memory; none of them are recognized by their uniqueness.[77]

Perhaps the incongruent, unique nature of its original historical context—the internecine Hasmonean war—motivated its passage to a more familiar historical backdrop, that of the Hasmonean victory or the destruction of the temple, and it was these secondary versions that were preserved in the YT.

Additional Types of Josephan Reworking of Ancient Legends

Apart from changes to content, Josephus typically imposes other types of reworking on early Jewish stories, just as he does on his historiographical sources. An example is his censoring of problematic statements regarding non-Jews. In two instances apologetic considerations can be identified as fueling the

---

[76] See Tuval, *Jerusalem Priest to Roman Jew*, 207–8 and the survey of the literature in n. 349 there.

[77] Funkenstein, *Perceptions of Jewish History*, 8. See Halbwachs, *Collective Memory*.

Table 7.1. Comparison of the Hasmonean Generations in the Josephan and Rabbinic Corpora

Generation and main figure	Second Temple legends	Josephus	Rabbinic literature
1. Judas Maccabeus	"Temple legend" that extols the victory of the first-generation Hasmoneans.	Glorifies this first-generation figure, censors elements potentially offensive to his non-Jewish readership.	Cherishes the memory of the glorious victory but erases any specific mention of the figures involved.
2. John Hyrcanus	Chronicles listing victories; "temple legend" praising the second-generation Hasmonean, John Hyrcanus.	Cited unchanged, linked to John's military-political exploits.	John is transformed into a sage and his military-political activity is played down. Prophecy is also attributed to the rabbis; at the same time, they announce that the era of prophecy has ended.
2–3. John Hyrcanus/ Janneus	Pharisaic story on the rupture with John/Janneus. The Pharisees are not to blame; the ruler was incited.	Adds an introductory remark praising the ruler and denigrating the Pharisees.	Heightened denigration of Janneus; introduction of the sages to the story.
3. Janneus	Pharisaic story on Janneus's deathbed instructions. The Pharisees are not guilty, they are generous, and it was Janneus who persecuted them. But he also sought reconciliation at the end.	Adds a remark denigrating the Pharisees.	Another version of the legend, including a biblical allusion.
4. Hyrcanus II and Aristobulus II	Pharisaic story on the loss of the commonwealth because of lack of unity.	Censors particularistic elements in favor of a universalistic lesson.	Addition of a halakhic message to the moral one; the phenomenon of the migration of traditions.

Josephan reworking of his source; of these, the definitive case is the Josephan omission of the abuse of the body of the Seleucid military leader Nicanor, which is preserved in all the rabbinic versions (Chapter 1). The second instance is more conjectural. In my reconstruction of the underlying story of the fratricidal Hasmonean war (Chapter 6), I suggested that the figure of the Greek-speaking old man, who appears solely in the BT, is integral to the story. I argued that Josephus deliberately omitted a dominant facet of the original story: the dangers posed by the foreign culture.

Another key phenomenon that has received insufficient attention in the scholarship is Josephus's propensity to strip the stories of their original biblical garb, turning them into dry, matter-of-fact accounts. Thus, for example, the rich biblical allusions of the original Nicanor tradition, the allusions to Korah and to the book of Esther in the story of the rupture with the Pharisees, and the reference to Zimri and Phinehas in the story of Janneus's instructions to his wife, are all missing from the Josephan account.[78] This phenomenon, a natural outcome of the transition from folktale to historical narrative, recalls Pierre Nora's observation: "Memory situates remembrance in a sacred context. History ferrets it out; it turns whatever it touches into prose."[79]

Josephus also intervenes by inserting explanatory comments into his sources. This type of treatment is prominent in the story of the rupture with the Pharisees (Chapter 3), into which Josephus introduces descriptions of the attributes of the Pharisees and the Sadducees. The same is true of the well-known passage appended to the story regarding the laws of the Pharisees and the attitude of the Sadducees toward the unwritten law (13.297–8).[80]

In other instances we can discern editorial intervention, such as the distribution of sections of one source among several passages, or the combination of different traditions. In the story of the pelting with citrons (*Ant.* 13.372–4; Chapter 4) I noted the double interpolation of two different traditions: one that recounts the episode of the citrons, and a second that recounts the questioning of Janneus's lineage. The discussion there also showed that the account of the erection of a wooden barrier in the temple by Janneus originally belonged to

[78] Feldman ("Josephus' Portrayal of the Hasmoneans," 58 and n. 18) ascribes a political motive to Josephus's deliberate omission of allusions to King David. I think, however, that this is a much broader phenomenon which is not restricted to the biblical David cycle but applies to biblical allusions in general.

[79] Nora, *Realms of Memory*, 1:3 (see the Introduction, sections B, G). Another feature of this Josephan shift is the tendency to interpret events rationally and to avoid theocentric explanations involving heavenly miracles. This is apparent not only in the Josephan transmission of the contents of the books of the Maccabees or the Letter of Aristeas, as others have shown, but also for the oral Jewish traditions that are our subject here. Thus, for example, Josephus appends two apologetic explanations to the story of the miracle of the rain in Herod's day: first of all, this story is not his but rather an ancestral tradition; second, he notes: "And this story, which our fathers have handed down to us is not at all incredible if, that is, one considers the other manifestations of power given by God" (*Ant.* 15.425).

[80] See Mason, *Josephus on the Pharisees*, 228, 230–40; and Chap. 4.

the first Jewish tradition. Josephus, however, detached it from its source, placing it after the second episode and also after a fact derived from Nicolaus: the killing of some 6,000 Jews. In the story of the fratricidal Hasmonean conflict (Chapter 6) I examined how Josephus inserted two different Jewish stories into the narrative—one on the siege and the sacrificial animals; the other, on the murder of Onias—and his clumsy attempt to link the two.

Josephus and the Pharisees

The journey we have undertaken in this volume may also contribute to the scholarly discussion of questions outside its direct purview. Identification of the Pharisaic nature of most of the stories that served Josephus and the rabbis impacts some of the fundamental questions that have engaged the scholarship for nearly two centuries. With respect to the rabbis, recent decades have called into question the longstanding viewpoint that the rabbis were the direct successors of the Pharisees,[81] and the presence of Pharisaic undertones in their literature contributes to the discussion. With respect to Josephus, the fact that he culled Jewish traditions from the Pharisaic milieu, notwithstanding the existence of a broad Jewish literature that emerged in non-Pharisaic circles and was preserved at Qumran and in apocryphal works, should carry weight in the debate over his identity.

The questions of Josephus's precise attitude toward the Pharisees, and whether or not he was affiliated with them, have long been the subject of scholarly debate.[82] On the one hand Josephus ostensibly attests that, after studying the three main sects, he decided to join the Pharisees (*Life* 12).[83] On the other, there is his asymmetrical description of the Pharisees, mainly in *Antiquities*, but also in *War* to a more limited extent. Alongside praise for Pharisaic expertise

---

[81] The questions of the identity of the Pharisees and the extent to which there was continuity between them and the rabbis have been comprehensively treated. Representative studies include Neusner, *From Politics to Piety*; Rivkin, "Defining the Pharisees"; Cohen, "Significance of Yavneh," 36–42; Flusser, "4QMMT," 97–103; Schäfer, "Vorrabbinische Pharisäismus," 125–75. For a viewpoint that detaches the Pharisees of the Second Temple period from the rabbinic establishment that flourished afterwards, see especially Morton Smith, "Palestinian Judaism"; Cohen, "Significance of Yavneh." For a more extreme view, which dates the beginning of rabbinic culture centuries after the destruction of the temple, see S. Schwartz, *Imperialism and Jewish Society*. For an up-to-date survey and bibliographical references, see Lapin, *Rabbis as Romans*, 46–9.

[82] For a detailed survey of the scholarship, see Mason, *Josephus on the Pharisees*, 18–39, 325–41; Regev, *Sadducees*, 23–4, 350–1; D. R. Schwartz, "Josephus on the Pharisees as Diaspora Jews," 137–8 nn. 1–6; Klawans, *Josephus and the Theologies of Ancient Judaism*. In what follows I will only mention several scholars who are definitive representatives of specific approaches.

[83] This is the explanation that has currently gained acceptance in the scholarship; however, Mason suggests a different reading, according to which Josephus does not attest in this text to voluntary adherence to the Pharisaic doctrines, but rather to public activity that forced him to obey the Pharisees, even without identifying with them. See Mason, "Was Josephus a Pharisee?" 12–30; idem, *Josephus on the Pharisees*, 357–71.

in ancestral tradition and their precise explication of pentateuchal law,[84] and attestation to their great influence on the masses,[85] Josephus also often attributes to them guile, quarrel-mongering, cruelty, and the pursuit of power.[86] It has also been noted that, as compared to the frequent, more detailed references found in *Antiquities* that cite Pharisaic power, influence, and involvement in many episodes, the descriptions of the Pharisees in *War* are few and brief, and do not parallel *Antiquities*.

How is this complexity to be interpreted? Many scholars indeed assume that Josephus was a Pharisee for most of his life.[87] Others suggest that only at a later stage, after the Pharisees enjoyed enhanced power in the post-destruction era, did Josephus seek to portray himself as a Pharisee for purposes of enhanced political advantage. They attribute the differences between *War* and *Antiquities* to the mature Josephus's new desire to conciliate the Pharisees by assigning to them political power—which in truth they did not possess—and to trigger a more favorable attitude toward them on the part of the Roman leadership.[88] Daniel R. Schwartz argues the opposite. In his opinion, the true portrait of the Pharisees as public leaders, and as involved up to the hilt in political processes, is found in *Antiquities*, and was penned by Josephus himself, whereas the hostile statements derive from Nicolaus. In *War*, which was written shortly after the First Jewish Revolt, Josephus sought to conceal Pharisaic political involvement for fear of the Romans.[89]

Schwartz grounds his argument in a comparison of *War* 1.67 and *Antiquities* 13.288, the section that precedes the story of the rupture with the Pharisees. Whereas *War* describes sedition (στάσις) on the part of his countrymen (ἐπι χωρίων) against John Hyrcanus, in *Antiquities* the grievance, without any mention of sedition, is ascribed to the Pharisees. According to Schwartz's reconstruction, in composing his later work Josephus copied *Antiquities* 13.288

[84] See *Life* 191; *War* 1.110, 2.162; *Ant.* 13.289, 408; 17.41; 18.12, 15.

[85] See *War* 1.110–14; *Ant.* 13.288, 296, 298, 401–2, 406; 17.41; 18.15, 17; *Life* 26.

[86] See *War* 1.110–14; *Ant.* 13.288, 401–2, 409–10, 423; 17.41; 18.17.

[87] See e.g. Feldman, "Torah and Greek Culture," 47–87; Rajak, *Josephus*, 33–4, 224–5.

[88] For the hypothesis regarding Josephus's late joining of Pharisaic circles and deliberate pro-Pharisaic propaganda, see Morton Smith, "Palestinian Judaism," 74–8; Neusner, "Josephus' Pharisees." For a survey of the many scholars who have adopted this viewpoint to varying extents, see D. R. Schwartz, "Josephus and Nicolaus," 164 n. 23; Mason, *Josephus on the Pharisees*, 35 n. 101. Recently, Klawans (*Josephus and the Theologies of Ancient Judaism*, 110–11, 134, 137–9, 168–70, 211–12) reiterated the viewpoint that Josephus was "truly" Pharisaic.

[89] D. R. Schwartz, "Josephus and Nicolaus," 169. In a subsequent article, Schwartz ("Josephus on the Pharisees as Diaspora Jews") suggests that the more positive portrait of the Pharisees that he identifies in *Antiquities* (discounting the negative remarks that he thinks originated with Nicolaus) is not grounded in identification with the Pharisees themselves, but with religious principles adopted by Josephus during his long years of exile, such as an identity grounded in study and religious law, rather than territory and temple, values identified with the Pharisaic outlook. In Tuval, *Jerusalem Priest to Roman Jew*, this was expanded to a comprehensive thesis that traces the development of Josephus's religious personality between the writing of *War* and *Antiquities*.

directly from Nicolaus, whereas *War* 1.67 is an abridgment of the same section of Nicolaus, in which Josephus deliberately censored Pharisaic involvement.[90]

These two main scholarly camps assume that Josephus the Pharisee, or Josephus who wished to portray himself as a Pharisee, sought to enhance the Pharisaic image and influence and to place this circle in a positive light, at least in his later works, *Antiquities* and *Life*. Accordingly, they stress the positive aspects of the Josephan description of the Pharisees in *Antiquities*: their political power and popularity, alongside their expertise in the Torah and ancestral tradition. The negative features attributed to them in those very same contexts—imperiousness, quarrel-mongering, envy, sedition—are downplayed by these scholars, or attributed to Josephus's sources, mainly Nicolaus.[91]

A cornerstone of the theory that attributes to Josephus deliberate aggrandizement of the Pharisees comes from the episode of Janneus's deathbed instructions to his wife (*Ant.* 13.400-4.; see Chapter 5). As we have seen, in this story, which is not found in the parallel in *War*, Janneus announces to Alexandra that she will be unable to rule without Pharisaic support, and that his abuse of the Pharisees endangered his rule (401-3). Morton Smith, and those who follow in his wake, interprets this story as deliberate propaganda by the mature Josephus, which aimed to convey to his Roman readers the notion that amity with the Pharisees was a precondition for establishing stable rule in the land of Israel.[92]

Steve Mason offers a counter-argument, maintaining that the descriptions of the Pharisees in *Antiquities* cannot be regarded as favorable propaganda. The opposite is the case. Pharisaic political power is portrayed there as the provocative power to do harm, and receives a reserved, hostile description. Mason ascribes these hostile statements to Josephus himself; accordingly, Josephus was neither a Pharisee nor a lover of the Pharisees, but a descendant and admirer of the Hasmonean dynasty, who attributed the dynasty's degeneration to the Pharisees.[93] Mason views the episode of the deathbed instructions not as pro-Pharisaic propaganda, but rather as an unsympathetic description of the Pharisees that paints them as cruel, elusive, power-hungry opportunists, penned

---

[90] Tuval, *Jerusalem Priest to Roman Jew*, 159, 169. Efron ("Simeon Ben Shatah and Jannaeus," 161–5) attributes section 288, which is hostile toward the Pharisees, to Nicolaus.

[91] For the scholarly literature on Nicolaus as a source for Josephus, see D. R. Schwartz, "Josephus and Nicolaus," 157 n. 1, and the Introduction, section D. One of the fathers of the approach that attributes hostile remarks to Nicolaus, mainly regarding the Hasmoneans but also the Pharisees on occasion, was Hölscher ("Josephus"). In more recent research, Daniel R. Schwartz is the definitive representative of this approach.

[92] Morton Smith, "Palestinian Judaism," 76; Neusner, "Josephus' Pharisees," 277–8, 286–8.

[93] Mason, *Josephus on the Pharisees*, passim. For an outstanding example, see p. 259. Tuval (*Jerusalem Priest to Roman Jew*) follows in his wake in assuming that Josephus was not a Pharisee and that the descriptions of the Pharisees in *Antiquities* were not fueled by manipulative political opportunism. See e.g. *Jerusalem Priest to Roman Jew*, 26 n. 95, 99 n. 42, 132–3, 142, and esp. 268–9, 284. Nonetheless, it appears that Tuval does not accept Mason's evaluation of the descriptions of the Pharisees in *Antiquities* as fundamentally negative, and points rather at positive trends, ascribing them to changes in Josephus's outlook.

by none other than Josephus.[94] Daniel Schwartz takes a similar stance regarding this source's hostility toward the Pharisees, but thinks that the story, which contains locutions very similar to the anti-Pharisaic section that precedes the story of the rupture with the Pharisees (*Ant.* 13.288), manifests Nicolaus's, not Josephus's, hatred of the Pharisees.[95]

Indeed, this section, which introduces the rupture tradition, is a bone of contention between the scholarly camps. As we saw in Chapter 3, the hostility displayed there toward the Pharisees, and its ascription to them of a tendency to sedition against kings and high priests, is in direct contradiction to the Jewish tradition that follows. Whereas most scholars assign this passage to Nicolaus, Mason strongly asserts that it is Josephan. Both of the passages at the heart of the scholarly debate regarding the image of the Pharisees in Josephus—the stories of the rupture and of the deathbed instructions—have been treated at length in this volume. In my opinion, both originated in external, apologetic Pharisaic traditions and were quoted and secondarily interpolated by Josephus into his narrative.

It is now possible to consider the implications of the Josephan use and treatment of these traditions for determining Josephus's attitude toward the Pharisees. I first note that the very fact that two pieces of openly pro-Pharisaic propaganda—the rupture and deathbed instructions traditions—were available to Josephus and that he chose to integrate them in his book at the very least indicates some affinity on his part to Pharisaic circles and their literature, as transmitted orally or in writing. As noted above (section A: "Pharisaic Legends"), most of the parallel stories found in Josephus and rabbinic literature—and not just the traditions concerning the Hasmoneans discussed here—are evidently Pharisaic, even if they do not explicitly mention the Pharisees or sectarian conflict.

Nonetheless, Josephus has chosen to embed these two pro-Pharisaic traditions in a hostile context. The rupture story is preceded by an introductory passage that displays hostility toward the Pharisees (*Ant.* 13.288; Chapter 3 above), and a statement that contradicts its original message has been inserted into the heart of the deathbed instructions story (*Ant.* 13.401–2; Chapter 5 above). As Schwartz and Mason have shown, these two additions are very similar in content and language.[96] Who, then, was responsible for these reworkings?

I return to my proposed analysis of the rupture story and its integration into the narrative. As shown in Chapter 3, Josephus wove the Jewish tale of the feast into a historical narrative that recounted a story of sedition (*stasis*; see *War* 1.67) against John Hyrcanus, and its source could have been Nicolaus. But the identification of the rebels, who in *War* are "his countrymen" (ἐπιχωρίων),

---

[94] Mason, *Josephus on the Pharisees*, 246–59. For a similar view, see also Tuval, *Jerusalem Priest to Roman Jew*, 206.

[95] D. R. Schwartz, "Josephus and Nicolaus," 159.

[96] Ibid. 159; Mason, *Josephus on the Pharisees*, 250.

with the Pharisees in *Antiquities*, and Josephus's erasure of the term *stasis* (mistakenly retained at the end of the story in *Antiquities*, section 299) were intended to create a clumsy connection between the historical-political description of a national revolt, which had its origins in Nicolaus, and the Jewish story of a feast and the Pharisees which Josephus inserted into the narrative sequence only in *Antiquities*. Awkward connections of this type between the historical-military framework and internal folkloristic Jewish anecdotes were unveiled in other chapters in this book (see Chapter 4). It is therefore difficult to accept Schwartz's contention that the Pharisaic political involvement in *Antiquities* reflects the original, and that the version in *War* underwent deliberate censorship. The opposite is true: the mention of the Pharisees, and their denigration in the introduction to the rupture story, is an attempt by the redactor—Josephus himself—to create a bridge between the framework and the interpolated Pharisaic-Jewish story.[97]

The discrepancies between the Jewish rupture legend and its hostile "shell" have long been noted in the scholarship, with most scholars ascribing the latter to Nicolaus, and a minority to Josephus.[98] But in the second instance—the story of Janneus's deathbed instructions—it appears that Josephus misled scholars. Failing to recognize this story as a Jewish source, scholars accordingly did not distinguish between it and the interpolated hostile remark, which contradicts the story's original pro-Pharisaic cast. This blurring between original story and editorial addition led to contrary evaluations: those who look at the overall picture view the story as pro-Pharisaic propaganda; those who assign great weight to the redactional comment identify it as crushing criticism of the Pharisees. This uncertainty gave rise to the contradictory ascriptions to Josephus on the one hand, and to Nicolaus on the other.

Based, however, on the argument put forth in this volume, that the story of the deathbed instructions is indeed a Pharisaic-Jewish tradition, as evidenced by its partial talmudic parallel and mainly by the affinity between its message and that of the rupture tradition (see Chapter 5), we must then assume that it was Josephus, not Nicolaus, who inserted this story into the narrative. After all, Nicolaus would not have been exposed to internal Jewish stories. If this indeed is the case, then the criticism of the Pharisees implanted in the heart of the story (13.401–2) was placed there by Josephus, just as he implanted the statement regarding the Pharisees in *Antiquities* 13.288. As noted, Schwartz and Mason alike have shown that the similar critical remarks on the Pharisees found in the introduction to the rupture episode (13.288) and in the heart of the deathbed instructions story (13.401–2) were penned by the same author. Were they

---

[97] Cf. Mason, *Josephus on the Pharisees*, 224. Note that Schwartz himself admits that, with regard to the presence of *stasis* in the episode in *War*, but not in *Antiquities*, the earlier version in this instance is the one in *War* ("Josephus and Nicolaus," 159).

[98] See the literature review in Mason, *Josephus on the Pharisees*, 219, and my survey in Chap. 3.

worded by Josephus himself as Mason suggests? Not necessarily. It is possible that the *wording* regarding Pharisaic power to cause harm and sedition, found in both units, originated in Nicolaus's workshop. Very similar content and wording are also found in the description of the Pharisees in *Antiquities* 17.41, in a Herodian context. There Schwartz presents convincing arguments for attributing the description to Nicolaus.[99] It is therefore possible that Josephus here employs locutions taken from Nicolaus. But we must separate the question of wording from the acts of redaction and interpolation. I argue for a reconstruction in which it was Josephus himself who inserted the hostile statements regarding the Pharisees into the stories of the Pharisaic rupture and the deathbed instructions. This indicates that Josephus had affinities to the Pharisees, was familiar with their traditions, and incorporated them into his book. Yet, in two instances in the context of the Hasmonean–Pharisaic relationship, Josephus tempered the pro-Pharisaic message of overtly pro-Pharisaic propaganda by inserting hostile statements (derived from Nicolaus?) before, or in, the tradition. This intervention allowed him to place the Hasmonean side of the equation in a more favorable light.

Although Josephus's sectarian affiliation is not the focus of this book, the discussion here may have contributed to the study of this question. The pool of Jewish traditions on which Josephus drew was definitively Pharisaic, and he apparently affiliated himself to the culture and knowledge of this group, who in his eyes represented the Jewish mainstream. It seems that Josephus wrote more expansively on the Pharisees in *Antiquities* because of its more comprehensive, more Jewish nature,[100] and not because of some deliberate manipulation that guided him when he wrote *War* or *Antiquities*. Nonetheless, Josephus did preface or insert harsh criticism of Pharisaic political activity into the Pharisaic sources he quoted. It is likely that the complex portrait of the Pharisees in *Antiquities* reflects their image in Second Temple Jewish society, which admired their religious intensity, knowledge of the Torah and ancestral tradition, and status as decisors, but feared their political clout and criticized their manipulative use of power.[101] Josephus was apparently torn between his affinity for the Pharisaic worldview and traditions, his admiration for Pharisaic prowess in interpreting the law, and the shared negative image of this group's political behavior in many Second Temple Jewish circles.[102] In conflictive contexts between the Pharisees and the Hasmonean dynasty, Josephus's reservations

[99] See D. R. Schwartz, "Josephus and Nicolaus," 159–69; for an opposing view, see Mason, *Josephus on the Pharisees*, 278–80.

[100] See the Introduction, section D, and similar approaches in Cohen, *Josephus in Galilee and Rome*, 144–51 and more recently in Tuval, *Jerusalem Priest to Roman Jew*.

[101] Intriguingly, a similar duality in the attitude toward the Pharisees is attested in other sources. See e.g. Matt 23:3. For a similar description of Josephan duality, see Mason, *Josephus on the Pharisees*, 334–5; Klawans, *Josephus and the Theologies of Ancient Judaism*, 7.

[102] On the usual criticism of the Pharisees as found in the DSS and the NT, see Chap. 3.

concerning the former were evidently also grounded in his well-known identification with the latter.

D. CONCLUSION

Notwithstanding their anecdotal folk nature, the legends of the Hasmoneans as
preserved in the Josephan and the rabbinic corpora provide an overarching view
of the rise and fall of the Hasmonean dynasty. A lost Aramaic chronicle that was
worded not long after the events in question listed the victories of the Hasmonean
house. Temple legends praised Judas's bravery in battle against the enemy that
threatened the temple, and highlighted John Hyrcanus's unique qualities as a
high priest and admired leader who merited a prophetic message in the temple
at a moment of national crisis. Another literary genre treated the Pharisaic–
Hasmonean relationship toward the end of John Hyrcanus's reign and during
that of Janneus. It attempted to limit the appearance of a rupture between them,
attributing the hostility to a misunderstanding and to instigators, and sought to
clear both parties: the Pharisees of accusations of rebellion and the Hasmonean
leader of malicious persecution. Finally, the fall of the dynasty, the loss of independence, and the threat to the temple were laid at the door of the sinful fourth
generation, Janneus's sons Hyrcanus and Aristobulus, who irresponsibly broke
internal Jewish unity.

These legends were embedded in Josephus's writings on the one hand, and in
rabbinic literature on the other. To a large extent both corpora inherited, and
reflect, the historical judgment of the ancient sources. Josephus and the rabbis
alike begin their accounts of the dynasty with praise and conclude with denigration. They celebrate first-generation Maccabean bravery; relate admiringly, albeit
with a hint of criticism, to John Hyrcanus; criticize Janneus and his attitude
toward the Pharisees; and attribute the fall of the dynasty and the loss of independence to the fourth-generation conflict between his sons. Both corpora mark
the end of John Hyrcanus's reign as the transitional point from days of glory to
incipient decline, laying the ultimate blame mainly at his descendants' feet.

Nonetheless, the treatment of these stories and their protagonists differs
in the Josephan and in the rabbinic corpora. Josephus heightens the glory of
the early generations and offers a restrained critique of the later ones. He
aggrandizes the figures of Judas and his brothers beyond what was found in the
material he inherited, and admiringly sketches John Hyrcanus and his long
reign, linking the legend of his prophetic powers to his historical persona as a
military and political leader. Where the Pharisaic tradition at his disposal was
hostile toward John, Josephus imposes on it a contrasting framework—penned
either by him or taken from Nicolaus—that accuses the Pharisees and justifies
the Hasmonean ruler. Josephus does censure the generations of Janneus and

his sons, in line with the ancient traditions. However, in this case as well he exhibits some leniency toward Janneus in his later, more independent work, by describing the difficult circumstances underlying Janneus's actions. Here too, into a Pharisaic tradition that is critical of Janneus he inserts statements that cast some of the blame for the dispute on the Pharisees, thus partially clearing the Hasmonean king. With respect to the last Hasmonean generation, in several places Josephus preserves the tradition that ascribes the fall of the dynasty to internecine warfare, even if he somewhat obscures this message as found in one of the ancient stories.

As for rabbinic literature, this examination showed that the redaction of the single story of a Hasmonean leader can serve as a metaphor for the overall attitude toward this figure and its generation; moreover, that this redaction shifts in relation to the Hasmonean generation being treated in the ancient tradition. We must distinguish between rabbinic literature's attitude toward the first generation of Hasmoneans, which is surprisingly incongruent, and its treatment of the stories of the next generations, which exhibit known phenomena typical of rabbinic literature. With respect to the first generation, the demonstrative erasure of Judas Maccabeus's name from the concrete tradition of Nicanor's defeat indicates that the absence of the names of the Maccabees from rabbinic literature is neither fortuitous nor the result of a lack of historical awareness, but deliberate, directed censorship. Surprisingly, the rabbis chose to celebrate the Hasmonean victory but to conceal the figures of its protagonists.

In contrast, the rabbinic treatment of the next three generations exemplifies prevailing currents in rabbinic literature: rabbinization and the creation of archetypal figures. Various scholars have already described the rabbinic tendency to "rabbinize" the stories they inherited.[103] The placement of the episode of John Hyrcanus's heavenly voice in a sequence of stories that treats the sages exemplifies the general trend that transformed this figure from political leader to early sage (Chapter 2). The story of the rupture with the Pharisees depicts them as the "sages of Israel," and their mass murder, which is recounted in the talmudic version, "desolates the world" in terms of Torah study. The halakhic content imposed on the story of the fratricidal Hasmonean conflict (Chapter 6) demonstrates a different means of moving dramatic events to the study house.

Jacob Elbaum, Shaye D. Cohen, and others have noted the rabbinic tendency to attribute many traditions to one archetypal figure and to create clusters of stories surrounding a single event.[104] The addition at the conclusion of the rupture legend (Chapter 3) illustrates the broad rabbinic tendency to strongly denigrate Janneus and to portray him as an enemy and persecutor of the rabbis. Other legends that attached themselves to this figure in the BT and the Scholion

---

[103] See n. 64. See also Kalmin, *Jewish Babylonia*; D. R. Schwartz, "Remembering the Second Temple Period."

[104] Elbaum, "Models of Storytelling," 71–7; Cohen, "Parallel Historical Tradition," 11.

are indicative of the propensity to ascribe a variety of negative traditions to Janneus, who represents—in the Scholion and in one instance in the BT—the prototypically evil king. In other instances, we witnessed the merging of different traditions. In the BT a tradition close to the Josephan one on the internecine struggle between the Hasmonean brothers was interwoven with a secondary tradition from the YT, which introduced motifs from the First Revolt into the story (the pig; see Chapter 6).

To my mind, it is not necessary to seek in these passages focused political opposition to the Hasmoneans and their deeds, or to their assumption of royalty, and certainly not to their achievement of national and political independence. The main force at play here is the rabbinic aspiration to ground their picture of the world in themselves and their doctrines, in line with "if I am here, everyone is here" (*b. Sukk.* 53a). Positive and negative personalities alike had to be placed in some sort of relationship to the rabbinic world. Where a positive hero fulfilled both a religious and a political function, it was possible to erase his secular roles and to emphasize his cultic functions, to anachronistically identify his religious activity with the ideal figure of the early sage. The rabbis encased a story containing a moral lesson that originally dealt with a threat to the temple with clusters of halakhot in order to bring it into the study house. Regarding the ambivalent relationship between the ruler and those identified as the predecessors of the rabbis, it was convenient for post-destruction redactors to assign this figure to the negative end of the spectrum, as the polar opposite of the world of the Second Temple sages as they imagined it. To make this work, the storytellers needed to identify with the figure of a sage who confronted the ruler. The most intriguing phenomenon is the treatment of the heroic figures of the Maccabees, whose names were proudly borne by one-third of the Jewish population, the rabbis among them. It was these very names that the rabbis deliberately sought to erase; in the absence of external sources, they would have succeeded. The rabbis cherished the Hasmonean victory and the national freedom to which it gave birth, but steadfastly refused to regard military-political leaders as figures worthy of emulation. Instead of idolizing a fighter, the leader of a rebellion, they preferred to ignore him as an individual and to praise an anonymous victory. Accordingly, the Maccabees—the military and political leaders who were the most significant, admired models during the Second Temple period—were erased and their names forgotten, simply because no way was found to bring them into the rabbinic camp.

Bibliography

Primary Sources

Manuscripts and early printed editions of rabbinic sources

Mishnah
Kaufmann A 50

Tosefta
Erfurt, Evangelisches Ministerium, Or. 2° 1220
London, British Library, Add. 27296 (Cat. Margoliouth 445)
Vienna, Österreichische Nationalbibliothek, Cod. Hebr. 20 (Saul Lieberman, *The Tosefta According to Codex Vienna...* [New York: Jewish Theological Seminary of America, 1962])
Editio princeps, Venice 1521–2

Scholia
Cambridge, University Library, Add. 648.9
(= hybrid edition)
[New York, Jewish Theological Seminary 10484.6 (formerly MS Vienna)]
Oxford, Bodleian Library, Michael 388 (Neubauer 867) = Scholion O
Parma, Bibloteca Palatina 2298 (De Rossi 117) = Scholion P
Editio princeps, Mantua 1514 (hybrid version)

Genesis Rabbah
Vatican, Biblioteca Apostolica, ebr. 30

Sifre Numbers
Vatican, Biblioteca Apostolica, ebr. 32

Jerusalem Talmud
Leiden, Universiteitsbibliothek, Scaliger 3 (*Talmud Yerushalmi: According to Ms. Or. 4720 [Scal. 3] of Leiden University Library with Restorations and Corrections,* introduction by Yaacov Sussmann). Jerusalem: Academy of the Hebrew Language, 2008
Vatican, Biblioteca Apostolica, ebr. 133 (*Sotah*)
Venice, printed edition, 1523

Babylonian Talmud
Cambridge, University Library, T-S Misc. 28.265 (Geniza fragment; *Qiddushin*)
Jerusalem, Yad Harav Herzog 1 (*Ta'anit*)
London, British Library, Harley 5508 (Margoliouth 400; *Sukkah* and *Ta'anit*)
Munich, Bayerische Staatsbibliothek, Cod. Hebr. 95

New York, Jewish Theological Seminary, Rab. 15 (*Sotah*)
Oxford, Bodleian Library, Heb. d. 20/25a-63 = Oxford 2675 (*Sotah*)
Oxford, Bodleian Library, Opp. 248 (Neubauer 367) = MS Oxford 367 (*Qiddushin*)
Paris, Alliance Israélite Universelle, H147A (*Menaḥot*)
Vatican, Biblioteca Apostolica, ebr. 110 (*Sotah*)
Vatican, Biblioteca Apostolica, ebr. 111 (*Qiddushin*)

PRINTED EDITIONS
Spanish: Guadalajara, 1480[?] (*Qiddushin*)
Venice, printed edition, 1520–3

Texts and Translations

Josephus
Josephus. *Jewish Antiquities.* Vols. 4–9 of *Josephus with an English Translation by H. St. J. Thackeray.* Loeb Classical Library. Cambridge, Mass.: Harvard University Press, 1930–65. Vols. 5–8, ed. and trans. Ralph Marcus.
Josephus. *The Jewish War.* Vols. 2–3 of *Josephus with an English Translation by H. St. J. Thackeray.* Loeb Classical Library. Cambridge, Mass.: Harvard University Press, 1956–59.
Mason, Steve, ed. *Flavius Josephus: Translation and Commentary.* Vols. 1B, 3–5, 9–10. Leiden: Brill, 2000–8.
Niese, Benedictus, ed. *Flavii Iosephi opera.* Berolini: Apud Weidmannos, 1887–95.
Ullman, Lisa, trans. *History of the Jewish War against the Romans.* Jerusalem: Carmel, 2009 (in Hebrew).

Philo
Philo of Alexandria. *The Embassy to Gaius.* Vol. 10 of the Loeb Classical Library edition. Trans. F.H. Colson. Cambridge, Mass.: Harvard University Press, 1962.
Philo of Alexandria. *On the Life of Moses.* Vol. 6 of the Loeb Classical Library edition. Trans. F.H. Colson. Cambridge, Mass.: Harvard University Press, 1935.
Philo of Alexandria. *On Rewards and Punishments.* Vol. 8 of the Loeb Classical Library edition. Trans. F.H. Colson. Cambridge, Mass.: Harvard University Press, 1939.

Dead Sea Scrolls
The DJD volumes of the Dead Sea Scrolls texts have been treated here as primary sources. Some editions appear both in primary and secondary sources because greater use was made of the monograph accompanying the text edition.

Allegro, John M. "Commentary on Isaiah (B)." In *Qumran Cave 4.I (4Q158–4Q186)*, 15–17. DJD 5. Oxford: Clarendon, 1968.
Alexander, P., and G. Vermes. "285. 4QSefer ha-Milḥamah." In *Qumran Cave 4.XXVI: Cryptic Texts*, ed. Stephen J. Pfann, 228–48. DJD 36. Oxford: Clarendon, 2000.
Baillet, Maurice. "13. Prophétie sacerdotale (?)." In *Les Petites Grottes de Qumran*, ed. M. Baillet, J.T. Milik, and R. De Vaux, 126–7. DJD 3. Oxford: Clarendon, 1962.
Baillet, Maurice, ed. *Qumran Grotte 4.III (4Q482–4Q520).* DJD 7. Oxford: Clarendon, 1982.

Berrin, Shani. *The Pesher Nahum Scroll from Qumran: An Exegetical Study of 4Q169.* STDJ 53. Leiden: Brill, 2004.

Charlesworth, James H., ed. *The Dead Sea Scrolls: Hebrew, Aramaic, and Greek Texts with English Translations.* 10 vols. Princeton Theological Seminary Dead Sea Scrolls Project. Tubingen: Mohr Siebeck, 1994–2011.

Elgvin, Torleif. "423. 4QInstruction[g] [Musar leMevin[g]]." In *Qumran Cave 4.XXIV: Sapiential Texts, Part 2, 4QInstruction [Musar LeMevin]: 4Q415 ff.*, ed. John Strugnell et al., 518–22. DJD 34. Oxford: Clarendon, 1999.

Eshel, Esther and Menahem Kister. "471a. 4QPolemical Text." In *Qumran Cave 4 XXVI: Cryptic Texts*, ed. Stephen J. Pfann, 446–9. DJD 36. Oxford: Clarendon, 2000.

Horgan, Maurya P. *Pesharim: Qumran Interpretations of Biblical Books.* Washington, DC: Catholic Association of America, 1979.

Martinez, Florentino Garcia, and Eibert J.C. Tigchelaar, eds. *Dead Sea Scrolls Study Edition.* 2 vols. Leiden: Brill, 1998.

Parry, Donald W., and Emanuel Tov, eds. *The Dead Sea Scrolls Reader: Parabiblical Texts.* Leiden: Brill, 2005.

Puech, E., ed. *Qumran Grotte 4.XVIII: Textes Hebreux (4Q521–4Q528, 4Q576–4Q579).* DJD 25. Oxford: Clarendon, 1998.

Qimron, Elisha. *The Dead Sea Scrolls: The Hebrew Writings.* 3 vols. Jerusalem: Yad Ben-Zvi Press, 2013 (in Hebrew).

Qimron, Elisha, and John Strugnell. *Qumran Cave 4.V: Miqsat Ma'aśê Ha-Torah.* DJD 10. Oxford: Clarendon, 1994.

Schuller, Eileen, and Moshe J. Bernstein. "372. 4Qnarrative and Poetic Composition[b]." In *Wadi Daliyeh II: The Samaria Papyri from Wadi Daliyeh and Qumran Cave 4. XXVIII. Miscellanea, Part 2*, ed. Douglas M. Gropp et al., 165–97. DJD 28. Oxford: Clarendon, 2001.

Steudel, Annette. "425. 4QSapiential-Didactic Work B." In *Qumran Cave 4.XV: Sapiential Texts, Part I*, ed. Torleif Elgvin et al., 203–10. DJD 20. Oxford: Clarendon, 1997.

Strugnell, John, and Daniel J. Harrington. "418a. 4QInstruction[e] (Musar leMevin[e])." In *Qumran Cave 4.XXIV*, ed. John Strugnell et al., 479–80. DJD 34. Oxford: Clarendon, 1999.

Yadin, Yigael, ed. *The Scroll of the War of the Sons of Light against the Sons of Darkness.* London: Oxford University Press, 1962.

Yadin, Yigael. *The Temple Scroll.* 3 vols. Tel Aviv: Israel Exploration Society, 1983.

Apocrypha

Charles, R. H. et al., eds. *The Apocrypha and Pseudepigrapha of the Old Testament in English.* 2 vols. Oxford: Clarendon, 1913.

De Jonge, Marinus. *The Testaments of the Twelve Patriarchs: A Critical Edition of the Greek Text.* PVTG, vol. 2, pt. 2. Leiden: Brill, 1978.

Goldstein, Jonathan A. *I Maccabees: A New Translation with Introduction and Commentary.* Anchor Bible 41. Garden City: Doubleday, 1976.

Goldstein, Jonathan A. *II Maccabees: A New Translation with Introduction and Commentary.* Anchor Bible 41A. Garden City: Doubleday, 1983.

Greenfield, Jonas C., Michael E. Stone, and Esther Eshel. *The Aramaic Levi Document: Edition, Translation, Commentary.* SVTP 19. Leiden: Brill, 2004.

Kisch, Guido, ed. *Pseudo-Philo's* Liber antiquitatum biblicarum. Publications in Medieval Studies 10. Notre Dame, Ind.: University of Notre Dame Press, 1949.

Rappaport, Uriel. *The First Book of Maccabees: Introduction, Hebrew Translation, and Commentary*. Between Bible and Mishnah: The David and Jemima Jeselsohn Library. Jerusalem: Yad Ben-Zvi Press, 2004 (in Hebrew).

Schwartz, Daniel R. *2 Maccabees*. CEJL. Berlin, New York: de Gruyter, 2008.

Stone, Michael E. *The Testament of Levi: A First Study of the Armenian MSS. of the Testaments of the XII Patriarchs in the Convent of St. James, Jerusalem; with Text, Critical Apparatus, Notes and Translation*. Jerusalem: St James, 1969.

Rabbinic Literature
Seder Olam Rabbah
Milikowsky, Chaim. *Seder Olam: Critical Edition, Commentary, and Introduction*. 2 vols. Jerusalem: Yad Ben-Zvi Press, 2013 (in Hebrew).

Megillat Ta'anit (Scholion)
Noam, Vered. *Megillat Ta'anit: Versions, Interpretation, History with a Critical Edition*. Between Bible and Mishnah: The David and Jemima Jeselsohn Library. Jerusalem: Yad Ben-Zvi Press, 2003 (in Hebrew).

English translation of *Megillat Ta'anit*: Noam, Vered. "Megillat Taanit: The Scroll of Fasting." In *The Literature of the Sages Second Part: Midrash and Targum, Liturgy, Poetry, Mysticism, Contracts, Inscriptions, Ancient Science and the Languages of Rabbinic Literature*, ed. Samuel Safrai, Zeev Safrai, Joshua Schwartz, and Peter J. Tomson. 2:339–62. CRINT. Assen: Royal Van Gorcum and Fortress, 2006.

MISHNAH
Albeck, Hanoch. *Shishah sidrei mishnah mefurashim bi-yedei H. Albek.* Jerusalem: Mossad Bialik, 1959.

English translations: Neusner, Jacob. *The Mishnah: A New Translation*. New Haven and London: Yale University Press, 1988.

Blackman, Philip. *Mishnayot*. 2d ed. 6 vols. New York: Judaica Press, 1964.

TOSEFTA
Lieberman, Saul. *The Tosefta: According to Codex Vienna, with Variants from Codices Erfurt, Genizah MSS. and Editio Princeps (Venice 1521)*. Vols. 1–3. 2nd revised ed. New York and Jerusalem: Jewish Theological Seminary of America, 1955–1973 (in Hebrew) (*Zera'im* to *Nashim, Neziqin*).

Zuckermandel, M.S. *Tosephta: Based on the Erfurt and Vienna Codices*. Rev. ed. Jerusalem: Wahrmann, 1970 (part of *Neziqin, Kodashim, Tohorot*).

English translation: *The Tosefta*. Translated by Jacob Neusner. 6 vols. New York: Ktav, 1977–86.

HALAKHIC MIDRASHIM
Sifra
Sifra de-ve rab hu sefer torat kohanim. Edited by Isaac Hirsh Weiss. Vienna: Schlossberg, 1862.

Sifre Numbers
Kahana, Menahem I. *Sifre on Numbers: An Annotated Edition.* 5 vols. Jerusalem: Magnes, 2011–15 (in Hebrew).
English translation. Levertoff, Paul P. *Midrash Sifre on Numbers: Selections from Early Rabbinic Scriptural Interpretations.* Translations of Early Documents, Series III. Rabbinic Texts. London: Society for Promoting Christian Knowledge, 1926.

Sifre Zuta Numbers
Sifre be-Midbar. Edited by H.S. Horovitz. Reprint, Jerusalem: Wahrmann, 1966.

Sifre Deuteronomy
Sifre on Deuteronomy. Edited by Louis Finkelstein. Reprint, New York: Jewish Theological Seminary of America, 1969 (in Hebrew).
English translation*: Sifre: A Tannaitic Commentary on the Book of Deuteronomy.* Translated by Reuven Hammer. New Haven: Yale University Press, 1986.

Sifre Zuta on Deuteronomy
Kahana, Menahem I. *Sifre Zuta on Deuteronomy: Citations from a New Tannaitic Midrash.* Jerusalem: Magnes, 2002 (in Hebrew).

JERUSALEM TALMUD
Talmud Yerushalmi: According to Ms. Or. 4720 [Scal. 3] of Leiden University Library with Restorations and Corrections, introduction by Yaacov Sussmann). Jerusalem: Academy of the Hebrew Language, 2008.
English translations: Neusner, Jacob, ed. *The Talmud of the Land of Israel: An Academic Commentary.* 35 vols. Atlanta, Ga.: Scholars Press, 1998–1999.
Guggenheimer, Heinrich W., ed. *The Jerusalem Talmud: Edition, Translation and Commentary.* 17 vols. Studia Judaica 18–21, 23, 29, 31, 34, 39, 43, 45, 51, 61, 68, 74, 80, 85. Berlin: de Gruyter, 1999–2015.

BABYLONIAN TALMUD
Talmud Bavli. Vilna: Romm, 1886.
English translation: *Hebrew-English Edition of the Babylonian Talmud.* Soncino edition. Translated into English with notes, glossary and indices under the editorship of Isidore Epstein. 35 vols. London: Soncino, 1948.

AGGADIC MIDRASHIM
Avot de-Rabbi Natan. Edited by Solomon Schechter. 2d ed. New York: Jewish Theological Seminary, 1997.
Bereshit Rabbah. Edited by J. Theodor and Ch. Albeck. 2d ed. 3 vols. Reprint, Jerusalem: Wahrmann, 1965.
Vayikra Rabbah. Edited by Mordecai Margalioth [Margulies]. 2 vols. New York: Jewish Theological Seminary of America, 1972.
Canticles Rabbah. Vilna: Romm, 1887.

Midrash Kohelet Rabbah 1–6: Critical Edition Based on Manuscripts and Genizah Fragments. Edited by Marc Hirshman with the assistance of Shaul Baruchi. The Midrash Project of the Schechter Institute of Jewish Studies. Jerusalem: Schechter Institute, 2016.

Eikhah Rabbah. Edited by Solomon Buber. Vilna: Romm, 1899.

Pesikta de Rav Kahana: According to an Oxford Manuscript. Edited by Bernard Mandelbaum. 2 vols. New York: Jewish Theological Seminary, 1962.

English translation: *Pesikta de-Rab Kahana: R. Kahana's Compilation of Discourses for Sabbaths and Festal Days*. Translated by William G. Braude and Israel J. Kapstein. Philadelphia: Jewish Publication Society, 1975.

Midrash Tanḥuma. Jerusalem: Levin-Epstein, 1969.

Midrash Tanḥuma. Edited by Solomon Buber. Reprint, New York, 1946.

English translations: *Midrash Tanhuma-Yelammedenu: An English Translation of Genesis and Exodus from the Printed Version of Tanhuma-Yelammedenu with an Introduction, Notes, and Indexes*. Translated by Samuel A. Berman. Hoboken, N.J.: Ktav, 1996.

Midrash Tanḥuma. Translated into English with Introduction, Indices, and Brief Notes (S. Buber Recension) by John T. Townsend. 3 vols. Hoboken, N.J.: Ktav, 1989–2003.

Pesiqta Rabbati. Edited by Meir Ish-Shalom [Friedmann}. Vienna, 1880. Reprint, Tel Aviv, 1963.

English translation: *Pesikta Rabbati*. Translated by William G. Braude. 2 vols. New Haven: Yale University Press, 1968.

Bemidbar Rabbah. Vilna: Romm, 1878.

English translation: *Midrash Rabbah*. Translated into English with notes, glossary and indices under the editorship of Rabbi Dr. H. Freedman and Maurice Simon with a foreword by Rabbi Dr. L. Epstein. 10 vols. London: Soncino: 1939–1951.

Shir ha-Shirim Zuta: Salomon Buber, ed. *Midrasch Suta*. Berlin: Itskowski, 1894.

TARGUMIM

Targum Pseudo-Jonathan: Deuteronomy. Translated with notes by Ernest G. Clarke. The Aramaic Bible, vol. 5B. Edinburgh: T & T Clark, 1998.

Medieval Literature

The Jossipon [Josephus Gorionides]. Edited with an introduction, commentary, and notes by David Flusser. 2 vols. Jerusalem: Bialik Institute, 1978–80.

Greek and Roman Authors

Dio Cassius. *Dio's Roman History*. Trans. Earnest Cary on the basis of the version of Herbert Baldwin Foster. 9 vols. Loeb Classical Library. London: Heinemann, 1968–70.

Polybius. *The Histories*. Trans. W. R. Paton; rev. Frank W. Walbank and Christian Habicht. 5 vols. Loeb Classical Library, 128, 137, 138, 160, 161. Cambridge, Mass.: Harvard University Press, 2010–12.

Suetonius. *Lives of the Caesars*. In *Suetonius: Volume II*. Trans. J. C. Rolfe. Loeb Classical Library. Cambridge, Mass.: Harvard University Press, 1997.

Tacitus. *The Annals*. Trans. with introduction and notes by A. J. Woodman. Indianapolis: Hackett, 2004.

Tacitus. *The Histories*. Trans. Clifford H. Moore. Loeb Classical Library. London: Heinemann, 1969.

Secondary Sources

Abegg, Martin G., James E. Bowley, Edward M. Cook, and Emanuel Tov. *The Dead Sea Scrolls Concordance*. 4 vols. Leiden and Boston: Brill, 2003–10.

Abel, Felix M. *Les livres des Maccabées*. Études bibliques. Paris: J. Gabalda, 1949.

Alon, Gedalyahu. "The Attitude of the Pharisees to Roman Rule and the House of Herod." In *Jews, Judaism and the Classical World*, trans. Israel Abrahams, 18–47. Jerusalem: Magnes, 1977.

Alon, Gedalyahu. "Biqoret: Sha'arei torat ereṣ yisrael." *Tarbiẓ* 12 (1940): 88–95 (in Hebrew).

Alon, Gedalyahu. "Did the Jewish People and Its Sages Cause the Hasmoneans to Be Forgotten?" In *Jews, Judaism and the Classical World*, trans. Israel Abrahams, 1–17. Jerusalem: Magnes, 1977.

Alon, Gedalyahu. "Iyyunim ba-sefarim ha-ḥiṣoniyyim." In *Studies in Jewish History in the Times of the Second Temple, the Mishna and the Talmud*, 1:177–93. Tel Aviv: Hakibbutz Hameuchad, 1957 (in Hebrew).

Alon, Gedalyahu. "Ha-yevanit be-ereṣ yisrael ha-yehudit." In *Studies in Jewish History in the Times of the Second Temple, the Mishna and the Talmud*, 2:248–77. Tel Aviv: Hakibbutz Hameuchad, 1958 (in Hebrew).

Amit, Yairah. "Dual Causality: An Additional Aspect." In *In Praise of Editing in the Hebrew Bible: Collected Essays in Retrospect*, trans. Betty Sigler Rozen, 105–21. Sheffield: Sheffield Phoenix Press, 2012.

Amusin, Joseph D. "The Reflection of Historical Events of the 1st Century B.C. in Qumran Commentaries (4Q161; 4Q169; 4Q166)." *HUCA* 48 (1977): 123–52.

Ankersmit, Franklin R. *Narrative Logic: A Semantic Analysis of the Historian's Language*. Martinus Nijhoff Philosophy Library. The Hague: Nijhoff, 1983.

Aptowitzer, Victor. *Parteipolitik der Hasmonäerzeit im rabbinischen und pseudo-epigraphischen Schrifttum*. Veröffentlichungen der Alexander Kohut Memorial Foundation 5. Vienna: Verlag der Kohut-Foundation, 1927.

Arav, Rami. "Evidence for Water Rituals at Bethsaida." *Eretz-Israel* 30 (2011): 357–69 (in Hebrew).

Assman, Jan, and John Czaplicka. "Collective Memory and Cultural Identity." *New German Critique: Cultural History/Cultural Studies* 65 (1995): 125–33. <http://web.ebscohost.com/ehost/pdfviewer/pdfviewer?vid=15&sid=92369b79-a989-40c7-bc3a-ce8fa9a4d0b6%40sessionmgr11&hid=22>.

Atkinson, Kenneth. *A History of the Hasmonean State: Josephus and Beyond*. T. & T. Clark Jewish and Christian Text Series 23. London: Bloomsbury T. & T. Clark, 2016.

Attridge, Harold W. *The Interpretation of Biblical History in the Antiquitates Judaicae of Flavius Josephus*. HDR 7. Missoula, Mo.: Scholars Press for HTR, 1976.

Avigad, Nahman. "A Bulla of Jonathan the High Priest." *IEJ* 25 (1975): 8–12.

Avigad, Nahman. "A Bulla of King Jonathan." *IEJ* 25 (1975): 245–9.

Avishur, Yitzchak. "Expressions Such as בין ידיים and Their Parallels in Semitic Languages." In *Comparative Studies in Biblical and Ugaritic Languages and Literatures*, 14–25. Tel Aviv: Archaeological Center Publication, 2007.

Avi-Yonah, Michael. *The Holy Land: A Historical Geography from the Persian to the Arab Conquest (536 B.C.–A.D. 640)*. Jerusalem: Carta, 2002.

Babota, Vasile. *The Institution of the Hasmonean High Priesthood*. JSJSup 165. Leiden: Brill, 2014.

Baer, Yitzhak. "Jerusalem in the Times of the Great Revolt." *Zion* 36 (1971): 127–90 (in Hebrew).

Barag, Dan B. "Alexander Jannaeus: Priest and King." In *"Go Out and Study the Land" (Judges 18:2): Archaeological, Historical and Textual Studies in Honor of Hanan Eshel*, ed. Aren M. Maeir, Jodi Magness, and Lawrence H. Schiffman, 1–5. Supplements of the Journal for the Study of Judaism 148. Leiden and Boston: Brill, 2012.

Bar-Asher, Moshe. "Divrei mavo le-mishnah ketav yad parma bet." In *Studies in Mishnaic Hebrew*, 1:131–61. Asuppot 4–5. Jerusalem: Bialik Institute, 2009 (in Hebrew).

Bar-Asher, Moshe. *Studies in Mishnaic Hebrew*. 2 vols. Asuppot 4–5. Jerusalem: Bialik Institute, 2009 (in Hebrew).

Bar-Kochva, Bezalel. *The Image of the Jews in Greek Literature: The Hellenistic Period*. Berkeley: University of California Press, 2010.

Bar-Kochva, Bezalel. *Judas Maccabaeus: The Jewish Struggle against the Seleucids*. Cambridge: Cambridge University Press, 1989.

Bar-Kochva, Bezalel. "On Josephus and the Books of the Maccabees, Philology and Historiography." *Tarbiz* 62 (1992): 115–32 (in Hebrew).

Batsch, Christophe. "Priests in Warfare in Second Temple Judaism: 1QM, or the 'Anti-Phinehas.' " In *Qumran Cave 1 Revisited; Texts from Cave 1 Sixty Years after Their Discovery: Proceedings of the Sixth Meeting of the IOQS in Ljubljana*, ed. Daniel Falk et al., 163–78. STDJ 91. Leiden: Brill, 2010.

Baumgarten, Albert I. "Rabbinic Literature as a Source for the History of Jewish Sectarianism in the Second Temple Period." *DSD* 2 (1995): 14–57.

Beer, Moshe. "The Term 'Crown of Torah' in Rabbinic Literature and Its Social Significance." *Zion* 55 (1990): 397–417 (in Hebrew).

Bendavid, Abba. *Biblical Hebrew and Mishnaic Hebrew*. Tel Aviv: Dvir, 1971 (in Hebrew).

Benovitz, Moshe. *BT Sukkah: Chapter IV and Chapter V*. Talmud Ha-Igud. Jerusalem: Society for the Interpretation of the Talmud, 2013 (in Hebrew).

Ben Shahar, Meir. "Biblical and Post-biblical History in Rabbinic Literature: Between the First and Second Destruction." Ph.D. diss., Hebrew University, 2011 (in Hebrew).

Ben Shahar, Meir. "The High Priest and Alexander the Great." In *Josephus and the Rabbis* by Tal Ilan and Vered Noam, 91–144. Jerusalem: Yad Ben-Zvi Press, 2017 (in Hebrew).

Ben Shahar, Meir. "The Prediction to Vespasian." In *Josephus and the Rabbis* by Tal Ilan and Vered Noam, 604–64. Jerusalem: Yad Ben-Zvi Press, 2017 (in Hebrew).

Ben-Shalom, Ram. *Facing Christian Culture: Historical Consciousness and Images of the Past among the Jews of Spain and Southern France during the Middle Ages*. Jerusalem: Ben-Zvi Institute, 2006 (in Hebrew).

Berkhofer, Robert F. "The Challenge of Poetics to (Normal) Historical Practice." *Poetics Today* 9 (1988): 435–52.

Bernstein, Moshe J. "Poetry and Prose in 4Q371–373 Narrative and Poetic Composition[a,b,c]." In *Liturgical Perspectives: Prayer and Poetry in Light of the Dead Sea Scrolls. Proceedings of the Fifth International Symposium of the Orion Center for the Study of the Dead Sea Scrolls and Associated Literature, 19–23 January 2000*, ed. Esther Chazon and with the collaboration of Ruth Clements and Avital Pinnick, 19–33. STDJ 48. Leiden: Brill, 2003.

Berrin, Shani L. *The Pesher Nahum Scroll from Qumran: An Exegetical Study of 4Q169*. STDJ 53. Leiden: Brill, 2004.

Berthelot, Katell. "4QTestimonia as a Polemic against the Prophetic Claims of John Hyrcanus." In *Prophecy after the Prophets? The Contribution of the Dead Sea Scrolls to the Understanding of Biblical and Extra-Biblical Prophecy*, ed. K. de Troyer and A. Lange (with L. L. Schulte), 99–116. Leuven: Peeters, 2009.

Betz, Otto. "The Death of Choni-Onias in the Light of the Temple Scroll from Qumran." In *Jerusalem in the Second Temple Period: Abraham Schalit Memorial Volume*, ed. A. Oppenheimer, U. Rappaport, and M. Stern, 84–97. Library of the History of the Yishuv in Eretz-Israel. Jerusalem: Yad Izhak Ben-Zvi, 1980 (in Hebrew).

Bilde, Per. *Flavius Josephus between Jerusalem and Rome*. JSPSup 2. Sheffield: JSOT, 1988.

Blau, J. "A Conservative View of the Language of of the Dead Sea Scrolls." In *Diggers at the Well: Proceedings of a Third International Symposium on the Hebrew of the Dead Sea Scrolls and Ben Sira*, ed. T. Muraoka and J. F. Elwolde, 20–5. STDJ 36. Leiden: Brill, 2000.

Bohak, Gideon. "A New Genizah Fragment of the Aramaic Levi Document." *Tarbiz* 79 (2010–11): 373–83 (in Hebrew).

Boyarin, Daniel. "Ha-midrash ve-ha-ma'aseh: Al ha-ḥeqer ha-histori shel sifrut ḥazal." In *Saul Lieberman Memorial Volume*, ed. Shamma Friedman, 105–17. New York and Jerusalem: Jewish Theological Seminary of America, 1993.

Braverman, Natan. "An Examination of the Nature of the Vienna and Erfurt Manuscripts of the Tosefta." *Language Studies* 5–6 (1992): 153–70 (in Hebrew).

Breuer, Yochanan. *The Hebrew in the Babylonian Talmud according to the Manuscripts of Tractate Pesaḥim*. Jerusalem: Magnes, 2002 (in Hebrew).

Brooke, George J. "The Kittim in the Qumran Pesharim." In *Images of Empire*, ed. Loveday Alexander, 135–59. JSOTSup 122. Sheffield: JSOT Press, 1991.

Brooke, George J. "Qumran Pesher: Towards the Redefinition of a Genre." *RevQ* 10 (1981): 483–503.

Brüll, Jacob. *Einleitung in die Mischnah*. 2 vols. Frankfurt am Main: published by author, 1876 (in Hebrew).

Chapman, Honora H. "By the Rivers of Babylon: Josephus and Greek Poetry." In *Josephus and Jewish History in Flavian Rome and Beyond*, ed. Joseph Sievers and Gaia Lembi, 121–46. JSJSup 104. Leiden: Brill, 2005.

Churgin, Pinkhos. *Studies in the Times of the Second Temple*. New York: Horeb Foundation, 1949 (in Hebrew).

Cohen, Shaye J. D. "Alexander the Great and Jaddus the High Priest according to Josephus." *AJS Review* 7–8 (1982–3): 41–68.

Cohen, Shaye J. D. "The Destruction: From Scripture to Midrash." *Prooftexts* 2 (1982): 18–39.

Cohen, Shaye J. D. *Josephus in Galilee and Rome: His Vita and Development as a Historian*. Columbia Studies in the Classical Tradition 8. Leiden: Brill, 1979.

Cohen, Shaye J. D. "The Modern Study of Ancient Judaism." In *The State of Jewish Studies*, ed. Shaye J. D. Cohen and Edward L. Greenstein, 55–73. Detroit: Wayne State University Press, 1990.

Cohen, Shaye J. D. "Parallel Historical Tradition in Josephus and Rabbinic Literature." In *Proceedings of the Ninth World Congress of Jewish Studies, Jerusalem, August 4–12, 1985, Division B, Volume 1*, 7–14. Jerusalem: World Union of Jewish Studies, 1986.

Cohen, Shaye J. D. "The Rabbi in Second-Century Jewish Society." In *The Cambridge History of Judaism*, vol. 3: *The Early Roman Period*, ed. William Horbury, W. D. Davies, and John Sturdy, 922–90. Cambridge: Cambridge University Press, 1999.

Cohen, Shaye J. D. "The Significance of Yavneh: Pharisees, Rabbis and the End of Jewish Sectarianism." *HUCA* 55 (1984): 27–53.

Cohen, Stuart A. *The Three Crowns: Structures of Communal Politics in Early Rabbinic Jewry*. Cambridge: Cambridge University Press, 1990.

Colautti, Federico. M. *Passover in the Works of Josephus*. Leiden: Brill, 2002.

Collins, John J. "Historiography in the Dead Sea Scrolls." *DSD* 19 (2012): 159–76.

Daube, David. "Typology in Josephus." *JJS* 31 (1980): 18–36.

De Certeau, Michel. *The Writing of History*. Trans. Tom Conley. European Perspectives. New York: Columbia University Press, 1988.

De Jonge, Marinus. *The Testaments of the Twelve Patriarchs: A Critical Edition of the Greek Text*. PVTG, vol. 2, pt. 2. Leiden: Brill, 1978.

Derenbourg, J. *Essai sur l'histoire et la géographie de la Palestine, d'après les Thalmuds et les autres sources rabbiniques*. Paris: Impr. impériale, 1867.

Destinon, Justus von. *Die Quellen des Flavius Josephus in der Jüdische Archäologie, Buch XII–XVII*. Kiel: Lipsius, 1882.

Dimant, Devorah. "Criteria for the Identification of Qumran Sectarian Texts." In *The Qumran Scrolls and Their World*, ed. Menahem Kister, 1:49–86. Between Bible and Mishnah. Jerusalem: Yad Ben-Zvi Press, 2009 (in Hebrew).

Dimant, Devorah. *History, Ideology and Bible Interpretation in the Dead Sea Scrolls: Collected Studies*. Tübingen: Mohr Siebeck, 2014.

Dimant, Devorah. "The Qumran Manuscripts: Contents and Significance." In *Time to Prepare the Way in the Wilderness*, ed. Devorah Dimant and Lawrence H. Schiffman, 23–58. STDJ 16. Leiden: Brill, 1995.

Dinur, Benzion. "Historiographical Fragments in Talmudic Literature and Their Investigation." In *Proceedings of the Fifth World Congress of Jewish Studies, 3–11 August 1969*, 2:137–46. Jerusalem: World Union of Jewish Studies, 1972 (in Hebrew).

Draper, J. A. " 'Korah' and the Second Temple." In *Templum Amicitiae: Essays on the Second Temple Presented to Ernst Bammel*, ed. William Horbury, 74–150. JSNTSup 48. Sheffield: JSOT Press, 1991.

Drory, Rina. *The Emergence of Jewish–Arabic Literary Contacts at the Beginning of the Tenth Century*. Literature, Meaning, Culture 48. Tel Aviv: Porter Institute for Poetics & Semiotics, Tel-Aviv University, 1988 (in Hebrew).

Drüner, Hans. "Untersuchung über Josephus." Ph.D. diss., Marburg, 1896.

Edrei, Arye, and Doron Mendels. "A Split Jewish Diaspora: Its Dramatic Consequences." *JSP* 16 (2007): 91–137.

Efron, Joshua. "Bar-Kokhva in the Light of the Palestinian and Babylonian Talmudic Traditions." In *The Bar-Kokhva Revolt: A New Approach*, ed. A. Oppenheimer and U. Rappaport, 47–105. Jerusalem, 1984 (in Hebrew).

Efron, Joshua. "The Hasmonean Revolt in Modern Historiography." In *Studies on the Hasmonean Period*, 1–32. SJLA 39. Leiden: Brill, 1987.

Efron, Joshua. "Psalms of Solomon and the Hasmonean Decline." In *Studies on the Hasmonean Period*, 219–86. SJLA 39. Leiden: Brill, 1987.

Efron, Joshua. "Simeon Ben Shataḥ and Alexander Jannaeus." In *Studies on the Hasmonean Period*, 143–218. SJLA 39. Leiden: Brill, 1987.

Efron, Joshua. *Studies on the Hasmonean Period*. SJLA 39. Leiden: Brill, 1987.

Elbaum, Jacob. "Models of Storytelling and Speech in Stories about the Sages." In *Proceedings of the Seventh World Congress of Jewish Studies*, 3:71–7. Jerusalem: World Union of Jewish Studies, 1981 (in Hebrew).

Eldar, Ilan. *The Hebrew Language Tradition in Medieval Ashkenaz (ca. 950–1350 C.E.)*. 2 vols. Publications of the Hebrew University Language Traditions Project (Edah ve-lashon) 5. Jerusalem: Hebrew University Language Traditions Project, 1979 (in Hebrew).

Elitzur, Brachi. "A Historic Overview of Approval and Criticism of the Zeal of Pinhas, (from Scripture to the Rabbinic Literature)." *Netuim* 17 (2011): 9–39 (in Hebrew).

Elitzur, Yehudah. "Tefisat ha-historiyah ba-miqra." In *Israel and the Bible: Studies in Geography, History and Biblical Thought*, ed. Yoel Elitzur and Amos Frisch, 253–60. Ramat-Gan: Bar-Ilan University, 1999 (in Hebrew).

Enelow, H. G., ed. *The Mishnah of Rabbi Eliezer or The Midrash of Thirty-Two Hermeneutic Rules*. New York: Bloch Publishing Co., 1933.

Epstein, J. N. *Introduction to the Mishnaic Text*. 3rd edn. Jerusalem and Tel Aviv: Magnes and Dvir, 2000 (in Hebrew).

Eshel, Esther. "Biblical Apocrypha and Pseudepigrapha in Light of the Qumran Scrolls." In *The Qumran Scrolls and Their World*, ed. Menahem Kister, 2:573–600. Between Bible and Mishnah. Jerusalem: Yad Ben-Zvi Press, 2009 (in Hebrew).

Eshel, Esther, Hanan Eshel, and Ada Yardeni. "A Scroll from Qumran Which Includes Part of Psalm 154 and a Prayer for King Jonathan and His Kingdom." *Tarbiz* 60 (1990–1): 295–324 (in Hebrew).

Eshel, Hanan. *The Dead Sea Scrolls and the Hasmonean State*. Trans. David Louvish and Aryeh Amihay. Series of Studies on the Ancient Period of Yad Ben-Zvi Press: The David and Jemima Jeselsohn Library. Grand Rapids, Mich.: Eerdmans, 2008.

Evans, Richard J. *In Defence of History*. London: Granta, 1997.

Feldman, Ariel. *The Rewritten Joshua Scrolls from Qumran: Texts, Translations and Commentary*. Boston: de Gruyter, 2014.

Feldman, Louis H. *Josephus and Modern Scholarship (1937–1980)*. Berlin: de Gruyter, 1984.

Feldman, Louis H. "Josephus' Portrayal of the Hasmoneans Compared with 1 Maccabees." In *Josephus and the History of the Greco-Roman Period: Essays in Memory of Morton Smith*, ed. Fausto Parente and Joseph Sievers, 41–68. StPB 41. Leiden: Brill, 1994.

Feldman, Louis H. *Josephus's Interpretation of the Bible*. Hellenistic Culture and Society. Berkeley: University of California Press, 1998.

Feldman, Louis H. "The Portrayal of Phinehas by Philo, Pseudo-Philo, and Josephus." *JQR* 92 (2002): 315–45.

Feldman, Louis H. "Prophets and Prophecy in Josephus." *JTS* 41 (1990): 386–422.

Feldman, Louis H. *Studies in Josephus' Rewritten Bible*. JSJSup. Leiden: Brill, 1998.

Feldman, Louis H. "Torah and Greek Culture in Josephus." *Torah U-Madda* 7 (1997): 47–87.

Finkelstein, Louis. *The Pharisees: The Sociological Background of Their Faith*. 2 vols. 3rd edn. Philadelphia: Jewish Publication Society of America, 1966.

Fisch, Yael. "The Brazenness of the High Priests." In *Josephus and the Rabbis* by Tal Ilan and Vered Noam, 526–43. Jerualem: Yad Ben-Zvi Press, 2017 (in Hebrew).

Flusser, David. "Apocalyptic Elements in the War Scroll." In *Judaism of the Second Temple Period.* Trans. Azzan Yadin. Vol. 1: *Qumran and Apocalyptism*, 140–58. Grand Rapids, Mich.: Eerdmans, 2007.

Flusser, David. "4QMMT and the Benediction Against the Minim." In *Judaism of the Second Temple Period.* Trans. Azzan Yadin. Vol. 1: *Qumran and Apocalyptism*, 70–118. Grand Rapids, Mich.: Eerdmans, 2007.

Flusser, David. "Jewish Messianism Reflected in the Early Church." In *Judaism of the Second Temple Period.* Trans. Azzan Yadin. Vol. 2: *The Jewish Sages and Their Literature,* 258–88. Grand Rapids, Mich.: Eerdmans, 2009.

Flusser, David. *Judaism of the Second Temple Period.* Trans. Azzan Yadin. 2 vols. Grand Rapids, Mich.: Eerdmans, 2007.

Flusser, David. "Pharisees, Sadducees, and Essenes in Pesher Nahum." In *Judaism of the Second Temple Period.* Trans. Azzan Yadin. Vol. 1: *Qumran and Apocalyptism*, 214–57. Grand Rapids, Mich.: Eerdmans, 2007.

Fox, Harry. "Biography, Stories, Tall Tales: Fishing for Gullibility." *Jewish Studies* 41 (2002): 104–41.

Fox, Harry. "'The Joy of the Place of Drawing' (Simḥat Beit Ha-Shoayvah)." *Tarbiẓ* 95 (1986): 173–216 (in Hebrew).

Fraade, Steven D. "'If a Case is Too Baffling for You to Decide'...(Deut 17:8–13): Between Constraining and Expanding Judicial Autonomy in the Temple Scroll and Early Rabbinic Scriptural Interpretation." In *Sibyls Scriptures, and Scrolls: John Collins at Seventy,* ed. Joel Baden, Hindy Najman, and Eibert Tigchelaar, 1:409–31. JSJSup 175. Leiden: Brill, 2017.

Fraade, Steven D. "Looking for Legal Midrash at Qumran." In *Legal Fictions: Studies of Law and Narrative in the Discursive Worlds of Ancient Jewish Sectarians and Sages,* 169–92. JSJSup 147. Leiden: Brill, 2011.

Fraenkel, Jonah. *Darkhei ha-aggadah ve-ha-midrash.* 2 vols. Givatayim: Yad La-talmud, 1991.

Fraenkel, Jonah. "Hermeneutic Problems in the Study of the Aggadic Narrative." *Tarbiẓ* 47 (1977–8): 139–72 (in Hebrew).

Friedlaender, Israel. "The Rupture between Alexander Yannai and the Pharisees." *JQR* n.s. 4 (1913): 443–8.

Friedman, Shamma. "From Here to Eternity: The Semantic Range of עולם." *Lešonenu* 70 (2008): 77–97 (in Hebrew).

Friedman, Shamma. "La-aggadah ha-historit be-talmud ha-bavli." In *Saul Lieberman Memorial Volume,* ed. Shamma Friedman, 119–64. New York and Jerusalem: Jewish Theological Seminary of America, 1993.

Friedman, Shamma. "The Transformation of עולם." In *Sha'arei Lashon: Studies in Hebrew, Aramaic and Jewish Languages Presented to Moshe Bar-Asher,* ed. A. Maman, S. E. Fassberg, and Y. Breuer, 2:272–85. Jerusalem: Bialik Institute, 2007 (in Hebrew).

Fuks, Gideon. "Josephus and the Hasmoneans." *JJS* 41 (1990): 166–76.

Funkenstein, Amos. *Perceptions of Jewish History.* Berkeley: University of California Press, 1993.

Furstenberg, Yair. *Purity and Community in Antiquity: Traditions of the Law from Second Temple Judaism to the Mishnah.* Jerusalem: Magnes, 2016 (in Hebrew).

Gafni, Isaiah M. "Ha-ḥashmonaim be-sifrut ḥazal." In *Yemei beit ḥashmona'i: Meqorot, siqqumim, parshiyot nivḥarot ve-ḥomer ezer*, ed. David Amit and Hanan Eshel, 261–76. Idan. Jerusalem: Yad Izhak Ben-Zvi, 1995.

Gafni, Isaiah M. "Josephus and I Maccabees." In *Josephus, the Bible and History*, ed. Louis H. Feldman and Gohei Hata, 116–31. Detroit: Wayne State University Press, 1989.

Gafni, Isaiah M. "On Talmudic Historiography in the Epistle of Rav Sherira Gaon: Between Tradition and Creativity." *Zion* 73 (2008): 271–96 (in Hebrew).

Gafni, Isaiah M. "Rabbinic Historiography and Representations of the Past." In *The Cambridge Companion to the Talmud and Rabbinic Literature*, ed. Charlotte E. Fonrobert and Martin S. Jaffee, 295–312. Cambridge: Cambridge University Press, 2007.

Gafni, Isaiah M. "Research on the Second Temple, Mishna and Talmud Period: The Contribution of Shmuel Safrai." In *Jews and Judaism in the Second Temple, Mishna and Talmud Period: Studies in Honor of Shmuel Safrai*, ed. Isaiah M. Gafni, Aharon Oppenheimer, and Menahem Stern, vii–xiii. Jerusalem: Yad Izhak Ben-Zvi, 1993 (in Hebrew).

Geiger, Abraham. *Urschrift und Übersetzungen der Bibel : In ihrer Abhängigkeit von der innern Entwicklung des Judentums*. 2nd edn. Frankfurt am Main: Madda, 1928.

Geller, M. J. "Alexander Jannaeus and the Pharisee Rift." *JJS* 30 (1972): 202–11.

Ginzberg, Louis. *A Commentary on the Palestinian Talmud: A Study of the Development of the Halakah and Haggadah in Palestine and Babylonia*. Vol. 3. Texts and Studies of the Jewish Theological Seminary of America. New York: Ktav, 1971.

Ginzberg, Louis. *The Legends of the Jews*. Trans. Henrietta Szold and Paul Radin. 2nd edn. 2 vols. Philadelphia: Jewish Publication Society of America, 2003.

Ginzberg, Louis. "Some Observations on the Attitude of the Synagogue towards the Apocalyptic-Eschatological Writings." *JBL* 41 (1922): 115–36.

Goldenberg, D. "The Halakha in Josephus and in Tannaitic Literature: A Comparative Study." Ph.D. diss., Dropsie College, 1978.

Goldstein, Jonathan A. "The Hasmonean Revolt and the Hasmonean Dynasty." In *The Cambridge History of Judaism*, ed. W. D. Davies and Louis Finkelstein. Vol. 2: *The Hellenistic Age*, 292–309. Cambridge: Cambridge University Press, 1989.

Goldstein, Leon J. *Historical Knowing*. Austin: University of Texas, 1976.

Goodblatt, David. *Elements of Ancient Jewish Nationalism*. New York: Cambridge University Press, 2006.

Goodblatt, David. *The Monarchic Principle: Studies in Jewish Self-Government in Antiquity*. TSAJ 38. Tübingen: Mohr Siebeck, 1994.

Goodblatt, David. "The Place of the Pharisees in First Century Judaism: The State of the Debate." *JSJ* 20 (1989): 12–30.

Goodblatt, David. "The Union of Priesthood and Kingship in Second Temple Judea." *Cathedra* 102 (2001): 7–28 (in Hebrew).

Goodman, Martin. *State and Society in Roman Galilee, 132–212*. 2nd edn. Parkes-Wiener Series on Jewish Studies. London: Vallentine-Mitchell, 2001.

Graetz, Heinrich. *Geschichte der Juden von den ältesten Zeiten bis auf die Gegenwart*. 5th edn. Leipzig: Leiner, 1906.

Graetz, Heinrich. *History of the Jews*. Trans. Bella Löwy. 6 vols. Philadelphia: Jewish Publication Society, 1956.

Gray, Rebecca. *Prophetic Figures in Late Second Temple Jewish Palestine: The Evidence from Josephus*. New York: Oxford University Press, 1993.

Green, William S. "Palestinian Holy Men: Charismatic Leadership and Rabbinic Tradition." *ANRW* 2 (1979): 619–47.

Hadas-Lebel, Mireille. *Jerusalem against Rome*. Trans. Robyn Fréchet. Interdisciplinary Studies in Ancient Culture and Religion 7. Leuven: Peeters, 2005.

Halbertal, Moshe, and Shlomo Naeh. "Ma'ayane ha-yeshu'ah: Satirah parshanit u-teshuvat ha-minim." In *Higayon L'Yona: New Aspects in the Study of Midrash, Aggadah, and Piyut in Honor of Professor Yona Fraenkel*, ed. Joshua Levinson, Jacob Elbaum, and Galit Hasan-Rokem, 179–97. Jerusalem: Magnes.

Halbwachs, Maurice. *On Collective Memory*. Trans. Lewis A. Coser. Chicago: University of Chicago Press, 1992.

Hallewy [Halevi], Elimelech E. *Ha-aggadah ha-historit-biografit: Le'or meqorot yevaniyyim ve-latiniyyim*. Tel Aviv: Niv, 1975.

Hallewy [Halevi], Elimelech E. "Concerning the Ban on Greek Wisdom." *Tarbiẓ* 41 (1972.): 269–74 (in Hebrew).

Halevy, Isaak. *Dorot ha-rishonim*. 6 vols. Frankfurt am Main: Golde, 1918.

Heinemann, Isaac. *Darkhei ha-aggadah*. 2nd edn. Jerusalem: Magnes, 1954.

Heinemann, Joseph. *Aggadah and Its Development*. Jerusalem: Keter, 1974 (in Hebrew).

Heinemann, Joseph. *Prayer in the Talmud: Forms and Patterns*. SJ 9. Berlin: de Gruyter, 1977.

Hengel, Martin. *Judaism and Hellenism: Studies in Their Encounter in Palestine during the Early Hellenistic Period*. Trans. John Bowden. 2 vols. Philadelphia: Fortress, 1974.

Herr, Moshe D. "The Conception of History among the Sages." In *Proceedings of the Sixth World Congress of Jewish Studies, 13–19 August 1973*, 129–42. Jerusalem: World Union of Jewish Studies, 1977 (in Hebrew).

Herr, Moshe D. "Continuum in the Chain of Torah Transmission." *Zion* 44 (1979): 43–56 (in Hebrew).

Herr, Moshe D. *The History of Eretz Israel: The Roman Byzantine Period: The Mishna and Talmud Period and the Byzantine Rule (70–640)*, ed. Moshe David Herr, 5:126–226. Jerusalem: Keter and Yad Izhak Ben-Zvi, 1985 (in Hebrew).

Hezser, Catherine. "The (In)significance of Jerusalem in the Talmud Yerushalmi." In *The Talmud Yerushalmi and Graeco-Roman Culture*, ed. Peter Schäfer and C. Hezser, 2:4–11. TSAJ 71, 79, 93. Tübingen, Mohr Siebeck, 2000.

Himmelfarb, Gertrude. "Telling It As You Like It: Postmodernist History and the Flight from Fact." In *The Postmodern History Reader*, ed. Keith Jenkins, 158–74. Routledge Readers in History. London: Routledge, 1997.

Himmelfarb, Martha. "Levi, Phinehas and the Problem of Intermarriage at the Time of the Maccabean Revolt." *JSQ* 6 (1999): 1–24.

Hirshman, Marc. *Torah for the Entire World*. Hellel ben-Hayyim. Tel Aviv: Hakibbutz Hameuchad, 1999 (in Hebrew).

Hollander, H. W., and Marinus de Jonge. *The Testaments of the Twelve Patriarchs: A Commentary*. SVTP 8. Leiden: Brill, 1985.

Hölscher, Gustav. "Josephus." *RE* 18 (1916): 1934–2000.

Hölscher, Gustav. *Die Quellen des Josephus für die Zeit vom Exil bis zum jüdischen Kriege*. Leiden: Teubner, 1904.

Honigman, Sylvie. *Tales of High Priests and Taxes: The Books of the Maccabees and the Judean Rebellion against Antiochos IV*. Oakland: University of California Press, 2014.

Horgan, Maurya P. *Pesharim: Qumran Interpretations of Biblical Books*. Washington, DC: Catholic Association of America, 1979.

Hurwitz, A. "Was QH a 'Spoken' Language? On Some Recent Views and Positions: Comments." In *Diggers at the Well: Proceedings of a Third International Symposium on the Hebrew of the Dead Sea Scrolls and Ben Sira*, ed. T. Muraoka and J. F. Elwolde, 110–14. STDJ 36. Leiden: Brill, 2000.

Ilan, Tal. "Ben Sira's Attitude to Women and Its Reception by the Babylonian Talmud." *Jewish Studies* 40 (2000): 103–11 (in Hebrew).

Ilan, Tal. "Herod's Deeds." In *Josephus and the Rabbis* by Tal Ilan and Vered Noam, 373–408. Jerusalem: Yad Ben-Zvi Press, 2017 (in Hebrew).

Ilan, Tal. *Integrating Women into Second Temple History*. TSAJ 76. Tübingen: Mohr Siebeck, 1999.

Ilan, Tal. "Jannaeus's Deathbed Instructions." In *Josephus and the Rabbis* by Tal Ilan and Vered Noam, 308–17. Jerusalem: Yad Ben-Zvi Press, 2017 (in Hebrew).

Ilan, Tal. "King David, King Herod and Nicolaus of Damascus." *JSQ* 5 (1998): 195–240.

Ilan, Tal. "King Jannaeus in the Babylonian Talmud." Appendix 2 to "The Rift with the Pharisees." In *Josephus and the Rabbis* by Tal Ilan and Vered Noam, 289–91. Jerusalem: Yad Ben-Zvi Press, 2017 (in Hebrew).

Ilan, Tal. *Massekhet Ta'anit: Text, Translation, and Commentary. A Feminist Commentary on the Babylonian Talmud*. Tübingen: Mohr Siebeck, 2008.

Ilan, Tal. "The Names of the Hasmoneans in the Second Temple Period." *Eretz-Israel* 19 (1987): 238–41 (in Hebrew).

Ilan, Tal. *Silencing the Queen: The Literary Histories of Shelamzion and Other Jewish Women*. TSAJ 115. Tübingen: Mohr Siebeck, 2006.

Ilan, Tal. "Titus's War Council." In *Josephus and the Rabbis* by Tal Ilan and Vered Noam, 731–40. Jerusalem: Yad Ben-Zvi Press, 2017 (in Hebrew).

Ilan, Tal. "The Trial of Herod/Jannaeus." In *Josephus and the Rabbis* by Tal Ilan and Vered Noam, 349–72. Jerusalem: Yad Ben-Zvi Press, 2017 (in Hebrew).

Ilan, Tal, and Vered Noam, in collaboration with Meir Ben Shahar, Daphne Baratz, and Yael Fisch. *Josephus and the Rabbis*. Jerusalem: Yad Ben-Zvi Press, 2017 (in Hebrew).

Ilan, Tal, and Vered Noam. "The Plot and Death of Herod/Jannaeus." In *Josephus and the Rabbis* by Tal Ilan and Vered Noam, 429–50. Jerusalem: Yad Ben-Zvi Press, 2017 (in Hebrew).

Ilan, Tal, and Vered Noam. "Remnants of a Pharisaic Apologetic Source in Josephus and in the Babylonian Talmud." In *Tradition, Transmission, and Transformation: From Second Temple Literature through Judaism and Christianity in Late Antiquity*, ed. Menahem Kister, Hillel Newman, Michael Segal, and Ruth A. Clements, 112–33. STDJ 113. Leiden: Brill, 2014.

Irshai, Oded. "The Priesthood in Jewish Society of Late Antiquity." In *Continuity and Renewal: Jews and Judaism in Byzantine-Christian Palestine*, ed. Lee I. Levine, 67–106. Jerusalem: Dinur Center, 2004 (in Hebrew).

Jawitz, Wolf. *Sefer toledot yisrael*. 4 vols. New edn. Tel Aviv: Am Olam, 1963.

Joosten, Jan. "Pseudo-Classicisms in Late Biblical Hebrew, in Ben Sira, and in Qumran Hebrew." In *Sirach, Scrolls, and Sages: Proceedings of a Second International Symposium on the Hebrew of the Dead Sea Scrolls, Ben Sira, and the Mishnah, Held at Leiden University, 15–17 December 1997*, ed. T. Muraoka and J. F. Elwolde, 146–59. STDJ 33. Leiden: Brill, 1999.

Kalmin, Richard. *Jewish Babylonia between Persia and Roman Palestine*. Oxford: Oxford University Press, 2006.

Kalmin, Richard. "Portrayals of Kings in Rabbinic Literature of Late Antiquity." *JSQ* 3 (1996): 320–41.

Kalmin, Richard. *The Sage in Jewish Society of Late Antiquity*. London: Routledge, 1999.

Kaufman, Asher S. *The Temple Mount: Where Is the Holy of Holies?* The Temple of Jerusalem. Jerusalem: Har Yera'eh Press, 2004.

Kimelman, Reuven. "Blessing Formulae and Divine Sovereignty in Rabbinic Liturgy." In *Liturgy in the Life of the Synagoguge: Studies in the History of Jewish Prayer*, ed. Ruth Langer and Steven Fine, 1–39. Duke Judaic Studies Series 2. Winona Lake, Ind.: Eisenbrauns, 2005.

Kister, Menahem. "Additions to the Article 'בשולי ספר בן-סירא'." *Lešonenu* 53 (1989): 36–53 (in Hebrew).

Kister, Menahem. "Aḥor va-qedem: Aggadot ve-darkhei midrash be-sifrut ha-ḥitsonit u-ve-sifrut ḥazal." In *Higayon L'Yona: New Aspects in the Study of Midrash, Aggadah, and Piyut in Honor of Professor Yona Fraenkel*, ed. Joshua Levinson, Jacob Elbaum, and Galit Hasan-Rokem, 231–59. Jerusalem: Magnes, 2006 (in Hebrew).

Kister, Menahem. "Biblical Phrases and Hidden Biblical Interpretations and Pesharim." In *The Dead Sea Scrolls: Forty Years of Research*, ed. Devorah Dimant and Uriel Rappaport, 27–39. STDJ 10. Leiden/Jerusalem: Brill/Magnes, 1992.

Kister, Menahem. "Legends of the Destruction of the Second Temple in Avot De-Rabbi Nathan." *Tarbiz* 67 (1998): 483–529 (in Hebrew).

Kister, Menahem. "Marginalia Qumranica." *Tarbiz* 57 (1987–8): 315–25 (in Hebrew).

Kister, Menahem. "Metamorphoses of Aggadic Traditions." *Tarbiz* 60 (1990–1): 179–224 (in Hebrew).

Kister, Menahem. "Notes on the Book of Ben-Sira." *Lešonenu* 47 (1983): 125–46 (in Hebrew).

Kister, Menahem. "The Scholia on Megillat Ta'anit." *Tarbiz* 74 (2005): 451–77 (in Hebrew).

Kister, Menahem. "Studies in 4QMiqsat Ma'ase Ha-Torah and Related Texts: Law, Theology, Language and Calendar." *Tarbiz* 68 (1999): 317–71 (in Hebrew).

Kister, Menahem, ed. *The Qumran Scrolls and Their World*. Between Bible and Mishnah. Jerusalem: Yad Ben-Zvi Press, 2009 (in Hebrew).

Klausner, Joseph. *Historiyah shel ha-bayit ha-sheni*. 5 vols. 3rd edn. Jerusalem: Ahiasaf, 1952.

Klawans, Jonathan. *Josephus and the Theologies of Ancient Judaism*. New York: Oxford University Press, 2012.

Knohl, Israel. "Axial Transformations within Ancient Israelite Priesthood." In *Axial Civilizations and World History*, ed. J. P. Arnason et al., 201–24. Leiden: Brill, 2005.

Koller, Aaron J. *Esther in Ancient Jewish Thought*. Cambridge: Cambridge University Press, 2014.

Krochmal, Abraham b. R. Nachman. *Commentaries and Notes on the Babylonian Talmud*. Facsmile of the Lemberg 1881 edition. Jerusalem: Makor, 1978 (in Hebrew).

Kugel, James. "How Old Is the Aramaic Levi Document?" *DSD* 14 (2007): 291–312.

Kutscher, Eduard Yechezkel. *Hebrew and Aramaic Studies*. Edited by Ze'ev Ben-Hayyim, Aharon Dotan, Gad Sarfatti, and with the assistance of Moshe Bar-Asher. Jerusalem: Magnes, 1977 (in Hebrew).

Kutscher, Eduard Yechezkel. *The Language and Linguistic Background of the Isaiah Scroll (1Q Isaᵃ)*. STDJ 6. Leiden: Brill, 1974.

Labendz, Jenny R. "The Book of Ben Sira in Rabbinic Literature." *AJS Review* 30 (2006): 347–92.

Lapin, H. *Rabbis as Romans: The Rabbinic Movement in Palestine, 100–400 CE*. New York: Oxford University Press, 2012.

Laqueur, Richard. *Der jüdische Historiker Flavius Josephus: Ein biographischer versuch auf neuer quellenkritischer Grundlage*. 2nd edn. Darmstadt: Wissenschaftliche Buchgesellschaft, 1970.

Leibner, Uzi. "The 23rd Day of Heshvan in Megillat Ta'anit." *Tarbiẓ* 71 (2002): 5–17 (in Hebrew).

Lévi, Israël. "Les sources talmudiques de l'histoire juive." *REJ* 35 (1897): 218–35.

Levine, Lee I. "Josephus' Description of the Jerusalem Temple: *War, Antiquities*, and Other Sources." In *Josephus and the History of the Greco-Roman Period: Essays in Memory of Morton Smith*, ed. Fausto Parente and Joseph Sievers, 233–46. StPB 41. Leiden: Brill, 1994.

Levine, Lee I. *Judaism and Hellenism in Antiquity: Conflict or Confluence?* Samuel and Althea Stroum Lectures in Jewish Studies. Seattle and London: University of Washington Press, 1998.

Levine, Lee I. "The Political Struggle between Pharisees and Sadducees in the Hasmonean Period." In *Jerusalem in the Second Temple Period: Abraham Schalit Memorial Volume*, 61–83. Jerusalem: Yad Ben-Zvi Press, 1980 (in Hebrew).

Levine, Lee I. *The Rabbinic Class of Roman Palestine in Late Antiquity*. Jerusalem: Yad Izhak Ben-Zvi, 1989.

Liddell, H. G., R. Scott, and H. S. Jones. *A Greek–English Lexicon*. 9th edn. Oxford: Clarendon, 1996.

Lieberman, Saul. *Greek in Jewish Palestine: Studies in the Life and Manners of Jewish Palestine in the II–IV Centuries C.E.* 2nd edn. New York: Feldheim, 1965.

Lieberman, Saul. *Hellenism in Jewish Palestine: Studies in the Literary Transmission, Beliefs and Manners of Palestine in the I Century B.C.E.–IV Century C.E.* 2nd edn. Texts and Studies of the Jewish Theological Seminary of America. New York: Jewish Theological Seminary of America, 1962.

Lieberman, Saul. *Studies in Palestinian Talmudic Literature*. Ed. David Rosenthal. Jerusalem: Magnes, 1991 (in Hebrew).

Lieberman, Saul. *Tosefta Ki-fshutah: A Comprehensive Commentary on the Tosefta*. 8 vols. 2nd ed. New York and Jerusalem: Jewish Theological Seminary of America, 1955–98 (in Hebrew).

Lim, Timothy H. "Kittim." In *Encyclopedia of the Dead Sea Scrolls*, ed. Lawrence H. Schiffman and James C. VanderKam, 1:469–71. New York: Oxford University Press, 2000.

Luria, Benzion. *Mi-yannai ad hordus: Meḥqarim be-toledot bayit sheni.* Jerusalem: Ha-ḥevrah le-ḥeqer ha-miqra bi-yisrael, 1974.

Mader, Gottfried. *Josephus and the Politics of Historiography: Apologetic and Impression Management in the Bellum Judaicum.* Mnemosyne. Supplementum 205. Leiden: Brill, 2000.

Main, Emmanuelle. "Les Sadducéens et l'origine des partis juifs de la période du Second Temple." Ph.D. diss., Hebrew University, 2004.

Main, Emmanuelle. "Les Sadducéens vus par Flavius Josèphe." *RB* 102 (1990): 190–202.

Marcus, Ralph, trans. *Jewish Antiquities*, vols. 5–8. Loeb Classical Library. Cambridge, Mass. and London: Harvard University Press and William Heinemann, 1998.

Mason, Steve. "Contradiction or Counterpoint? Josephus and Historical Method." *Review of Rabbinic Judaism* 6 (2003): 145–88.

Mason, Steve. *Flavius Josephus on the Pharisees: A Composition-Critical Study.* StPB 39. Leiden: Brill, 1991.

Mason, Steve. "Introduction to the *Judean Antiquities*." In *Flavius Josephus: Translation and Commentary*, ed. Steve Mason. Vol. 3: *Judean Antiquities 1–4*. Leiden: Brill, 2000.

Mason, Steve. "Was Josephus a Pharisee? A Re-Examination of Life 10–12." *JJS* 40 (1989): 12–30.

Meir, Ofra. "The Acting Characters in the Stories of the Talmud and the Midrash (A Sample)." Ph.D. diss. Hebrew University, 1977 (in Hebrew).

Meshorer, Ya'akov. *Jewish Coins of the Second Temple Period.* Trans. I. H. Levine. Tel Aviv: Am Hassefer, 1967.

Meshorer, Ya'akov. *A Treasury of Jewish Coins: From the Persian Period to Bar Kokhba.* Jerusalem: Yad Ben-Zvi Press, 2001.

Milikowsky, Chaim. "'Seder 'Olam' and Jewish Chronography in the Hellenistic and Roman Periods." *PAAJR* 52 (1985): 115–39.

Milikowsky, Chaim. *Seder Olam: Critical Edition, Commentary, and Introduction.* 2 vols. Jerusalem: Yad Ben-Zvi Press, 2013 (in Hebrew).

Milikowsky, Chaim. "The 'Status Quaestionis' of Research in Rabbinic Literature." *JJS* 39 (1988): 201–11.

Miron, Guy. "Memory, Historiography and What Lies Between Them: Three Decades Since Zakhor." *Zion* 78 (2013): 107–21 (in Hebrew).

Muraoka, T. "Hebrew." *Encyclopedia of the Dead Sea Scrolls*, 1:344. Oxford: Oxford University Press, 2000.

Nakman, David. "The Halakhah in the Writings of Josephus." Ph.D. diss., Bar-Ilan University, 2004 (in Hebrew).

Neusner, Jacob. *From Politics to Piety: The Emergence of Pharisaic Judaism.* Englewood Cliffs, N.J.: Prentice-Hall, 1973.

Neusner, Jacob. "Josephus' Pharisees: A Complete Repertoire." In *Josephus, Judaism, and Christianity*, ed. Louis H. Feldman and Gohei Hata, 274–92. Detroit: Wayne State University Press, 1987.

Neusner, Jacob. *The Rabbinic Traditions about the Pharisees before 70*. 3 vols. Leiden: Brill, 1971.

Noam, Vered. "Agrippa/Jannaeus and the Nazirites' Offerings." In *Josephus and the Rabbis* by Tal Ilan and Vered Noam, 493–507. Jerusalem: Yad Ben-Zvi Press, 2017 (in Hebrew).

Noam, Vered. "Did the Rabbis Cause the Hasmoneans to Be Forgotten? A Reconsideration." *Zion* 81 (2016): 295-333 (in Hebrew).

Noam, Vered. "In the Wake of the New Leaf of Megillat Ta'anit and Its Scholion." *Tarbiz* 77 (2007–2008): 411–24 (in Hebrew).

Noam, Vered. "Introduction." In *Josephus and the Rabbis* by Tal Ilan and Vered Noam, 1–90. Jerusalem: Yad Ben-Zvi Press, 2017 (in Hebrew).

Noam, Vered. "Josephus and Early Halakhah: The Exclusion of Impure Persons from Holy Precincts." In *"Go Out and Study the Land" (Judges 18:2): Archaeological, Historical and Textual Studies in Honor of Hanan Eshel*, ed. Aren M. Maeir, Jodi Magness, and Lawrence H. Schiffman, 133–46. JSJSup 148. Leiden: Brill, 2012.

Noam, Vered. "Lost Historical Traditions: Between Josephus and the Rabbis." In *Sibyls, Scriptures, and Scrolls: John Collins at Seventy*, ed. Joel Baden, Hindy Najman, and Eibert Tigchelaar, 2:991–1017. JSJSup 175. Leiden: Brill, 2017.

Noam, Vered. "Megillat Taanit: The Scroll of Fasting." In *The Literature of the Sages Second Part: Midrash and Targum, Liturgy, Poetry, Mysticism, Contracts, Inscriptions, Ancient Science and the Languages of Rabbinic Literature*, ed. Samuel Safrai, Zeev Safrai, Joshua Schwartz, and Peter J. Tomson, 2:339–62. CRINT. Assen: Royal Van Gorcum and Fortress, 2006.

Noam, Vered. *Megillat Ta'anit: Versions, Interpretation, History with a Critical Edition*. Between Bible and Mishnah: The David and Jemima Jeselsohn Library. Jerusalem: Yad Ben-Zvi Press, 2003 (in Hebrew).

Noam, Vered. "The Miracle of the Cruse of Oil: The Metamorphosis of a Legend." *HUCA* 73 (2002): 191–226.

Noam, Vered. "The Rift with the Pharisees." In *Josephus and the Rabbis* by Tal Ilan and Vered Noam, 255–85. Jerusalem: Yad Ben-Zvi Press, 2017 (in Hebrew).

Noam, Vered. "A Statue in the Temple." In *Josephus and the Rabbis* by Tal Ilan and Vered Noam, 454–86. Jerusalem: Yad Ben-Zvi Press, 2017 (in Hebrew).

Noam, Vered. "The Story of King Jannaeus (*b. Qiddušin* 66a): A Pharisaic Reply to Sectarian Polemic." *HTR* 107 (2014): 31–58.

Noam, Vered. "Why Did the Heavenly Voice Speak Aramaic? Ancient Layers in Rabbinic literature." In *The Faces of Torah: Studies in the Texts and Contexts of Ancient Judaism in Honor of Steven Fraade*, ed. Michal Bar-Asher Siegal, Tzvi Novick, and Christine Hayes, 157-68. JAJSup 22. Göttingen: Vandenhoeck and Ruprecht, 2017.

Noam, Vered. "'Will this one never be brought down?': Reflections of Jewish Hopes for the Downfall of the Roman Empire in Biblical Exegesis." In *The Future of Rome: Concepts of Historical Time under the Roman Empire*, ed. Jonathan J. Price and K. Berthelot. Forthcoming.

Nora, Pierre, *Realms of Memory: Rethinking the French Past*. 3 vols. Ed. Lawrence D. Kritzman. Trans. Arthur Goldhammer. New York: Columbia University Press, 1996.

Olick, Jeffrey K., and Joyce Robbins. "Social Memory Studies: From 'Collective Memory' to the Historical Sociology of Mnemonic Practices." *Annual Review of Sociology* 24 (1998): 105–40. <http://www.jstor.org/stable/223476>.

Orian, Matan. "Hyrcanus II versus Aristobulus II and the Inviolability of Jerusalem." *JSQ* 22 (2015): 205–42.

Petersen, Hans. "Real and Alleged Literary Projects of Josephus." *AJP* 79 (1958): 247–59.

Porter, James I. "Reception Studies: Future Prospects." In *A Companion to Classical Receptions*, ed. Lorna Hardwick and Christopher Stray, 469–81. Oxford: Blackwell, 2007.

Price, Jonathan. "Introduction." In *Yosef Ben Matityahu, History of the Jewish War against the Romans*, trans. Lisa Ullman, 21–79. Jerusalem: Carmel, 2009 (in Hebrew).

Qimron, Elisha. "Concerning 'Joshua Cycles' from Qumran." *Tarbiẓ* 53 (1994): 503–8 (in Hebrew).

Qimron, Elisha. "The Nature of DSS Hebrew and Its Relation to BH and MH." In *Diggers at the Well: Proceedings of a Third International Symposium on the Hebrew of the Dead Sea Scrolls and Ben Sira*, ed. T. Muraoka and J. F. Elwolde, 232–44. STDJ 36. Leiden: Brill, 2000.

Qimron, Elisha. "Observations on the History of Early Hebrew (1000 B.C.E.–200 C.E.) in the Light of the Dead Sea Documents." In *The Dead Sea Scrolls: Forty Years of Research*, ed. Devorah Dimant and Uriel Rappaport, 349–61. STDJ 10. Leiden: Brill, 1992.

Qimron, Elisha. "עמות and Its Kindred Forms." *Lešonenu* 67 (2004): 21–6 (in Hebrew).

Rabin, Chaim. "Alexander Jannaeus and the Pharisees." *JJS* 7 (1956): 3–11.

Rabin, Chaim. "Hebrew and Aramaic in the First Century." In *The Jewish People in the First Century: Historical Geography, Political History, Social, Cultural and Religious Life and Institutions*, ed. S. Safrai and M. Stern, 2:1007–39. CRINT. Philadelphia: Fortress, 1976.

Rabin, Chaim. "The Historical Background of Qumran Hebrew." *Scripta Hierosolymitana* 4 (1958): 144–61.

Rabinowitz, Zvi M. *Halakha and Aggada in the Liturgical Poetry of Yannai*. Tel Aviv: Kohut Foundation, 1965 (in Hebrew).

Rajak, Tessa. *Josephus: The Historian and His Society*. Classical Life and Letters. London: Duckworth, 1983.

Rappaport, Solomon. *Agada und Exegese bei Flavius Josephus*. Veröffentlichungen der Oberrabbiner Dr. H. P. Chajes-Preisstiftung an der Israelitisch-Theologischen Lehranstalt in Wien. Vienna: Alexander Kohut Memorial Foundation, 1930.

Rappaport, Uriel. *The House of the Hasmoneans: The People of Israel in the Land of Israel in the Hasmonean Period*. Series of Studies on the Ancient Period/The David Jemima Jeselsohn Library. Jerusalem: Yad Izhak Ben-Zvi, 2013 (in Hebrew).

Rappel, D. "Hokhmat Yevanit: Rhetoric?" *Jerusalem Studies in Jewish Thought* 3 (1983): 317–22 (in Hebrew).

Raveh, Inbar. *Fragments of Being: Stories of the Sages—Literary Structure and World View*. Or Yehuda: Kinneret, Zmora-Bitan, Dvir, 2008 (in Hebrew).

Reeg, Gottfried. *Die Ortsnamen Israels nach der rabbinischen Literatur*. Beihefte zum Tübinger Atlas des vorderen Orients. Wiesbaden: L. Reichert, 1989.

Regev, Eyal. *The Hasmoneans: Ideology, Archaeology, Identity*. Journal of Ancient Judaism Supplement Series 10. Göttingen: Vandenhoeck und Ruprecht, 2013.

Regev, Eyal. "The Hasmoneans' Self Image as Religious Leaders." *Zion* 77 (2012): 5–30 (in Hebrew).

Regev, Eyal. *The Sadducees and Their Halakhah*. Jerusalem: Yad Ben-Zvi Press, 2005 (in Hebrew).

Rendsburg, Gary A. "The Galilean Background of Mishnaic Hebrew." In *The Galilee in Late Antiquity*, ed. Lee I. Levine, 225–40. New York: Jewish Theological Seminary of America, 1992.

Rivkin, Ellis. "Defining the Pharisees: The Tannaitic Sources." *HUCA* 40–1 (1970): 205–49.

Rofé, Alexander. "The Beginnings of Sects in Postexilic Judaism." *Cathedra* 49 (1988): 13–22 (in Hebrew).

Rokeah, David. *Jews, Pagans and Christians in Conflict*. StPB 33. Jerusalem/Leiden: Magnes/Brill, 1982.

Rokeah, David. "The War of Kitos: Towards the Clarification of a Philological-Historical Problem." *Scripta Hierosolymitana* 23 (1972): 79–84.

Rosenblum, Jordan. "'Why Do You Refuse to Eat Pork?': Jews, Food, and Identity in Roman Palestine." *JQR* 100 (2010): 95–110.

Rosenthal, Eliezer Shimshon. "Ha-moreh." *PAAJR* 31 (1963): 1*–71* (in Hebrew).

Rosenthal, Yoav. "A Newly Discovered Leaf of Megillat Ta'anit and Its Scholion." *Tarbiz* 77 (2007–8): 357–410 (in Hebrew).

Rosen-Zvi, Ishay. "Bodies and Temple: The List of Priestly Bodily Defects in Mishnah Bekhorot, Chapter 7." *Jewish Studies* 43 (2005): 49–87 (in Hebrew).

Rosen-Zvi, Ishay. *The Mishnaic Sotah Ritual: Temple, Gender and Midrash*. Trans. Orr Scharf. JSJSup 160. Leiden: Brill, 2012.

Rubenstein, Jeffrey L. *The History of Sukkot during the Second Temple and Rabbinic Periods*. BJS 302. Atlanta, Ga.: Scholars Press, 1995.

Rubenstein, Jeffrey L. "King Herod in Ardashir's Court: The Rabbinic Story of Herod (B. Bava Batra 3B-4A) in Light of Persian Sources." *AJS Review* 38 (2014): 249–74.

Rubenstein, Jeffrey L. *Rabbinic Stories*. The Classics of Western Spirituality. New York: Paulist Press, 2002.

Rubenstein, Jeffrey L. "The Sadducees and the Water Libation." *JQR* 84 (1994): 417–44.

Safrai, Shmuel. *In Times of Temple and Mishnah: Studies in Jewish History*. 2 vols. Jerusalem: Magnes, 1994 (in Hebrew).

Safrai, Shmuel. *Pilgrimage at the Time of the Second Temple*. 2nd edn. Jerusalem: Akademon, 1985 (in Hebrew).

Samet, Nili. "New Light on the Administrative Term *ben bayit* in Biblical and Rabbinical Sources." *Tarbiz* 84 (2016): 283–93 (in Hebrew).

Sarfatti, Gad B. "The Inscriptions of the Biblical Period and Mishnaic Hebrew." *Language Studies* 5–6 (1992): 41–65 (in Hebrew).

Sarfatti, Gad B. "Pious Men, Men of Deeds, and the Early Prophets." *Tarbiz* 26 (1957): 126–53 (in Hebrew).

Schäfer, Peter. *The History of the Jews in the Greco-Roman World*. Trans. David Chowcat. London and New York: Routledge, 2003.

Schäfer, Peter. *Jesus in the Talmud*. Princeton: Princeton University Press, 2007.

Schäfer, Peter. "Research into Rabbinic Literature: An Attempt to Define the 'Status Quaestionis.'" *JJS* 37 (1986): 139–52.

Schäfer, Peter. "Der Vorrabbinische Pharisäismus." In *Paulus und das Antike Judentum: Tübingen-Durham-Symposium in Gedenken an Den 50. Todestag Adolf Schlatters (Mai 1938)*, ed. Martin Hengel and Ulrich Heckel, 125–75. WUNT 58. Tübingen: J. C. B. Mohr, 1988.

Schalit, Abraham. "Domestic Politics and Political Institutions." In *The Hellenistic Age: Political History of Jewish Palestine from 332 B.C.E. to 67 B.C.E.*, vol. 6 of *The World History of the Jewish People*, ed. Abraham Schalit, 253–97. London: W. H. Allen, 1972.

Schiffman, Lawrence H. *Sectarian Law in the Dead Sea Scrolls: Courts, Testimony and the Penal Code*. BJS 33. Chico, Calif.: Scholars Press, 1983.

Schremer, Adiel. "The Name of the Boethusians: A Reconsideration of Suggested Explanations and Another One." *JJS* 48 (1997): 290–9.

Schremer, Adiel. "The Religious Orientation of Non-Rabbis in Second-Century Palestine." In *"Follow the Wise": Studies in Jewish History and Culture in Honor of Lee I. Levine*, ed. Zeev Weiss, Oded Irshai, Jodi Magness, and Seth Schwartz, 319–41. Winona Lake, Ind.: Eisenbrauns, 2010.

Schürer, Emil. *The History of the Jewish People in the Age of Jesus Christ (175 B.C.–A.D. 135)*. 3 vols. New English version revised and edited by Geza Vermes and Fergus Millar. Edinburgh: T. & T. Clark, 1973–87.

Schwartz, Barry. "Collective Memory and History: How Abraham Lincoln Became a Symbol of Racial Equality." *The Sociological Quarterly* 38 (1997): 469–96. <http://www.jstor.org/stable/pdfplus/4121155.pdf?acceptTC=true>.

Schwartz, Daniel R. "Composition and Sources in *Antiquities* 18: The Case of Pontius Pilate." In *Making History: Josephus and Historical Method*, ed. Zuleika Rodgers, 125–46. JSJSup 110. Leiden: Brill, 2007.

Schwartz, Daniel R. *Flavius Josephus, Vita: Introduction, Hebrew Translation, and Commentary*. Between Bible and Mishnah: The David and Jemima Jeselsohn Library. Jerusalem: Yad Ben-Zvi Press, 2007 (in Hebrew).

Schwartz, Daniel R. "From Alexandria to Rabbinic Literature to Zion: The Jews' Departure from History, and Who It Is Who Returns to It?" In *Zionism and the Return to History: A Reappraisal*, ed. S. N. Eisenstadt and Moshe Lissak, 40–55. Jerusalem: Yad Ben-Zvi Press, 1999 (in Hebrew).

Schwartz, Daniel R. "From Priests at Their Right to Christians at Their Left? On the Interpretation and Development of a Mishnaic Story (m. Rosh HaShanah 2:8–9)." *Tarbiz* 74 (2005): 21–41 (in Hebrew).

Schwartz, Daniel R. "Introduction: Was 70 CE a Watershed in Jewish History? Three Stages of Modern Scholarship, and a Renewed Effort." In *Was 70 CE a Watershed in Jewish History? On Jews and Judaism Before and After the Destruction of the Second Temple*, ed. Daniel R. Schwartz, Zeev Weiss, and in collaboration with Ruth Clements, 1–19. Ancient Judaism and Early Christianity 78. Leiden and Boston: Brill, 2012.

Schwartz, Daniel R. "Josephus and Nicolaus on the Pharisees." *JSJ* 14 (1983): 157–71.

Schwartz, Daniel R. "Josephus, Catullus, Divine Providence, and the Date of the Judean War." In *Flavius Josephus: Interpretation and History*, ed. Jack Pastor, Pnina Stern, and Menahem Mor, 331–52. JSJSup 146. Leiden: Brill, 2011.

Schwartz, Daniel R. "Josephus on Albinus: The Eve of Catastrophe in Changing Retrospect." In *The Jewish Revolt against Rome: Interdisciplinary Perspectives*, ed. Mladen Popovic, 291–309. JSJSup 154. Leiden: Brill, 2011.

Schwartz, Daniel R. "Josephus on Hyrcanus II." In *Josephus and the History of the Greco-Roman Period: Essays in Memory of Morton Smith*, ed. Fausto Parente and Joseph Sievers, 210–32. StPB 41. Leiden: Brill, 1994.

Schwartz, Daniel R. "Josephus on the Pharisees as Diaspora Jews." In *Josephus und das Neue Testament*, ed. Christfried Boettrich, Jens Herzer, and Torsten Reiprich, 137–46. WUNT 209. Tubingen: Mohr Siebeck, 2007.

Schwartz, Daniel R. "Κατὰ τοῦτον τὸν καιρόν: Josephus' Source on Agrippa II." *JQR* 72 (1982): 241–68.

Schwartz, Daniel R. " 'Kingdom of Priests': A Pharisaic Slogan." In *Studies in the Jewish Background of Christianity*, 57–80. WUNT 60. Tubingen: J. C. B. Mohr, 1992.

Schwartz, Daniel R. "Law and Truth: On Qumran-Sadducean and Rabbinic Views of Law." In *The Dead Sea Scrolls: Forty Years of Research*, ed. Devorah Dimant and Uriel Rappaport, 229–40. STDJ 10. Leiden: Brill, 1992.

Schwartz, Daniel R. "Mah beyn maqqabim aleph u-maqqabim bet, o: ha-maqaf ha-me'atger she-be-ṣerufim kegon 'mamlakhti-dati', dati-leumi' ve-ṣiyoni-dati." In *Ha-moreshet ha-yehudit be-olam ḥinukhi mishtaneh: Sugyot be-histalmuyot morim*, ed. Miriam Barlev. Vol. 10:11–20. Jerusalem: Misrad Hahinukh and the Hebrew University, 2005.

Schwartz, Daniel R. "On Pharisaic Opposition to the Hasmonean Dynasty." In *Studies in the Jewish Background of Christianity*, 44–56. WUNT 60. Tubingen: J. C. B. Mohr, 1992.

Schwartz, Daniel R. "On the Question of the Opposition of the Pharisees to the Hasmonean Dynasty." In *The History of the Hasmonean State against the Background of the Hellenistic Era*, ed. Uriel Rappaport and Israel Ronen, 442–53. Jerusalem and Tel Aviv: Yad Izhak Ben-Zvi and the Open University, 1993 (in Hebrew).

Schwartz, Daniel R. *Reading the First Century: On Reading Josephus and Studying Jewish History of the First Century*. WUNT 300. Tübingen: Mohr Siebeck, 2013.

Schwartz, Daniel R. "Remembering the Second Temple Period: Josephus and the Rabbis, Apologetics and Rabbinical Training." In *Erinnerung als Herkunft der Zukunft: Zum Jubiläumssymposium des Instituts für Jüdisch-Christliche Forschung an der Universität Luzern (17.–19. September 2006)*, ed. Verena Lenzen, 63–83. Judaica et Christiana 22. Bern: P. Lang, 2008.

Schwartz, Daniel R. "Sources and Composition: Josephus' Account of the Clash between Samaritans and Galileans in the Days of Cumanus." *Te'uda* 25 (2012): 125–46 (in Hebrew).

Schwartz, Joshua. "Once More on the Nicanor Gate." *HUCA* 62 (1991): 245–83.

Schwartz, Seth. *Imperialism and Jewish Society, 200 B.C.E. to 640 C.E.* Jews, Christians, and Muslims from the Ancient to the Modern World. Princeton: Princeton University Press, 2001.

Schwartz, Seth. *Josephus and Judaean Politics*. Columbia Studies in the Classical Tradition 18. Leiden: Brill, 1990.

Scott, James M. "Korah and Qumran." In *The Bible at Qumran: Text, Shape, and Interpretation*, ed. Peter W. Flint and with the assistance of Tae Hun Kim, 182–202. Studies in the Dead Sea Scrolls and Related Literature. Grand Rapids, Mich.: Eerdmans, 2001.

Seeman, Chris. *Rome and Judea in Transition: Hasmonean Relations with the Roman Republic and the Evolution of the High Priesthood*. New York: Peter Lang, 2013.

Segal, Moses H. [Moshe Zvi]. "The Descent of the Messianic King in the Testaments of the Twelve Patriarchs." *Tarbiẓ* 21 (1950): 129–36 (in Hebrew).

Segal, Moses H. [Moshe Zvi]. *Dikduk leshon ha-mishnah*. Tel Aviv: Dvir, 1936.

Segal, Moses H. [Moshe Zvi]. *A Grammar of Mishnaic Hebrew*. Oxford: Clarendon, 1927.

Shahar, Yuval. "*Har Hamelekh*: A New Solution to an Old Puzzle." *Zion* 65 (2000): 275–306 (in Hebrew).

Sharon, Nadav. "The Kittim and the Roman Conquest in the Qumran Scrolls." *Meghillot* 11 (2016): 357–88 (in Hebrew).

Shatzman, Israel. "The Hasmoneans in Greco-Roman Historiography." *Zion* 57 (1992): 5–64 (in Hebrew).

Shemesh, Aharon. *Halakhah in the Making: The Development of Jewish Law from Qumran to the Rabbis*. Taubman Lectures in Jewish Studies 6. Berkeley: University of California Press, 2009.

Shemesh, Aharon. "The Origins of the Laws of Separatism: Qumran Literature and Rabbinic Halacha." *RevQ* 18 (1997): 223–41.

Shemesh, Aharon. "The Scriptural Background of the Penal Code in the Rule of the Community and Damascus Document." *DSD* 15 (2008): 191–224.

Shemesh, Aharon, and Cana Werman. "Hidden Things and Their Revelation." *RevQ* 18 (1998): 409–27.

Shoshany, Ronit. "The Story of the Carpenter's Apprentice." *Sidra* 21 (2006): 87–98 (in Hebrew).

Sievers, Joseph. "Josephus, First Maccabees, Sparta, the Three Haireseis—and Cicero." *JSJ* 32 (2001): 241–51.

Sievers, Joseph. *Synopsis of the Greek Sources for the Hasmonean Period: 1–2 Maccabees and Josephus, War 1 and Antiquities 12–14*. SubBi 20. Rome: Editrice Pontifico Istituto Biblico, 2001.

Simon-Shoshan, Moshe. *Stories of the Law: Narrative Discourse and the Construction of Authority in the Mishnah*. Oxford: Oxford University Press, 2012.

Smith, Mark S. *The Origin and Development of the Waw Consecutive: Northwest Semitic Evidence from Ugarit to Qumran*. HSS 39. Atlanta, Ga.: Scholars Press, 1991.

Smith, Morton. "Palestinian Judaism in the First Century." In *Israel: Its Role in Civilization*, ed. Moshe Davis, 67–81. New York: Seminary Israel Institute of the Jewish Theological Seminary of America, 1956.

Sokoloff, Michael. *A Dictionary of Jewish Babylonian Aramaic of the Talmudic and Geonic Periods*. Dictionaries of Talmud, Midrash and Targum III and Publications of the Comprehensive Aramaic Lexicon Project. Ramat-Gan, Baltimore, and London: Bar-Ilan University Press; Johns Hopkins University Press, 2002.

Sokoloff, Michael. *A Dictionary of Jewish Palestinian Aramaic of the Byzantine Period*. 2nd edn. Dictionaries of Talmud, Midrash and Targum II and Publications of the Comprehensive Aramaic Lexicon Project. Ramat-Gan, Baltimore, and London: Bar-Ilan University Press; Johns Hopkins University Press, 2002.

Stemberger, Günter. *Jewish Contemporaries of Jesus: Pharisees, Sadducees, Essenes*. Trans. Allan W. Mahnke. Minneapolis: Fortress, 1995.

Stemberger, Günter. "The Maccabees in Rabbinic Tradition." In *The Scriptures and the Scrolls: Studies in Honour of A. S. van der Woude on the Occasion of his 65th Birthday*, ed. F. Garcia Martinez, A. Hilhorst, and C. J. Labuschagne, 193–203. VTSup 49. Leiden: Brill, 1992.

Stemberger, Günter. "Narrative Baraitot in the Yerushalmi." In *Talmud Yerushalmi and Graeco-Roman Culture*, ed. Peter Schäfer, 1:63–81. TSAJ 71. Tübingen: Mohr Siebeck, 1998.

Stern, Menahem, ed. *Greek and Latin Authors on Jews and Judaism*. 3 vols. Jerusalem: Israel Academy of Sciences and Humanities, 1976.

Stern, Menahem. *Hasmonaean Judaea in the Hellenistic World: Chapters in Political History*. Ed. Daniel R. Schwartz. Jerusalem: Shazar, 1995 (in Hebrew).

Stern, Menahem. "Nicolaus of Damascus as a Source of Jewish History in the Herodian and Hasmonean Age." In *Studies in Jewish History: The Second Temple Period*, ed. Moshe Amit, Isaiah Gafni, and Moshe D. Herr, 445–64. Jerusalem: Yad Izhak Ben-Zvi, 1991 (in Hebrew).

Stern, Sacha. *Jewish Identity in Early Rabbinic Writings*. AGJU 23. Leiden: Brill, 1994.

Sternberg, Meir. *The Poetics of Biblical Narrative: Ideological Literature and the Drama of Reading*. Indiana Literary Biblical Series. Bloomington: Indiana University Press, 1985.

Sussmann, Yaakov. "The History of *Halakha* and the Dead Sea Scrolls: A Preliminary to the Publication of 4QMMT." *Tarbiz* 59 (1989–1990): 11–76 (in Hebrew).

Sussmann, Yaakov. "'Torah she-be-al peh' peshutah ke-mashma'ah—koho shel qoso shel yod." In *Mehqerei Talmud: Talmudic Studies Dedicated to the Memory of Professor Ephraim E. Urbach*, vol. 3, part 1: 209–384. Jerusalem: Magnes, 2005 (in Hebrew).

Tabory, Joseph. *Jewish Festivals in the Time of the Mishnah and Talmud*. 3rd rev. edn. Jerusalem: Magnes, 2000 (in Hebrew).

Tal, Avraham. "The Infinitival Forms in Strata of Palestinian Jewish Aramaic." In *Hebrew Language Studies: Presented to Professor Zeev Ben-Hayyim*, ed. Moshe Bar-Asher et al., 201–18. Jerusalem: Magnes, 1983 (in Hebrew).

Tal, Avraham. "Strata of Palestinian Jewish Aramaic: The Paragogic Nun as a Criterion." *Lešonenu* 43 (1979): 165–84 (in Hebrew).

Talshir, David. "Ha-ivrit bi-yemei ha-bayit ha-sheni: Beit gidulah ve-gilguleha." In *Mehqerei Talmud: Talmudic Studies Dedicated to the Memory of Professor Eliezer Shimshon Rosenthal*, ed. Moshe Bar-Asher and David Rosenthal, 2:284–301. Jerusalem: Magnes, 1993.

Taran, Anat. "Remarks on Josephus Flavius and the Destruction of the Second Temple." *Zion* 61 (1996): 141–57 (in Hebrew).

Tcherikover, Victor. *Hellenistic Civilization and the Jews*. Trans. S. Applebaum. Philadelphia: Jewish Publication Society, 1959.

Teeter, Andrew. "Isaiah and the King of As/Syria in Daniel's Final Vision: On the Rhetoric of Inner-Scriptural Allusion and the Hermeneutics of 'Mantological Exegesis.'" In *A Teacher for All Generations: Essays in Honor of James C. Vanderkam*, vol. 1, ed. Eric F. Mason, Samuel I. Thomas, Alison Schofield, and Eugene Ulrich, 169–99. JSJSup 153/I. Leiden: Brill, 2012.

Tepper, Yigal, and Yuval Shahar. "He'arot historiyot-geografiyot le-kerav hadashah le-or ituro shel 'ma'aleh hadashah.'" In *Ma'alot kedumim li-yerushalayim*, ed. Yigal Tepper and Yuval Shahar, 6–23. Tel Aviv: Ha-mador li-yedi'at ha-ares be-verit ha-tenu'ah ha-kibbusit, 1988.

Thackeray, H. St John. *Josephus: The Man and the Historian*. New York: Jewish Institute of Religion, 1929.

Thoma, Clemens. "John Hyrcanus I as Seen by Josephus and Other Early Jewish Sources." In *Josephus and the History of the Greco-Roman Period: Essays in Memory of Morton Smith*, ed. Fausto Parente and Joseph Sievers, 127–40. StPB 41. Leiden: Brill, 1994.

Tropper, Amram. *Simeon the Righteous in Rabbinic Literature: A Legend Reinvented*. Ancient Judaism and Early Christianity 84. Leiden: Brill, 2013.

Tuval, Michael. *From Jerusalem Priest to Roman Jew: On Josephus and the Paradigms of Ancient Judaism*. WUNT 2.Reihe. Tübingen: Mohr Siebeck, 2013.

Urbach, Ephraim E. "Ha-derashah ki-yesod ha-halakhah u-va'ayat ha-sofrim." In *The World of the Sages: Collected Studies*, 50–66. 2nd edn. Jerusalem: Magnes, 2002 (in Hebrew).

Urbach, Ephraim E. *The Halakhah: Its Sources and Development*. Trans. Raphael Posner. Yad La-Talmud. Jerusalem: Massada, 1986.

Urbach, Ephraim E. "Matai paskah ha-nevu'ah." In *The World of the Sages: Collected Studies*, 9–20. 2nd edn. Jerusalem: Magnes, 2002 (in Hebrew).

Urbach, Ephraim E. "The Role of the Ten Commandments in Jewish Worship." In *Collected Writings in Jewish Studies*, ed. Robert Brody and Moshe D. Herr, 289–317. Jerusalem: Magnes, 1999.

Urbach, Ephraim E. "The Talmudic Sage: Character and Authority." In *Collected Writings in Jewish Studies*, ed. Robert Brody and Moshe D. Herr, 404–7. Jerusalem: Magnes, 1999.

Vermes, Geza. *Jesus the Jew: A Historian's Reading of the Gospels*. New York: Macmillan, 1974.

Vidas, Moulie. "Greek Wisdom in Babylonia." In *Envisioning Judaism: Studies in Honor of Peter Schäfer on the Occasion of His Seventieth Birthday*, ed. Ra'anan S. Boustan et al., 1:287–305. Tübingen: Mohr Siebeck, 2013.

Von Rad, Gerhard. *Old Testament Theology*. Trans. D. M. G. Stalker. 2 vols. London: SCM, 1982.

Walfish, Avraham. "Approaching the Text and Approaching God: The Redaction of the Mishnah and Tosefta Berakhot." *Jewish Studies* 43 (2005–2006): *21–*79 (English section).

Walfish, Avraham. "The Poetics of Mishnah." In *The Mishnah in Contemporary Perspective*, ed. Jacob Neusner and Alan J. Avery-Peck, 2:153–89. Handbook of Oriental Studies; Section 1: The Near and Middle East 65, 87. Leiden: Brill, 2006.

Weiss, Isaac H. *Dor dor ve-dorshav*. 5 vols. New York: Platt & Minkus, 1924.

Weiss, Ruhama. *Meal Tests: The Meal in the World of the Sages*. Tel Aviv: Hakibbutz Hameuchad, 2010 (in Hebrew).

Wellhausen, Julius. *The Pharisees and the Sadducees: An Examination of Internal Jewish History*. Trans. Mark E. Biddle. Mercer Library of Biblical Studies. Macon, Ga.: Mercer University Press, 2001.

Werblowsky, R. J. W. "Greek Wisdom and Proficiency in Greek." In *Paganisme, Judaïsme, Christianisme: Influences et affrontements dans le monde antique: Mélanges offerts à Marcel Simon*, 55–60. Paris: De Boccard, 1978.

Werman, Cana, and Aharon Shemesh. *Revealing the Hidden: Exegesis and Halakha in the Qumran Scrolls*. Jerusalem: Bialik Institute, 2011 (in Hebrew).

White, Hayden. "The Historical Text as Literary Artifact." In *Tropics of Discourse: Essays in Cultural Criticism*, 81–100. Baltimore and London: Johns Hopkins University Press, 1978.

White, Hayden. *Tropics of Discourse: Essays in Cultural Criticism*. Baltimore and London: Johns Hopkins University Press, 1978.

Wiesenberg, Ernest. "Related Prohibitions: Swine Breeding and the Study of Greek." *HUCA* 27 (1956): 213–33.

Wilk, Roman. "The Abuse of Nicanor's Corpse." *Sidra* 8 (1992): 53–7 (in Hebrew).

Wilk, Roman. "When Hyrcanus was Besieging Aristobulus in Jerusalem." In *Dor Le-Dor: From the End of Biblical Times Up to the Redaction of the Talmud Studies in Honor of Joshua Efron*, ed. Aryeh Kasher and Aharon Oppenheimer, 99–104. Jerusalem: Bialik Institute, 1995 (in Hebrew).

Williamson, H. G. M. "The Historical Value of Josephus' *Jewish Antiquities* XI. 297–301." *JTS* 28 (1977): 49–66.

Windschuttle, Keith. *The Killing of History: How Literary Critics and Social Theorists Are Murdering Our Past.* 1st pbk. edn. San Francisco: Encounter, 2000.

Yalon, Hanoch. *Introduction to the Vocalization of the Mishna.* Jerusalem: Bialik Institute, 1964 (in Hebrew).

Yassif, Eli. *The Hebrew Folktale: History, Genre, Meaning.* Trans. Jacqueline S. Teitlelbaum. Folklore Studies in Translation. Bloomington: Indiana University Press, 1999.

Yerushalmi, Yosef Hayim. *Zakhor: Jewish History and Jewish Memory.* Samuel and Althea Stroum Lectures in Jewish Studies. Seattle and London: University of Washington Press, 1982.

Zeitlin, Solomon. *The Rise and Fall of the Judaean State: A Political, Social and Religious History of the Second Commonwealth.* Philadelphia: Jewish Publication Society, 1962.

Zohar, Noam. *Secrets of the Rabbinic Workshop: Redaction as a Key to Meaning.* Jerusalem: Magnes, 2007 (in Hebrew).

Zucker, Moshe. "Le-fitron ba'ayat 32 midot u-'mishnat Rabbi Eliezer.'" *PAAJR* 23 (1954): 1–40 (Hebrew section).

Index Locorum

General Index

rabbinic literature (*cont.*)
  dependence on Josephus 18
  early features of 23–7
  parallels with Josephus 9–13, 17–19
  preserving superior traditions 23–4
  priestly temple genre in 188–91
  use of Aramaic chronicles 186–7
  views on historiography 6–7
rabbinization 83n, 99n, 133, 206n, 220

Salome (Herod's sister) 25n, 122, 140
Salome (Aristobulus I's wife) 23n
Scaurus, Aemilius 162
Shelamzion, *see* Alexandra
Simeon ben Shataḥ 80, 86, 92n, 103, 113,
  122–3, 161, 169
Simeon the Righteous of the Alexander
  legend 25n, 51, 70n, 188
Simeon the Righteous mentioned in
  '*Abot* xiii, 70n
Simeon the Righteous of the Caligula
  legend 70, 71, 73n, 187, 189, 190n

Targum Pseudo-Jonathan 61
Temple legends 58–9, 63, 75, 186–8, 190, 193,
  196, 202, 206–7, 219
temple motif:
  in the Hyrcanus legend 63, 66
  in the Nicanor legend 50–1

in the priest pelted with citrons
  legend 136
use of the genre 190–1
theodicy, theodicean legends 31, 157, 186, 194,
  198, 209

Urim and Thummim 65, 70

War (Josephus) 5, 8, 9, 15, 18n, 20, 40, 60,
  63n, 92, 126, 140, 167n, 218
  as a source for *Antiquities* 3, 16, 86–9, 92,
    198–9
  comparison to *Antiquities* 3n, 16–17, 19–20,
    69, 86–7, 89, 124–6, 132, 135, 141, 163, 167,
    198, 207, 213–15, 217
  early Aramaic or Hebrew version of 11,
    18n, 90
  help of assistants in writing 17
  Jewish identity in 17
  sources used in 16, 39, 43n,
    124n, 198
water libation ceremony 128–31

Yehudah ben Gedidya/Gudgeda 25–6, 80, 83,
  95–6, 100–1
Yehudah ben Pachura 108n

Zimri 25, 139, 146–7, 149–52, 154–5,
  192, 212

|||||||||||||||||||||

Printed in the USA/Agawam, MA
April 26, 2022

792221.012